The Real Fidel Castro

The Real Fidel Castro

Leycester Coltman

With a Foreword by Julia E. Sweig

Yale University Press
New Haven and London

For information about this and other Yale University Press publications, please contact:
U.S. Office: sales.press@yale.edu   yalebooks.com
Europe Office: sales@yaleup.co.uk   www.yaleup.co.uk

Set in Adobe Garamond by Northern Phototypesetting Ltd, Bolton, Lancs
Printed in the United States of America

Library of Congress Cataloging-in-Publication Data
Coltman, Leycester.
   The real Fidel Castro / by Leycester Coltman.—1st ed.
     p. cm.
   ISBN 0–300–10188–0 (cloth: alk. paper)
   1. Castro, Fidel, 1926– 2. Cuba—History—1933–1959. 3. Cuba—History—1959–
4. Heads of state—Cuba—Biography. I. Title.
   F1788.22.C3C59 2003
   972.9106′4′092—dc21   2003012942

A catalogue record for this book is available from the British Library

10 9 8 7 6 5 4 3 2 1

Contents

Illustrations

Foreword

In *The Real Fidel Castro*, Sir Leycester Coltman offers a unique contribution to the literature on the Cuban revolution and the political life of its leader Fidel Castro. Since the early 1960s American readers have been limited to biographical and historical treatments of Castro written mainly by North Americans excessively distracted by the questions and concerns of the Cold War or by Cuban exiles with an axe to grind. Sir Leycester's perspective offers a welcome new depiction of recent Cuban history and of Fidel Castro Ruz, the man most associated with that country's successes and failures over the last forty-five years. And the book provides an excellent complement and update to a work published fifteen years ago by Wayne S. Smith, the retired US diplomat who served two tours of duty, first as a junior officer in the late 1950s and later as President Carter's envoy during that administration's attempt to improve relations with Cuba in the late 1970s.

Whereas Smith left Havana in 1981, resigning from the US Foreign Service in protest over the Reagan administration's reversals of the Carter initiative, Coltman began his service as British Ambassador there ten years later, in 1991, and stayed until 1994. Other than the years 1959 to 1962, which saw the birth and radicalisation of the revolution, the emergence of a counter-revolution, the Bay of Pigs, the Cuban Missile Crisis, and the beginning of Soviet sponsorship, I can think of no other three-year period which was as significant in terms of recent Cuban history.

During Coltman's stay, the world changed for Cuba. The Soviet Union withdrew its troops and eliminated its multi-billion dollar annual subsidy to the island; the US tightened its trade embargo; thousands of Cuban troops returned from Angola, the country's last major international mission; Fidel Castro adopted a series of economic reforms that, while stopping far short of full blown liberalisation, converted a solidly statist economy into a mixed economy and began, in the Pope's subsequent formulation, to open Cuba to the world.

Coltman brings a keen, wry and subtle eye to these critical events, to Castro's decision-making process, and to many other dimensions of the revolution's history, narrating the story with a mixture of insight drawn from his personal interaction with Castro and a scholar's approach to history. Like the great British historian of Cuba, Hugh Thomas, Coltman's voice is particularly refreshing for the American reader precisely because he is, well, not American. Yet he is a close enough cousin to provide an analysis of Fidel Castro as a politician without having to qualify, demonise and caveat his way through the story.

The full history of British relations with Latin America during the Cold War period has yet to be written. Given a further opportunity Sir Leycester Coltman may have shared more observations of his own country's approach to Cuba and to the hemisphere. His book is a careful and highly readable, if modestly indirect, introduction to this wider story.

Julia E. Sweig
Senior Fellow, Council on Foreign Relations and author of
Inside the Cuban Revolution (2002)
July 2003

Preface

Leycester Coltman was born in 1938 and educated at Rugby School and Magdalene College, Cambridge. He later spent a sabbatical year at the Manchester Business School.

After joining the British Diplomatic Service he served in Copenhagen, Cairo, Brasilia, Mexico City, Brussels and latterly as British Ambassador in Havana (1991–4) and Bogota (1994–8). During spells in the Foreign Office in London he served in the Eastern Department (on the Jordan desk), in the Permanent Under-Secretary's Department (responsible for liaison with the Intelligence Services), as Deputy Head of the Southern European Department, as Head of the Mexico and Central America Department (during the period of the Contra war in Nicaragua and the invasion of Panama) and, before being posted to Cuba, as Head of the Latin America Department.

An important part of a diplomat's work is to sift through a mass of information, misinformation, press reports, rumours and gossip in order to separate fact from fiction and provide an accurate and balanced account of what is really going on in the country at issue. In a closed society like that of Cuba this is a difficult task requiring knowledge and experience. Much of Coltman's diplomatic career had been spent on political work, especially in Latin America. He was ideally placed to understand and describe the complex historical and psychological forces which moulded Fidel Castro.

During Coltman's service both in London and in Cuba he had access to information additional to that obtained from direct contacts with Castro and others. This gave him a unique perspective from which to assess the credibility of the many witnesses who have written or talked about their particular encounters with Castro. Coltman accompanied many visitors in calls on Castro and saw how the Commandant behaved with both friends and enemies. And Castro would often visit the ambassador's residence for lengthy and relaxed conversations with Coltman. He was therefore unusually well-placed to make sense of the apparent contradictions in Castro's personality.

Leycester Coltman died, sadly and unexpectedly, shortly after having delivered the typescript of this book to his literary agent, Andrew Lownie. He did not have the opportunity to make final alterations to the script or add a full list of annotations. Requiring only light editing by the publisher, the book is presented here as Coltman wrote it and, as far as possible, as he would have wished.

Piedad, Beatrice, Roland and Stephen Coltman
London, July 2003

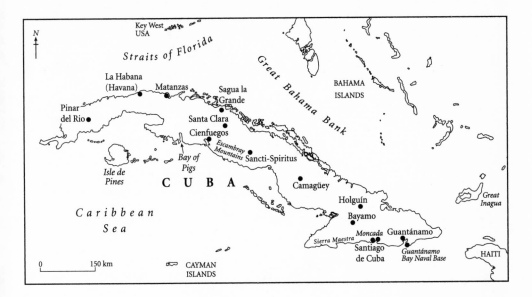

1 Rebel in Search of a Cause

In July 1992 Fidel Castro, then aged sixty-four, visited for the first time the small stone house where his father was born, in the north-west of Spain. The occasion made him drop for a few moments his usual insistence on not talking about his family and private life. How did he feel entering his father's house? 'Full of love . . . The old man used to feel homesick. He used to tell me things about when he was a soldier in Cuba during the war with the United States. He wanted to return, and he did. My father was very poor but a hard worker. He had a group of peasants. There was one who looked after the cattle and he had sciatica. By then things had improved and this man became a cook in the house . . . He had a bad temper. I always remember that he reprimanded us. I also remember my father's sadness. But why am I telling you this . . . ?'

Angel Castro, Fidel's father, was born in 1875 to a peasant family in rural Galicia, one of the poorest regions of Spain. As a young man Angel was tough, self-reliant, taciturn, hard-working and shrewd. But being barely literate and owning no land, he had no alternative but to work for wealthier farmers nearby as a hired agricultural labourer.

In 1895, when Angel was twenty, the leaders of the independence movement in Cuba launched the final stage of the war against Spanish rule. Cuba was the most valuable and prized part of what remained of Spain's once mighty overseas empire. The government in Madrid was determined not to let it go. More and more troops were shipped to Cuba in the effort to crush the insurrection. Angel Castro was conscripted into the army and sent to Cuba.

Cuba was a long way from Spain, but very close to the United States. Public opinion in the United States, whipped up by press reports of Spanish atrocities, increasingly favoured intervention to end Spanish rule. In 1898 a massive explosion destroyed the American battleship *Maine* in Havana harbour, with heavy loss of life. It was probably an accident; but the US government blamed the Spanish authorities, declared war on Spain and soon inflicted a crushing defeat on the Spanish navy. The Spanish land forces, exhausted by three years of bitter fighting against the rebel guerrillas, now also had to face a fresh and eager American expeditionary force which disembarked in Cuba. Spain was soon forced to surrender to the United States and handed over to them the administration of Cuba. The American flag, not the flag of an independent Cuba, was raised over the Governor's palace in Santiago. The Spanish administrators and military, including Angel Castro, returned to Spain. Many Spanish landowners also left, selling their estates and properties at knock-down prices, usually to Americans. The Spaniards and the Cubans now had something in common: they both felt they had been cheated and humiliated by the United States. It was a humiliation which Fidel would later feel as keenly as if he had suffered it in person.

In Washington there were conflicting views on whether to annex Cuba to the Union or to allow independence. The view prevailed that a friendly independent Cuba, open to American capital and subject to American influence, would be preferable to a reluctant and rebellious dependency. In 1902, after four years of direct United States rule, during which new institutions were created on the American model, the independent Republic of Cuba was finally proclaimed. But its independence was limited. The United States retained a large naval base at Guantánamo and the right, enshrined in the Cuban constitution at American insistence under the so-called Platt Amendment, to intervene should its interests in Cuba be threatened. A commercial treaty ensured favourable American access to the Cuban market.

With peace and American tutelage, Cuba seemed set to enjoy economic growth and prosperity. Labour was in short supply. Like thousands of other Galicians in these years Angel Castro, who had been encouraged by what he had seen of Cuba as a soldier, decided to emigrate. An uncle had emigrated to Cuba a few years earlier.

If in the United States ambitious immigrants went west, in Cuba they were more likely to go east. Oriente, the large easternmost province of Cuba, was the most undeveloped part of the island, but it had great agricultural and mineral potential. Inhabited largely by former slaves, with a tradition of unruliness and rebellion, the province had been devastated by the successive phases of the independence wars. American companies, notably United Fruit, had bought vast tracts of land, cleared forest and built sugar mills, railways and roads.

Angel Castro did various jobs, sometimes as an employee of the Nipe Bay Railway Company, a subsidiary of United Fruit, and sometimes on his own. During some of his early years he travelled around the countryside with a cart, selling lemonade from a barrel to labourers working in the sugar cane plantations and woodlands. Later he set up a store in the town of Guaro, selling various goods and equipment needed by peasants in the area. With the profits from these activities he was able to lease from United Fruit some land planted with sugar cane. He employed a group of peasants, mostly recent immigrants, to work the plantation. He also hired them out to do other jobs such as loading transport or felling timber. He acquired a small sawmill, selling wood to the nearby sugar mills. According to some accounts he was no respecter of legal niceties, often pinching equipment from United Fruit installations. He took the view that Cuba had been stolen from Spain by the Americans, and that there was no harm in taking a few bits and pieces back.

By hard work and austere living he accumulated enough money to achieve his ambition of becoming a landowner. He bought a farm called Birán, some ten miles from the Bay of Nipe on the north coast, and gradually expanded it over the years, sometimes (according to one of his neighbours) by quietly moving his border posts during the night. It was mostly good flat land, suitable for sugar cane, not far from a dirt road and the railway line used to transport cane to the sugar mills. He built a large wooden house, on stilts so that animals could shelter under the house as in Galicia. It had wide verandas and large bedrooms. Angel bred cattle and various types of poultry, planted sugar cane, maize and other crops, married a Cuban schoolteacher called María Luisa Argota and had two children, Pedro Emilio and Lidia. He employed several servants at the farmstead.

After a few years of marriage María Luisa left Birán, Angel having turned his attention to a girl called Lina Ruz, who was working in the household as a maid and cook. Lina was thirty years younger than Angel. She had been born in Pinar del Rio, at the westernmost end of Cuba. Her parents had trav-elled with their large family through almost the whole length of the island, sometimes in an ox-drawn cart, ending up near Birán. There her father earned a meagre living transporting cane by cart to the sugar mills. Lina's father asked Don Angel to employ one of his daughters. Angel chose Lina, then aged about fifteen. On María Luisa's departure Lina took over the running of the house and was treated as Angel's wife. She gave birth to three sons and four daughters. After Angela and Ramón came her third child, Fidel, born on 13 August 1927.

Shortly before Fidel's birth, Angel became friendly with a businessman and local politician called Fidel Pino. Angel lent money to Pino, who had lost a fortune in a failed speculation. Angel nevertheless looked up to Pino as a man of higher social status. Angel calculated that it would serve his interests to have Pino as godfather to his third son. Hence the name Fidel. But Fidel Pino showed little interest. After all, the boy's parents were not even properly married. For the baptism to take place Angel needed to get a priest and the prospective godfather together in a church with the child. This never happened. It was not until seven years later that Fidel Castro was baptised, with a different godfather.

Fidel's earliest years were mostly happy and problem-free. He could run around wherever he wanted with his brothers and sisters. The farm animals and surrounding countryside provided plenty of entertainment. He swam in a nearby river and tried to catch birds using a sling-shot or bow and arrow. He played also with other children, including the children of the black labourers, mostly Haitian immigrants, who lived in palm-thatched huts near the railway line. But everyone knew that he was the son of the big boss, Don Angel, and treated him accordingly. He got used to always getting his way. On the rare occasions when he did not, he was liable to throw a tantrum. When Ramón or Fidel behaved badly, their mother sometimes threatened to beat them with a belt, but Fidel usually escaped punishment. He learnt that if he listened to his mother's scoldings with a serious expression, and did not contradict her, her anger quickly passed.

His father, who was already fifty-two when Fidel was born, was rather remote and uncommunicative, usually busy with the running of the farm, and sometimes showing an explosive temper, for example when he lost at dominoes. In later years, when Fidel had become a Marxist, he sometimes referred to his father in disparaging terms. He wanted to distance himself politically from a landowner who exploited peasants and paid no taxes. He once recounted how as a child he had seen his father opening his safe at election time to hand out money to the traditional fixers whose job was to bring out the vote for the government. But it is unlikely that he felt any disapproval at the time. The balance of evidence, including statements by Angel's other children, is that there was never a seriously bad relationship between Fidel and his father. Angel ran his farm in a typically macho authoritarian style, but he was usually indulgent towards his children. By the standards of most Cuban landowners he was also good-natured towards his workers. Fidel later recalled that his father had his cane-fields weeded more often than was necessary, in order to give work to cane-cutters from neighbouring American-owned plantations who were left without employment during the months between harvests. 'I can't recall his ever failing to find a solution whenever somebody came to him for help. Sometimes he grumbled and complained but his generosity always got the upper hand.'

Despite Angel's occasional angry rebukes, Fidel was never ill-treated as a child. If anything, he was spoiled. The earliest photographs of him show a well-scrubbed little boy with a self-satisfied expression and expensive-looking clothes, more Little Lord Fauntleroy than peasant boy. When dressed up like this he must have offered a stark contrast to his bare-footed Haitian playmates. A later photograph shows little Fidel in a Panama hat, sitting proudly on a tractor. In quarrels with his father Fidel nearly always ended up getting his way. His home life was almost certainly not, as some biographers have speculated, a cause of his subsequent rebelliousness against authority figures.

During Fidel's childhood Angel's prosperity continued to grow. In addition to the 1,800 hectares he owned, he leased a further 10,000 hectares mainly from United Fruit, making his farm one of the biggest in the region. Most of this additional land was hilly and unsuitable for sugar cane, but it could be used for timber and grazing animals. As the household expanded, new rooms and an office were added to the house. Several new farm buildings were put up. There was a cock-pit near the house where on Sundays during the cane harvest workers could spend their wages on cock-fights, remaining penniless if they lost and getting drunk on rum if they won. During the harvest some 600 labourers worked on the estate. Despite their wealth, Angel and Lina did not acquire any middle-class attitudes. They made no pretence of having social graces or intellectual interests. Most of the rooms in the house were in a state of chaotic untidiness, with chickens roosting in several of them. The family and the numerous servants often ate meals together and retained their rough country manners.

Near the farmstead there was a one-room hut which served as a school-room. A young woman teacher, employed by the state, came from Santiago, the regional capital, to give lessons to some twenty local children of different ages. Most of the children were poor and would stop going to the schoolroom as soon as they were old enough to do manual work. From the age of about three Fidel attended the school, together with his elder brother Ramón and sister Angela. Being the youngest pupil he was put in a chair at the front of the class. The children were taught some reading, writing and arithmetic, and kept occupied with activities such as singing the national anthem. In the class Fidel would not sit still and was quarrelsome, often trying to defy the teacher's authority. Sometimes, when the teacher annoyed him, he would yell at her and then run home as fast as he could.

There was no religious instruction in the school and no nearby church. Fidel's only early contact with religion was through his mother. She prayed vigorously every day, trying to persuade various saints to fulfil her wishes. There was probably an element of Afro-Cuban *santería* (devotion to the saints) in Lina's concept of Christianity. Reminiscing later about his child-hood, Castro said he did not know whether his father had any religious convictions; his father simply never mentioned the subject.

When Fidel was aged six, he was sent with his sister Angela (and later also Ramón) to live with the teacher in Santiago. The teacher had told Fidel's parents that he was clever and that she could prepare him at home to go later to a good school in Santiago. In later years Fidel said he thought the teacher's main interest was to get her hands on the 40 pesos a month (a peso was equivalent to a dollar) which his father sent to cover his board and lodging. He disliked intensely being away from home. The teacher lived in a small, damp, dilapidated house, together with her father and sister, neither of whom had any income. Five people (later six) had to live off the teacher's salary, which was meagre and often paid late, and the money received from Angel Castro. Fidel complained that he never had enough to eat. He was frequently reprimanded, told not to shout and not to beg, and was sometimes spanked. Teaching was sporadic and consisted mainly of practising handwriting and learning arithmetical tables.

For a time, Fidel's parents brushed aside his complaints about the way he was treated by the teacher. But eventually the children's scraggy appearance made their mother realise that something was indeed wrong. They were brought back to live at home in Birán. Angel remonstrated with the teacher. The teacher explained her difficult situation, and there was a reconciliation. To Fidel's dismay, the children were sent back to live with the teacher again in Santiago. However, conditions in the teacher's house improved when the teacher's sister got married to the honorary consul of Haiti, bringing more money into the household.

After a year in Santiago Fidel was at last baptised. The honorary consul acted as godfather. Fidel was pleased and relieved to be baptised. When he had been unbaptised, other children had called him a Jew. He confused the word *judío* (Jew) with a similar word, *jote*, which was the name of a large black bird. He thought it must have been these unpleasant birds which had 'killed Christ'. In any event he understood that being a 'Jew' was something distinctly undesirable.

Baptism was a requirement for entering a Catholic school. It was also possibly to ensure the children's acceptance in a Catholic school that at this time Angel and Lina underwent a formal religious marriage. (It was evidently agreed by those conducting the ceremony that Angel's first marriage could be treated as dissolved, or perhaps his first wife's existence was just quietly forgotten.) After eighteen months in Santiago, now legitimate and baptised a Christian, Fidel began to attend the La Salle school run by the Marian Christian Brothers, together with Ramón and later his younger brother Raúl. He went to school in the morning and returned to the consul's house at lunch-time.

He was still an unruly pupil who talked a lot and reacted badly to being told off. He also continued to resent the efforts of his former teacher, and of the consul and his wife, to control and repress his boisterous and rebellious spirit. They threatened that if his behaviour did not improve, he would be sent to his school as a boarder. He decided that this would be preferable. He deliberately behaved badly and was duly sent to La Salle as a boarder, his father agreeing to pay the modest additional cost. He disliked the discipline and the boring classes, but he had friends among the boarders and plenty of free time to practise sports such as baseball and soccer, at both of which he showed considerable talent. The boarders were also taken on excursions which he enjoyed, especially a twice-weekly boat trip to a nearby island with a recreation centre.

At La Salle Fidel was often in trouble with his teachers. He organised protests about the food, and was several times involved in fights with other boys. When a teacher slapped his face, he reacted violently, trying to punch and bite the teacher. His brother Ramón acquired a reputation as a trouble-maker and bully. After three years the school sent Angel Castro a report saying that the boys' performance was unsatisfactory: if they were to stay at the school, they must take their studies more seriously, and improve their behaviour.

When Angel received this report, he was furious. He told the boys that because of their poor behaviour they would not go back to school. Ramón was quite content to stay on the farm. He had little interest in studying and wanted to spend more time with the daughter of a Haitian cane-cutter who lived nearby. Fidel however objected vociferously to being kept away from school. He blamed the teachers for his behaviour, and claimed to be the victim of injustice. He threatened to burn down the house if he was kept at home. Again he got his way, mainly through the intercession of his mother. Fidel's younger brother Raúl was Lina's favourite son because he was more gentle and loving than the other two, but she recognised that Fidel was exceptionally bright and strong-willed. She had no formal education herself but was determined that Fidel should get the best possible education. She talked her husband round to this view.

So Fidel was packed off to the Dolores school, also in Santiago, a prestigious college run by Spanish Jesuits and attended by the sons of wealthy local businessmen and landowners. No one ever talked of a colour bar, but it was taken for granted that only white boys went to the school, despite the high proportion of blacks and mestizos in Oriente province. Fidel went first as a day boy, on a trial basis, living at the house in Santiago of a business acquaintance of his father who acted as guardian. His sister Angela, attending a girls' school in Santiago, was living in the same house. He again had a bad relationship with the new guardian, becoming angry and resentful when pocket money was withheld as a punishment for bad behaviour or for getting poor marks at school. When the guardian locked him in his room to force him to do his homework, he deliberately did no work at all. He told his teacher that he had lost his report booklet. When they gave him a new one he used the old one to forge better marks than he had actually received. He fell behind even more when he got appendicitis and had to spend three months in hospital due to a post-operational infection. He enjoyed this period since he could spend the time reading comics, talking to other patients and toying with the idea of becoming a doctor or surgeon.

Things improved when he became a boarder at Dolores. He liked and admired the Jesuit priests who taught him. As Castro himself later often acknowledged, the priests were extremely dedicated, taking a real interest in the welfare and progress of their pupils. By encouraging outdoor activities and group competitions, they stimulated a spirit of adventure, and tried to impart the qualities of courage, honesty, moral rectitude and a willingness to make sacrifices in a noble cause. Fidel began for the first time to get good grades, displaying an impressive memory and greater interest in school work, especially history. Growing tall and strong like both his parents, he excelled at sports. He enjoyed swimming and going on hikes in the nearby mountains. As in most boys' boarding schools, proficiency at games made him popular and a natural leader. A few fellow pupils claimed later that at school Fidel was boastful, moody and aggressive. But these accounts seem to have been influenced by hostility to Castro's subsequent political career. His Jesuit teachers singled him out as a boy of exceptional talent and promise.

Despite having insisted on being sent to boarding school, Fidel always looked forward to his holidays at home in Birán. Carrying a hunting-knife and shotgun, and accompanied by one of his dogs, he would walk or ride up the pine-covered hills in his father's huge estate, shooting at birds or other wild animals or any other target on which he could practise his aim. When one of his sisters seemed likely to tell his parents that he had been shooting at the farm hens, he persuaded her to take a shot herself so that she could not inform on him.

He showed a keen curiosity about the flora and fauna on the estate. He was also intrigued by the deposits of iron and nickel ore which were visible on the surface not far from his home. He listened on the radio to what was happening in the world. In 1940, when he was fourteen, he wrote a letter to President Roosevelt, in passable English, saying that he had heard on the radio about his election and asking the President to send him a 10-dollar note, since he did not have one. He added that if the President needed iron to build his battleships, he could show him a good mine. He was pleased to receive a polite acknowledgement (which duly impressed his classmates) but disappointed that the reply did not enclose the requested dollar bill.

Until he was fourteen, Castro had never left the province of Oriente. But at Dolores he heard a lot about an even more prestigious Jesuit school, the

Belén college in Havana. He asked to be transferred there, and as usual he got his way. To be admitted in the second grade, a pupil needed to be at least fifteen years old. Since Fidel was still only fourteen, his father paid a bribe to get a new birth certificate giving his year of birth as 1926 rather than 1927. To avoid the embarrassment of acknowledging this fraud, Fidel spent the rest of his life claiming to be a year older than he really was. His fiftieth birthday was celebrated in style when he was in fact forty-nine.

Standards at Belén were high, in sports as well as academic studies. He had to practise hard to get into the college basketball team. He also devoted a lot of time to athletics, baseball and table tennis. Still keen on swimming and mountain climbing, he joined an association called 'The Explorers' and eventually became its 'general'. He liked to climb mountains on his own. On one excursion he miscalculated the time he would take and kept the school bus waiting for two hours. On another occasion he jumped into a swollen river to rescue a Jesuit teacher who had got into difficulty trying to cross it.

The time and energy which he devoted to these sporting and outdoor activities caused his academic performance to suffer. He tended to daydream in classes that did not interest him. He was warned that he was heading for failure in several exams. But by dint of intensive last-minute cramming, using his almost photographic memory, he in fact got good marks, especially in maths, physics and geography.

His favourite subjects at Belén were history and debating. From early childhood he had been fascinated by stories of wars and battles. His interest in history continued to be mainly focussed on the military aspects. He studied the careers of great military leaders of the past, and spent a lot of time conducting imaginary battles and planning how he would achieve victory. The Second World War was raging, and Castro made maps and charts to follow its progress. He was usually bored by religious instruction, but liked the Old Testament accounts of battles and conflicts, especially when a small force achieved victory against the odds by a bold and sudden stroke, such as Joshua bringing down the walls of Jericho. These interests stayed with him all his life. In his old age he would on the smallest pretext launch into an analysis of the campaigns of Alexander the Great, or the struggle for power between Mark Antony and Octavian, or the rights and wrongs of the war strategies of Napoleon or Stalin.

At Belén he joined a debating society, seeing oratory as a sort of verbal warfare. He always liked talking and trying to win people over to his viewpoint. He was passionately keen to win the argument, at this stage not so much because of any strong beliefs but simply because he liked to win. He collected speeches by Demosthenes and Cicero, and tried to imitate their florid style. He practised his delivery in front of a mirror. A photograph of him giving a speech at Belén college shows a slim, quite elegant young man in a self-consciously relaxed but dignified posture.

It has been suggested that Castro's subsequent political development was influenced by his contacts at school with wealthy upper-class boys. The argument is that they looked down on Castro as a rough-mannered provincial boor, or possibly made fun of his illegitimate background, and that as a result he harboured a resentment against the rich and powerful in Cuban society. There is however little evidence for this. He sometimes said that he felt more at ease with 'ordinary' people, and also that, unlike some children of rich parents, he had lots of contact with poor people in his childhood. But such comments were a typical politician's means of showing that he was a man of the people. In Cuba in the 1950s a young man did not need to suffer social rejection to become a Communist, any more than did a son of wealthy parents at Cambridge University in the 1930s.

While at Belén college he still had relatively little interest in politics. In later years he sometimes tried to give the impression that even as a teenager he had felt sympathy for left-wing causes. In a speech at Havana University in 1995 he claimed to have been shocked and indignant when a Spanish teacher at Belén told him about the large number of Republican prisoners who were executed by the Franco government at the end of the Civil War. But this indignation may have been less strong at the time than he wanted his audience to believe. The weight of evidence is that he generally accepted without question the conservative assumptions of his teachers. The Jesuits at Belén were very different from the Jesuits of a later generation who often supported revolutionary causes. Castro himself said that they were all right-wing and supporters of Franco, teaching that Communism was something profoundly evil, responsible for the killing of priests and similar atrocities.

Among the political texts which Castro studied at Belén with apparent approval and admiration were the speeches of José Antonio Primo de Rivera, the founder of the Spanish Falange. José Antonio denounced both Marxism and the decadent materialism of the parliamentary democracies. Fidel was later converted to Marxism, but he always retained José Antonio's belief in 'strength through unity', and contempt for multi-party democracy. As a Marxist, he perforce became a philosophical materialist; but he never lost his scorn for materialist moral values. In 1998, after decades of persecuting and reviling the Catholic Church in Cuba, he would talk at great length about how much he shared with Pope John Paul a conviction that spiritual values were being corrupted by the consumerism and materialism of the industrialised world.

José Antonio also promulgated the notion of *hispanidad* (Hispanic culture), arguing that all the Spanish-speaking countries formed a single spiritual, cultural and even racial community. The young Castro felt a natural affinity for this doctrine. He was a Cuban patriot, but felt no embarrassment about his father's Spanish birth. On the contrary, if the Spanish-speaking countries did not stick together, they would inevitably be absorbed or dominated by the new empire of the United States. It was only later that Castro learnt to reject any attitude tinged with Fascism.

As for religion, Castro's attitude at this stage seems to have been a fairly conventional mix of compliance and boredom. In accordance with the school routine he had to go to mass every day, and he was sometimes seen praying privately. He would later say that he repeated the prayers and catechism mechanically, not thinking of the meaning, and that on the annual three-day 'spiritual retreat', which called for long periods of silence and self-inspection, he just waited for the next meal and daydreamed. Again, this indifference may have been exaggerated with the benefit of Communist hindsight. But it would not have been particularly surprising or unusual. Wealthy parents sent their sons to Belén because of its educational reputation and social cachet rather than for religious reasons. The Jesuits were well aware of this. They hoped that the seed of religion would take root among their pupils, but they knew that they had to tread cautiously and not push Catholic indoctrination too hard.

In any event Castro's religious attendance was good enough to earn favourable mention in the entry about him in the 1945 Belén College Year Book. The report also described him as an excellent student and outstanding athlete. It concluded that he would study law at university and expressed confidence that he would 'write brilliant pages in the book of his life'.

On 13 August 1996, officially Castro's seventieth birthday, a Cuban journalist reminded him of the entry in the Belén College Year Book. Had he fulfilled the prediction that he would write brilliant pages in the book of life? This was one of the rare occasions on which Fidel was in the mood to reminisce about his childhood.

FC: 'It was very generous of them to write that. They did it because I practised sports. I had good grades at school in general, but I was no model student. I did sports and other activities most of the year. People in school appreciated that . . . The priest who wrote the report was very fond of me . . .'

CJ: (Cuban journalist): 'Why?'

FC: 'It was his Spanish nature. He taught me discipline, studies, sports and outdoor activities.'

CJ: 'Were you a very serious boy when you were young in Birán? People there told us you were very serious.'

FC: 'Everyone has his version of events.'

CJ: 'What is your version? That's the one that's missing.'

FC: 'If I was serious? For my age I was. I was as serious as a young man could be at that age. I was always involved in adventures . . . At the age of five or six I was sent away. The teacher played a diplomatic role with my parents. My father had a good business sense, and it made good business sense to send the boys away to study. It's true. In my house there was no electricity. We used candles, lamps. Many places had electricity, but we lived in the middle of the countryside . . . One day my father bought a radio. In those days, radios were big monstrosities. The only one who could turn it on was him. I used to read. I'm talking about a different period now, when I was a bit older. I slept downstairs and my father slept upstairs. I took my books to my room. I read the ten-volume history of the French Revolution there. However, when the radio started broadcasting baseball games, I put my books aside and listened to the radio . . .'

CJ: 'You were keen on baseball, because you were a good pitcher.'

FC: 'No, I wasn't a good pitcher.'

CJ: 'You weren't? Then they're flattering you over there.'

FC: 'I'm being flattered right here. They make out that I was a professional player.'

CJ: 'Why don't you go to Birán?'

FC: 'May I finish telling this story, or do you want me to start on something else?'

CJ: 'Please carry on.'

FC: 'We used to take our gloves, ball and everything else with us when we went home from the teacher's small house . . . It was then that our parents realised that we were being mistreated. We were very skinny, and our hair was very long, because we were not even taken to the barber. I had to sew my own shoes, with the risk of being scolded for breaking the needle or something else. My shoes were very worn out. I had only one pair . . . Then we were taken back there. We were waging a war against the teacher. On one occasion we pelted the school with stones. She didn't like noise much. So we threw hundreds of stones, while hiding behind some trees. It was our revenge . . .'

CJ: 'Against the teacher?'

FC: 'I was only six years old . . .'

It was mainly Angel Castro's 'business sense' that made Fidel choose to study law after leaving Belén. Fidel later regretted not having studied a more 'useful' subject such as science. But at the time the law looked a natural choice. It offered a very respectable career, and one which gave plenty of scope for Fidel's passion for gladiatorial debate. As he himself recalled, people said: 'He talks a lot. He should be a lawyer.' But his father's encouragement was probably the decisive factor. A landowner can easily get embroiled in disputes over contracts or boundaries. Having a lawyer in the family could be very useful.

Fidel's younger brother Raúl followed him to Belén, but was much unhappier there. He complained bitterly about the prison-like atmosphere, the constant prayers and the fear of God. Fidel would later also attack the emphasis in Catholic schools on sin and punishment, which he described (in retrospect) as spiritual terrorism. But at the time he took it in his stride. He absorbed completely his Jesuit teachers' view that honour and integrity were much more important than material wealth or success. The personal honour which he learnt to respect at school, and always tried to demonstrate, meant above all not submitting to superior force. He admired the band of Spartans who defended the pass of Thermopylae against overwhelming odds, and his Iberian forebears in Numantia who perished to a man rather than surrender to the invading Romans. He had no death wish or desire for martyrdom. On the contrary, he always believed that any amount of trickery or deception was legitimate in order to survive to fight another day. But surrender and submission were shameful. One of the words which he used most often and most emotionally, especially in his old age, was *verguenza*, meaning the sense of shame. Not to have *verguenza* was the worst of sins.

Most of Castro's contemporaries at Belén college, both pupils and teachers, would become his political enemies when he turned Cuba into a Communist state. Many went into exile. Some spent long years in prison. But there is a surprising degree of convergence between their recollections of Castro as a schoolboy and his own reminiscences in old age. As a teenager he had been subject to conflicting influences. He had a mother who was warm, extrovert and loving, always ready to support and defend him. But he had been taken away from his home at an early age and spent many years in the environment of an all-male boarding school, where he learned to be hard and emotionally self-reliant. It is not surprising that his personality showed paradoxes and apparent contradictions. At Belén he could impress both teachers and boys as being intelligent and reasonable, but could also engage in acts of reckless exhibitionism, such as when he rode his bicycle at full speed downhill and through a narrow gate, hitting the gatepost and spending three days in the school infirmary recovering from his injuries. Garrulous and pushy, he was also very much a loner, difficult to influence and obstinately determined to take his own decisions. He had followers and admirers but no really close personal friends. A talented and fanatically keen participant in team sports, he was a poor team player, usually wanting to take the lead and do everything his way. Lazy and self-absorbed much of the time, he could also be fiercely hard-working, dedicated and loyal. He could be generous and magnanimous, but also vindictive and unforgiving. He always had a keen sense of humour and could laugh at himself (despite many assertions to the contrary). But he was a bad loser and could react with ferocious rage if he thought that he was being humiliated.

When he left Belén he had great belief in himself and was encouraged in this by the teachers who said he had a brilliant future. At the graduation ceremony he was not top of the graduating class, but he received the loudest applause, no doubt due to his sporting prowess. He certainly showed no sign of having felt socially ostracised by the more upper-class boys. On the contrary he felt he had become part of the elite. His parents might be rough and unpolished, but he had distinguished himself at the best school in the country. He thought he could achieve great things. At the same time he did not yet know what they were. He may have allowed his teachers and parents to influence his choice of a subject to read at university simply because he did not yet know what he wanted to do and be in life. Politics was not a high priority. When he arrived at the university he was, as he often subsequently said, politically illiterate. But the pattern of his future life was in fact already beginning to take shape.

He needed a cause to which he could attach his energy and determination. How could he make a name for himself? What could he do for his country? He had studied and admired the exploits of the heroes of Cuba's independence movement, and also the history of the American and French Revolutions. The United States had made itself a great world power. But Cuba in 1945 seemed pretty small and insignificant on the world scene. His Jesuit mentors had talked about the Hispanic world, but Latin America was in reality weak, poor and divided. Why were the English-speaking Americas so strong and the Spanish-speaking Americas so weak?

Cuba's greatest national hero was José Martí, whose writings in exile provided much of the political and intellectual inspiration for the independence movement. Martí had landed on the coast of Oriente and died soon afterwards, charging on a white horse towards the Spanish lines. Castro began to study the writings of Martí at Belén with an enthusiasm which would continue and grow throughout his life. It was Martí who made Castro start thinking that the United States was the cause of many of Cuba's weaknesses and deficiencies. Martí had lived in New York, 'in the belly of the beast', and warned of the danger for Cuba and Latin America of American expansionism.

Why had the United States intervened against Spain just when the Cuban nationalists seemed on the brink of success? And when independence finally came, why had it not brought the justice, prosperity and dignity which the patriots had fought for? Why had the country's wealth fallen increasingly into the hands of North Americans? When there was an economic down-turn, and measures were introduced to protect Cuban jobs, this did not affect the Americans running the sugar mills in Oriente. It was instead the poor Haitian cane-cutters working on Angel Castro's farm who were liable to be rounded up and deported. Why was this? Why were successive Cuban governments so willing to dance to the Americans' tune? These were the sort of questions that were gnawing at Castro at the time when he moved from college to university.

It has often been argued that Castro as a politician was inspired less by ideology than by hostility to the United States. He would devote his entire political life to fighting the United States, making propaganda against the United States, seeking to weaken American power and influence wherever and whenever he could. His intensely emotional hostility to the Unites States was however intellectual in origin. In his youth he had very little direct contact with Americans. There was no childhood incident which influenced his attitude. He was in fact not being hypocritical when in later years he protested that his battle against 'imperialism' did not mean any dislike of Americans as a people or the United States as a country.

Castro in fact always admired American qualities: the strength of their institutions, their patriotism, their hard work and self-reliance and above all their technology. He has told politicians and diplomats from English-speaking African countries that they were lucky to have been colonised by the British rather than the Spanish, demonstrating the point by contrasting North American power and prosperity with Latin American failure. But already by the time he was eighteen, under the influence of Martí and others, the United States was beginning in his mind to take the form of the 'empire', the great imperious force which dominated and exploited weaker countries like Cuba. His attitude to it was that of a pugilist confronting a large and powerful opponent. He does not necessarily hate him, and may feel a healthy respect for him. But the stronger the man facing him, the more determined he is to use every ounce of his strength and cunning, every skill and trick that he knows, to thwart and ultimately defeat his opponent. Throwing off the yoke of American domination was to become his cause, his mission in life.

2   Alone on the Beach

In 1945, when Castro enrolled in the Faculty of Law at Havana University, the state of Cuba seemed in many respects quite favourable. The Second World War had pushed up the price of most important commodities, including sugar. Cuban export industries were booming. Although much of the wealth being created went abroad, a lot also came to the capital. To many outsiders Havana looked one of the most dynamic, prosperous and pleasure-loving cities in Latin America. Democracy seemed alive and well, with a new government elected the previous year on a platform of popular reforms.

These circumstances did not, however, create an atmosphere of peace and contentment at Havana University. Since the time of independence, university students had tended to see themselves as the country's conscience, speaking out against the corruption, incompetence and servility of successive governments. Being a focus of opposition, students were also often the victims of repression. This repression had reached unprecedented heights of brutality during the government of General Gerardo Machado, who used gangs of hired thugs to kill or terrorise troublesome student leaders.

Machado's dictatorship collapsed in chaos in 1933. But the events that followed left a sense of anger and frustration which was still keenly felt by the generation of students which Fidel Castro joined in 1945. Much of this anger and frustration was directed towards the United States.

The United States maintained that it had the right to intervene in Cuba's affairs whenever this was necessary to ensure 'a government adequate for the protection of life, property and individual liberty'. When Machado departed, the US Ambassador tried to patch together a new government, which would be more broad-based but still conservative-minded and pro-American. The Student Directorate, which had borne the brunt of opposition to Machado, now led opposition to the Ambassador's role, demanding the establishment of a genuinely independent and nationalistic government. For a while the Ambassador lost control. The armed forces, a traditional bastion of conservatism, were weak and ineffective. The officer corps had been discredited by their support for the hated Machado, and demoralised by his fall. Taking advantage of this situation, Sergeant Fulgencio Batista, a handsome *mestizo* (half-caste) with considerable charm and intelligence, organised a 'sergeants' revolt', and took control of the army. He made common cause with the Student Directorate. Amid scenes of wild enthusiasm, a Revolutionary Directorate took power, led by Dr Ramón Grau, a popular university lecturer. The new government proceeded to promulgate a flurry of radical measures, including agrarian reform, voting rights for women, minimum wages and minimum working hours, and new trade union rights.

The US Ambassador was deeply worried by the new government's 'communistic' programme. He withheld recognition from it, and urged his own government to prepare for a direct intervention by the US Marines. The threat proved sufficient. Batista, now a colonel, agreed to take power himself, and to throw out the Revolutionary Directorate. Once again, student leaders became the target of violent repression. Professor Grau organised his supporters into the Authentic Cuban Revolutionary Party, known as the *Auténticos*, and bided his time.

Batista proved a skilful politician. He operated at first behind the façade of a civilian government. He made a tactical alliance with the Communists, and used them to enhance his control of the labour movement. At the same time he reassured the Americans during a successful visit to Washington in 1938. He organised elections to a Constituent Assembly which drew up a new and admirably democratic constitution. In 1940 he was elected President of the Republic.

Batista's supporters also won the parallel elections to the Congress. Fidel Castro, then aged fourteen, had a direct glimpse of how the electoral system worked. His half-brother Pedro Emilio was standing as an alternate candidate of the *Auténtico* party in Oriente province. Pedro Emilio asked Fidel to call on all the people at Birán on the electoral roll and to explain to them, many being illiterate, how to vote and where to put their cross on the ballot paper to elect Castro. Fidel carried out this task diligently. He had been promised a horse if his half-brother were successful. However, as often happened in the countryside, a detachment of Rural Guards arrived at the polling station, and only allowed people to vote if they supported the government.

By 1944 Batista had become over-confident. Presiding over a booming economy, and believing that he was genuinely loved by the Cuban people, he staged relatively free and fair elections. To his surprise and disgust, he lost. Dr Grau returned to power. But Grau was a changed man, less the idealistic academic, more the pragmatic politician. In an attempt to consolidate his shaky power base, he gave money and jobs to some of his old student supporters, and a green light to use violence against his political enemies, both inside and outside the university. The activities of the pro-government 'action groups' provoked other young political activists to adopt the same methods, spawning more armed gangs.

The university provided an ideal base for such activities. It occupied a large area on a hill in a prosperous suburb of the city. In the Latin American tradition the University was 'autonomous', and the national police and army were not allowed to enter its precincts. There was a special university police force, responsible in theory to the Rector, but it was small, ineffective and often in cahoots with the gangs. Privately owned weapons could easily be stored and protected. The large student body was under no effective supervision. Students had programmes of lectures and examinations but tended not to be under the direction of any particular professor or tutor. There were many 'professional' students, men already well into their thirties who enrolled every year but only to have the university as a base for other activities.

By the time Castro entered the university the action groups had degenerated into outright gangsterism. While their members still professed political ideals and objectives, usually on radical nationalistic lines, most of their activities were directed to securing power and financial benefits for themselves. By threats and intimidation they virtually controlled the sale and distribution of textbooks. They influenced frightened professors into giving good grades to their members and supporters. Above all they tried to get their members elected to the top posts in the Federation of University Students (FEU), the officially recognised organisation representing the student body and a good launching-pad for a career in national politics. The gangs' worst violence was directed against each other rather than against their supposed ideological opponents. Beatings, shootings and even murders were quite commonplace.

Before joining the university, Castro had led a sheltered existence. He wanted to make his mark on a bigger stage, and was certainly not intimidated by the university's reputation for violence. He spent the summer of 1945 at home in Birán, restless and impatient to start his new life. He insisted to his father that at the university he would need a car. Angel resisted for a while, but finally bought Fidel a new Ford. Fidel drove to Havana with his sister Angela. The journey took three days, Fidel learning to drive on the way. In Havana they rented a small flat. In September he enrolled in the Law Faculty, and immediately plunged into university politics, his aim from the start being to become the President of the FEU. He looked up the records of his fellow law students in order to judge better how to enlist their support. His first circle of acquaintances were mainly like himself from Catholic schools, and with them he presented himself as representing the Catholic interest.

In his first months at university Castro also devoted a fair amount of time to sports and athletics. But soon politics took over almost completely. He became a voracious reader of newspapers, political journals and books about current affairs. He showed little interest in his legal studies, attending lectures only rarely and relying, as he had done at school, on last-minute cramming to pass exams. Most of his time was devoted to making himself known among his fellow students and campaigning for office in the FEU. He spent many hours in the faculty cafeteria and in other cafeterias in Havana where students gathered. He talked unstoppably about politics, with much gesticulating, often standing up and pacing around. He stood out in a crowd. Tall and with handsome features, he often made a point of wearing a dark suit and tie, which was unusual in the hot climate and generally informal atmosphere of Havana. Far from wanting to blend in with his peers, he wanted to be different. Despite the formal dress, his lifestyle was scruffy and Bohemian. He tended to leave papers on the floor, cigar ash everywhere and shoe-marks on the beds where he would throw himself down fully clothed. He confidently assumed, as he would for the rest of his life, that others could adapt to him rather than the other way round.

At this period Castro had little knowledge of economic or social questions, and showed little interest in them. His focus was on the practicalities of obtaining and wielding power. He presented himself as the man who would be most energetic and most effective in defending the students' interests, and in promoting the values of honesty, decency and justice. His attitude towards authority, both at national and university level, was contemptuous and adversarial. At his Jesuit boarding-school he had learned to respect above all austerity, honour and moral rectitude. The big world of Havana mostly reflected very different values. Life was to be enjoyed. Money was what counted. Governments governed by buying favours. Those who supported authority could expect to be rewarded. Those who opposed authority could expect to feel the weight of a police truncheon. In the wider world the United States was top dog. It was common sense to keep on good terms with the Americans, and comply so far as possible with their wishes.

Castro detested these attitudes. In the university he soon lost what remained of his religious faith, but he retained the outlook of a religious zealot in denouncing the immorality of the authorities. In his eyes police brutality, government corruption and Cuban subservience to the United States were all symptoms of the moral rottenness at the core of the Cuban body politic.

Most Cubans and even many students accepted United States dominance as a fact of life which it was futile to resist. But few liked the spectacle of their country's subservience. Most politically active students considered themselves to be 'anti-imperialist'. This did not necessarily have any Marxist connotation. It meant little more than opposing United States domination. The numerous American interventions in Cuba's history had left many Cubans with a deep sense of national humiliation. They saw Cuba's experience as being typical of the whole region. The United States had engineered the splitting off of Panama from Colombia in order to build and control the Panama Canal. It had effectively annexed Puerto Rico. In 1930 United States Marines in the Dominican Republic had helped establish the government of General Trujillo, who became one of the most brutal dictators in the history of Latin America. American military and economic power had been frequently exercised to ensure that the governments of Central America favoured United States interests.

Castro's anti-imperialism was therefore neither original nor unusual. But in his case it was exceptionally passionate and single-minded. He joined the University Committee for the Independence of Puerto Rico and the Committee for Democracy in the Dominican Republic (i.e. for getting rid of Trujillo's government). If there were any meetings or protests about the nefarious actions of the United States in the region, Castro would seek to take a leading role. He even liked the idea of working for a political federation of the Caribbean states, including Central America, Colombia and Venezuela, which would constitute a regional power and be strong enough to stand up to United States pressure.

What did Castro's fellow students make of him? As always with Castro, subsequent recollections have inevitably been coloured by attitudes to his later career. Some of his colleagues found him self-centred, pretentious and domineering. His hyper-activism and extreme views made some regard him as 'crazy', a maverick. But even some who later became bitter enemies acknowledged that at the University he was already beginning to show his famously charismatic qualities. He had charm, wit, insatiable energy and a great histrionic sense. He quickly made himself a centre of attention.

The appointment of the top officers in the FEU was the outcome of a sequence of elections starting at the bottom. Students following a particular course elected a delegate from their year. The various course delegates then elected from among their number a representative of their year within their faculty. The representatives of each year (five in the case of the Law Faculty) then chose from among their number the President of the Faculty. The thirteen Faculty Presidents finally elected the President, Secretary General and other national officers of the FEU.

This system of indirect elections looked democratic enough but was in practice much more susceptible to manipulation than a system of direct elections would have been. It was easier to influence the votes of three out of five year representatives than to influence a mass election. The system was in force at this period in many authoritarian countries, such as Franco's Spain, where student bodies were in practice under tight government control. It would indeed become the typical process of election in the Communist state established in Cuba by Castro.

Castro got himself elected as course delegate (by those studying legal anthropology) and then as representative of his year in the Law Faculty. But he did not get the vote of any of the other year representatives to become President of the Law Faculty. In his second year he helped a friend from Oriente to get elected as representative of the new first year. This gave Castro two out of five votes, but the other three, while all claiming to be independent and opposed to government control of the FEU, argued that Castro was too extreme and controversial to represent the faculty effectively. Castro was persuaded to go along with the appointment of the fourth year representative, on the understanding that he would vote against the pro-government candidates in the FEU elections.

Some months later, when the slate which Castro considered to be pro-government had been re-elected to the top FEU posts, Castro and his supporters, having talked round two more year representatives, summoned an extraordinary assembly of the Law Faculty students, said that the Faculty President had breached the undertakings on which he had been elected and that as a consequence the four other year representatives had elected Castro to replace him. The existing President did not accept this and appealed to the University Council, i.e. the Rector. For a short time there were two rival Presidents. Then the Council ruled that the extraordinary meeting was unconstitutional, that the statutes of the university made no provision for removing duly appointed officers before the end of their term and that the election of Castro was invalid.

Castro believed that his failure to achieve his ambition of becoming FEU President (or even accepted as President of the Law Faculty) was due to foul play and outside pressures, especially pressure from gangs close to the authorities. But the cause lay at least partly in his own personality. He was a loner who always wanted to get his own way and was reluctant to do deals or negotiate compromises. At meetings he was impatient of procedural rules and usually tried to dominate the proceedings. The political associations and action groups saw him as a talented agitator, a useful man to have on their side, but also as a loose cannon, someone who could not be trusted to follow an agreed line.

From an early date Castro's political activism attracted the attention of the Cuban Communist Party. Alfredo Guevara, an influential Party member, heard about the rambunctious new activist in the Law Faculty. He walked round from the neighbouring Faculty of Philosophy and Letters to introduce himself, and to see whether Castro might be suitable material for recruitment.

His impression was that Castro was extremely unsuitable. With his dark suit and tie, and aristocratic bearing, he seemed the epitome of aggressive Catholic conservatism. Castro remained on friendly personal terms with Guevara, as he did with some other Communist students, but the Communists regarded him as a potentially dangerous political opponent. It would be several years before there was a meeting of minds.

Castro also had dealings with two of the main action groups which were active inside the university. These were the Socialist Revolutionary Movement (MSR) and the Insurrectional Revolutionary Union (UIR). The President of the FEU when Castro arrived at the University, and the man whose job he wanted, was Manolo Castro (no relation), one of the leading figures in the MSR and already in his thirties. He had been appointed a police lieutenant in Grau's 1933 government but returned as a student in the Faculty of Engineering when that first Grau government collapsed. Fidel had at first an ambivalent attitude to Manolo Castro and the MSR. He had no objection at all to 'action', including violence, if it seemed to him to be in a good cause. One of his first initiatives was to lead a group of fellow law students which violently broke up a meeting of alleged 'Fascists'. The MSR purported to be anti-government, anti-Communist and anti-imperialist, all of which fitted Fidel's own position. One of the principal specific avowed objectives of the MSR was the overthrow of the Trujillo dictatorship in the Dominican Republic, a cause which Fidel enthusiastically supported. Fidel realised moreover that his chances of becoming President of the FEU would be greater if he could persuade Manolo Castro to back him as his successor than if he ran against him or against his chosen successor.

At the same time Fidel was suspicious of the MSR's close links with members of the Grau government. He knew that MSR members took government money in return for doing Ministers' dirty work, including the pursuit of personal vendettas. The MSR for their part did not trust Fidel. He was aggressively independent and unlikely to accept the discipline of a tightly controlled and secretive organisation such as the MSR. They may have known or suspected that Fidel was also in friendly contact with members of the MSR's deadly rivals, the UIR.

In his first year Fidel was close enough to Manolo Castro to be among three students invited by Manolo to accompany him in a call on Carlos Miguel de Céspedes, a right-wing politician with a reputation for corruption. Céspedes was thinking of standing as a candidate to be Mayor of Havana. He had contacted the President of the FEU to seek student support for his campaign. An account of the meeting was published soon afterwards in a student magazine, probably written by Fidel himself. Certainly Castro was given the best lines. According to the article, Céspedes explained his programme and asked for the students' support. When Fidel's turn came to speak, his first few words seemed positive and encouraging. He said that he would support Céspedes (pause for effect) but on three conditions (another pause for effect). The three conditions were: first, that the student leaders killed by previous right-wing governments should be brought back to life; second, that Céspedes and his friends should return to the national Treasury all the money which they had stolen from the people; and third, that history should be turned back a hundred years. If these conditions were met, said Fidel, he would willingly sell himself as a slave to the colony into which Céspedes wanted to turn Cuba. He then walked out.

In November 1946 Castro, then aged nineteen (officially twenty), made his first public speech to attract significant attention outside the university. He was one of the speakers at an annual ceremony organised by the university to mark the anniversary of the execution by the Spanish authorities in 1871 of eight medical students convicted of desecrating the grave of a Spanish officer. The event took place in the cemetery of the fashionable suburb of Vedado. After paying tribute to the student martyrs, Castro launched into a fierce attack on the Grau government; he accused Grau of planning to run for an illegal second term as President in 1948; he said that ministers were systematically stealing public funds for their own private purposes, while the poor starved; he claimed that violent gangs were run from the inner circles of the government; and he urged the Cuban people not to be intimidated into apathy and inaction, but to fight with all their strength against the tyranny being imposed on them.

Partly because of Castro's outspoken contribution, the ceremony at the cemetery took the front page of some newspapers the following day. His name began to be known. The event made enough of a splash to be the subject of a report to London by the British Ambassador, who said it illustrated the growing disgust felt in some circles over the corruption and high-handedness of the Grau administration.

A month after his Vedado speech Castro, according to some accounts, took part in an assassination attempt against a gun-toting member of the UIR, Lionel Gómez. Gómez was about to join the university, and had boasted that he intended to take over the Presidency of the FEU. Castro viewed Gómez as an obstacle to his ambitions. He warned Gómez not to use his strong-arm tactics to try to influence the FEU elections. Gómez treated the warning with derision. Then, when Castro and two companions saw Gómez in a sports stadium, they decided on the spur of the moment to kill him. As Gómez and members of his gang were leaving the stadium, Castro and his friends fired several shots, before fleeing. But Gómez was only wounded. Another student accompanying him was also wounded in the leg. According to some versions of the incident, Castro and his two colleagues were acting on behalf of Manolo Castro. Another version is that Manolo Castro was not involved but that Fidel had hoped to gain Manolo's support by killing one of his dangerous enemies. Others argued that the story of Castro's involvement was a fabrication by his political enemies.

If Castro did indeed shoot and wound Gómez, the outcome in the ensuing months was the opposite of what might have been expected. Castro's relationship with the MSR grew more distant and more antagonistic, while his relations with the UIR, to which Gómez belonged, grew closer. He appeared to be well liked by the head of the UIR, Emilio Tró, a man in his thirties who had fought with the Anarchists in the Spanish Civil War and with the United States army in the Second World War. The UIR had no significant ideological differences with the MSR, but opposed it on the grounds that it acted as a cat's-paw and enforcer for the government. Tró admired Castro's independence and courage, and took the view that Gómez was himself partly responsible for the shooting incident, through his boastful and provocative behaviour. Whether and when Castro actually joined the UIR is debatable. Friends of Castro deny that he ever belonged to the UIR or any other gang. A leading member of the UIR said later in exile that Castro had 'used us for his own political battles in the university, but never really identified himself with the UIR'. In any event, once Castro began to associate closely with the leaders of the UIR, being seen visiting Tró in his office and sometimes travelling in a UIR car, he was perceived by the student body to be for all practical purposes a member.

Castro was never a believer in non-violence. Both by instinct and by conviction he favoured hitting back. Violence for him was therefore either good or bad depending on the motive. He saw no inconsistency in constantly attacking and denouncing the gangs in the university, while himself belonging to the UIR, or at least associating with it. Commenting on this period of his life he wrote: 'This evil . . . had its origins in the resentment and hatred which Batista sowed during eleven years of abuses and injustices. Those who saw their comrades assassinated, wished to avenge them. A regime which was incapable of imposing justice permitted vengeance. The blame does not lie with those young men . . . They wanted to make a revolution at a moment when this was impossible. Many of those who died as gangsters, victims of illusion, would today be heroes.'

Castro never directly refuted the various allegations which have been made about his involvement in violence at the University. By contrast he often publicly took pride in never having been bought off by the authorities. Writing in 1955, only five years after graduating, he said: 'Thousands of students who are today professional men saw my actions for five years . . .

These men can be witnesses to my conduct . . . In an era of unprecedented corruption, when many student leaders had access to dozens of government jobs and so many were corrupted, to have led protests against the regime for several years, without ever having appeared on a government payroll, is worthy of some merit.'

Castro always described himself as the victim of violence, rather than as an instigator. As he put it in 1959: 'I was the Quixote of the University, always the target of blows and bullets.' There were some others who also saw him in this light. He had a band of enthusiastic followers, and increasing success in attracting media publicity. In January he was one of thirty-four student leaders who signed a declaration denouncing Grau's plans to seek re-election as President. They undertook to continue the struggle against re-election even if it cost them their lives, adding the words used by Bolívar in the South American War of Independence: 'It is better to die on our feet than live on our knees.' Soon after this Castro took a group of students to the Isle of Pines to look at what was supposed to be a show-piece prison. In both design and organisation it had been copied from a prison in the United States, and was trumpeted by the government as a 'model penitentiary'. Castro and his friends found what they expected and no doubt wanted: that conditions for the inmates were in fact barbarous. They protested vigorously and publicly and got their findings written up in various newspapers in Havana.

In the spring of 1947 Castro got involved for the first time in national politics. One of the very few established politicians whom he admired was Eduardo (Eddy) Chibás, a wealthy, quarrelsome and eccentric senator. Like Castro, Chibás had been educated at the Dolores and Belén Jesuit schools. He was imprisoned for a time under Machado and was a member of the Student Directorate which nominated Grau as President in 1933. He was again imprisoned briefly in the ensuing repression under Batista. He was always on the radical wing of Grau's *Auténtico* party, insisting that the movement of 1933 was not a revolt but a revolution. A flamboyant orator, he presented himself as a brush sweeping away the dirt and rubbish which polluted the corridors of power. The accession of Grau to the Presidency in 1944 did not stop Chibás from pursuing his long-running campaign against government corruption and abuses. He had a weekly radio programme in which he denounced ministers for taking cuts on government contracts, diverting state pension funds to private purposes, putting friends on the government payroll to draw salaries without working, creaming off profits from lottery and gambling operations, and similar abuses. His slogan *Verguenza contra dinero* (Shame against money) was exactly in tune with Castro's sentiments.

Chibás finally withdrew completely from the *Auténticos*. On 15 May 1947 he summoned a large meeting to announce the launch of a new party, the

Party of the Cuban People (PPC). It became known as the *Ortodoxos,* on the grounds that the *Auténticos* had strayed away from the principles of Martí which it claimed to represent, and that the *Ortodoxos* were the true orthodox representatives of Martí's thinking. The party would stand for 'nationalism, anti-imperialism, socialism, economic independence, political liberty and social justice'. Castro was the only prominent student leader who attended the launch of the new party. He immediately joined and became an enthusiastic supporter. His time with the *Ortodoxos* would be the only period in which he tried to achieve his political aims through the ballot box. Even in this period, however, he showed little confidence in the conventional democratic process. He and some other students set up a faction of the youth wing of the *Ortodoxos,* naming it Radical Orthodox Action (ARO). The ARO under Castro's influence was soon moving away from the main party, advocating the seizure of power by revolutionary rather than electoral means. Chibás welcomed Castro's support, but had a poor opinion of his judgement. He was irritated by Castro's efforts to push him into a more radical posture, and into rejecting tactical links with wealthy and more conservative sympathisers.

Meanwhile the battle of the gangs was moving into a new and even more violent phase. In an attempt to exercise greater control, President Grau appointed the main protagonists of the gangs to lucrative posts in the government machine. Manolo Castro was made National Sports Director, which meant that he finally had to relinquish his post as President of the FEU. Mario Salabarría, the man with direct control of the MSR's racketeering and intimidation, became a police major and head of the Police Bureau of Investigation in Havana. Emilio Tró was also appointed a police major, and given the job of Director of the National Police Academy. Grau hoped that these appointments would give him an instrument for controlling and intimidating the labour unions. He did not want to use the army, whose loyalty was still suspect. But the predictable outcome was that gang violence, now between rival police forces, increased in ferocity.

In the university Castro took part in a series of meetings of students and academic staff aimed at agreeing a range of reforms. He continued to argue in favour of direct elections to the FEU, but without success. Elections went ahead on the old system. Once again, the MSR was pitted against the UIR. The MSR, recognising that they might not be able to impose all their own men, supported a fairly broad-based slate which included some Communists. A rival slate, in which Castro stood for the post of Secretary-General, was supported by the UIR and many Catholics, but was defeated. The new President of the FEU, Enrique Ovares (later given a long prison sentence under Castro), was at that time a relatively uncontroversial moderate Socialist. The new Secretary-General, occupying the post sought by Castro, was Castro's Communist friend Alfredo Guevara.

A special assembly was held on 16 July 1947 to announce the university reforms that had been drawn up. Castro was one of the speakers. He made the most of his opportunity. His style was more formal and grandiloquent than in later years, but the content included most of the elements that would come to constitute a typical Castro speech. He raised the emotional temperature by recounting the fate of students killed by past oppressive governments. He then launched a sweeping attack on the Grau government, accusing it of using corrupt gangs to terrorise and intimidate the Cuban nation.

This was too much for the authorities, and in particular for the new head of the Police Bureau of Investigation in Havana, Major Salabarría, who was clearly Castro's principal target. Castro received a sharp ultimatum. In his second year he had been so totally absorbed in politics that he had not even registered for the annual exams, and was therefore technically not eligible to attend university classes. Using this as a pretext, Salabarría conveyed the message that Castro must stay away from the university altogether. If he did not, he was made to understand in the language of the gangs that he would be killed.

Speaking about this episode in 1961 Castro said:

> The atmosphere in the university had been contaminated by the sickness of national politics. My impetuosity, my desire to excel, made me determined to fight. My straightforward character soon brought me into conflict with the environment, the venal authorities, the corruption and the gang-ridden system that dominated the university. At the instigation of corrupt politicians, the gangs threatened me and prohibited me from entering the university. This was a moment of great decision . . . Alone on the beach, facing the sea, I examined the situation. Personal danger, physical risk, made my return to the university an act of extraordinary temerity. But not to return would be to give in to threats, to give in to bullies, to abandon my ideals and aspirations. I decided to go back and went back . . . with weapons in my hands . . .

Castro often contrived to convert the critical moments of his life into part of a heroic myth. In later life he would accept intellectually the Marxist view of history, the belief that it was economic and social conditions that slowly but surely determined trends and movements in the history of nations. But emotionally he remained attached to the view of history which had aroused his passionate interest in childhood and adolescence, the view in which heroic and exceptional individuals were able, through will-power, determination and good fortune, to change the course of history. Standing alone was an essential ingredient in the drama. He often praised great men of the past, both of thought and action, but seldom acknowledged much personal debt to them. 'I have been my own teacher all my life.' He was the small boy alone defying the authority of a bullying teacher, the solitary student on the beach facing the apparatus of a brutal police, the commander-in-chief of only two men facing the might of Batista's army, the little country standing up to the bullying and intimidation of its all-powerful neighbour. The smaller the David and the bigger the Goliath, the greater the merit of fortitude and resistance. He did not seek isolation, but if it came, it brought its political and emotional compensation.

Of course there could be only one David. In later life Castro never showed much sympathy with individuals who risked prison or worse rather than submit to his own authoritarian state power. For him such individuals were always, even if they themselves did not realise it, pawns of the great imperialist power against which his little island was fighting. However idealistic and honest their motivation, Castro could turn against them all the anger and vindictiveness which he felt for traitors bought and corrupted by the imperialist enemy.

No doubt in the summer of 1947 Castro did indeed stand alone on the beach, contemplating how he would respond to the threat against his life. But the picture of isolation given in the 1961 interview was overdone. He gave a fuller and probably more accurate account of this incident in a talk to the university of Havana in 1995. He said that after receiving the threat he wept, because he thought he would die. But having decided not to submit, he went to see 'an older friend' (presumably Emilio Tró). The older friend gave him a fifteen-round Browning pistol. Castro said this gave him a lot of confidence. He was a good shot, having often practised with various weapons at the farm in Birán. How did he survive the day of his return to the university? 'The truth was that one friend had other friends, and there were various people, various organisations and lots of people armed everywhere. Some were young, highly esteemed, courageous young men. My friend took the initiative as he had very good relations with the students and said to me: "You cannot sacrifice yourself like this." He persuaded another seven or eight people to come with me, people whom I did not know. They were excellent . . .'

In his 1995 account, Castro said that when he entered the university there were about fifteen members of the 'mafia' waiting for him. But when they saw that he was surrounded by a substantial number of armed men, they backed off. Subsequently he often went without a weapon, because he feared that Salabarría might induce the university police to arrest him for the illegal possession of arms. He relied on safety in numbers, being always accompanied by colleagues. On one occasion a large part of his anthropology class accompanied him to his apartment, after a rumour circulated that he would be attacked there. However, within days of his dramatic 'return' to the university, he was involved in an entirely new project, his first incursion into international politics.

3 Lessons in Revolution

In June 1947 Castro got wind of plans for an international expedition to overthrow the dictator of the Dominican Republic, General Rafael Trujillo. For years Dominican exiles and left-wing organisations throughout the Caribbean had been pressing for action against Trujillo. It was a particular objective of the MSR action group. What made it possible for the MSR to move from words to deeds was the appointment as Minister of Education of Julián Alemán, an ambitious and notoriously corrupt friend of President Grau. Alemán had close ties with the MSR leaders. His access to the budget and other resources of the Education Ministry made him a powerful ally.

Alemán persuaded the President that there would be political and economic benefits in supporting the expedition. He argued that the action would be popular in Cuba, and that a new Dominican government could be expected to give commercial advantages to the people who had helped it to power. The expedition would have to be prepared in secret, both to take Trujillo by surprise and to prevent the United States from intervening. The Americans were unlikely to sit idly by while one Caribbean country took military action to overthrow the government of another Caribbean country. But Trujillo had become an embarrassment to his one-time American sponsors. Alemán believed that once the deed was done, and Trujillo removed from power, no one would complain seriously and most would applaud.

After all, the Trujillo government had become a byword for the worst sort of repressive brutality, and was detested by most sections of world opinion from the far left to the moderate democratic right. The Dominican Republic was seen as a country whose wealth went into the pockets of a few big corporations, and of the family and cronies of the dictator, while the majority of the population lived in squalor and poverty. A ruthless secret police routinely resorted to torture and killings to root out any focus of opposition.

Alemán thought that the expedition would also help him to secure fuller control over the action groups. In return for his providing finance, weapons and other supplies, the MSR and its allies would use their muscle to help Alemán's personal ambitions, which included running for the Presidency in 1948.

The man put in charge of planning and leading the expedition was General Juan Rodríguez, a Dominican exile. From a military viewpoint the proposed expedition looked perfectly feasible. The Dominican Republic was less than 200 miles from the eastern tip of Cuba. The Dominican army and police were effective against unarmed civilians, but had never had to confront a well-armed and determined military force. It was expected that once a beach-head was established, the local population would give enthusiastic support to the invaders, and that the initial landing could if necessary be followed by further waves of volunteers. Alemán started importing large quantities of weapons from Argentina, storing them in various secret locations.

When Fidel Castro heard about the expedition, he immediately wanted to join. He had become the President of the University Committee for Democracy in the Dominican Republic. In this capacity he had got to know many of the leading Dominican exiles. A military expedition formed by volunteers from all over the Caribbean perfectly fitted his ideal of region-wide joint action against 'imperialism'. The problem for Castro, however, was that the Cuban body most directly involved in the project was the MSR, the organisation which had declared war on him and whose threats he had defied by returning to the university.

To overcome this obstacle, Castro sought the help of some friends who were taking a leading role in the organisation of the expedition. These were in particular Juan Bosch, a prominent Dominican intellectual, and Enrique Ovares, the new President of the FEU. These two talked on Fidel's behalf to Rolando Masferrer, the head of the MSR, and to Manolo Castro, the preceding FEU President. Ovares told Manolo Castro that personal differences between him and Fidel should not prevent them from working together to get rid of Trujillo. Manolo Castro agreed: 'Fidel is a shit, but he is right on this.' He and Masferrer gave an assurance that Fidel Castro would come to no harm from the MSR, at least while he was engaged on the Dominican enterprise.

When Fidel's parents heard that he was planning not to spend his summer holiday at home, but instead to take part in the invasion of a neighbouring country, they were horrified. They contacted Bosch and tried to persuade him to discourage Fidel from participating. Accompanied by Fidel's elder brother Ramón, they appealed to Fidel to desist. His father offered financial inducements if he would withdraw. His mother got emotional, saying that if the Dominicans did not kill Fidel, Masferrer would.

There was never a chance that these efforts would succeed. Fidel believed that his parents were well-meaning but completely incapable of understanding the political importance of what he was doing. He told them that Máximo Gómez, one of the heroes of the Cuban War of Independence, was a Dominican. The Cubans owed the Dominicans a debt. Unless the peoples of the Caribbean showed solidarity with each other, they would remain weak, divided and exploited by the United States. There was no meeting of minds. Fidel knew that if he failed to join the expedition, his reputation as an anti-imperialist revolutionary would be seriously tarnished. As if to demonstrate that nothing would deflect him from his purpose, he wrote a last will and testament, bequeathing his collection of books to various student friends.

The participants in the expedition gathered towards the end of July 1947 at a farm near Holguin, a town in Oriente province. There were about 1,200 men, mostly Dominicans and Cubans but also a sprinkling of exiles and volunteers from other countries in the region such as Venezuela, Guatemala, Costa Rica and Honduras. The organisers wanted to give the expedition as international a flavour as possible. In Holguin the men were organised into platoons and issued with uniforms and weapons. Castro was put in charge of a mixed-nationality platoon.

With such a large and diverse contingent, it was difficult to restrict knowledge of what was afoot. Rumours spread widely in Cuba and were soon picked up in Miami and further afield. Those within the Cuban army who knew about the operation were distinctly unenthusiastic. The Chief of Staff, General Pérez Dámera, was supposed to be helping to organise the expedition. But he was privately suspicious that Grau and Alemán might try to use the force to promote their own interests inside Cuba. He said that it was dangerous and insecure to have this relatively large irregular force on the Cuban mainland. He insisted that it should move to a more secluded offshore location.

On 29 July the expeditionary force was transported at night on three boats to Cayo Confites, one of hundreds of small uninhabited islands off the north coast of Cuba. There they stayed for fifty-nine days, burnt by the relentless tropical sun, bitten by swarms of mosquitoes, receiving supplies, undergoing training, and waiting impatiently for the order to set sail for the Dominican Republic. During this time things started to go seriously wrong. The Dominican and United States governments both had intelligence sources within the Dominican exile community and within the Cuban army. They knew exactly what was happening. As a bait Trujillo sent his private yacht to the waters off the eastern tip of Cuba, and spread the rumour that he was aboard. The force on Cayo Confites duly sent a fast launch to try to capture Trujillo, thereby confirming their presence and intentions. Trujillo pressed the US government to take action to stop the invasion. The Cuban army, except for a few officers with specially close links with the government, was increasingly hostile. Chief of Staff Pérez Dámera was summoned to a meeting in Washington and on return urged his government forcefully to call off the expedition.

The MSR's involvement in the expedition was also becoming a liability, due to developments in Havana. Police Major Salabarría of the MSR accused Police Major Tró of the rival UIR of murdering one of his officers. While Tró was dining with the Chief of Police of Marianao, policemen under Salabarría surrounded the house and a three-hour gun battle took place. Tró died riddled with bullets. Four innocent bystanders, including a woman, were killed and others wounded. The 'Orfila massacre' shocked even the hardened and cynical people of Havana. The army was outraged and secured the government's agreement to the arrest of Salabarría, who was later sentenced to thirty years in prison.

Hard-pressed by the United States and the Cuban army, President Grau on 20 September ordered the cancellation of the expedition. General Rodríguez was summoned to Havana and a naval frigate was sent to Oriente. When the order came to call off the expedition, some men left Cayo Confites and disbanded. Others including Castro embarked on a freighter, hoping to go ahead with a scaled-down operation under the command of Juan Bosch. But the freighter was intercepted by the naval frigate near the Gulf of Nipe. Most of those on board were arrested and taken to Havana. Some escaped. Fidel Castro, wanting to avoid the humiliation of arrest and possibly fearing that the MSR might now feel released from any obligation not to take action against him, decided to escape during the night, exploiting the fact that he happened to be off the familiar shoreline near his home. He swam ashore, carrying a sub-machine gun strung round his neck. He hid his gun and walked to the house of a family friend, who provided a change of clothes. He stayed only one night in Oriente before moving on. He was eager and impatient to get back to Havana.

The shambolic failure of the Cayo Confites expedition did not lead Castro to change his political views. On the contrary, the experience confirmed his belief that military action by revolutionaries from different countries was both possible and desirable. He regarded it as self-evident that a ruthless dictatorship like that of Trujillo could not be overcome by fine words and diplomatic pressure. In Castro's view the mission had not failed. It had been betrayed. Grau and Alemán had set it up, but when circumstances became difficult they shamefully pulled the plug on it. General Pérez Dámera had pretended to support the expedition, but from the start he had been 'bought' by Trujillo. Castro concluded that a traditional professional army could never be trusted to support revolutionary action.

Castro was also indignant over the lack of adequate security. Little was done to ensure that the numerous participants from many countries did not correspond with their relatives or friends, including people abroad. For the revolutionary seizure of power, Castro concluded, secrecy was more important than numbers. A small highly motivated armed group could achieve more by a sudden bold stroke than could a larger force which had lost the element of surprise. The lesson of the French Revolution, which he had studied from his childhood, was that success needed the combination of two circumstances: mass discontent with a discredited government, and a dedicated revolutionary leadership willing to act with speed and boldness.

Two days after swimming ashore in Oriente, Castro was back in the thick of political activity in Havana University. Colleagues were stunned to see him. Reports had arrived that he must have drowned in the Gulf of Nipe. With the main action group leaders either dead or under arrest, the atmosphere for Castro at the university was less tense and threatening than when he had left. He launched himself into an intensive spiral of political agitation. At a student rally he denounced Grau and Alemán for betraying the cause of Dominican liberation. Meanwhile, Castro's political mentor Eddy Chibás was promoting a censure motion against Alemán in the Senate, alleging misuse of public funds and other abuses.

Alemán responded defiantly to these criticisms, redoubling his efforts to promote his Presidential ambitions. He organised a motorcade parade through Havana, ending with a rally in front of the presidential palace. Near the university one of the cars stalled, and some hostile students seized the opportunity to pelt it with stones. Nervous bodyguards opened fire and killed one of the students. Despite this death, Alemán went ahead with the rally outside the palace, receiving a public tribute from President Grau. Hours later hundreds of students, with Castro in the front row, marched past the palace carrying the dead student in a coffin, shaking their fists and shouting for Grau to resign. Back at the university Castro harangued the crowd, saying that Grau was directly responsible for the student's death. He said that the next day the criminals in Grau's government would be celebrating a national holiday with illuminations and champagne, while the students and workers mourned a dead colleague. Carried along on the tide of emotion, the official leadership of the students ordered a forty-eight-hour national strike. Over several weeks there were marches and demonstrations, with Castro usually playing a prom-inent role.

In this period Castro still often carried a weapon. On one occasion a lieutenant of the university police tried to disarm him. After an argument the policeman challenged Castro to a personal pistol duel in a remote corner of the campus. Castro accepted the challenge but, suspecting a trap, took a group of armed students with him. The policeman was also accompanied by several armed accomplices. Castro assumed that the police had planned to assassinate him. They fled when they saw that Castro was with other armed men.

In early November Castro conceived a plan to bring down the Grau government. The idea came paradoxically from President Grau himself. Grau had wanted to display at one of his rallies the bell which Carlos Manuel de Céspedes, the hero of the Cuban independence struggle, had struck in 1868 to signal the start of the First War of Independence. The famous bell had been taken from Céspedes's estate of Demajagua in Oriente province to the nearby town of Manzanillo, and placed in the charge of the town council. It was incorporated into a shrine dedicated to the heroes of the independence movement. Grau wanted to use the bell of Demajagua to demonstrate his nationalist credentials. But when his representative arrived in Manzanillo, the town council refused to release the bell. Manzanillo was a stronghold of the radical wing of the sugar-cane workers' union. The Mayor was a Communist strongly opposed to the Grau government.

Castro realised that while the town council of Manzanillo was unwilling to let the President exploit the sacred piece of the national heritage, they might well lend the bell to Grau's political opponents. Castro was friendly with several Communist students whom he enlisted into his scheme. The idea was to take the bell with maximum publicity to a mass demonstration in front of the presidential palace. The bell would be tolled while the crowd demanded Grau's resignation. Castro's Communist friend Alfredo Guevara secured the support of the rest of the FEU leadership for the project. The leaders of the *Ortodoxo* party agreed to meet the costs of bringing the bell to Havana and of arranging suitable publicity.

Castro went to Manzanillo with another Communist student friend, Leonel Soto, picked up the bell, and travelled back by train with two representatives of the Manzanillo town council. At Havana railway station the bell and its bearers were greeted tumultuously by hundreds of students. The bell was transported in a large open car in a slow triumphal parade to the university, where it was stored for safe keeping in the Martyrs' Gallery adjacent to the Rector's office. Castro made yet another speech, praising the citizens of Manzanillo for having refused to hand over the symbol of Cuba's independence to puppets in the service of foreigners. During the night the students argued over the organisation of the anti-Grau demonstration planned for the following day. Castro's proposition was that they should resolve to toll the bell until Grau relinquished power. More and more people would join the crowd until they became an irresistible force. If necessary, the crowd would storm and occupy the Palace. The event would be Cuba's storming of the Bastille.

Other students argued that Castro's idea was impracticable and that the objective should be a more realistic political one, to discredit Grau and his Ministers and show up their subservience to imperialism.

When the Rector's office was opened the following morning, the bell was missing. It was assumed that the police had surreptitiously removed it during the night. FEU President Enrique Ovares delivered a letter to the Rector holding him responsible for the theft. Castro went to an anti-government radio station and announced that government agents had stolen the bell of Demajagua. He named various police officers who had been seen near the university during the night of the bell's disappearance.

In the evening Castro again addressed a large gathering of students at the university. It was his first speech to have a distinctly leftist slant. Hitherto his attacks on the Grau government had been primarily over the abuse of power, the theft of public funds and the use of violence to intimidate opponents. More recently he had been accusing Grau of betrayal – of betraying the 1933 revolution, of betraying those who had voted for him in 1944, of betraying the democrats of the Dominican Republic. Now he talked more about the social and economic failures of Grau's government. The peasants were as poor and landless as ever, while ever more of the country's resources were in foreign hands. Public health and public education had been neglected, while large resources were lavished on the armed forces. True independence would not be achieved without economic as well as political liberation. Castro was not yet expressing a Marxist viewpoint, but he was moving in that direction.

The Demajagua bell affair made the government look petty and vindictive, but it did not spark a revolution, as Castro had hoped. It was one more factor strengthening the determination of the government and army to crack down on the Communist influences which they blamed for many of their difficulties. There was particular concern, reflected in the conservative media, that the trade unions, long a Communist stronghold, were beginning to form an alliance with the largely middle-class students.

The first years of Grau's administration had coincided with the years in which Communists around the world were enjoying the reflected glory of the Soviet Union's heroic victory over Nazi Germany. Grau had negotiated a political deal by which he allowed the Communists to consolidate their position in the trade unions, in return for Communist support in the Congress for his government's programme. By late 1947, however, the tide had turned. The Soviet Union had dismayed its Western allies by imposing Communist regimes in the countries of eastern Europe which it occupied. The Cold War was beginning with a vengeance. Much of the Cuban media joined the hue and cry against Communist influence and infiltration. The US Embassy lost no opportunity to warn of the dangers of co-operating with Communists.

Grau began to respond to these internal and external pressures. He and his Labour Minister Carlos Prío now made it a top priority to try to curb Communist influence in the trade union movement.

It was in Manzanillo, the town that had refused to lend the bell of Demajagua to Grau, that the crackdown on Communism came to a head. On 22 January 1948 police in Manzanillo tried to arrest Jesús Menéndez, a black Communist leader of the sugar workers' union who was also a congressman. Menéndez claimed that the attempt to arrest him was a violation of his congressional immunity. When he walked away he was shot in the back and killed. This event polarised opinion further. General Pérez Dámera, the army chief of staff, answered criticism by saying that the police officer had been carrying out his duty and had shown an example which others should follow. The left made Menéndez a martyr. His ashes were placed in the Capitol in Havana and thousands filed past in a public tribute. The students of Havana were in the forefront of the tributes to Menéndez and of the protests at his death.

On 11 Febuary the growing student activism reached a new pitch. A demonstration against police brutality turned into a violent rampage in which cars and other property were smashed. The police charged in force, chasing the rioting students into the university precincts. The police officer in charge, a Major Carames, caught a disabled student and beat him with his pistol on the famous *escalinata,* the broad stairway leading up to the main university buildings. The next day students provocatively mounted a machine-gun at the top of the *escalinata* to deal with any further police intrusion. Other students staged a march into the town to protest at the violation of the university's autonomy. Castro was in the truck of a group of protesters carrying the Cuban flag, singing the national anthem and shouting 'Out with Carames! Down with Grau!' In the ensuing police baton charge Castro was struck on the head. He went with some fellow students to a nearby hospital, not to get treatment (the injury was slight and superficial) but to talk to journalists and photographers who had been summoned to see his bandaged and bloodstained head.

On 22 February Manolo Castro, the National Sports Director and Fidel's old adversary in the MSR, was lured out of a cinema and gunned down in the street. A press report, probably emanating from the MSR, said that the assassins belonged to a group headed by Fidel Castro. Hearing this news, Castro went with two companions to a police station. He made a statement that he had nothing to do with the killing and that witnesses could testify that he had been in a cafeteria when the murder took place. He was told that there was no warrant for his arrest, and that he could leave. Two days later, however, he was picked up in the street by a police patrol car and taken to a police station for questioning about the murder of Manolo Castro. He was subjected to a test for traces of explosives which proved negative. After he made a statement about his movements, the investigating judge ordered his release on provisional liberty, the conditions for which were that he could not leave the country and had to report back to the police at a later date.

Although Castro probably did not directly participate in the assassination, he may well have been involved in discussions and planning of the attack. In any event, fearing that MSR members might take the law into their own hands, he went into hiding, moving from one address to another. He was pleased when an opportunity arose for him to make his second attempted incursion onto the international stage.

In March 1948 a delegation headed by the President of the Foreign Relations Committee of the Argentine Senate arrived in Havana and set up shop in the National Hotel. They had been sent by President Perón on a tour of Latin American countries to enlist support for a congress to be held in the autumn in Buenos Aires to set up a new Latin American student organisation. Students throughout the region were overwhelmingly 'anti-imperialist', and Perón was confident that a regional student organisation would give strong support to his campaign to regain the Islas Malvinas (Falkland Islands).

Many of the students at Havana University were reluctant to get too closely involved with a project promoted by Perón. Virtually all of them approved of Perón's anti-imperialist line, including his efforts to assert Argentina's sovereignty over the Malvinas. Many on the left feared, however, that Argentina's campaign over the Malvinas would divert attention from what they considered to be the most important threat. Old-fashioned European colonialism appeared to be weak and on the way out, whereas United States imperialism was strong and expanding. The students were also concerned by reports of the arrest and imprisonment of dissident labour leaders in Argentina. They knew that Perón had been ostentatiously friendly to General Franco's regime in Spain, at a time when Franco was suffering almost complete international ostracism. To many Cuban radicals, Perón's government looked more Fascist than revolutionary.

Significantly, Castro felt few such scruples. For him the overriding need was for Latin American solidarity and co-operation. Only through working together could the region achieve real political and economic independence. That was the message preached by Martí. And like Martí, Castro already saw Cuba as too small a stage for his ambitions. Cuba on its own could not change the world.

What kept the countries of Latin America weak and backward? For Castro, it was the divisions between them, and within them, both exploited by the United States. The imperialists could easily dominate a divided continent;

and in each country they had the services of a corrupt ruling class which cared only for its own comfort and self-interest. There was no conflict between nationalism and internationalism. A truly revolutionary government would work for the whole nation, ending divisions of class and race; and it would work for all the poor and oppressed countries of the world, ending the divisions between exploiters and exploited.

Listening to this grandiose talk, some of Castro's fellow students were impressed, seeing him as a visionary. Others thought he was a self-important windbag. The Communists liked his line on imperialism, but thought some of his ideas were too much akin to Fascism. Castro in turn agreed with the Communists on many issues, but disliked their servile obedience to the Soviet Union, changing their line whenever Stalin gave the word. Castro told Alfredo Guevara: 'I would be a Communist if I could be Stalin.'

Against this background, if there was one ruling government in the world in 1948 with an outlook which seemed close to Castro's, it was the Argentine government. Perón was nationalistic and anti-imperialist. He had not been afraid to nationalise American- and British-owned utilities. His corporatist ideas, rejecting the political influence of both foreign monopolies (working in the interests of Washington) and Communist trade unions (working in the interests of Moscow) appealed strongly to Castro, as did his campaign for Latin America to act together as an independent force between the two superpowers. Perón was above all a man of action, of practical achievements. As for the Malvinas, Castro shared Argentina's indignation over Britain's maintenance of an anachronistic colony in the Western hemisphere. In later years Castro would describe his dealings with the Peronists as having been 'tactical'. But in 1948 he did not see things that way.

When Castro and some UIR colleagues went to the National Hotel to meet the visiting Argentine delegation, there was an enthusiastic meeting of minds. Castro suggested that as part of the preparations for the autumn congress in Buenos Aires, there should be a meeting of student delegates in Bogotá in April to coincide with a hemispheric conference which was to establish the Organisation of American States (OAS). The idea behind the OAS, strongly pushed by the Truman administration in Washington, was that the countries of the Americas should close ranks against international Communism, while the United States provided economic and other aid to its poorer Latin American partners.

The Peronists were not keen on this agenda, which marginalised their campaign over the Falklands. The Argentines and Cuban students hoped that their proposed meeting in Bogotá, coinciding with the OAS conference, would help to whip up opposition to United States plans in Latin America, and support for an alternative agenda favoured by both the Argentine authorities and the Cuban students. The four causes which they agreed to promote were: an end to Britain's colonial occupation of the Malvinas, the return of the Panama Canal to Panama, an end to the military dictatorship in the Dominican Republic, and independence for Puerto Rico.

In accordance with plans agreed with the Argentines, Castro set off with a fellow UIR student, Rafael del Pino, on a trip to Venezuela, Panama and Colombia. In a press interview many years later he was defensive about how this journey was financed. He claimed to have bought the air tickets with his own money. He admitted that the hotel where he stayed in Bogotá was 'pleasant', but claimed that prices in Bogotá were low and that the exchange rate was favourable. If one had some dollars, as he had, they went a long way. Another story circulated later was that one of Castro's sisters sold a refrigerator to help finance the trip. However, it seems rather unlikely that Castro financed this lengthy journey with the money he received from his father for his expenses as a student, or with help from other members of the family. His explanations on this point were probably 'tactical'. He did not want to appear to have been acting as the paid agent of a foreign government, least of all of a military government which later fell into ignominy. But it was probably the Argentine Embassy which in fact provided the funds for the journey.

On 19 March Castro went with del Pino to Havana airport to take a flight to Caracas. At the airport he was arrested for attempting to violate the terms of provisional liberty on which he had been released after questioning about the murder of Manolo Castro. He told a judge indignantly that he was travelling on an important mission to improve relations between the countries of Latin America, and that the stories linking him to the death of Manolo Castro were a blatant fabrication by his political enemies. The judge was evidently impressed, and let him go.

In Caracas Castro and del Pino were given a friendly reception by Venezuelan student supporters of the Social Democratic President-Elect, Rómulo Gallegos. A group of students took Castro to meet the editors of the main pro-Gallegos newspaper, where they explained the project for the student meeting in Bogotá. They failed to get an interview with Gallegos himself but left a message enlisting his support for their plans. They then went to Panama, seeking publicity by visiting a student who had been wounded by police in a demonstration over the Canal. Castro was outraged and disgusted by the large number of bars and brothels servicing the American troops in Panama. They finally flew to Bogotá, booking in at the Claridge Hotel.

The politically active students in Bogotá were mostly left-wing Liberals, supporters of the Liberal Party's Presidential candidate, Jorge Eliécer Gaitán. Gaitán was the great hope of a wide spectrum of Colombians from the moderate centre to the left. A brilliant and impassioned orator, he seemed the man who might at last end the long history of Colombian instability and fratricidal violence. He promised radical reforms to bring about greater social justice. He aroused intense loyalty and enthusiasm among his followers, and was expected to win the presidential election due later that year. Castro was soon infected by the enthusiasm of his new Colombian companions.

He had not been long in Bogotá before he was in trouble with the police. With some Colombian students he and del Pino went to a special performance in the city's grandest theatre, the Colón, attended by many government and society leaders. From the gallery they threw down leaflets denouncing the United States and calling for support for the students' anti-imperialist causes. Castro and del Pino were arrested, had their hotel room searched, and were taken to a police cell for questioning. After explaining at length their actions and plans, they were released. As Castro said many years later, apparently without irony: 'After all, handing out pamphlets isn't a criminal offence anywhere in the world, except under a repressive government.'

Castro and del Pino had been going to meetings presenting themselves as representatives of the students of Cuba, but without consulting the official FEU leadership in Havana. When the President and Secretary-General of the FEU (Enrique Ovares and Alfredo Guevara) arrived in Bogotá, there was soon a dispute over who should speak on behalf of the Cuban students. Castro argued vehemently that since he had done most of the work and preparations, he should be the spokesman. According to Castro, the FEU leadership had been lukewarm about the Bogotá meeting and only decided to turn up when they saw that it was likely to be a success. For the sake of peace and harmony, Ovares agreed that Castro should represent the Cuban students, in particular in contacts with Gaitán. On 7 April the Colombian student leaders took Castro and del Pino to a meeting with Gaitán, who promised to support the student congress and to speak himself at the closing rally in a public square. He asked the Cubans to see him again in the offices of *El Tiempo* newspaper at 2 p.m. on 9 April to confirm the details of his participation.

On 9 April Castro and del Pino had lunch at their hotel and then set out to walk to the appointment with Gaitán. Suddenly people started running in all directions, shouting that Gaitán had been assassinated. It was assumed that Gaitán's enemies in the right-wing 'oligarchy' had hired the assassin, who was lynched by the furious crowd. Soon anger turned to generalised violence and looting. People broke into government offices and started smashing furniture and equipment, and starting fires. This was the beginning of the *Bogotazo*, two days of anarchic rioting which left a huge trail of destruction and some 3,000 people dead.

Castro saw an enraged man in the street trying to smash a typewriter, but without much success. He showed him that the best way was to throw it in the air and let it drop. He and del Pino walked to the square where the Colombian Congress was located. People were shouting and throwing stones. Furniture was being hurled from the upper windows of the building. Someone was trying to address the crowd from a balcony but no one paid any attention. A popular uprising was taking place but it appeared to have no direction and no leadership. Some police units had joined the rebellion against the Conservative government, but the attitude of the army was unknown.

What to do? Castro and del Pino decided to go to the boarding-house where Ovares and Guevara were staying. While they were talking they saw a large crowd, armed with sticks, metal bars and a few rifles, marching purposefully down the street. Hearing that the crowd were going to collect weapons from a nearby police station, Castro and del Pino decided to join them. When the crowd arrived at the station it had already been occupied and the rifles there distributed. Castro looked upstairs but could only find a tear-gas launcher. He put on a coat and tried to change into a pair of police boots, but desisted when the owner protested. Downstairs an officer who had joined the rebellion was organising squads. He gave Castro a rifle and some bullets. Groups set off in different directions. Castro's group, hearing that the National Broadcasting Station had been taken by students but was now under attack, set off to help. When they passed the Ministry of War a few soldiers were hanging about outside. Castro jumped on a bench to harangue them, but had to stop to catch up with the rest of the group who had not waited. When a large body of organised and armed troops went by, Castro's group took cover and kept their heads down, having (as Castro said) too few weapons to confront them.

Seeing a bus going in the right direction, Castro and some others boarded it. At this point he became separated from del Pino. In the bus his wallet was stolen. At the radio station there was a lot of shooting going on. Castro's group could not get near. They decided to go to the university. There also confusion reigned. Hearing about another police station that had joined the rebellion, they went there. Castro told the officer in charge who he was, and offered to help. The officer set off with a bunch of volunteers including Castro to the Liberal Party headquarters, but was apparently unable to obtain any guidance or instructions. On the way back one of the jeeps in which they were travelling broke down. Castro and some others were left stranded. Some policemen passing on foot told them that they were going to the Fifth Divisional Police headquarters, which was also supporting the rebellion. Castro went with them. Six hours had passed since the rioting began, and it was now dark.

At the headquarters there were some 400 armed men being organised by a senior officer. Castro 'got in line and got organised along with them'. He was assigned to a group defending the second floor. It had become evident by now that the army had rallied behind the government. During the night there were frequent false alarms that the army was about to launch an attack on the building.

The next morning Castro tried to persuade the police commander that they should take some sort of offensive action, such as occupying the presidential palace. He said he had studied the French Revolution and other popular uprisings. Sitting passively in a defensive position was a recipe for failure. The commander was not impressed, but agreed that Castro and some others should patrol the high ground overlooking the headquarters. He returned to the headquarters when night fell.

At dawn the next day it was announced (misleadingly) that an agreement had been reached between the government and the units which had rebelled. In fact the Liberal Party leadership had agreed with President Ospina that constitutional legality must be upheld and order restored. The civilians in the police station, including Castro, were told to leave. He returned to his hotel, where he rejoined del Pino. He was told that people had been looking for him and talking about Cuban agitators involved in the riots. It seemed safer to go to the boarding-house where Ovares and Guevara were staying. The owner of the house was denouncing the rioters. Castro vehemently disagreed, where-upon he and del Pino were thrown out into the street. They had only a few minutes to find safe refuge before a curfew came into force, after which they would be liable to be shot at sight. They went to the hotel where the Argentine student delegation were staying. From there an Argentine diplomatic car took them to the Cuban Consulate. The diplomatic number plates enabled them to pass without difficulty through several roadblocks. The Cuban consul, an amiable old gentleman, judged it best to get the Cuban students out of Colombia as quickly as possible. The Cuban government, in view of the chaotic situation in Bogotá, had sent an aircraft to pick up any Cubans needing evacuation.

In talking later about his involvement in the *Bogotazo*, Castro emphasised his personal isolation. At the most difficult moment, at the police headquarters waiting 'like sitting ducks' for an army attack, he was the only Cuban present, ready to fight alongside complete strangers, under a commander who seemed to him highly incompetent:

During the night while we waited for an attack I thought of Cuba, of my family and everyone, and I felt very alone. There I was with my rifle and a few bullets. I asked myself, 'What am I doing here? I've lost contact with everybody, with the students and the chief of police. Here I am in a mouse-trap. This is completely wrong. It's wrong to sit here waiting for an attack instead of going out to attack . . .' I started to wonder if I should leave. But I decided to stay . . . I thought: 'Well, the people here are the same as the people in Cuba, the same as people everywhere. These people are oppressed and exploited.' I argued to myself: 'Their main leader has been assassinated and this uprising is absolutely justified. I may die here but I'm staying.' I made my decision knowing that it was a military disaster, that those people were going to lose, that I was alone, and that these were Colombians, not Cubans. However, I reasoned that people were the same everywhere, that their cause was just and that it was my duty to stay. So I stayed all night, waiting until dawn for an attack.

In subsequent years all sorts of inaccurate stories were put about relating to Castro's role in the *Bogotazo*. Usually these were designed to demonstrate that Castro was part of a pre-planned Communist plot. One supposed witness claimed that Castro had a document identifying him as an agent of the 'Third Front of the USSR'. Even after the end of the Cold War, books and articles were published perpetuating the myth of the *Bogotazo* as a Communist conspiracy. Another story given currency after the *Bogotazo* was that Castro had killed several priests. In fact none was killed by anyone. But when it came to black propaganda Castro could give as well as he got. In an early interview he said he had heard that priests had fired on the crowd, and he could well believe it.

The murder of Gaitán strengthened Castro's conviction that real change could not be achieved in Latin America through the ballot box. It also demonstrated how easily popular discontent could degenerate into aimless violence, looting and personal vengeance. Even among the police who supported the rebellion, there was no discipline. Castro witnessed a scene at the police headquarters in which a group of police were savagely beating a fellow policeman accused of being a Conservative. For Castro the lack of discipline certainly contributed to the failure of the uprising. Although the Colombian high command was mostly Conservative, Castro's Colombian friends told him that many younger officers supported Gaitán. They might have brought a significant part of the army to support a Liberal takeover of power. But the spectacle of looting and indiscriminate violence made most army officers decide that the restoration of order had to be the first and only priority.

For many years Castro said little about his role in the *Bogotazo*. His silence allowed all sorts of wild stories to flourish. In old age, however, he became more forthcoming. He made no attempt to deny that he had actively helped to promote an armed revolution. On one occasion, talking in front of Alfredo Guevara, he said that the Communists had been useless. While he was trying to arm and organise the insurrection in Bogotá, the Communists like Alfredo Guevara did nothing but sit round a table and discuss the situation. Guevara, now well used to acting as a butt for Castro's humour, smiled wanly.

4 Part-time Husband and Lawyer

By the time Castro arrived back in Havana in mid April 1948, press reports in both Colombia and Cuba had mentioned the involvement of two 'Cuban Communists' in the Bogotá riots. The real Cuban Communists were aggrieved. Not for the first time, they were being blamed for action which they had in fact carefully avoided. Alfredo Guevara remained friendly and good-humoured with Castro, but reported to his fellow Communists that Castro had confirmed his tendency to 'adventurism'.

Castro's political hero Eddy Chibás, leader of the *Ortodoxo* party, was a candidate in the 1 June presidential elections. Castro campaigned for him with his usual fiery energy. He accompanied Chibás on a tour of Oriente, Castro's home province, and sometimes spoke from the platform as a warm-up for Chibás. But Chibás was too eccentric and unpredictable for most Cubans. The government candidate for the Presidency, Labour Minister Carlos Prío (Grau and Alemán having decided not to run), won by a comfortable margin.

During the campaign Castro continued to accuse police officers of corruption and other abuses. The police in turn regarded him as a dangerous and malicious enemy, and looked for an opportunity to hit back. A week after the presidential election a police sergeant in Havana was shot dead. Before he died, according to the police, he identified Castro as his assailant. Another student was produced as a witness identifying Castro as the gunman. Castro was arrested. He claimed that the allegations were fabricated to discredit him. Luckily for him, the witness changed his story before the trial began, saying he had been bribed by the police to accuse Castro. The judge dismissed the case.

Castro spent the summer holiday of 1948 at home in Birán. Havana enjoyed a few months of peace and quiet. But when the student agitators returned in September, trouble soon flared up again. The government had used the quiet season to authorise the national bus company to raise bus fares. Buses were the only means of transport by which many workers and students could get to work. The cost of transport was a significant element in their budget. The fare increases sparked immediate violent protests, led by both trade unions and students. Several buses were burnt. Castro was soon in the thick of the action. Another leading agitator was his friend Justo Fuentes, a self-taught black man and a leading member of the UIR action group. Castro and Fuentes had a regular fifteen-minute slot on a radio station which supported the *Ortodoxos*. They used their broadcasts to fan the flames of discontent over bus fares. The government feared that the situation could degenerate into riots on the scale of the *Bogotazo*. To avoid this they backed off and cancelled the fare increases.

When not occupied with political agitation, Castro was going out with a female student in the Faculty of Philosophy and Letters. She was Mirta Díaz-Balart, the sister of Castro's friend and fellow law student Rafael Díaz-Balart. Fidel and Mirta were introduced in the cafeteria of the Law Faculty, and immediately took a strong liking to each other. She conformed to the type of woman who, as time would prove, always attracted Castro: a girl from a 'good family', petite, pretty, quite cultured and sophisticated, with light brown hair and upper-class manners. Her father was the mayor of Banes, the town in Oriente province which was the centre of United Fruit activities in Cuba. He had a successful legal practice, General Batista being among his friends and clients.

On 11 October 1948, two days after the inauguration of President Prío, Fidel and Mirta got married in the Catholic church of Banes. Fidel's parents were delighted that their talented but wild and uncontrollable son had at last done something sensible, namely marrying into a well-connected and influential family from Oriente. Mirta's father was less enthusiastic, having heard of Castro's reputation as an agitator at the university. He also considered that Angel and Lina Castro, with their uncouth peasant manners, were not quite suitable to display in the polite middle-class society of Banes.

Before his marriage Fidel had had relatively little contact with women. His adolescence had been spent at all-male boarding schools, with holidays on the large but isolated rural family estate. Years later Castro criticised all-male schools because they caused boys to spend a lot of time fantasising about women. It is reasonable to assume that he did his share of fantasising. The Jesuit priests' warnings about sensuality no doubt had their effect in tightening the stress between desire and puritanical inhibitions. At university he had more opportunity to have girlfriends, but did not show much interest. Pushy and supremely self-confident with men, he struck his colleagues as astonishingly awkward and shy with attractive girls. He never danced and had little social small talk. When other students were chatting up girls or dancing at clubs, Castro would be at political meetings. During his first year at university he briefly went out with a couple of girls, but he often missed dates and never developed a serious relationship. It is probable that Mirta was the first person with whom he had sexual relations. If he did have any other sexual relationships during his years at university, they must have been confined to purely physical one-off encounters.

Fidel and Mirta went on a three-month honeymoon in the United States, with generous gifts of money from their parents and other well-wishers. Batista, then living in self-imposed exile in the United States, gave $1,000. They spent some weeks in Miami and then went on to New York, where they stayed at a flat rented by Mirta's brother Rafael. Fidel tried to improve his English, setting himself the task of learning two hundred words a day. He also made up lost ground in his law studies. He bought Marx's *Das Kapital* in a New York bookshop, and was intrigued at the thought of acquiring such a subversive work in the heart of the capitalist world. He had a strong sense of following in the footsteps of José Martí, who had lived in New York before returning to Cuba to launch the war of independence. Fidel showed his care-free attitude towards money and contempt for personal financial manage-ment. He bought a showy Lincoln convertible car, but found himself with insufficient funds to pay the customs duty due before it could be transported to Cuba. He had to appeal urgently to his father for more money.

On return to Havana Fidel and Mirta rented a small flat near the sea in the prosperous suburb of Vedado. Mirta seemed happy and in love. She was glad to be away from her home in Banes, where she had been given a hard time by a domineering stepmother. With Mirta, Fidel was usually loving and protec-tive, in a courtly Spanish manner. It soon became apparent, however, that his personality and lifestyle were highly unsuited to married life. Like many idealistic and charismatic people, he was at the same time monumentally egocentric. He could wax indignant about the downtrodden and oppressed in general, while showing no concern for the sensibilities of the particular people closest to him. He often failed to turn up to meals at home, preferring to spend his evenings at the *Ortodoxo* party headquarters or in cafeterias frequented by fellow students. If he did come home, he would often bring a bunch of political followers, and expect Mirta to cater for them. If he had money, he would spend it on his political projects rather than on his wife and home.

In this fourth year at university Castro devoted more time and effort to his legal studies. He had missed exams in the two preceding years, but managed to make up lost ground by intensive cramming. Studying and marriage were, however, only a partial distraction from his obsession with politics. In January 1949, when the government again raised bus fares, he leapt into action, leading a detachment which hijacked eight buses and took them to the university, knowing that the national police were prohibited from entering the university precincts. The buses were covered with flags and anti-government slogans. When the buses were taken back during the night by the bus company, Castro railed against the traitors in the university who had allowed this to happen. There were more marches into the centre of Havana, and more stoning of the police.

When the excitement over bus fares was beginning to fade, an incident occurred which provided a new focus for agitation. Some drunken American sailors climbed onto the statue of Martí in central Havana, and one of them urinated on its base. Cuban bystanders were outraged. Police had to intervene to protect the sailors and accompany them to a police station, where a crowd gathered shouting insults. When Castro heard the news he and some friends formed a 'guard of honour' which stood 'protecting' the statue throughout the following night. The next morning students staged a noisy demonstration in front of the US Embassy, hurling stones and demanding that the American sailors be handed over for trial in Cuba. Police charged and dispersed the demonstrators. Several students including Castro were beaten in the tumult. Later Castro and his Communist friends Alfredo Guevara and Lionel Soto went round the newspaper offices of Havana delivering an inflammatory protest, accusing the Americans of treating Cuba with arrogance and contempt, and accusing the Cuban authorities of shameful servility.

Attacking the United States was a relatively uncontroversial and risk-free activity. But attacking the police, and especially accusing named officers of corruption, meant living dangerously. Castro was regarded as a leading member of the UIR gang. The rival MSR, which still had strong links to the police, had not forgotten or forgiven the crimes which they attributed to the UIR, including the murder of Manolo Castro. Fidel Castro was aware of the dangers. He kept his movements as unpredictable as possible. However, everyone knew that he and Justo Fuentes gave a broadcast at the same time every week at a particular private radio station. In April 1949 a group of MSR thugs lay in wait outside the radio station. By chance Castro was not present on the day in question. Fuentes was shot dead as soon as he stepped onto the street.

The murder of Fuentes caused outrage even outside the university. President Prío found himself under pressure to take action against the gangs. As Labour Minister in the previous administration he had sometimes used the gangs in his efforts to eliminate Communist influence in the trade union movement. But like Grau before him, he found that the gangs were a monster which, once unleashed, was difficult to control.

By this time Fidel Castro's links with the UIR had in fact become tenuous. His politics were moving further to the left. Marriage to a girl who reflected the attitudes and values of the Cuban upper class did nothing to soften his radicalism. On the contrary, he was reading Marx and Engels, and studying the social inequalities visible in Havana. He had always admired the ringing rhetoric of the Communist Manifesto and Lenin's *What Is to Be Done?* He now tried to work his way through heavier material such as *Das Kapital.* He visited the poorer districts of the town and became active in the University Committee for the Struggle against Racial Discrimination. His radio broadcasts supported Chibás but, unlike Chibás, he never criticised Communism. He was focussing less on the hypocrisy and iniquities of particular politicians, more on the need for structural changes to end the exploitation and humiliation of workers, peasants and the unemployed. Marxism offered a rational and scientific explanation for events which had seemed haphazard and perplexing. As he later put it: 'In the midst of a forest of events, where it was very difficult to understand anything, and where everything seemed due to the wickedness of men – their defects, perversity and immorality – I started to identify other factors not dependent on the attitudes and morals of particular individuals ... I began to understand human society, the historical process and the social divisions that I saw every day.'

Fidel and Mirta (the latter six months pregnant) spent the 1949 summer holiday in her home town of Banes. The town was divided into two parts by a small river. The well-connected Díaz-Balarts had houses in both halves. One half of the town was almost entirely the property of the United Fruit Company. Here the executives of United Fruit lived in their comfortable American houses, went to American shops to buy goods imported from the United States, played polo in American clubs and swam from the private Puerto Rico beach, protected from unwanted Cuban intruders by armed guards employed by United Fruit. Castro was coldly furious at the evidence that Cubans were second-class citizens in part of their own country. Ten years later one of his first acts after the Revolution would be to unlock the gate which excluded unauthorised Cubans from the beach used by the Americans.

In September Mirta gave birth to a son, Fidelito. The couple moved to a slightly larger flat in Havana, directly opposite a military barracks. Castro told visitors that he was well protected thanks to the presence of soldiers on guard duty outside his block. He also told them cheerfully that he was close enough to the President's house to take a pot shot at him with a rifle from his balcony. The couple were joined for a time by Fidel's younger brother Raúl, who was due to start studying sociology at the University the following year. Raúl was bright but, unlike Fidel, he had not distinguished himself at Belén College. He was a poor sportsman and had found the discipline and religious instruction suffocating. Compared to the earnest and domineering Fidel, Raúl struck visitors as warm, easy-going and unpretentious.

For Castro the big political event of that autumn was what came to be known as the Pact of the Action Groups. President Prío made a two-pronged attempt to end gangsterism. A few notorious gunmen were arrested and given prison sentences. Then all the main action groups were secretly offered well-paid sinecure jobs in different government ministries in return for their abstaining from violence. Most accepted the money, but there was little discernible reduction in violence. Coinciding with this development, many of the non-violent student activists, including both Communists and *Ortodoxos*, formed a new organisation, the 30 September Movement, dedicated to opposing the influence of the gangs in the university.

Castro wanted to join the 30 September Movement. The committee of the Movement were not at all keen to admit him. Castro was assumed to be a member or supporter of the UIR, despite his denials. Alfredo Guevara of the Communists and Max Lesnick of the *Ortodoxos* tried to put him off. They said a condition of membership was never to carry a weapon. Castro said he would stop carrying a weapon. They said that the committee intended to denounce the Pact of the Action Groups and to name the people involved, including UIR members. Castro volunteered to make the public denunciation himself. His association with the UIR had been due to his personal friendship with Emilio Tró. When Tró was killed, Castro lost interest. He was now quite willing to denounce UIR members who had sold out to the government. In the end his offer was accepted. He was given the task of delivering a speech at a special assembly in the Martyrs' Gallery at the university on 13 November 1949.

Castro's speech made a big impact. It exposed the membership of the gangs and their secret deals with the government. The speech was published in the national press and enhanced Castro's reputation as a person bold to the point of foolhardiness. It was confidently predicted that the gangs would take some drastic action against him. He went into hiding for a fortnight in Lesnick's flat. From there he was smuggled out to the province of Matanzas and from there took a train to Oriente. At home in Birán he persuaded his father to give him enough money to finance a period of exile in the United States. He followed the route of his honeymoon the previous year, going to Miami and then to New York. There he lay low, studying law and reading politics. After some weeks, when the dust had settled, he returned to Havana. He led a comparatively quiet life and graduated as a Doctor in Law in September 1950. His father gave him a new Pontiac car as a graduation present.

With the help of his wife's family, Castro could have got a well-paid job in a prosperous legal partnership. He chose a quite different course. He suggested to two of his fellow law graduates, Jorge Azpiazu and Rafael Resende, that they set up a legal partnership which would help poor people to assert their rights. Azpiazu and Resende were both from a poor background and had left-wing sympathies. Azpiazu had voted against Castro in FEU elections on the grounds that Castro was from a family of rich landowners. The two accepted the proposal and the law firm of Azpiazu, Castro and Resende duly set up shop in a small, sparsely furnished office in a run-down area of Old Havana.

Castro maintained the contempt for money which he had shown as a student. At home in Oriente his father owned virtually everything and he could simply take or borrow what he wanted. When he needed to buy something he asked his father for money, but felt little gratitude when he received it. At school the Jesuits had taught that it was spiritual values that mattered and that worldly goods were a snare and delusion. At the university he had spent much of his time denouncing the greed of money-grubbing politicians, unscrupulous businessmen and exploitative landowners.

Against this background it was not surprising that his law business earned little money. His most important client was a Spanish timber merchant who employed Azpiazu, Castro and Resende to recover debts from carpenters who had not paid for their timber purchases. Castro's approach was to ask the indebted carpenters for a list of the people who had not paid for the carpenters' work, and then put pressure on the latter to pay up. The Spanish merchant paid for Castro's services in wood to furnish the law firm's offices. Castro also took up the defence of peasants expelled from their land, workers dismissed for striking, and students imprisoned for rioting. He represented the market stall-owners who frequently suffered harassment and extortion from the police. He took payment from the stall-owners only in goods. He liked to walk around the market helping himself to food and receiving the grateful smiles of the stall-owners. In another quixotic and fruitless venture, he tried to take legal action against the American-owned Cuban Telephone Company on behalf of subscribers who claimed that the tariffs were too high. He also represented some slum-dwellers whose buildings were due to be demolished to make space for a public square, securing a small payment of compensation for those evicted.

When a young friend borrowed and then crashed Castro's car, the friend's wealthy father offered to pay for the damage. Castro brushed aside the offer, saying the only thing that concerned him was his friend's injuries. The other side of the coin of this grand disdain for money was Castro's indifference to the material needs of his loyal and long-suffering wife. They had bought furniture for the flat on an instalment plan but Castro ignored the reminders to pay. When he was engaged in political activities away from Havana the furniture company came to the flat and removed all the furniture. Castro's partner Azpiazu received a telephone call from a tearful Mirta who found herself without even a cot for the baby. On at least two occasions the electricity was cut off because Castro had failed to pay the electricity bills. Mirta complained that she was sometimes short of money even to buy food for the baby.

In November 1950 Castro was arrested in the town of Cienfuegos. He had gone there to support high-school students who were protesting over a decision by the Education Ministry to prohibit student associations in schools. There was a four-hour running battle between students and police. Castro strode into the mêlée, was beaten, charged with using violence against the police, and taken to the provincial capital of Santa Clara. In his weekly broadcast Eddy Chibás protested at the arrest of his young supporter. There was a demonstration in front of the prison where Castro was held. Castro issued a defiant statement to the press. Being a qualified lawyer, he insisted on conducting his own defence at his trial. In court he embarked on a long harangue against the government and the police. The magistrate, perhaps unhappy to be providing a platform for Castro's political campaigning, dismissed the charges and ordered his release.

Castro found other ways to keep himself in the public eye. He became friendly with the editor of the newspaper *Alerta,* Ramón Vasconcelos, a disillusioned former minister in Prío's government. *Alerta* had a modest circulation of about 30,000, but the editor was constantly looking for ways to increase it. He hoped that coverage of Castro's activities in support of quixotic causes would be good for circulation. The paper made a big story of a legal action brought by Castro against a fruit-canning company which had dismissed long-established workers in order to take on new workers at a lower salary, in breach of labour legislation. Another story reported Castro suing a landowner who had got some peasants into debt and then used these debts as a means of taking possession of their land.

Castro still spent plenty of time on activities that had nothing to do with his legal profession. He was active in the Cuban Peace Committee, part of an international network of organisations supporting the campaign of Bertrand Russell and other left-leaning Western liberals against the war in Korea. He attacked the Cuban government for supporting the American position on Korea, and for planning to send Cuban troops to fight as 'cannon fodder' alongside the Americans. He contemptuously rejected allegations that the peace committees were front organisations manipulated by the Soviet Union.

Castro's hopes of transforming the Cuban political scene were still centred on Eddy Chibás, leader of the *Ortodoxos.* But in the summer of 1951 Chibás made a fatal error. Falling into a trap, he believed some information leaked to him about Education Minister Aureliano Sánchez. In the Senate he accused Sánchez of having bought a ranch in Guatemala with funds misappropriated from his ministerial budget. He repeated the charge in one of his Sunday broadcasts. In fact Sánchez was one of the cleanest members of the government, having put an end to the corrupt practices of his predecessor Alemán. Chibás had chosen a bad target. The government demanded that he substantiate his allegations. Some congressmen had promised to provide Chibás with documentary proof, but failed to come up with it.

With Chibás unable to prove his allegations, the government went on to the offensive, saying that he was a muckraker and proven liar. Chibás had his back to the wall. On 5 August he made an emotional broadcast defending his honour. He was accompanied in the studio by several *Ortodoxo* colleagues, including Castro. He insisted that his allegations against Sánchez would be found to be true. Galileo was right to say that the earth went round the sun, even though he could not prove it. He called on the Cuban people to sweep away the thieves in the government. He ended shouting: 'This is my last wake-up call!' He then drew a pistol and shot himself in the stomach. Castro, who was standing nearby when the shot rang out, rushed to fetch a car, helped to carry Chibás into a hospital, and spent a long time at his bedside. It is possible that Chibás meant only to injure himself, as a dramatic gesture. However, the bullet wound caused an infection, and after eleven days in hospital he died.

There was an argument among *Ortodoxo* leaders over where Chibás's body should lie in state. The Capitol was too much associated with the government. The *Ortodoxo* party headquarters was too small for the number of people who would want to pay their respects. As a result the party leadership accepted a suggestion that the youth section take charge of the ceremony, and hold it in the Great Hall of Havana University. Castro formed part of the guard of honour. After the lying in state, Castro had another of his ideas for instant revolution. He proposed to fellow members of the youth wing that instead of going with the body to the Colón cemetery, they should take it to the presidential palace. With the coffin of Chibás as a standard and rallying point for the huge crowd attending the funeral, they would demand Prío's resignation, and occupy the palace. Castro's colleagues said he was crazy: there would be lots of armed police around the palace; an attempt to storm the building would provoke a bloodbath. Castro tried to argue that the police would not dare to fire on a large and determined crowd; Prío was near the end of his term of office, and had sent plenty of money abroad; if in danger, he would flee the country. But Castro was overruled. The body was taken straight to the cemetery for burial.

Having studied the Marxist view of 'bourgeois democracy', Castro thought the only possibility of securing real change in Cuba was through revolution, rather than through elections. He felt frustrated by the caution and timidity of Chibás's successor as *Ortodoxo* leader, the worthy but uninspiring Roberto Agramonte. However, the *Ortodoxos* still seemed the only viable instrument for fulfilling Castro's political ambitions. The Communist Party was tainted by its links with the Soviet Union. Castro judged that in the atmosphere of the Cold War, the Communists had no chance of gaining enough mass following to carry through a successful revolution. The country was being bombarded with propaganda alleging that Communism meant abolishing private property, seizing peasants' land, prohibiting religion, making children inform on their parents, taking orders from Moscow, and so on. The best hope was that events would push the *Ortodoxos* towards a more radical and revolutionary position.

Castro therefore stuck with the *Ortodoxos,* and outwardly accepted the party's discipline. But he was constantly looking for ways to raise the temperature. He started an investigation of the President's personal finances, discovering that he had bought a large farm near Havana and used army personnel to build an approach road and to refurbish the farmhouse. He discovered also that Prío as a lawyer had represented a rich businessman who had been sentenced to six years in prison for rape. As President, Prío had used his presidential prerogative to grant a pardon to the rapist, who in gratitude gave him an extensive piece of land. Castro wanted to expose all this in one of the *Ortodoxo* party's regular radio broadcasts. But the new party leadership, remembering what had happened to Chibás, was unwilling to approve Castro's plan. They thought he would embroil the party in damaging litigation. Castro had to buy time on another radio station to make his accusations. They were given front-page coverage in *Alerta.* Castro then presented charges in a criminal court against two police officers whom he held responsible for the death of a worker killed in an anti-government demonstration.

Castro wanted to run for Congress in the June 1952 elections. He saw himself as a leading light in the *Ortodoxo* party, and as the spiritual heir of Chibás. The party leadership, however, had a different view. They thought that he was too young, immature and headstrong to be given an important role. His past association with the UIR action group was damaging. The allegations that he had been involved in two murders while at the university, whether true or not, were a liability. When Agramonte announced the party's candidates for senatorial and gubernatorial posts, Castro's name was not on the list. The best he could hope for was to be a candidate for the House of Representatives. For that he had to be nominated as an 'aspirant' by one or more branches of the party.

It was at about this time that Castro had a meeting with General Fulgencio Batista, who had returned to Cuba in 1948 and won a seat in the Senate. With some friends Batista established the Unitary Action Party, as a vehicle to get himself elected again to the Presidency. Batista was always on the lookout for useful allies and agreed to a suggestion by Castro's brother-in-law, Rafael Díaz-Balart, that he should meet Castro. Rafael Díaz-Balart, the son of Batista's lawyer, had become head of the youth wing of Batista's party. He now tried to enlist Castro's support for Batista. Castro led Díaz-Balart along by remarking enigmatically that if Batista wanted to stage a coup against Prío, 'then he can count on me'. Castro agreed to call at Batista's luxurious villa. But the meeting did not get beyond polite generalities. Both men were fishing for information, neither wanting to reveal their real political intentions. Castro admired the books in Batista's library and casually expressed surprise that Batista evidently did not have Malaparte's *Technique of the Coup d'Etat*. Batista suspected that Castro was an *agent provocateur*. He told Díaz-Balart afterwards that his young friend was very intelligent, but dangerous.

Despite his lack of visible support from the *Ortodoxo* leadership, Castro pressed ahead in trying to gain election to the House of Representatives. He had successfully cultivated grassroots support in the *Ortodoxo* headquarters of the poorest districts of Havana. Three of these districts gave him their backing. Leaving his wife at home with Fidelito, he threw himself into the campaign with enormous energy, sending out a mimeographed letter in blue ink addressed personally to each of the 80,000 *Ortodoxo* party members registered in Havana. In Cuba in 1952 this sort of personalised electioneering was unprecedented. Without obtaining permission he used the party's congressional franking stamp to give his letters a more official appearance. He made numerous long speeches, using his faction of the party's youth wing as his personal machine to organise and direct rallies and meetings.

Castro had completely given up his legal practice, except to the extent that it could further his political ambitions. In January 1952 he presented an indictment of President Prío to the Tribunal of Accounts (the body responsible for supervising the government's financial management) accusing him of five misdemeanours, namely using the presidential pardon in return for financial favours, violating labour laws on his properties, using soldiers as labourers, dismissing lawful workers to replace them with forced military labour, and selling farm products at below the legitimate cost of production. He followed up a month later by announcing on the radio that he would publicly expose the President's links with the armed gangs. After this trailer, the exposure was published in *Alerta*. There Castro gave details of the phoney jobs given to the gang members, the ministries on whose payroll they appeared, and the salaries they received. He said the President's personal secretary, Orlando Puente, distributed each month sixty envelopes containing cash for the gang members. All this was little more than a rehash of the exposure already made by Castro two years earlier in the university, but it nevertheless caused a considerable stir. He next announced that he would expose the scandalously luxurious lifestyle which the President enjoyed without the public's knowledge. Posing as a gardener he had taken photographs of the President's country mansion, and the lavish parties staged there.

Although Castro was campaigning as a member of the *Ortodoxo* party, his aims were already revolutionary. He considered that outside Havana the *Ortodoxos* had fallen under the control of traditional middle-class liberals, but that in Havana there was a solid base of support for a radical programme. His game plan was to help Agramonte and the *Ortodoxos* to victory and then to form a breakaway faction in the Congress with a new revolutionary platform, seeking support from workers, peasants, intellectuals, teachers, the unemployed and other 'progressive' forces.

There is a fair chance that the *Ortodoxos* and Castro would both have succeeded in the election. Prío and his government were deeply discredited. The *Auténtico* presidential candidate, Carlos Hevia, was relatively honest but unimpressive. After eight years of corruption and abuse of power, the *Auténticos* were regarded as virtually irredeemable. The Party had moreover suffered another serious split, with Prío distancing himself from his predecessor Grau. Attempts were made to charge Grau with embezzling public funds. Amid mutual recriminations Grau decided to set up a separate party. Later there was a reconciliation. But most predictions and opinion polls still favoured Agramonte. The Communists decided not to put forward their own Presidential candidate, recommending their supporters to vote for Agramonte.

Batista was standing as the candidate of his Unitary Action Party. He had not developed much of an electoral machine, having been encouraged to believe that his name and reputation would be enough to win him the presidency. His friends thought that people would look back on his period of government as a time of peace and prosperity, and that they would flock to support him. As the campaign progressed, however, it became apparent that these hopes were misplaced. The opinion polls suggested that he would get a bare 10 per cent of the vote.

From an early stage Batista had been approached by groups of army officers urging him to lead a coup. They were mostly middle-ranking and junior officers who had been passed over for promotion during the eight years of *Auténtico* government. They argued that a military coup was the only way to avoid either a continuation of graft, corruption and gangsterism under the *Auténticos,* or a leap into the dark under the untried and unpredictable *Ortodoxos*. At first Batista graciously turned down these approaches, believing he could win in a fair election. But as his chances of electoral victory slipped away, he changed his mind. He may have believed stories that President Prío was himself planning to take unconstitutional action if this seemed the only way to keep out the *Ortodoxos*. In any event, on 10 March he decided that the moment had come for direct action.

5 The Movement

Whether or not Batista had read *The Technique of the Coup d'Etat,* he was always extremely proud of the speed and efficiency with which he took power in the early hours of 10 March 1952. In fact most of the preparations had been undertaken by others. Some were old Batista supporters who had been purged from the army. Others were disgruntled officers resentful at seeing less competent but more pliant colleagues now enjoying the good life and privileges which went with senior rank. Even some of the generals appointed during the period of *Auténtico* rule felt little loyalty to the graft-ridden and discredited government of President Prío. The plotters were so determined to get rid of the politicians that they had contemplated going ahead on their own if they had failed to persuade Batista to lead the coup.

On Sunday 9 March Batista went to a political rally in Matanzas, fifty miles east of Havana, and talked as if his mind was only on the elections due in June. In the evening he returned to his villa near Havana. Shortly after midnight three Buicks slipped quietly out of the villa. They contained Batista, six serving officers and four retired officers. They drove to Camp Columbia, the huge military barracks where more than half of the Cuban army was based, the place where nineteen years earlier the then Sergeant Batista had master-minded the 'sergeants' revolt'. The officer on duty at the barracks, one of the plotters, let them in and proceeded with his co-conspirators to take command of the four infantry battalions in the barracks. The houses of the top generals were surrounded and the generals arrested. The wife of General Cabrera, the Chief of Staff, urged him to resist, but he said: 'Old girl, when things have reached this stage, all is lost.'

At the given word, other officers in the plot proceeded to take control of La Cabaña fort at the mouth of Havana harbour, the main naval headquarters, and other key command posts. Police Lieutenant Salas, one of the two police officers against whom Castro had lodged a criminal suit for responsibility for the death of a worker killed in a demonstration, took over the central telephone exchange, where his men listened in to communications from the presidential palace and government offices. Over the next hours troops and police moved into bus and railway stations, airports, electricity plants and radio transmission centres. The entrances to ministries and political party headquarters were sealed, and soldiers turned away anyone trying to enter them. Police were given a list of politicians and known agitators who were to be detained until the situation had been stabilised.

The arrested generals all went quietly, but General Cabrera's wife, evidently made of sterner stuff than her husband, managed to telephone her daughter, whose boyfriend telephoned the presidential palace with news of the takeover in Camp Columbia. A message was passed to the President, who drove from his residence to the palace and summoned his cabinet colleagues. Presidential officials tried to find out what was happening at other military bases. The colonels commanding the military garrisons in the central provinces of Matanzas and Las Villas telephoned to declare their loyalty.

Batista, informed through Lieutenant Salas of Prío's desperate attempts to rally support, sent a small squad to the palace, ostensibly to strengthen the guard. But the guard suspected that the soldiers had come to arrest the President, and shot the lieutenant commanding them. Batista then sent tanks which surrounded the palace, but then withdrew. At this point a student delegation headed by the FEU President, Alvaro Barba, arrived to urge President Prío to resist the coup. Prío said he would indeed resist, but from one of the loyal garrisons. The palace was too vulnerable. The students asked the President to give them arms with which to defend the constitutional order. Prío said he would send a consignment of weapons to the university. The students returned to the university to await the arrival of the weapons, which never came. Prío and his Prime Minister were driven in disguise eastwards towards Matanzas, where they discovered that the garrison commander had been arrested by officers supporting Batista. They drove on towards Camaguey, but before arriving learnt that supporters of the coup had also taken control of that garrison. They turned back towards Havana and sought asylum in the Mexican Embassy, where they discovered that several ministers had preceded them.

The leadership of the trade union confederation met early on the morning of 10 March and declared a general strike in protest at the illegal seizure of power by Batista. But in the general confusion and lack of information about what was happening, the strike call had little effect. Students were congregating at the university, waiting in vain for the weapons promised by the President. Several politicians and trade unionists disposed to fight against the takeover went to the university, which seemed the only place likely to provide a centre of resistance. For the most part the people of Havana went about their business as if nothing unusual had happened.

Fidel Castro was asleep in bed on the morning of 10 March when a friend, René Rodríguez, called at his flat with news of the coup. Thinking (rightly as it proved) that he was a likely candidate for arrest by the military government, he put on dark glasses and walked the few blocks to the flat of his half-sister Lidia. His aim was to avoid arrest for as long as possible, while organising resistence. His brother Raúl, who was also staying at the flat and who was still an enrolled student, went to the university. Only Mirta and little Fidelito were present when police arrived looking for the Castro brothers.

From Lidia's flat Castro sent Rodríguez to the university and to the home of *Ortodoxo* leader Roberto Agramonte to report back on developments. At midday radio stations interrupted the music which had been playing all morning to announce the formation of a new government, composed mainly of old Batista stalwarts who had served in his 1940–4 administration. Batista had tried briefly to find a respectable civilian politician willing to front for him as provisional President, but then decided to do the job himself. Soon afterwards the government issued a declaration saying they had acted to put an end to a regime of crime and corruption, and to pre-empt plans by Prío to retain power by unconstitutional means. Presidential and Congressional elections would be held in November 1953. Meantime constitutional guarantees, including the right to strike and to engage in party political activities, were suspended. The Congress was dissolved pending new elections, but Congressmen would continue to receive their salaries (a characteristic Batista detail).

Rodriguez returned to report that Agramonte had said that the *Ortodoxos* would condemn the coup, but would use only civic resistance. He had no particular message or guidance for the party. At this Castro flew into a violent rage, shouting obscenities and calling Agramonte a coward. He was even more disgusted when he learnt how quickly Batista had succeeded in neutralising opposition from the trade unions. Some militant trade unionists were arrested. Batista then sent a reassuring message to Eusebio Mujal, the Secretary-General of the Trade Union Confederation, saying that existing legislation enshrining trade union rights would be respected. Mujal contacted Prío in the Mexican Embassy. Having established that Prío was not in a position to offer any resistance to the coup, he concluded that the only sensible course for the unions was to do business as usual with the new government.

Since Lidia's flat was an obvious place for Castro to go, he decided it would be safer to spend the night at the Andino hotel, a cheap boarding-house where he had stayed when a student. The next morning he and Rodríguez took a bus to the flat of another *Ortodoxo* activist, Eva Jiménez, who lived in a quiet middle-class suburb. There he spent two days drafting a proclamation denouncing Batista's seizure of power, entitled *Revolución no, Zarpazo!*, a *zarpazo* being an animal's sudden blow with its paw. His theme was that the coup was not, as Batista claimed, a true revolution aimed at establishing social justice and honest government, but a crude grab for the spoils of power. Castro called for active resistance. He promised that, as in the past, there would be young men willing to die a martyr's death in the fight against a brutal and oppressive government. There was no more bitter experience for a people, he wrote, than to go to bed free and wake to slavery.

Rodríguez and Eva Jiménez took the proclamation to the newspaper *Alerta* and tried to persuade Ramón Vasconcelos to publish it. On previous occasions Vasconcelos had published material by Castro which no other journal would accept. But now he baulked at printing Castro's proclamation. With the suspension of constitutional guarantees, press controls had been imposed. Vasconcelos feared that publication of the proclamation would simply lead to his paper's being closed down. Unable to find a publisher, Castro decided to print the proclamation himself. Helped by his brother Raúl and by Nico López, a black print worker who had helped with his election campaign, he made 500 copies of the proclamation by hand on a mimeograph machine.

On the 16th of every month the *Ortodoxo* faithful gathered for a ceremony of commemoration at the grave of Eddy Chibás in Colón cemetery. Castro and his friends used the gathering on 16 March, six days after the coup, as an opportunity to hand out copies of his proclamation. *Ortodoxo* leader Agramonte was also present, but infuriated Castro again by saying that the struggle against Batista would be non-violent. Castro jumped on a tombstone and shouted that Batista had taken power by force and that he must be thrown out by force.

Many in the crowd of bystanders applauded Castro's intervention. Like him they were angry and frustrated. They had confidently expected to win the election due in June, and now their hopes had been crushed. Outside the circle of *Ortodoxo* militants, however, Castro's extreme rhetoric made little impact. The mood of the country was one of resignation and apathy. Castro and, especially, his hero Chibás had helped to create this mood. For years they had conducted an unceasing campaign of vilification not just against Prío's government, but against the whole political set-up, describing it as being riddled with corruption, nepotism, fraud, violence, injustice and dishonest patronage. Now, when Batista had indeed 'swept away the corrupt politicians' (as Chibás advocated) Castro suddenly described the old order as representing freedom. The Communists were rather more consistent. They condemned the coup, but said it represented no real change from the bad old system of the preceding *Auténtico* governments. The Communists' low-key reaction was seen by some as a signal that they might be willing to co-operate with Batista as they had done a decade earlier.

Batista had taken power swiftly, smoothly and virtually without violence. He claimed to have acted only because he had information that Prío was planning to find a pretext to cancel the elections and extend his own period in office. He promised to restore the democratic rights and freedoms established in the 1940 Constitution, which had moreover been largely his own creation. He skilfully played on public disillusion with the old politicians, digging up and publicising more dirt about their public and private lives. He undertook to end the gang violence which had characterised the *Auténtico* years of government. He promised that government contracts would be honoured, as would the country's international obligations. He would hold free elections in twenty months' time. With those assurances and explanations, was it worth sacrificing one's life in a completely unrealistic effort to overthrow the new government by force, as Castro wanted? Most people thought not.

After three days Batista felt secure enough to start relaxing some of the measures adopted on the day of the coup. He accepted a request from the Mexican Ambassador to give ex-President Prío a safe conduct to fly to Mexico and thence to Miami. Several other prominent *Auténtico* politicians fled the country. Hostile politicians who stayed in Cuba, including the leadership of the *Ortodoxo* Party, were subjected to a mixture of threats and blandishments. Agramonte was summoned to the offices of the SIM (secret police), who said he was under close surveillance and that there would be serious consequences if he did not abide by the new government's dispositions.

The new government broadcast messages of support from various governors, mayors, businessmen and other prominent citizens. The Havana Chamber of Commerce and other business organisations expressed their approval of the Batista government and support for the measures he proposed to take. The banking community made it known that they had confidence that Batista would provide the stable conditions necessary for good economic management. Some of the old politicians, notably the leadership of the small Liberal and Democrat Parties, openly welcomed the coup. The Catholic Church was ambivalent, with only a few individual churchmen speaking out against Batista. Most government officials remained at their desks, as did the judiciary. When the leaders of the *Auténtico* and *Ortodoxo* parties filed a suit in the Court of Constitutional Guarantees, alleging that Batista had violated the 1940 Constitution, the Court rejected the suit, arguing that the 'Revolution' was now itself the source of law.

Fidel Castro was not content merely to associate himself with his party's legal action. He separately presented criminal charges against Batista in the Court of Urgencies, arguing that the sentences prescribed in the penal code for actions taken by Batista amounted to more than 100 years in prison. He said threateningly that a regime that seized power by force had no moral or legal basis to condemn others who might use force against it. He brought suits against various ministers for violating the labour legislation which Batista had promised to uphold. The government paid little heed to these pinpricks, and the courts simply ignored him. Such was the general tranquillity in the country, and Batista's confidence, that some newspapers were able to report anti-government activities, including actions taken by Castro in the courts, without suffering any reprisal. In May some of the constitutional guarantees which had been suspended at the time of the coup were restored, at least in theory.

International recognition further strengthened the new government. The military dictatorships in Venezuela, Nicaragua and the Dominican Republic were the first to give General Batista formal recognition. Several more Latin American and European governments followed suit when it had become evident that Batista was in effective control of the country. The discussion within the United States government on whether to grant recognition centred not on Batista's democratic credentials, but on his likely attitude towards Cuba's international obligations and towards Communism. Although Batista had co-operated with the Communists in the war years, State Department officials felt confident that in the new international climate he would be robustly anti-Communist. Batista quickly provided reassurance on this point. On 27 May the United States government, setting aside the views of Cuba's two largest political parties, conveyed formal recognition. The relative speed with which the United States recognised the Batista government, in contrast to their prolonged refusal to recognise the revolutionary government of 1933, strengthened Castro's belief that 'imperialism' was the real and ultimate enemy against which he would have to fight.

It has sometimes been suggested that Castro may have been privately pleased at Batista's coup. He had for years been advocating the revolutionary path to power. It would be easier to justify the violent overthrow of a military dictator than of a democratically elected government, however flawed. As Lenin said, the worse, the better. But the weight of evidence is that Castro was genuinely enraged over the coup. He had been working feverishly to get himself elected to Congress, in order to have a platform in the public eye from which to gather mass support for a revolutionary programme. In these months of electioneering he had been able to canvas openly, to give radio broadcasts, and to disseminate his views in *Alerta*. These avenues were now closed. He said later: 'When the coup took place, everything changed. As a first step, I thought we should have to go back to the previous constitutional stage.' He decided, however, that it would be pointless to work with the official *Ortodoxo* party. In his view it had fallen almost completely into the hands of weak and ineffectual middle-class liberals. Instead, he would form an entirely new organisation from among the radical supporters whom he had got to know while electioneering in Havana.

He now set out to construct what he called, with deliberate vagueness, 'the Movement'. It would be a twin-track organisation, with a civil committee and a military committee, both tightly controlled by himself. The civil committee would conduct political agitation, through an underground newspaper and such political activities as were possible under the Batista regime. The military committee would prepare, train and eventually arm a secret force able to take violent action to destabilise and ultimately bring down the Batista government. The Movement was to be organised on a cell structure already familiar in revolutionary movements which had operated against authoritarian regimes in many parts of the world, including Cuba during the dictatorship of Machado. Each cell would comprise about ten men, who would have no knowledge of the existence and activities of the other cells. The only person who would know everyone and everything would be Castro himself.

The idea of the Movement was born when Castro met a small group of personal friends, all young *Ortodoxos* living in Havana, who had already decided to try to do something more effective against Batista than futile protests. The leading lights of the group were a twenty-four-year-old accountant in a car dealership, Abel Santamaría, and his sister Haydée Santamaría. From his first long conversation with Castro, Santamaría became a devoted and ardent supporter, and in effect Castro's deputy. The Santamarías' small flat was the principal base for the Movement's activities. Castro had been introduced to Santamaría by another important early member, Jesús Montané, a junior manager in General Motors whom Castro had approached during his electoral campaign in an attempt to exchange his old car for a more serviceable one. Montané contrived to obtain a car for the Movement and his job provided good cover for secret revolutionary activities.

Castro demanded secrecy and total commitment from his followers. Members of the Movement were required to live an austere life, abstaining from alcohol and dedicating themselves wholly to working for the overthrow of Batista. Strict discipline was maintained. Any indiscretion, or failure to attend meetings at exactly the time prescribed, could be grounds for expulsion. Melba Hernández, an *Ortodoxo* lawyer some years older than Castro, later described joining the Movement as almost a religious experience. Listening to Castro's soft, compelling, urgent voice, suddenly life took on a new meaning and a new purpose. The conspiratorial secrecy was part of the experience. 'Castro spoke in a very low voice . . . came close as if to tell you a secret; and then you suddenly felt you shared the secret.'

Melba Hernández in turn brought into the Movement another important member, a young teacher and poet called Raúl Gómez. Montané brought in his close friend Boris Luis Santa Coloma, who was the fiancé of Haydée Santamaría. Castro himself also brought in the printer Nico López and two or three other trusted friends. These dozen people constituted the nucleus of the Movement. The initial four-person leadership was formed by Castro, the two Santamarías and Melba Hernández, but Castro was always totally and indisputably in overall command. Melba Hernández's parents were sympathisers and offered their flat as an alternative meeting-place. Castro's half-sister Lidia was also sufficiently sympathetic and trusted for her flat to be used occasionally for meetings of the Movement's leadership. Montané and Santamaría later secured the use of a smart office near the Malecón seafront, which provided the best cover. Castro never used his own flat for meetings of more than two or three people.

After July 1952 the pace of recruitment was stepped up. Within a year Castro had enrolled some 1,200 people into the Movement, organised in more than a hundred cells. Some of the cells were pre-existing circles of like-minded friends who joined as a group. The formal leadership now comprised ten people, six in the political committee and six in the military committee, Castro and Abel Santamaría having membership of both committees. The great majority of grassroot members were from the poorer districts of Havana, people who had been attracted by Castro's campaign to become a Congressman. There were street vendors, drivers, shop assistants, waiters, mechanics and some unemployed. Many were loners, with few family or other ties, and no loyalty to other organisations such as trade unions. A typical early member was Ramiro Valdés, a twenty-one-year-old assistant truck driver who many years later would be the feared and highly efficient head of President Castro's secret police. Valdés had been impressed by Castro's diatribes on the *Ortodoxo* radio programme and asked to meet him. He found Castro dressed, despite the stifling July heat, in his familiar dark woollen suit. But Castro's conservative appearance only served to emphasise the quiet passion with which he set out his revolutionary objectives. Valdés became a dedicated member and helped to recruit many more members from the impoverished slums of the Artemisa district near Havana.

Castro deliberately avoided trying to recruit members of the Communist Party. He was secretly closer in ideology to the Communists than to the mainstream *Ortodoxos*. But he knew that the Communists had their own plans and agenda, and would not submit to the discipline of any other political organisation. The Communists had moreover become isolated from other left-wing movements by the pressures of the Cold War. They had lost ground even in the university. Castro's old Communist friend Alfredo Guevara tried, on instructions from the Party, to coax him into an alliance with the Communists. Castro calculated, however, that any Communist involvement in the

Movement would be a potential liability, frightening away the social moderates whose support he still needed. Two Communists would at a late stage join the Movement, but in both cases the circumstances were exceptional. One was a middle-aged worker whose Communist affiliation had somehow been overlooked. The other was Raúl Castro, who consorted closely with Communist fellow-students throughout 1952. Raúl spent the spring of 1953 attending a Communist-front peace conference in Vienna and visiting various East European countries. In June 1953, following his return to Cuba, he applied to join the Communist Youth movement. But Fidel had not involved Raúl in the inner circles of the Movement. He knew that in any conflict of loyalty he could count on Raúl to submit to his older brother's domineering personality.

There were relatively few students or people with a university education in the Movement. This also was deliberate. People with a university education tended to have an opinion about everything and to argue the toss. That was not what Castro wanted in the Movement. He wanted people who would give unconditional support to his leadership and direction. He recruited students or graduates only when they had some technical knowledge or contacts that were especially useful.

Apart from building up membership, the political activity of the Movement in its early days was concentrated on the production and distribution of an underground newspaper. Before Santamaría and Montané joined forces with Castro, they had bought a second-hand printing machine with which they produced an anti-Batista news-sheet called *Son Los Mismos* ('They are just the same'). Castro wrote articles for this publication under the pseudonym of Alejandro, but he disliked the title and with the poet Raúl Gómez he started a second publication called *El Acusador* ('The Accuser').

After a while *Son Los Mismos* was dropped and *El Acusador* became the sole mouthpiece of the Movement, with Castro writing much of the content himself. Most of the news-sheet consisted of fairly crude invective against Batista and his cronies. There was less about what the Movement actually favoured. It called for an end to the abusive treatment of workers and peasants, improved wages, and respect for the rights of women. Castro wrote that after the Revolution the land of the big absentee landowners (mostly foreign) would be taken over and distributed to the smallholders and peasants who worked on it. But there was no talk of Communism or even Marxism. The hero and model most quoted was the one accepted by virtually all Cubans, José Martí. If *El Acusador* did not give a full picture of Castro's intentions, he justified this to himself with Martí's axiom that to achieve one's goals, one must conceal them.

As well as a printed mouthpiece, Castro was keen to obtain a clandestine broadcasting facility. He had recruited to the Movement a forty-one-year-old physician, Dr Mario Muñoz, who lived in the town of Colón in central Cuba. Muñoz was an ardent revolutionary, but also a ham radio enthusiast. He constructed two simple transmitters, which were used to broadcast announcements and declarations by the Movement. The broadcasts were advertised in the Movement's news-sheet, but proved difficult to hear.

The first anniversary of the death of Eddy Chibás was on 16 August 1952. A large meeting of *Ortodoxo* supporters was to take place at Chibás's grave in Colón cemetery. Castro planned to turn the event into a big propaganda platform for the Movement. Ten thousand copies of the third issue of *El Acusador* were printed for distribution at the ceremony, which included a fierce attack on the weakness and cowardice of the official *Ortodoxo* leadership. However, it became apparent that the SIM had penetrated at least partially the Movement's organisation. The printing machine was found in the flat of a Movement member called González, and smashed. A large stack of copies of *El Acusador* was seized and destroyed. As some leading Movement members approached the Colón cemetery carrying copies of *El Acusador,* they were arrested. Melba Hernández and another woman were released later the same day and alerted Castro about the arrests. The next day Castro and Hernández went to the police station in their capacity as lawyers to seek the release of those who had been arrested. They were shocked to find that several members of the Movement's leadership not involved in any way with the Colón ceremony, including Montané and Raúl Gómez, had also been arrested. It was clearly a co-ordinated police action. Soon afterwards one of the Movement's radio transmitters was found by the police and destroyed.

Luckily for Castro, the police evidently did not think that his bunch of amateur revolutionaries constituted a serious threat. For the secret police the most dangerous threat to the Batista regime would lie in any disaffected group within the army itself, and secondly in the established political parties, especially *Auténtico* groups financed by ex-President Prío. The odd collection of people producing *El Acusador* did not fall into these categories, and they were released without charge after a few days. Shortly afterwards Fidel Castro and Abel Santamaría were stopped by a police patrol car, taken to a police station and searched. But nothing incriminating was found on them and they too were released. Despite intensive efforts, Castro was never able to establish whether the police action was due to treachery from within or was simply the result of police surveillance of people distributing the Movement's news-sheet.

The arrests in August did not affect the incipient military activities of the Movement, which now became Castro's top priority. The key development in this field was the recruitment in September of Pedro Miret, an engineering student and armaments expert who owned a collection of fairly ancient rifles and shotguns. He had been giving instruction in weapons handling to anti-Batista students in the little-used basements of some university buildings, and occasionally out of sight on the roof. Soon after joining the Movement Miret became a member of the six-man military committee, together with Castro, Abel Santamaría, José Luis Tasende (a factory worker), Ernesto Tizol (a chicken farmer who had formed his own little political group before joining forces with Castro) and Renarto Guitart (a commercial apprentice from Santiago). The military training of Movement cells took place in the autumn of 1952 either in the university (it was dangerous to take weapons out of the university precincts) or at night in farmland near Havana. In the university recruits were taught to dismantle and assemble Miret's rifles. On secluded farmland they were taught to crawl commando-style over obstacles, carrying a mock weapon. After January 1953 all training was done outside the university, in locations frequently changed to maintain security. Cell members travelled individually by bus to the countryside and then followed instructions on how to arrive at their rendezvous.

For both security and financial reasons there was very little actual shooting practice. Oscar Alcalde, a Movement member who was a junior official in the Finance Ministry, joined a hunting club and used this as a pretext to invite guests to practise shooting with a shotgun. For a time Miret was assisted in his training programme by a man called Isaac Santos who had served in the US army in Korea and taught infantry and commando skills. Santos was later dropped on the suspicion that he might be a plant of either the Batista police or the CIA. Castro himself and Abel Santamaría were seldom present at military training sessions. Detailed co-ordination of training sessions, including the issuing of code-words, was handled usually by Tasende and Tizol. The usual intermediary for carrying messages between Castro and other Movement leaders was Nico López, partly because a black workman looked unlikely to be the associate of an aristocratic-looking young lawyer.

A critical problem for the Movement was the lack of money to acquire weapons. Most of the weapons they were able to purchase were sporting guns. Military rifles in reasonably good condition were difficult to find on the black market, and very expensive, as was ammunition for military weapons. At one time Alcalde was sent to a clandestine meeting, set up by a third party, with a Spanish Republican who was said to be offering to sell ten second-hand Thompson sub-machine guns. Some men hanging about the rendezvous made Alcalde suspect that the meeting was a SIM trap. He fled without meeting the Spaniard.

The Movement had no seriously wealthy members who might have solved its financial problems. Castro himself was earning virtually nothing and would later jokingly describe himself as the Movement's only paid employee, since he lived off money borrowed from colleagues. His father was reluctant to meet his requests for large sums of money, especially since he knew that Fidel could be earning a good income if he had been willing to work seriously as a lawyer. Fidel approached his older brother Ramón, who had taken over the running of the farm in Birán. Fidel said he urgently needed money for an action which he was planning, without revealing the nature of the action. With some reluctance, Ramón gave him 140 pesos, which Fidel accepted but without gratitude. Several Movement members mortgaged their properties or sold furniture to raise money. When Montané left General Motors, he gave all of his 4,000 pesos severance pay to the Movement.

In November 1952 Castro attended the annual celebration organised by Havana University to commemorate the death of the eight students executed by the Spanish colonial authorities. It was on this occasion that he met Naty Revuelta. She was a beautiful society girl married to a successful and hard-working young cardiologist. She had a rebellious spirit, and plenty of time on her hands. She had joined several political organisations and become an enthusiastic supporter of the most radical wing of the *Ortodoxos*. When Batista staged his coup, Naty feared that the *Ortodoxo* radicals would become the target of police persecution. She had copies made of her flat key and sent them to three well-known militants in Havana, including Castro, so that they could use her flat as a safe refuge. He had sent a message of thanks but had not previously met Naty in person.

Fidel found Naty extremely attractive. He used all his charm and humour on her, with great success. They laughed a great deal that evening, as Naty later recalled. She was at the time happily married with a young daughter, but she fell besottedly in love with Fidel and would remain so throughout her life, despite many years of neglect and virtual ostracism. Naty's husband at first assumed benevolently that Naty's enthusiasm for Castro was political, and for a time he went along with it. Naty was so keen to support the Movement that she sold her jewellery to help buy weapons.

As for Castro's long-suffering wife Mirta, she remained loyal and supportive, but Castro told her little about his political activities and objectives. Her brother Rafael was by now Under-Secretary of the Interior in Batista's government, and she was caught between conflicting pressures. Accustomed to a comfortable middle-class life, Mirta was suffering the consequences of Castro's lack of income. According to a credible anecdote, Castro came home late one night with his friend Pedro Trigo to find the electricity cut off in his flat due to the non-payment of bills, his three-year-old son Fidelito ill with a high temperature, and his wife with no money to buy medicine. He arranged to send Fidelito to a nearby hospital and borrowed 5 pesos from Trigo for his wife to buy medicine. He in fact had 100 pesos in his pocket, but this had been donated for the purchase of weapons, and that purpose for Castro took precedence over all other considerations.

In January 1953 Castro made his final break with the official *Ortodoxo* party leadership. A special meeting of the party had been summoned to discuss a proposal to participate in a multi-party alliance against Batista. Castro and other radicals thought that such an alliance would destroy the party's independence and represented a sell-out. He led a walk-out, shouting that 'these politicians' would achieve nothing. At the same time Castro was playing a double game with the Communists. He himself never took part in Communist activities, but he did nothing to discourage his brother Raúl from doing so. Raúl was often in the forefront of Communist demonstrations both inside and outside the university. He took a leading role in a student protest when the white marble statue of a Communist hero was found covered in black paint. The protest turned into a major riot. Failing to keep control with tear-gas and truncheons, the police opened fire and killed one of the protesters. Thirty students were arrested and taken to a police station. At this late stage Fidel Castro, *deus ex machina,* turned up at the police station in his capacity as a registered lawyer to demand the release of the detained students.

The centenary of the birth of José Martí fell on 28 January 1953. It was a big occasion. Every political faction in Cuba, from left to right, laid claim to Martí's spiritual inheritance. Batista organised lavish official celebrations, starting at the presidential palace. Opposition groups organised counter-celebrations. Fidel Castro, who passionately believed that he was the true heir of Martí, agreed to participate in a mass torchlight parade through the streets of Havana. About 500 members of the Movement took part, marching in disciplined ranks, shouting 'Revolution!' and 'Liberty!' All the Movement members carried flaming torches designed to double up as weapons in the event of a police attack. Not for the first time Castro seemed to be modelling his publicity tactics on those of Hitler and Mussolini.

The Batista police, wanting to show their best face to the foreign guests invited to Havana for the official Martí celebrations, took no action against the marchers. The well-organised and disciplined ranks marching behind Castro were assumed by many onlookers to be Communists. Those who knew Castro, but were not in the Movement, assumed that he was once again getting on any opposition bandwagon that was available. Since he was a great talker and attention-seeker, no one suspected, despite the evidence before their eyes, that he was also the commander of a secret army.

Shortly after the Martí centenary, Castro got a signed article published in the national media for the first time since the Batista coup a year earlier. The article, appearing in the popular weekly *Bohemia,* described the destruction by the police of the studio of a left-wing sculptor. Compared with Castro's usual fulminations, for example when he was producing *El Acusador,* the article in *Bohemia* was pretty tepid. It marked another tactical turning point in Castro's leadership of the Movement. As he stepped up preparations for military action, he wanted to show himself to be busy with what the police would regard as fairly innocuous political activity.

Castro's Movement was by no means the only clandestine organisation aiming to overthrow Batista. Another such group was the National Revolutionary Movement (MNR), led by a professor of philosophy, Rafael García Bárcena, who had been a co-founder of the *Ortodoxo* party in 1947 with Eddy Chibás and was regarded by some as the rightful successor to Chibás. He had taught for six years in the Higher School of War and had built up a following among young military officers. García Bárcena hoped to engineer a bloodless seizure of power on similar lines to Batista's own coup. Unlike Castro's Movement, the MNR was a largely middle-class organisation, with many professionals and students among its members.

García Bárcena approached Fidel Castro in March 1953, seeking his support for an attempt to seize the Camp Columbia military base with help from officers inside the barracks. Castro prevaricated. He claimed later to have been willing in principle to support García Bárcena but to have warned him that the MNR was talking to too many people and that their security was probably compromised. This may have been true, but it also gave Castro a pretext for avoiding involvement with an enterprise which he did not control and considered to be ill-conceived. In any event, on the day when García Bárcena was planning to seize control of Camp Columbia, police surrounded the house where the plotters had assembled, and arrested all those inside. García Bárcena and some others were severely tortured to reveal accomplices. Fourteen were put on trial and given prison sentences. Some of the MNR militants not in jail decided later to join Castro's Movement. Some accused him of treachery. He had known the planned date for the MNR's action, and had taken care to ensure that he and all the other members of the Movement's leadership were a long way from Havana on the day in question.

In June 1953 a meeting was held in Montreal, Canada, of representatives of all the non-Communist political parties and organisations opposed to Batista. The purpose was to work out a strategy to restore democracy in the island. Castro, having virtually excluded himself from the *Ortodoxo* party, was not invited to attend, but called on some of the participants after their return to Cuba. The former head of the *Ortodoxo* youth wing, Max Lesnick, hinted that action was afoot and that the supply of weapons would not be a problem. Lack of weapons was a big problem for Castro, but he remained determined not to join forces with any other group outside his control. On the contrary, the suspicion that others might soon be launching action against Batista may have induced him to bring forward his own plans in order to get in first. The plan that he had been nurturing for several months was to attack the Moncada military barracks at Santiago in Oriente province, and simultaneously the smaller Cespedes military post at Bayamo, a town some sixty miles from Santiago which controlled the main road into the province from the West.

Until the last moment Castro told only five other members of the Movement about his scheme to attack Moncada. But throughout his life he would combine extreme secrecy and deceptiveness with occasional flashes of apparently foolhardy openness. In June he approached an *Ortodoxo* professor of military history, Portell Vilá, and asked him about the feasibility of a surprise attack on the Moncada barracks by a group of armed volunteers. Portell Vilá said that without inside help it was bound to fail.

Castro was not convinced. He stuck to his belief, based in particular on events in the French Revolution, that boldness and surprise were the secrets of success. As he himself put it, previous attempts at revolution in Cuba had been undertaken with or without the established army, but never against it. It was assumed that the army could stop any attempt to seize power, and that the army must therefore be induced at least to stand aloof if an uprising was to be successful. The failed MNR attempt would have depended for success on help from army officers. Castro believed that this sort of action with military support would be no more than a putsch, and that the military would be left with the real power, as happened in 1933 when the Revolutionary Directorate took power with help from Batista's soldiers, only to be ousted themselves a few months later.

Castro thought he could prove wrong the assumption of the army's invincibility. The Moncada barracks were normally occupied by about 400 men, but he expected that the men would be in a low state of alert, and that on 25 July, the festival of St James (Santiago), most officers would be on leave or celebrating in the town late into the night. The attackers would arrive at dawn on 26 July in a group of cars, dressed in army uniforms, and seize control of the barracks before the alarm could be raised. They would break into the armoury and leave the barracks with the weapons quickly, before other army or air force units had time to react. If time and circumstances permitted, they would send confusing messages to other military bases suggesting that the action had been taken by junior ranks inside the barracks.

Santiago was carefully chosen as the target for the operation. Oriente had throughout Cuba's history been the most turbulent and revolutionary part of the country. Its poverty and lack of development, and the concentration of land in the hands of a few people, mostly foreign corporations, had long made it a breeding ground for discontent. In Oriente could be seen the worst social consequences of the seasonal nature of Cuba's principal product, sugar. For the cane-cutters (mostly the descendants of slaves) there was back-breaking work from dawn to dusk during four months of the year, and usually unemployment during the remaining eight months. Oriente consti-tuted the bony head of the crocodile which forms the shape of Cuba, the area most remote from the main centres of military and political power in Havana in the crocodile's tail. A successful sudden stroke against the Moncada barracks could, Castro believed, spark a widespread popular uprising in the province before the authorities had time to move troops to the east. The weapons in the Moncada armoury would multiply by several times the Move-ment's fire-power, and enable it to arm local volunteers. Castro was consciously following in the footsteps of the Cuban independence fighters who had armed themselves by surprise attacks on Spanish military posts in the east of the island. If the attack failed, the nearby Sierra Maestra, the highest and wildest mountain range in Cuba, would provide the best possible area in which the attackers could seek refuge and reorganise themselves.

Immediately after the capture of Moncada Castro planned to occupy a radio station in Santiago from which to broadcast the Movement's manifesto. The manifesto had been drafted by the poet Raúl Gómez and edited heavily, as usual, by Castro. It contained nine paragraphs of grandiose and apparently jejune rhetoric, with a strong dose of self-glorification. '. . . The Revolution is born in the soul of the Cuban people, from the vanguard of young men seeking a new Cuba free of past errors and sordid ambitions . . . It has been prepared with the patience, bravery and determination of those who dedicate their life to an ideal . . .' The manifesto said that the Revolution favoured virtue, honour, economic prosperity, social justice and the 1940 Constitution (even Batista could agree with that) but gave little idea how these things were to be attained. All this was less simplistic than it looked. Castro was deter-mined not to tie his hands. The manifesto declared that the *Ortodoxo* party was the true inheritor of the ideals of Martí. But this indirect appeal for *Orto-doxo* support involved no real allegiance. The manifesto also said that the Revolution was independent of both foreign governments and national politi-cians. Naty Revuelta had been charged with obtaining material to broadcast before and after the manifesto: records with suitably stirring revolutionary music by Beethoven and other classical composers, the national anthem and songs of the independence wars, and a recording of the last radio broadcast of Eddy Chibás before his suicide.

A member of the military committee, Ernesto Tizol, rented a 2-acre farm near the Siboney beach ten miles from Santiago, ostensibly to rear chickens (his normal activity) but in reality to provide a base for the storage of weapons and the assembly of the attacking force. From mid-July weapons and army uniforms were transported from Havana and hidden in a dry well concealed under the floorboards of an improvised chicken-house in the Siboney farm. The Movement had obtained about 100 uniforms on the black market. Haydée Santamaría and Melba Hernández had made a few more, and sewn on suitable badges of rank. Renato Guitart, the only member of the military committee who came from Santiago, supervised preparations in Santiago, including transport plans and routes. He was able to buy locally a large quantity of shotgun ammunition. He arranged for another man from Santiago to survey the exterior of the barracks and make a careful note of the movements and routines of the soldiers on guard. He rented rooms in various hotels and boarding-houses in Santiago and Bayamo, ostensibly for friends who were coming to participate in the Santiago annual festival. Most of the leadership were booked into the Rex Hotel, which conveniently did not insist on having the names of all the people in the party of visitors. On 16 July Abel Santamaría travelled to Santiago to assume command until Fidel's arrival. He rented and moved to Siboney a large number of mattresses, and ordered supplies of food and milk.

Before leaving Havana to head the military operation, Castro had an intensive week of meetings, some only indirectly related to the operation. He went to the Communist bookshop in Havana and asked a friend there to set up a meeting with a senior representative of the Communist Party. He duly met Carlos Rafael Rodríguez, who was the Party's leading intellectual and had served as a Minister in Batista's 1940 government. They had a long talk about the state of the country. Castro gave no hint of his impending action to overthrow Batista, but indicated that he had a lot of sympathy with Communist ideology. His objective in this discussion was to ensure that the Communists would react positively to the Moncada action, or at least not condemn it out of hand. Castro had no intention of subordinating his Movement to international Communism, but he already saw the Communists as long-term allies.

He also called on his brother-in-law and former friend, Rafael Díaz-Balart, now Under-Secretary in the Interior Ministry with direct responsibility for the police. Castro pretended to be interested in the fate of a client who had been arrested some days earlier. He asked for information about where the man was held and what charges were to be brought against him. This interest was a cover to enable Castro to check out whether the authorities had any knowledge of his own plans. He left satisfied that the government had no suspicions.

Castro had chosen 165 people to take part in the operation, 138 in Santiago and the remaining 27 in Bayamo. Most were young men from Havana and the Western province of Pinar del Rio. There were two lawyers

(Castro himself and Hernández), one doctor, one dentist, five accountants and six students (including Raúl Castro), most of the rest being non-unionised workers such as drivers, cooks, carpenters, bricklayers, mechanics and farmworkers. Apart from Castro himself, none of those selected had children. He knew that he was putting the lives of all the participants at risk, and did not want to create orphans. In a slightly macabre touch of paternalistic sentiment, he insisted that a young man who was engaged should get married before leaving Havana, so that if he died he would at least have had the pleasure of a wedding night. The main body of the assault force then travelled from Havana in pairs or small groups by car, bus and train, mostly over the period 22 to 24 July. All had been given addresses in Santiago or Bayamo where they should stay before being picked up and taken to the assembly points. They knew that they were to take part in a military operation, but most were told of the specific target only on the day of the action.

On the morning of Friday 24 July Castro went with his 'chauffeur', Teodulfo Mitchel, a black lorry-driver who was a recent recruit to the Movement, to hire a large Buick car which he said he needed for a weekend in the tourist resort of Varadero. Mitchel then drove him to various locations in or near Havana to co-ordinate last-minute arrangements. He called on Naty Revuelta to pick up retyped copies of the Moncada manifesto and the recordings which she had prepared to accompany the broadcasting of the manifesto. He told Naty to deliver copies of the manifesto to selected newspapers and politicians at precisely 5 a.m. on Sunday 26 July.

Late on the evening of 24 July Castro and Mitchel finally set out on the 560-mile road to Santiago. During the night they stopped and took a brief rest in Colón at the house of Dr Mario Muñoz, who agreed to travel separately in his own car to a rendezvous in Santiago. After another long drive they stopped in the town of Santa Clara. It was now the morning of Saturday 25 July. Castro went to an optician. In the hectic round of last-minute meetings in Havana he had forgotten to pick up his glasses, which he seldom wore in public but would need to conduct an armed military assault. He obtained a substitute pair of glasses and they drove on, arriving at Bayamo in the early evening. They went to the Gran Casino Hotel where the Bayamo contingent, led by Raúl Martínez, had assembled during the preceding two days. Castro spent some hours giving instructions and encouragement for the planned attack on the Bayamo garrison the next morning. He said that even if the attack failed, it would contribute to the certain eventual overthrow of Batista. He then set out again, arriving at the Siboney farm shortly before midnight. He was met at the entrance by Montané, who was on guard. About 120 men had already arrived. A few more would straggle in by car over the next hours. The cars were all concealed in chicken houses. The lights in the house were all out except in one small room where Melba Hernández and Haydée Santamaría had been preparing food and ironing the army uniforms.

After greeting all those present Castro went into a huddle with Abel Santamaría and Guitart, whom he had not seen for more than a week. They went over the military plan. The object of the attack, the Moncada barracks, was a sprawling group of buildings and training areas inside a 6-hectare irregular rectangle, the perimeter formed in part by a high fence and in part by the exterior wall of the main fortress-like building. It was the headquarters of a 380–strong infantry regiment and a twenty-six-man detachment of the Rural Guard. There were four entrances to the compound. The one chosen by Castro was gate no. 3, which gave access to a courtyard in the principal headquarters building.

The plan was that twenty-one men should occupy a civilian hospital that overlooked the Western wall of the barracks, from the rear windows of which they could give diversionary fire if necessary. Another smaller group was to take up position on the roof of the three-storey Palace of Justice, one block south of the barracks, from where they could give cover to the main attacking party who would arrive in a convoy of cars at the no. 3 entrance. The three soldiers on guard duty would be seized and disarmed before they could raise the alarm, the iron chain across the entrance would be lifted, and several vehicles would drive into the courtyard inside. The attackers would storm into the adjacent dormitory and capture and disarm the soldiers there. Other attackers would take control of the barracks radio transmitter. Others again would break into the armoury and load weapons into the vehicles. As soon as this had been done the whole attacking party would withdraw from the barracks and disperse in their respective vehicles. The attackers were to try to achieve their objectives without bloodshed, but would be ready to shoot if they met armed resistance.

Abel Santamaría had assumed that he would lead the main attack group and that Fidel as overall commander would remain outside with the back-up vehicles. Haydée and Melba Hernández agreed with Abel that for the sake of the future of the Movement, Fidel should not expose himself unnecessarily. Castro insisted, however, that he would lead the main attack, and that Abel should lead the group occupying the hospital. He instructed that in the event of his own death, Abel should take over the leadership of the Movement. He was at first opposed to allowing the two women to take part in the operation, but eventually agreed with a suggestion by Dr Mario Muñoz that they should go with him to the hospital in the last car. Muñoz would be dressed as a doctor in a white coat and the women could help him to deal with any casualties.

These points having been settled, Castro set out again by car to visit Luis Conte Aguero, an *Ortodoxo* friend and broadcaster who had a house in

Santiago. From a discussion a few days earlier in Havana, Castro believed that Conte would be in Santiago for the festival. He intended to ask Conte to use his radio expertise to co-ordinate the broadcasting of the Moncada manifesto. But this time Castro's secretiveness defeated his purpose. Conte had remained in Havana and Castro had to return empty-handed to Siboney.

Shortly after Castro's return, weapons and uniforms were handed round. The uniforms were to be put on over the men's ordinary clothes, so they could be discarded if necessary. Castro had reserved a large uniform for himself but had neglected to try it on. It was still too short. He had shaved off his moustache to help conceal his identity but he was worried that an ill-fitting uniform might arouse suspicion. Some last-minute efforts were made to adjust it. Castro also thought that Abel Santamaría looked unconvincing in his sergeant's uniform and jokingly ordered him to adopt a more military posture. Renato Guitart, impatient for the action to start, had already put on a uniform some hours earlier.

Most of the weapons issued were shotguns or light .22 rifles. There were only a very few heavier weapons. There was a moment of intense alarm when a young man accidentally pulled the trigger of his loaded weapon. Everyone remained silent and motionless for several minutes until they concluded that no one outside the farm had heard the shot.

At about 4 a.m. Castro finally gathered everyone together and, while the women handed round milk, told them for the first time the target of the operation and how it would be carried out. He said that if all went well there would be no bloodshed and the whole operation would be over in 10 minutes. Most officers would probably be either away from the barracks or sleeping off the effects of the carnival the previous night. The seizure of weapons from Moncada would ignite a rebellion in Oriente which would spread to the rest of Cuba. There were obviously risks that something could go wrong. For security reasons he had not been able to tell them earlier about the target of the operation. But everyone present had joined the Movement voluntarily, and all those taking part in the action should also do so voluntarily. If anyone was reluctant and wanted to pull out, there was still time to do so.

Castro no doubt genuinely did not want reluctant heroes who might let the team down at a critical moment. But he was surprised as well as disgusted when ten men, the representatives of two cells including the only student cell, came up to him after the briefing to say that they wanted to drop out. They thought that the rebels' numbers and weapons were inadequate to take on such a powerful and well-protected target. These men were taken into a back room and placed under armed guard. Castro ordered that they could leave in the two cars in which they had come, but only after the whole convoy of the attack force had left the farm. After this difficult moment the atmosphere recovered and the rest of the party remained solid.

Shortly before 5 a.m., amid nervous and excited whispers, Castro gave his final pep-talk. His words were later learnt in schools all over Cuba, and the approved version sounds like one of the fictitious orations before battle in a Roman history. But that was the way Castro liked to speak at 'historic' moments, and the text is probably in fact close to what he actually said.

> In a few hours you will be victorious or defeated, but regardless of the outcome – listen well, friends – this Movement will triumph. If you win tomorrow, the aspirations of Martí will be fulfilled sooner. If we fail, our action will nevertheless set an example for the Cuban people, and from the people will arise fresh young men willing to die for Cuba. They will pick up our banner and move forward . . . The people will back us in Oriente and in the whole island. As in '68 and '92, here in Oriente we will give the first cry of Liberty or Death!

The party then moved out of the house to board the cars assigned to them. Decades later some of the survivors would still talk about the intensity of this moment, the clear star-covered sky just before dawn, the palm trees lit up in the lights of the emerging cars, the sense above all of being engaged in an enterprise which seemed much bigger and better than anything they had previously done.

6 Moncada Lives!

Just before 5 a.m. on 26 July 1953, sixteen cars, each packed with armed rebels, set out from the Siboney farm and drove in a convoy towards Santiago. Right from the start things went wrong. A car broke down with a punctured tyre. Four of the occupants managed to squeeze into other cars, but four others had to be left behind. Another car with eight men took a wrong turning in Santiago and became detached from the main convoy. The car containing the six-man group which was to occupy the Palace of Justice (under the command of Lester Rodríguez and including Raúl Castro) also got lost in the streets of Santiago, and arrived late. The group commanded by Abel Santamaría arrived on time at the civilian hospital, which the men occupied without mishap or opposition. They explained that they were part of a rebel organisation which was taking control of the Moncada barracks.

The first car in the main attack group, containing eight men commanded by Renato Guitart, drew up outside gate no. 3 of the barracks, a few minutes after the scheduled time of 5.15 a.m. They dismounted and Guitart, dressed in a sergeant's uniform, shouted: 'Attention! The general is coming!' As the three guards stood to attention, Jesús Montané, Ramiro Valdés and José Suárez grabbed the guards' Springfield rifles and hustled the men through the gate. Guitart and four others lifted the chain across the entrance to the barracks and ran up a flight of stairs leading (as they mistakenly thought) to the headquarters communications room. At this point the rest of the cars, the first driven by Fidel Castro, should have driven through the gate and into the courtyard. But they failed to appear.

Castro had stopped 150 yards away, opposite the military hospital, and was thinking what to do about a mobile patrol of two soldiers with sub-machine guns who had appeared unexpectedly in the street. The soldiers were looking suspiciously at what was happening at the gate, with their backs towards Castro. Castro drove his large Buick slowly towards the soldiers, with the car door open, hoping to jump them before they could raise the alarm. When one of them turned round, Castro accelerated, but he was holding a large pistol in one hand and drove the car hard into a high curb. The engine stalled. Now a sergeant appeared in the street and raised his pistol towards Castro's car. The men in the car behind Castro opened fire and the sergeant fell. Next a soldier started shooting from the window of the military hospital. Castro and the other five men in his car jumped out, took cover and started firing back. The men in the other cars followed suit. Then a loud alarm bell started ringing in the barracks. That marked the end of any realistic chance of success for the operation.

Soon more rifle fire was coming from both the windows of the military hospital and the windows and roof of the headquarters building. A heavy machine gun opened up from the top of a tower 200 yards away inside the barracks compound. Castro shouted to his men to run towards the gate, but in the smoke, half-light and noise of gunfire from both sides, no one reacted. The rebels continued firing at the barracks, but they remained pinned down behind either their cars or a fence and trees on the other side of the street.

Meantime, the men in the first car, the only ones who actually got inside the barracks, found that about fifty soldiers were sleeping in camp beds in the courtyard. Contrary to Castro's belief that the garrison would be under-manned, it was crowded with additional soldiers from outlying districts who had moved to Moncada for the Santiago carnival. The unarmed soldiers in the courtyard surrendered to the rebels, but after a few minutes, when the alarm sounded, armed soldiers from other parts of the barracks appeared on the scene, and heavy shooting broke out. Guitart and three others were killed. The remaining rebels from the first contingent shot an officer and several soldiers but, finding themselves with no back-up and cut off from the rest of the party, they were forced to retreat to the street.

When Castro saw that his men were outgunned and outnumbered, he signalled to them to withdraw. Some got away in their cars, carrying several injured men. Some fled on foot. Castro was unable to restart his own car but clambered into one of the cars which were backing out of the street. Pedro Miret and two others kept firing from their positions to cover the withdrawal of the main party.

The group on the roof of the Palace of Justice saw what was happening and tried to give covering fire. But they were soon silenced by much heavier return fire. When the main force withdrew, they discarded their weapons and uniforms, and walked through the building and out into the street, where they dispersed. Raúl Castro set out with the aim of covering on foot the fifty odd miles from Santiago to the family farm in Birán.

Abel Santamaría's group in the civilian hospital fired towards the head-quarters building, but they could not see what was happening in the street in front of the barracks. By the time they realised that the main rebel force had withdrawn, it was too late for them to leave the hospital without running into soldiers. Abel told Haydée and Melba to move away from the men and to try to escape. He said that if the men were killed, it was important that someone should survive to say what had happened. They went to the children's ward and tried to calm the babies who were crying for food and attention. Most of the men then got into beds and pretended to be patients. Some well-disposed nurses helped them to put on hospital clothes and bandages. Soon afterwards a squad of soldiers went through the hospital, and at first noticed nothing suspicious. However, the Moncada barracks press officer happened to have been in the hospital, and he pointed out the rebels to the soldiers, including the two women. The men were dragged out, severely beaten with rifle butts, and then taken to the Moncada barracks. Dr Muñoz protested at the soldiers' behaviour. He was shot in the back ('trying to escape') and died instantly. He was the first to be killed after the fighting had ended. The army had suffered greater casualties than the rebels – nineteen dead and twenty-seven wounded, as against six dead and fifteen wounded – and the soldiers were bent on revenge.

In the course of the rest of the day, and of the following day, all twenty-two rebels in the hospital were killed, usually after undergoing horrendous tortures at the hands of interrogators charged with extracting confessions of links with political parties inside or outside of Cuba. More than thirty rebels from the main force suffered the same fate. Some died under torture. Others were finished off with a pistol shot. Haydée and Melba saw the poet Raúl Gómez alive, but with his face so smashed that at first they did not recognise him. He was later shot dead. The women heard soldiers talking about how a rebel was tortured to death by SIM interrogators, and realised from the description of his two-toned shoes that it was Haydée's fiancé Boris Santa Coloma. When Melba said that the rebels' objective had been to capture the garrison without bloodshed, an enraged soldier said: 'You didn't want bloodshed? Well, now you can see blood.' They were taken into the barber's shop, which had been used for the torture sessions. There was dried blood everywhere, even on the walls. Fresh blood on a narrow balcony outside the room was so deep that ripples were formed on it by the wind. Haydée started retching. Even one of the soldiers appeared to go into shock, repeating to himself: 'This I don't like. This can't be true.'

The attack on the Bayamo garrison was as unsuccessful as the attack on Moncada. A gate which the rebels expected to be open was found padlocked. When they tried to climb over a wall some horses were disturbed, and a man guarding the horses challenged them. An undisciplined rebel fired a shot towards the man, which alerted the soldiers in the garrison. After exchanging fire for about fifteen minutes, the rebels were forced to retreat. Ten escaped.

Of the twelve captured, most were killed. One man survived despite being tied to a rope and pulled along behind a jeep. Five had earlier decided not to take part.

By mid-afternoon on 26 July, about forty exhausted rebels, including Fidel Castro, had made their way back to the Siboney farm. Some were wounded. Others were very demoralised and decided to surrender, or to give up the struggle and return to Havana. Only nineteen were willing to accompany Castro when he set out towards the rugged Gran Piedra mountain a few miles to the north, in the hope of establishing a guerrilla base. One fell out almost immediately with painful feet. The column stopped briefly at the house of an old black woman, who told her grandson to guide the men into the mountains. After a few miles Castro told the boy to return home, since he did not want anyone to know the final route which they took. By the next morning they had reached a village high up on the mountainside. They were desperately tired and hungry. After being turned away from several shacks, they finally found a black peasant willing to kill a pig for them. He said he had lived there all his life, but that he was subjected to harassment and extortion by the landowner. Castro gave him a pistol and said, according to his own account: 'If they come and bother you, open fire with this . . . Defend what is yours!'

Later in the day, in another peasant hut, the group heard General Batista on a portable radio talking about the Moncada attack. He said the rebels were very well-armed mercenaries, and that the attack had been planned and organised by millionaires living in exile, i.e. former President Prío. Communist propaganda had been found at the farm where the rebels assembled. (This was a book by Lenin which Abel Santamaría had taken to Santiago as bedtime reading. The authorities made great play with the discovery, although it did not easily square with the theory that the main instigator was the staunchly anti-Communist Prío.) Batista said that the rebels had committed numerous atrocities, stabbing several injured men to death in the military hospital. The army had proved loyal and courageous in fighting off the rebel assault.

It was natural that both sides should give a propagandistic account of the event. There were plenty of arguments that could be used to condemn the rebels' action. But in fact all the atrocities came from the army and SIM police. A few army officers and military doctors were horrified by the violence of the repression, and tried to save some of the rebels' lives. But the soldiers were mostly ill-disciplined and enraged by the death of their comrades. Their ferocity was whipped up further by their commanding officer, Colonel Chaviano, who made it known that he wanted ten rebels killed for every one of his soldiers. Captain Lavastida, a notoriously brutal and corrupt SIM officer, encouraged his interrogators to show no restraint. There are conflicting versions on how far Batista personally knew and approved what was happening, but he certainly raised the temperature by putting the army on nation-wide alert, declaring martial law, imposing strict censorship and demanding to be informed who was behind the attack. Among the emergency measures introduced was the suspension of a prison code under which police and servicemen were held responsible for the lives of prisoners in their charge. This looked like a deliberate measure to legitimise the murder of prisoners by Colonel Chaviano's men.

News of the brutality in Santiago soon started spreading, despite tightened government censorship. A young woman journalist smuggled out of Moncada photographs of bodies showing marks of torture, and of prisoners still alive who were later declared to have died in the attack. Some men entirely unconnected with the attack were arrested and beaten, simply because of their suspicious appearance, for example if they had a bandaged arm or leg. Prominent *Ortodoxo* and Communist politicians in Santiago were arrested and questioned, in an attempt to prove a link with the rebels. Initial public disapproval of the action of the rebels soon turned to shock and anger at the army's ruthless response. The Governor of Oriente province tried without success to persuade the army to show greater restraint. On 28 July Archbishop Pérez Serantes (who had baptised Fidel Castro twenty years earlier) summoned a meeting of civic leaders in Santiago which called for an end to the killings. He issued a statement entitled 'Enough Blood,' and undertook to urge the rebels still at large to surrender if the army would respect their lives. There was growing anger even in Havana over the treatment of the rebels. Under this public pressure the Army Chief of Staff finally issued orders to Colonel Chaviano to preserve the life of captured rebels.

On 29 July Raúl Castro, who was about half way in his long walk to Birán, was picked up at a police roadblock. He had no documentation and was jailed until his identity could be confirmed. The next day a travelling salesman identified him as Fidel Castro's brother, and he was sent to Moncada. Colonel Chaviano was now under orders to hand over prisoners to the city jail. The rebels who, like Raúl, had managed to avoid capture during the four days following the attack, were treated correctly.

Fidel Castro was still at large, and was now the most wanted man in Cuba. The army was concentrating its efforts on capturing him, even using spotter aircraft. Archbishop Pérez, possibly distrusting the assurances which he had received from Colonel Chaviano, drove for several hours along the Gran Piedra mountain road, stopping every few hundred yards to appeal over a megaphone for the rebels to surrender, and giving his personal promise that he would guarantee their safety.

Castro and his companions had been moving along the Gran Piedra range, in increasingly poor shape and suffering from severe hunger. On successive days groups of men had decided to leave the column and return to Santiago. Hearing in a peasant's hut about Archbishop Pérez's actions and promises, Castro encouraged most of the remaining men to surrender. With just two companions, Oscar Alcalde and José Suárez, he planned to move across to the nearby Sierra Maestra range, and start the slow process of building up a guerrilla force. But at dawn on 1 August a sixteen-man Rural Guard squad found the three rebels sleeping in a mountain hut.

At this point Castro's chances of survival looked poor. The soldiers knew that Colonel Chaviano, despite the order not to kill prisoners, would be delighted to hear that the man mainly responsible for the death of his troops had himself been killed resisting arrest. The Colonel's deputy had asked another squad returning with a prisoner: 'Why did you bring this one in?' There were moreover social reasons why the soldiers should be happy to do away with Castro. All the members of the Rural Guard squad, including the officer in charge, were black, like most of the rural population of Oriente province. Black soldiers tended to identify with Batista, who was a mulatto and former sergeant, against the white traditional ruling class of Spanish origin, of which Castro and his two companions were typical representatives.

On finding the three rebels, a corporal suggested they 'kill the whites' without more ado, and some soldiers prepared to do so. But the officer in charge, a gruff, taciturn, fifty-three-year-old lieutenant called Pedro Sarría, shouted an order not to shoot. He was one of the officers who had tried to stop the killings in Moncada, and had with difficulty saved the lives of two rebels picked up in the streets of Santiago. He also wanted to deliver these three rebels alive. Castro pretended to be a local farmer called Rafael González but, unknown to Castro, Sarría had seen him some years earlier, when he was doing a legal course at Havana University. Sarría recognised Castro immediately. On the way down the mountain Castro admitted that he was indeed Fidel Castro, and asked why Sarría had not killed him. Sarría said: 'Listen boy, I'm not that sort of person.' Castro said that if Sarría went on like that, the army would kill him. 'Let them kill me', was Sarría's only reply. In later years Sarría denied having any political sympathy with Castro. He said that Castro was a human being and that professional soldiers 'should not commit crimes', Sarría never rose above the rank of captain, but when he died in retirement twenty years later, the then President and Commander in Chief did not forget to attend his funeral.

On the way back along the road to Santiago, the Rural Guard squad saw a group of five rebels who had broken away from Castro's column the previous day. They were hiding in long grass, and the soldiers started to shoot at them.

Then Archbishop Pérez appeared on the scene, and interposed himself. The rebels surrendered to the Archbishop, while the soldiers shouted insults. The Archbishop told Lieutenant Sarría that the rebels were under his protection. Sarría said 'You should tell Colonel Chaviano, not me.' The Archbishop insisted that Sarría should deliver the prisoners to the city jail, rather than to the Moncada barracks, and Sarría readily agreed to do so.

After the horrors which Melba and Haydée had been through, their only remaining hope was that Fidel had somehow survived, and would be brought alive to the city jail. From their cell they peered through the grating in the window to see every new arrival. After days of waiting their hopes faded. The local newspaper announced in a huge headline that Fidel Castro was dead. 'Then one day,' recorded Haydée, 'we heard footsteps, and voices louder and more excited than usual. Something big was happening. But if something big, what could it be? Then in a moment I saw some hands in motion, some fingers. I don't know how I knew, but – they were Fidel's . . . We had been neither dead nor alive. Now we broke free of that thing – you must experience it to know it – that is neither life nor death. And from that moment the question whether we lived or died no longer mattered. Fidel was alive. Moncada lived!'

When Castro arrived at the city jail, Colonel Chaviano personally conducted the interrogation. Castro concealed nothing. He gave a long account of how he had organised the Movement, and how he had planned to overthrow the Batista government, in order to install an entirely new political system. Chaviano naively thought that these admissions would damn Castro, and redound to the credit of the army. He gave a summary of Castro's statements to the press, allowed journalists to interview Castro, and even arranged for Castro to speak on the radio. The effect was the opposite of what Chaviano had assumed. Castro was changing, in the eyes of public opinion, from an obscure extremist into a significant political figure, with a vision of a new and perhaps better Cuba.

The authorities soon realised that giving Castro the oxygen of publicity was a very bad idea. The rebels were transferred to a prison north of Santiago. Castro was placed in solitary confinement, and censorship prevented any further media coverage of his views and actions. Raúl Castro and Pedro Miret informally took over the leadership of the rebel prisoners. Planning for the forthcoming trial, they interviewed each person and built up a large dossier of information about the atrocities committed by the army. By small favours they enlisted the help of some common criminals in the jail in communicating scraps of paper to and from Fidel Castro. Fidel recommended that the leaders of the Movement, and those rebels whose participation in the Moncada attack could easily be proved, should confirm openly their actions and take pride in them. Those who had been picked up on suspicion, but against whom there was no firm evidence, should deny everything, since they would be more useful to the Movement if acquitted.

When Fidel's wife heard about his participation in the Moncada affair, she contacted the Archbishopric of Havana, seeking information. The Archbishop of Santiago later telephoned her to confirm that Fidel was alive and well. Mirta went to Santiago, as did Fidel's mother Lina and half-sister Lidia, but they were not allowed to see him.

After a fortnight Fidel was allowed to write to his family. His letters to his wife were mostly devoted to requests for things to be sent to him, including his favourite dark blue pinstriped suit, but mainly books. His first request was for two books of philosophy, the plays of Shakespeare, and 'any novels which you think might interest me'. There was a certain stiffness and lack of warmth in the correspondence. Mirta tried to be loyal and supportive, but must have been deeply hurt by Fidel's lack of confidence in her during the long preparations for Moncada. For Castro, politics was the most important thing in life; and the mere fact that Mirta was a member of the Díaz-Balart family, a family of close Batista supporters, put a chill into the relationship. Mirta could not change her middle-class attitudes, and was not willing to break completely with her family. Fidel's letters to her express more concern about the welfare of little Fidelito than of his wife. Even when consoling Mirta, he seemed to have Fidelito's interests in mind. 'I am well. You know that prison bars cannot break my spirit, my determination, or my conscience . . . Be calm and courageous. Above all, you must think about Fidelito. I want him to go to the school you have chosen . . . When you come, bring him with you.'

In letters to his older brother Ramón, Fidel also wrote more about his son than about his wife, saying that he was glad that Fidelito had enjoyed his stay at Birán. 'Mirta wants to send him to school, I mean private school. We shall see whether this is possible.' (Even in Cuba in 1953 the issue of private schools was a problem for left-wing intellectuals.) Fidel wanted Ramón to convince their parents that being in prison was not something 'horrible and shameful'. If one went to prison for a noble cause, it was 'a very honourable place'. In another letter he asked: 'Do they understand that I am imprisoned for doing my duty?' He asked Ramón to send more cigars. He had finished the box sent earlier and it was 'often necessary to give cigars to people who help us'.

On 21 September the trial of the rebels began in the Palace of Justice in Santiago. There were 122 defendants, including *Auténtico*, *Ortodoxo* and Communist politicians arrested due to the authorities' dogged insistence that there must have been 'intellectual authors' more important than Castro. All were charged under a code which prescribed from five to twenty years of prison for 'organising an uprising of armed persons against the Constitutional Powers of the State'. One of the three presiding judges was reputed to be pro-Batista, but all three were professional lawyers who evidently wanted to maintain an appearance of legality, and to impose normal court practices and procedures, including allowing the defence lawyers to question witnesses. The courtroom was packed with armed soldiers, but civilians including journalists were also admitted. The result was catastrophic for the Batista government.

Castro, acting as his own defence counsel, persuaded the judges to overrule the army's decision that the defendants should be kept in handcuffs throughout the trial. He argued that he had led an uprising not against the Constitutional Powers of the State, but against General Batista, who was transparently an unconstitutional ruler who had seized power by violence and maintained it by every sort of crime, abuse and deception. Asked who were the intellectual authors of the Moncada action, Castro said there was only one intellectual author, José Martí, the Apostle, the Master, whose words he went on to quote, eloquently justifying the use of force to overthrow a tyrannical and unjust government.

The judges instructed the defendants to confine themselves to answering the questions put to them; but this did nothing to prevent the proceedings from becoming in practice a trial of the regime and of the army. Under questioning, both the defendants and some army witnesses revealed the tortures and murders committed in the Moncada barracks. Montané testified that a soldier had boasted of having used a razor to cut off the genitals of his friend Boris Santa Coloma, and threatened that Montané would also be castrated if he did not talk. Haydée Santamaría confirmed that Santa Coloma had been tortured to death. She said her brother Abel had had his eyeball gouged out while he was still alive. Questioned about this, an army witness disclosed that interrogators had extracted both Abel's eyes with a bayonet. After more such revelations, Castro interjected that the evidence presented to the court proved that the army authorities had committed serious criminal offences. He asked that the court should order that the evidence be gathered and collated, in order to bring appropriate prosecutions. The flustered judges, unable to think of a good reason to reject this request, accepted it and instructed that the evidence be examined with a view to possible prosecutions.

The government and army were appalled at what was becoming a public relations disaster. Although censorship blacked out news of the court proceedings, the absence of published news gave greater credence to the revelations spread by word of mouth by journalists and others. After five days Colonel Chaviano, on orders from Havana, persuaded two prison doctors to certify that Fidel Castro was too ill to attend the trial. The doctors did so reluctantly, trying to salve their consciences by telling Castro that it was the only way to save him from the fury of the officers whom he was denouncing. Castro would not let the doctors off the hook, saying that he was doing his duty and they should do theirs. During the evening he smuggled a note to another prisoner, who conveyed it to Melba Hernández.

When the trial resumed on 26 September, Fidel Castro was not present. An officer representing Colonel Chaviano explained that Castro was ill, and produced the medical certificate. Melba Hernández then stepped forward, pulled Castro's note from under her hair, and gave it to the judges. She said the medical certificate was a lie. It had been written under duress and was a device to cover the army's intention to murder Castro. (Castro did indeed believe that the army planned to kill him. A prison officer called Yanes, who would later become Castro's chief bodyguard, was dismissed after telling Castro that he had been ordered to poison him. The army also circulated false documents purporting to come from friends of Castro who planned to 'rescue' him from prison.) Castro's slip of paper addressed to the judges included a quotation from Martí: 'A just cause from the depths of a cave is stronger than an army.'

The judges ordered an independent medical examination of Castro. When this showed that he was in perfect health, they ordered that he be returned to the court. The prison authorities, under emphatic orders from the government in Havana, moved Castro to a more distant isolation cell, and flatly refused to let him leave the prison. The judges, whose courage and independence had their limits, accepted a 'compromise', under which Castro would be tried separately the following month.

The authorities now tried to bring the trial to a rapid conclusion. On 28 September Raúl Castro protested at Fidel's continued absence, and said the army was conspiring to assassinate him. The judge ordered Raúl to sit down and keep quiet, but added that the court had 'taken all measures necessary for the protection of the defendant'. On 5 October the trial ended. The prosecution agreed to drop the charges against the politicians who had been accused of moral responsibility. The rebels whom Castro had advised to deny involvement were acquitted. The prosecutor, somewhat grotesquely, praised the twenty-nine men who had with 'honour and nobility' acknowledged their 'guilt'. The judges then sentenced Raúl Castro, Pedro Miret, Ernesto Tizol and Oscar Alcalde to thirteen years in prison. Twenty other men received ten-year sentences; three got three years; Melba Hernández and Haydée Santamaría seven months.

Fidel Castro was brought to trial separately on 16 October, in a nurses' room in the civilian hospital near the Moncada barracks. The hospital was chosen as a venue to maintain the fiction of Castro's illness, and no doubt also to restrict access. The small room, with an instructional human skeleton and a picture of Florence Nightingale, was densely packed with court officials, soldiers and observers, including six journalists.

The proceedings advanced very rapidly. Fidel was asked if he had led the Moncada attack, and if his objective had been to overthrow the government. He answered yes to both questions. Colonel Chaviano and some other witnesses made very brief statements. In a speech lasting two minutes the prosecutor said the defendant had admitted his guilt, and asked for the maximum sentence of twenty years. Castro remarked that two minutes was not much time in which to justify sending a man to prison for nearly a quarter of a century. He asked the judges to accept his right to put the defence case fully and without interruption. He then launched into a two-hour speech. Reconstructed after the event from memory, and entitled 'History will absolve me!' it is the most famous speech by one of history's most famous (or notorious) speechmakers.

Some commentators have questioned whether the text that was circulated in 1954 is really what Castro actually said at the trial in 1953. But its importance is as the first full exposition of his political thinking, and it scarcely matters whether he composed it in 1953 or 1954. In any case there is no reason to doubt that what Castro wrote from memory, and circulated, is at least close to what he said at the trial. He may have added a few extra bits after the event, but it was already fairly polished. He spent weeks preparing it, even keeping a fellow prisoner awake at night practising his delivery. He had a very accurate memory for such things. When leaving the court afterwards he asked Marta Rojas, a young journalist, whether she had made full notes. She had.

In his address Castro started by denouncing the methods used by the authorities to deny him a fair trial. He had been kept in solitary confinement for months, and allowed to speak to a lawyer only in the presence of SIM policemen. The government had used a fraudulent medical certificate to keep him away from the main trial. 'Here was a regime afraid to bring an accused man before the court; a regime of blood and terror which shrank in fear of the moral conviction of a defenceless man, a man unarmed, slandered, isolated . . . I warn you, I have only started . . . I know that I will be silenced for many years. They will try to hide the truth by every possible means . . . But my voice will not be drowned. Strength gathers in my heart even when I feel most alone . . .' He described the torture and murder of his colleagues, their bodies thrown into unmarked graves. 'Some day these men will be disinterred. Then they will be carried on the shoulders of the people to a place beside the tomb of Martí, and their liberated land will surely erect a monument to honour the memory of the Martyrs of the Centennial.' He did not seek vengeance for his dead friends. The common soldiers were not to blame. 'They believed they were doing their duty . . . When Cuba is freed we shall respect, shelter and aid the wives and sons of the courageous soldiers who died fighting against us. They are not to be blamed for the misery of Cuba. They are also victims . . .' Castro praised the correct behaviour of three officers, including Lieutenant Sarría. But he predicted that the officers responsible for unspeakable cruelties, the brutal criminals responsible for maintaining Batista's tyranny, would meet a day of reckoning. 'You yourselves (the judges) will be judged, not once but many times, as often as this trial is held up to scrutiny in the future.'

Castro ridiculed the efforts of the authorities to claim that the rebels had no popular support. Their support came from the 700,000 unemployed, the 500,000 impoverished farm workers, the 400,000 underpaid and ill-housed industrial workers, the 100,000 exploited tenant farmers, the 30,000 undervalued teachers, the 20,000 small businessmen worn down by debt and venal officials, the 10,000 doctors, engineers and other professionals unable to use their skills and training. He set out the rebels' political programme, starting with five Revolutionary Laws which would be promulgated when they obtained power, involving mainly land redistribution and profit-sharing for workers. They rejected the doctrines of 'absolute freedom for enterprise, the law of supply and demand, and guarantees to investment capital'. Measures to be introduced would involve radical educational and health reforms, the nationalisation of utilities and telephone companies, social housing, rent control, reafforestation, and the establishment of agricultural co-operatives. 'To those of you who call me a dreamer, I quote the words of Martí: "The dream of today will be the law of tomorrow."'

In his final section Castro returned to the theme of the just use of force to overthrow a tyrant. He quoted a long string of writers, philosophers and even theologians, from John of Salisbury to John Milton, from the Jesuit Juan Mariana to the US Declaration of Independence. He concluded with an oratorical flourish possibly borrowed from Hitler, but expressed rather better: 'I do not fear prison. I do not fear the rage of the miserable tyrant who took the lives of seventy of my comrades. Condemn me. It does not matter. History will absolve me.'

In this speech, which was to become the most sacred text of a Communist regime, there was no mention of Marx or Lenin, or even of the word Socialism. In 1953 Castro was still playing down his Marxist sympathies. But he was already proposing a radical transformation of society, and rejecting the Western concept of democracy. 'I earnestly believe revolution to be the source of legal right.' He gives a vague commitment to restore the 1940 Constitution, but offers no time-frame for this, and says nothing about the rights and freedoms of political parties. On the contrary, 'there being no organisation for holding elections to accomplish this (the fulfilment of the 1940 Constitution) the revolutionary movement, as the incarnation of the people's sovereignty, the only source of legal power, would assume . . . the legislative, executive and judicial powers'. He clearly foreshadowed the arguments used by his subsequent Communist government to exclude the possibility of putting back the clock on revolutionary change. 'The first popularly elected government would have to respect these laws (introduced by the revolution) . . . because when people achieve something they have sought for generations, no force in the world is capable of taking it away.'

His intention from the start was to introduce *irreversible* revolutionary change.

According to Marta Rojas, everyone in the stuffy hospital room in Santiago, including the soldiers and court officials, listened to Castro's performance with rapt attention. When he finally came to an end and sat down, there was a long moment of silence. The judges then held a brief whispered consultation, before the presiding judge announced the Court's verdict: fifteen years in prison. After four hours it was all over. With a sigh of relief the Batista government went back to their rum cocktails and games of canasta, hoping to hear no more of the troublesome and turbulent young lawyer from Birán.

7   Prison and Exile

Fidel Castro and twenty-five fellow conspirators were sent to serve their sentences in a hospital wing of the Model Prison in the Isle of Pines (now Isle of Youth), a large island fifty miles south of the Cuban mainland, where tourists now go for scuba-diving. Castro had visited the prison as a student, in order to denounce conditions there in an anti-government publicity stunt. In 1953 conditions for the Moncada prisoners were in fact relatively humane, at least at first. They could exercise, read, cook food, receive family visits once a month and, subject to censorship, send and receive mail. They had access to the prison library, and could receive books from outside. Fidel and Raúl received a regular supply of food and cigars from their brother Ramón.

Castro's mind, in prison as elsewhere, was always on politics. What could be done? The first requirement was to sustain so far as possible the morale and cohesion of his small group of fellow revolutionaries. They would constitute the nucleus of a rebuilt Movement, now called the 26 July Movement after the date of the attack on the Moncada barracks. Castro's men turned their prison wing into a school, which they named the Abel Santamaría Ideological Academy. There were five hours of classes a day. Fidel taught philosophy and modern history; Pedro Miret taught ancient history; Montané taught English; some others taught whatever they knew.

Castro also set out energetically to improve his own education. His principal interests remained history and philosophy. He continued to study Martí and Lenin, and retained his schoolboy fascination with the great conquerors of history. He especially admired Napoleon, seeing him as a military genius who also had qualities of humanity and vision. He was unimpressed by Freud, and admitted to falling asleep over Kant's *Transcendental Aesthetics of Space and Time,* but was enthusiastic about Karl Marx's study of Napoleon III. He acquired several books about developments in the Communist world, such as *The Secret of Soviet Strength* by the 'Red' Dean of Canterbury. Even when reading ancient history, or classical literature like Shakespeare, his aim was to elucidate the processes of historical development. Was Julius Caesar just an autocratic tyrant, or a progressive revolutionary figure brought down by aristocratic reaction?

He also read a large number of novels, mainly because they were available in the prison library, but partly also in response to the enthusiastic interest of Naty Revuelta. He and Naty exchanged long letters commenting on the books they were reading. He read classics like Dostoyevski, Balzac and Thackeray, and also contemporary best-sellers like Axel Munthe's *The Story of San Michele,* A. J. Cronin's *The Citadel* and Somerset Maugham's *The Razor's Edge.* In novels, as in everything else, he looked for political and social lessons; but his political enthusiasms did not always blunt his critical sense. He recognised the power and psychological depth of Dostoyevski, despite Dostoyevski's 'reactionary' outlook. He liked the politics of Hugo's *Les Miserables,* but pointed out to Naty its 'excessive romanticism, verbosity and tedious and exaggerated erudition'.

Castro wrote frequently to a few political friends and sympathisers outside the prison. His tone was sometimes light-hearted, sometimes earnest and demanding. Parts of his letters, such as when he praised the honesty and decency of the prison staff, were aimed mainly at the prison censor. Under the surface, however, he was always pursuing a political objective. He was desperately keen to keep alive public awareness of the Moncada affair, and sympathy with the fate of the Moncada prisoners. He urged friends to pursue the prosecution of those responsible for the murder of prisoners in Moncada. He himself instituted legal action in a local court in the Isle of Pines, accusing Batista and three generals of responsibility for murder and torture.

Another prime objective was to maintain his own tight control of the residual Movement. He realised that with prison censorship, and the general state of repression in the country following Moncada, there was little he could do in the short term to restructure the Movement outside the prison, or to attract new members. But he tried to ensure that his leadership position was not usurped in his absence. He warned his supporters against taking initiatives without consulting him. 'It is no good if everyone thinks they have the right to make declarations, without consulting anyone. You can't expect much from an organisation of anarchic people, each of whom takes whatever path he thinks best . . .' He responded negatively when some friends proposed joining a broad-based 'civic movement'. He argued that such a body would try to encompass 'too many opinions and interests', and lack revolutionary unity. In other words, it would not be under his control.

During his first months in prison Fidel wrote regularly to his wife Mirta. Whereas his letters to Naty were long and rambling, those to Mirta consisted mainly of curt requests and instructions. He also received visits from Mirta and Fidelito, and his half-sister Lidia, and was able to use Mirta and Lidia to convey messages and texts that might not pass the censor. Perhaps by mistake, perhaps deliberately, the prison authorities on one occasion sent a letter addressed to Mirta to Naty, and a letter for Naty to Mirta. Mirta was aggrieved to see that Castro wrote more warmly and affectionately to Naty than to her. He also revealed more of his political thinking to Naty. One long letter to Naty showed how far he had come to accept the Marxist view of history, and his ambivalent attitude to creative artists. Prompted by Naty's question whether Rolland would have been a great writer if born in another era, Castro wrote:

Human thought is always conditioned by the circumstances of the epoch. In the case of a political genius, I would say that it depends exclusively on that. Lenin in the era of Catherine would have been a vigorous defender of the Russian bourgeoisie. If Martí had lived at the time of the occupation of Havana by the English, he would have been at the side of his father defending the Spanish flag. Napoleon, Mirabeau, Danton and Robespierre, what would they have been in the time of Charlemagne but humble servants in . . . some feudal castle? The crossing of the Rubicon by Julius Caesar would not have occurred in the first years of the Republic, before the sharpening of the intense class struggle which shook Rome, and before the development of the great plebeian party . . . But what is clear for the political genius is not so for the artistic genius. I agree with Victor Hugo: in the poet and artist lies the infinite. And it is the infinite which gives them their uncompromising greatness. The infinite that exists in art is alien to progress . . . It doesn't depend on any possible improvement of the future, on any transformation . . . Having in itself the unmeasurable and the uncountable, it . . . is equally pure, equally complete, equally divine . . . whether in a period of complete barbarism or of complete civilisation. It is the beautiful, varied depending on the character of different creative geniuses, but always the same as itself . . . Rolland could have been born a century earlier and been as brilliant as . . . Voltaire, although with ideas different from those of this century, just as I would say different things if I was writing to another woman . . .

In February 1954 there was a dramatic worsening in Castro's prison conditions. General Batista visited the Isle of Pines, and his programme included the inauguration of a power plant at the prison. When Batista was within earshot the twenty-six Moncada rebels started singing their anthem, the 'March of 26 July'. At first Batista thought the prisoners were paying him a tribute, but when he heard the words, denouncing the insatiable tyrants who had plunged Cuba in evil, he furiously left the prison. The prison authorities were enraged that their big day had been ruined. The author of the anthem, a young self-taught composer, was beaten and whipped on successive days, on one occasion being left unconscious. Several ringleaders were given two weeks solitary confinement. Prison privileges were suspended. Fidel Castro was consigned to indefinite solitary confinement.

Despite his tumultuous political career, Castro was always emotionally a loner, and he survived many months of solitary confinement without losing his spirit and determination. His main problem was the lack of light. Daylight came through the one small window in his cell, but there was no electric light, and he damaged his eyes trying to read at night with a tiny oil lamp. But his letters mostly remained resolutely cheerful. When he was allowed to sit in the sun, he wrote that he felt as if he were on holiday. 'What would Marx think of such a revolutionary?' If nothing else occurred to him to write about, he would just ramble, describing in satirical detail the activities of any birds or insects within view of his cell. Only occasionally did he strike a more despondent note. 'You can't imagine how this solitude devours energy . . . I always try to do something, I invent my own worlds and I think and I think, but this is precisely why I am so exhausted.'

Like many prisoners, the Moncada group got satisfaction from developing methods of communicating without the knowledge of the authorities. Messages were conveyed to Fidel inside cigars and matchboxes with false bottoms, sometimes through Mirta, who was still allowed to pay short visits. A kindly warder agreed to take a plate of food to Castro; and although he found a message inside the mashed potato, Castro persuaded him not to report the incident. The rebels played on their patio with a rag ball which from time to time landed on a roof near Castro's cell. A prisoner asked permission to climb onto the roof to fetch the ball, and from there he threw it to the patio where Castro was allowed to exercise.

Castro consumed a large number of lemons, and for a time no one questioned this unusual taste. He was writing in lemon-juice between the lines of letters to his wife and others. When the letters were heated, the lemon-juice writing could be read. Partly by this means the long text of *History Will Absolve Me* was laboriously transmitted to Castro's followers over a period of more than three months. The journalist Marta Rojas, who was in touch with Mirta and later with Melba Hernández, confirmed the accuracy of Castro's reconstruction of the Santiago speech.

Although Castro felt frustrated by the constraints of prison, his political situation was in some ways improving. After the Moncada trial he was more famous than he had ever been when free and active. In February 1954 Melba Hernández and Haydée Santamaría finished their sentences, and Melba became an extremely energetic and effective advocate for Castro and the other prisoners. Batista had announced elections for November 1954; and although most politicians were unwilling to participate in what seemed likely to be a farce, Batista had eased press censorship and was trying to give an impression of democratic normality. This opened opportunities for public pressure. At an *Ortodoxo* function in a Havana theatre, Mirta was invited to read a message from Fidel. At Fidel's suggestion, Mirta and Lidia wrote to the popular weekly magazine *Bohemia,* complaining about Fidel's conditions in jail. The magazine sent reporters to interview him, the authorities evidently thinking that the reality would be seen to be less grim than his family had claimed. The interview was published in early June, with photos of Castro in his prison cell. The magazine had earlier proclaimed Castro one of the twelve outstanding world figures of 1953, along with personalities such as Queen Elizabeth II (just crowned), the Shah of Iran (just restored) and Soviet secret police chief Beria (just executed).

Castro always felt confident that he had 'the people' behind him, even if many members of his own family and social class were opposed. 'With what joy I would bring revolution to this country from top to bottom! I am sure that it would bring happiness to the Cuban people. For the sake of this I should be willing to incur the hatred of one or two thousand people, among them some relatives, half my friends, two-thirds of my colleagues and four-fifths of my old colleagues at university.' Soon after writing this, his alienation from some of his family and old friends became even greater. He heard on the radio that his wife Mirta had been dismissed from her job in the Ministry of the Interior. Unknown to Castro, Mirta had earlier been persuaded by her brother, the Deputy Minister of the Interior, to be put on the Ministry's payroll, as a means of providing her with a steady income. Although she was receiving an allowance from Fidel's father Angel, she evidently thought it was inadequate. On Fidel's instructions she had publicly criticised the prison service, which was the responsibility of Interior Minister Hermida. When Hermida discovered that Mirta was on the Ministry payroll, he ordered that the arrangement be ended.

Castro could not believe that Mirta had ever been on the Ministry payroll. For him accepting surreptitious money from the Batista government would be the grossest form of unfaithfulness. He assumed that Hermida had concocted the story as a dirty trick to discredit him, to make people believe that the wife of the self-styled revolutionary had been taking money from the government. He immediately wrote to Mirta, in a hectoring tone, demanding that she sue Hermida for libel. Giving vent to the homophobic prejudices which in this period he shared with many Cuban men, he ranted about Hermida's 'sexual degeneration'. In letters to others he wrote that Mirta was 'too intelligent to be seduced by her brother, consenting to be on the government payroll, no matter how hard her economic situation . . . Anger blinds me and I can scarcely think . . . The prestige of my wife and my honour as a revolutionary are at stake. Let them see me dead a thousand times rather than suffer impotently from such an insult.'

However, after a few days Fidel's half-sister Lidia informed him that Mirta had indeed been on the Ministry payroll. Lidia reported that Mirta's father and brothers had visited her, and that she had gone with them to the family beach-house. Mirta did not want to involve herself any more in Castro's political activities. Castro's red-hot rage turned to a cold and bitter anger, mixed with self-pity. He blamed his brother-in-law more than Mirta, but soon afterwards instituted divorce proceedings. For Mirta, Fidel's reaction had been the last straw, and she also started divorce proceedings.

Interior Minister Hermida was upset by Castro's allegations that he had used Mirta as a propaganda weapon. Accompanied by two other Cabinet Ministers, he visited Castro on the Isle of Pines, and was all courtesy and goodwill. He said he had nothing to do with Mirta's being on the payroll. It was a stupid thing done by her brother Rafael without his knowledge. Castro, said the Minister, had an unblemished record as a man of honour. No one would question his honour. Hermida himself had been a political prisoner under Machado. He understood Castro's feelings and respected his integrity. Castro accepted the Minister's explanations with reasonably good grace, saying glumly that Hermida at least had acted correctly. His quarrel was not personal, but with the system.

Hermida's visit was followed by some improvements in Castro's prison conditions. His brother Raúl was allowed to share his cell. Raúl had learnt deaf and dumb sign language from a Larousse dictionary, and was able to communicate with the rest of the group through Pedro Miret, who had also learnt the system. An electric light was put in the Castros' cell, and they were provided with fresh water, clean clothes and better food. 'We don't even have to pay rent,' wrote Fidel, reporting the improvements. For a few weeks he continued to pour out grief and anger over Mirta. He suffered especially from the thought that his son Fidelito was now being looked after by the treacherous Díaz-Balart family. But he soon came to terms with the break with Mirta. He wrote to Lidia: 'Don't worry about me. You know I have a heart of steel.' However, several people who knew Castro in the first years of his marriage believe that at that time he was genuinely in love with Mirta, that perhaps she was the only woman he ever loved deeply, and that some permanent scar must have been left by the break-up.

Mirta was granted a divorce, and custody of Fidelito. The news about Fidelito plunged Fidel again into gloom and rage. 'One day I'll be out of here and I'll get my son and honour back, even if the earth is destroyed in the process.' He instituted legal proceedings to regain custody and to obtain authority to designate a school where Fidelito could be educated away from the influence of the Díaz-Balarts. 'I'm going to do whatever is necessary and I don't care if the suit lasts until the end of time. If they think they can wear me down and that I'll give up the fight, they're going to find out that I've acquired an Asiatic patience. I shall re-enact the Hundred Years War, and I'll win it.'

In November 1954 Batista carried out his promise to hold elections. The result was a foregone conclusion, and no serious politician was prepared to play Batista's game by standing against him. However, the run-up to the election gave Castro's supporters an opportunity to step up the campaign for an amnesty for the Moncada prisoners. Since their release from prison, Haydée Santamaría and Melba Hernández had been tireless in organising demonstrations demanding an amnesty. Now political rallies were often interrupted by shouts of 'Fidel Castro!' An Amnesty Committee for Political Prisoners was established, including two young women who would be very important in the Castros' lives: Vilma Espin (Raúl's future wife) and Celia Sánchez (Fidel's future secretary and partner). From prison Fidel encouraged two Moncada veterans who had escaped to Mexico to return openly to Cuba, the idea being to force the government either to start another trial, with all the embarrassing revelations which that would again involve, or to grant a general amnesty.

In March 1955 some members of Congress tabled an amnesty bill. The government said it would support the bill if the Moncada prisoners undertook not to attempt any further insurrection. Castro did not like the condition. All the prisoners signed a declaration rejecting it as an attempt to force them to repudiate their past actions. 'We shall not give up our honour as the price for our freedom. We will suffer a thousand years of imprisonment rather than humiliation! A thousand years of imprisonment rather than sacrifice our dignity!'

Batista's attitude to the amnesty campaign was one of mild irritation rather than serious worry. His position looked very comfortable. The economy was thriving. Impressive skyscrapers were filling the Havana skyline. Crowded casinos were making Havana the Las Vegas of Latin America. Maurice Chevalier, Lena Horne and Nat King Cole were among the celebrities who graced the city's famous nightclubs. Batista was good for business, and was basking in American approval. Carlos Prío, the elected President whom Batista had overthrown, was arrested in Miami and charged with violating the US Neutrality Act. Vice-President Nixon visited Havana and toasted Batista's electoral success, ignoring the fact that no opposition figures had stood against him. Next CIA director Allen Dulles, fresh from his success in overthrowing the left-wing government of President Arbenz in Guatemala, visited

Cuba to encourage the Batista government's good work in rooting out Communism. In this situation of prosperity and approval, it seemed sensible not to allow the atmosphere to be spoilt by misguided public sympathy for a few immature revolutionaries. The government therefore decided to get shot of the issue. A bill for an unconditional amnesty was approved by the Congress and signed by Batista. On 15 May 1955 the prisoners were released.

Emerging from jail, Castro greeted his supporters like a conquering hero. Haydée wept with emotion, as did Lidia and Fidel's younger sister Emma. He gave press conferences and radio interviews, both on the Isle of Pines and on his return to Havana. Students carried him on their shoulders on the journey to Lidia's flat, where he was to stay. Lidia later made discreet arrangements for Fidel to see Naty Revuelta privately in the empty flat of a mutual friend. Fidel and Naty made love (probably for the first time) and she conceived Alina. But Naty was not the only girl with whom he had a relationship in these weeks. Another attractive political supporter, Maria Laborde, conceived a child who would be named Jorge Angel Castro.

Castro was now busy reconstructing the Movement. He held meetings with the remnants of García Bárcena's MNR and agreed to fuse the two organisations, in effect recruiting the key MNR leaders into his own Movement. He later formally established an eleven-person National Directorate of the 26 July Revolutionary Movement (MR-26-7 for short), with a mixture of Moncada stalwarts and new blood from the former MNR, including two men who were to play a key role in the future, the law student Armando Hart and the Santiago student leader Frank Pais.

After the initial euphoria, however, Castro's return to active politics did not have the dramatic impact for which he had hoped. The rebellious students now had new leaders, notably José Antonio Echeverría, the charismatic President of the FEU. Other opposition leaders found Castro inflexible and contemptuous of compromise. His followers circulated thousands of copies of *History Will Absolve Me,* but it was old news and made little impression. His deliberately provocative posture – 'Next time we shall not fail' – was out of tune with a public mood which was tired of violence. Potentially most serious of all, splits were appearing in the Movement. Some of Castro's supporters had become restless at his autocratic leadership. Raúl Martínez, who had led the attack in Bayamo, was annoyed by Castro's tendency to play up the heroism of the attack on Moncada, while saying nothing about Bayamo. Castro for his part criticised Martínez and others for having established friendly contact in Mexico with supporters of ex-President Prío. Eleven of Fidel's followers presented a paper suggesting changes to the Movement. They proposed that it should have a more democratic structure, and be directed by a board rather than one man. Castro rejected the proposal out of hand, asking scornfully when a successful revolution had ever been run by a committee. As a result, a few of the Moncada veterans broke with Castro. Others who had signed the paper backtracked and stayed with him, but he would never again completely trust them.

On top of these internal difficulties, conditions for the opposition in general again took a turn for the worse. A series of violent student demonstrations and bomb explosions ushered in another period of tightening repression. Without formal press censorship, pressure was put on newspapers and radio stations not to provide an outlet for extremists like Castro. The newspaper *La Calle*, which had been publishing a daily article by Castro, was closed down. Days later *Alerta*, which had continued to publish news about Castro, was also closed, the government alleging that it was controlled by Communists. Raúl Castro was publicly accused of involvement in a bomb attack. The government was outraged when Fidel suggested that the bombs were planted by the authorities themselves, to justify clamping down on opposition. There were rumours of police plans to stage an incident in which Fidel would be killed. Raúl, Nico López and Jesús Montané formed an armed bodyguard to protect Fidel in Lidia's flat. Then Raúl, hearing that he was about to be arrested, asked for political asylum in the Mexican Embassy, and left for exile in Mexico.

The Cuban Communist Party, hearing that Fidel also planned to leave, urged him to stay in Cuba and join a broad-front campaign against Batista. But Castro had made up his mind and formed his plans. On 7 July 1955 he followed Raúl into exile. Lidia fetched Fidelito from his school to say goodbye to his father, before she went with Fidel to the airport. In a parting declaration, Castro said that the government was determined to retain power by any means, and had blocked the possibility of peaceful opposition. It was time for people to demand their rights rather than plead for them. He was leaving to live temporarily in another part of the Caribbean. From such a journey 'one either does not return, or returns with the tyranny decapitated at one's feet'.

Castro left secret instructions to the MR-26-7 Directorate. Those remaining in Cuba had the job of building up its organisation, preparing cells for revolutionary action in all the main towns of Cuba. They were also to collect money to finance the activities of the MR-26-7 in Mexico. The MR-26-7 section in Mexico would organise, train and arm a military force, which would travel by sea to Oriente. There it would start a guerrilla war against Batista's army, spreading from the Sierra Maestra to take over the whole country. While the invasion force was establishing itself in the Sierra Maestra, the local MR-26-7 organisation in Santiago, headed by Frank País, would distract the army with a spate of strikes and armed attacks on government buildings.

This was the plan which Castro was refining as he set off for a new life in Mexico. Mexico had a tradition of offering asylum to left-wing exiles. It had provided a friendly haven to thousands of Spanish Republican exiles, and to refugees from the numerous right-wing dictatorships now established in Latin America. It had for decades been the natural first choice for left-wing Cubans escaping from persecution. Castro had some friends and contacts there, as well as rivals.

In Mexico City Fidel rented a small, cheap room. He often ate his meals in the flat of María Antonia González, the Cuban wife of a Mexican wrestler, who provided a sort of meeting place and free hotel for Cuban and other exiles. In the exile community it was taken as normal and natural that those who had money, or a spouse earning money, should help out those who had none. Castro got to know a number of prominent exiles from the Caribbean, and struck up a friendship with the wife of one of his heroes, Pedro Arbizu, the leader of the Puerto Rico independence movement, who was serving a long prison sentence in the United States.

Raúl Castro, who had earlier joined the café society of the exile community, struck up a friendship with a young Argentine doctor, Ernesto Guevara. Guevara had a low-paid job in a hospital laboratory, and also worked sporadically as a news agency photographer. As a medical student in Buenos Aires, he had travelled widely throughout the continent, by train, bus, bicycle or motorbike, often cleaning plates or doing other menial jobs to pay his way. He spent a long vacation drifting through Chile, Peru, Colombia and Venezuela, before returning via Florida to Argentina. After qualifying as a doctor in 1953 he still did not want to settle down. He set off to Bolivia, and from there to Central America. He was living in Guatemala with a Peruvian woman called Hilda Gadea, who had a job in the left-wing government of President Arbenz, when the CIA engineered an invasion which overthrew the government. Guevara and his partner left for Mexico. He told Raúl that in Costa Rica he had met some Cubans who belonged to a revolutionary organisation led by Fidel Castro. They were Nico López and some others who had escaped from Cuba after the Moncada attack. At Guevara's request Raúl took him to meet Fidel at María Antonia's flat.

Guevara was a committed Marxist–Leninist. His manner was quiet and self-effacing, and unlike Fidel he was more inclined to listen than to talk. He had many intellectual interests and, again unlike Castro, his conversation was by no means obsessively centred on politics. He read poetry and books on archaeology, as well as Karl Marx. But he was, as Fidel put it, 'a more advanced revolutionary than I was'. His aim in life, as yet vague and unfocussed, was to do something to help Latin America to throw off the yoke of American imperialism, the complex and pervasive system of control and exploitation which, as he saw it, enabled the United States to prosper at the expense of the poverty and misery of the peoples of Latin America.

Castro asked Guevara about his experiences while travelling in Latin America. Guevara painted a gloomy picture. There was a small elite who lived like North Americans, and directly or indirectly served North American interests; and then the masses, uneducated, impoverished, brutalised. It was the United States which had turned Central America into a string of 'banana republics', controlled by companies like United Fruit. It was to serve US economic interests that the Americans had broken off a chunk of Colombia and turned it into the pseudo-independent republic of Panama. When President Arbenz of Guatemala started a reform programme which threatened the interests of United Fruit, the US government had no scruples about using the CIA to overthrow Arbenz, and put in his place a colonel willing to serve US interests. Guevara criticised Guatemalan Communists who had fled the anti-Communist crackdown instituted by the CIA. The only honourable course, he thought, would have been to stay behind in the jungles and mountains, fighting a guerrilla war against the new puppet government.

That was also Castro's view. He had seen how United Fruit operated in Cuba. It was only one of many US corporations which dominated and exploited Latin America, but it was a powerful symbol. United Fruit owned all the land around the Castro farm in Birán. Some local farmers owned their own sugar cane, but they could sell it only to the United Fruit sugar mill. They could transport it only by the United Fruit railway. Batista's power came originally from the US Ambassador. His secret police, who tortured and killed Castro's followers, were advised and trained by the CIA. And the hated Díaz-Balart family, who had stolen Castro's son, had their home in the United Fruit town of Banes, where Cubans could not go to the beach, *their* beach, without permission from a United Fruit guard.

Castro told Guevara about his plans for revolution in Cuba. There were many drifters in Mexico City who talked about revolution. But for Guevara, Fidel was different. He was very self-confident and determined. He looked like someone who would indeed, whether for his son or for Latin America, re-enact the Hundred Years War and win it. Guevara knew that Castro had few followers, no money and no weapons. But the liberation of Latin America had to start somewhere. Guevara and Castro talked all night and by the morning, as Guevara said, he belonged to Castro's project. Since he was an Argentine, his Cuban friends called him Che. When he became part of the Cuban heroic legend, he would be just The Che.

At a meal some days after Che's first meeting with Fidel, Che's partner Hilda (later his wife) asked Fidel why he had gone into exile, instead of fighting the Batista regime inside Cuba. The question touched the highly sensitive issue of Castro's courage and honour. 'That's a good question,' said Fidel; and he proceeded (as Hilda later recorded) to spend four hours answering the question. The gist was that the extent and depth of US influence in Cuba made it impossible to overthrow Batista without bringing a force of armed men from abroad. Castro's task was to organise the expedition, which would land in Oriente and set off a national uprising.

Che wanted to join the expedition as a fighter, not just as a doctor. His medical knowledge would be useful, even if he was a highly inexperienced specialist in allergies. The first requirement, however, was to find a man who could convert Castro's motley band of left-wing exiles into a fighting force. Pedro Miret had done his best to train the men of Moncada, but he had never been a real soldier. Castro soon identified the man he wanted. It was Colonel Alberto Bayo. Born in Cuba of Spanish parents, Bayo had fought with the Spanish army against rebels in Morocco, studied guerrilla warfare at the Spanish Military Academy, and then fought on the Republican side in the Spanish Civil War. Exiled after Franco's victory, Bayo had obtained various teaching jobs in Mexico City, and given military instruction to a variety of would-be revolutionaries in the Caribbean. Castro visited the old man and persuaded him to undertake, when the men and facilities were ready, the training of an expeditionary force to overthrow Batista.

Bayo later wrote: 'Wasn't it amusing? He was asking whether I would commit myself to teach guerrilla tactics to his future soldiers, when he had recruited them and when he had collected the money to feed, dress and equip them, and buy ships to transport them to Cuba. Come on, I thought, this young man wants to move mountains with one hand. But what did it cost me to please him? "Yes," I said, "Yes, Fidel, I promise to instruct these boys the moment it is necessary."' When Castro was in a position to ask Bayo to fulfil his promise, the colonel explained that his private business and other teaching commitments meant that he could only devote three hours a day to teaching Castro's men. Castro insisted that he must work full-time. 'Sitting in front of me, Fidel Castro was shouting at me in my own house, gesticulating violently, as if we were in the middle of a great quarrel: "You are a Cuban, you have an absolute duty to help us!"' Castro got his way. 'I became infected with his enthusiasm. I got caught up in his optimism. Then and there I promised Fidel to resign from my classes and to sell my business.'

While preparing the Mexican side of the operation, Castro was also busy with events in Cuba, sending a stream of instructions to the MR-26-7 leaders in Havana and Santiago. A major objective was to infiltrate the youth wing of the *Ortodoxo* party, and win over the organisation, or as many members as possible, to Castro's political line. He issued Manifesto no. 1 to the Cuban people, containing much the same programme as *History Will*

Absolve Me, but with more emphasis on the need for rapid industrialisation and state control of natural resources. He had been studying the economic measures adopted after the Mexican Revolution, notably the nationalisation by President Lázaro Cárdenas of British and American oil companies. He also played up the importance of rural electrification, and of ending racial and sexual discrimination.

In Cuba, Pedro Miret and Frank Pais were working in great secrecy on plans for the landing of Fidel's expeditionary force. Celia Sánchez, who knew the geography of Oriente well (as a teenager she had climbed Cuba's highest mountain to place a bust of Martí on the summit), obtained detailed marine and tidal charts of the coastline where Castro planned to land. They studied the requirements for men and vehicles for concerted action at the moment of Castro's arrival. Frank Pais had considerable success in building up clandestine support for the MR-26-7 among the traditionally militant workers of Manzanillo and other towns in Oriente.

Castro's biggest problem, as so often in the past, was money. Many of his supporters were in Mexico on short-term tourist visas. Money was needed not only for living and accommodation expenses, but also to bribe the police to grant visa extensions. The Mexican *mordida* (bite) was as pervasive as ever. The money arriving from Cuba was hopelessly inadequate for Castro's needs. Having with limited success begged and borrowed from sympathetic individuals in Mexico, he set off in October 1955 on a six-week fundraising tour of the United States. He addressed meetings of Cuban exiles in New York, Miami, Tampa and other towns. He was generally given a warm reception, tinged with some scepticism about his ability to deliver on his grandiose promises. In Miami he was reunited with Fidelito. Lidia had taken Fidelito out of his school (probably without Mirta's permission) to see his father in Florida. When the six-year-old Fidelito started playing with money collected in a hat at a fundraising meeting in the Flagler Theatre, Fidel shouted: 'Don't touch it, Fidelito. That money belongs to Cuba!'

Batista's agents, as well as the FBI, were keeping an eye on Castro during his time in the United States. The Cuban government were keen to puncture Castro's reputation as a young man who was misguided but idealistic. Stories were circulated that he was misappropriating funds donated by political well-wishers. When he returned to Mexico, he found that a lot of hostile articles had been appearing in the Cuban media. *Bohemia* attacked his arrogant assumption that only he knew what was good for Cuba. It predicted that if he gained power, he would be God and Caesar in one person, executing anyone he judged immoral. Other newspapers accused Castro of hypocrisy and double-dealing, suggesting that his fundraising had been only a means of lining his own pockets.

These articles made little impact on Cuban public opinion, but they certainly distracted and enraged Castro himself. For a man of his gigantic ego, attaching as much importance as he did to personal honour, the allegations of embezzlement were outrageous and galling. He devoted a great deal of time and energy to issuing public rebuttals. His Manifesto no. 2 to the Cuban people, and a string of letters to the press, were mainly devoted to a defence of his own actions and integrity. He described in laborious detail the many occasions in his career when he could have obtained money or influence by dishonourable means, but had scorned to do so. He had collected 20,000 pesos to finance the attack on Moncada, and had spent none of it on himself. 'Yet how many times were we short of milk for my son! How many times did the hard-hearted electric power company cut off my electricity! I still keep the wretched court papers by which the landlord tried to evict us from the house. I had no personal income, and practically lived off the charity of my friends. I know what it is to have a son suffering from hunger, while having in my pockets money belonging to the cause.'

It would have been good news for Batista if Castro had indeed been spending his funds on personal indulgence. In fact he was using the money collected in the United States mainly to buy weapons. He had approached a wealthy Cuban living in Mexico, Orlando de Cárdenas, who had purchased weapons on a large scale for ex-President Prío. After initial reluctance, and being subjected to Castro's well-tried persuasive techniques, de Cárdenas agreed to use his contacts to buy weapons for the MR-26-7. Castro also spent money renting 'safe houses' in Mexico City, where groups of his followers lived in a regime of monastic discipline, studying and preparing for the coming revolution. Colonel Bayo visited the houses as an 'English teacher,' and gave lessons in weapon-handling, map-reading and other military skills. Later Castro rented a farm near the town of Chalco, south-east of Mexico City, where Bayo could undertake more serious military training. The men went on arduous hikes up the slopes of the Popocatépetl volcano. Castro was in a hurry. During his tour of the United States he had promised to liberate Cuba before the end of 1956. He was determined not to miss this self-imposed deadline.

Castro had sympathisers who acted as informants in the government in Havana, and in the Cuban Embassy in Mexico City. Through this private intelligence network he heard a rumour that the SIM were planning to get rid of him. With logistical support from the Cuban naval attaché, two agents dressed as Mexican policemen would 'arrest' him, take him to a remote location, and kill him, while a forged letter purporting to come from Castro would reach his associates, saying that he had left on a secret mission abroad. Castro decided that the best way to forestall such an attempt was to publicise it, which he did.

However, Castro's security was far from perfect. Perhaps through treachery, or more probably because the Cuban Embassy was outbidding Castro in payments to the Mexican police, a safe house in the Polanco district of Mexico City was raided, large quantities of weapons were seized, and several leading MR-26-7 members were detained. Castro and two colleagues were surrounded by police in the street, disarmed, and taken to a police station. A few days later the farm near Chalco was raided, and more arrests were made. Altogether some forty of Castro's men (but not Raúl Castro) were under detention.

Press reports in both Mexico and Cuba, based mainly on briefing from the Cuban Embassy, announced that a group of Cuban Communists, including Fidel Castro, had been arrested for plotting against the Batista government. Batista knew that the Cuban Communists, firmly committed as they were to a long-haul policy of non-violent political action, did not in fact constitute any immediate danger. But he was happy to play up the Communist threat in order to consolidate US support, and strengthen his request for Castro's extradition. Castro denied being a Communist. He said that his links with the Communists were less than those of Batista, whose election posters in 1940 appeared next to the hammer and sickle and who included Communists in his first government.

The Mexican authorities were tolerant of foreign political activists, even if they were Communists, but this tolerance did not stretch to allowing private armies. The police threatened to extradite Castro and his men to Cuba. Castro said that in Cuba they would be executed. His Mexican friends and lawyers went to work to stop extradition. A judge ordered their release, but the Interior Ministry refused to accept the validity of the judicial order. There were several days of confusion over the legal situation. In the end the decisive factor was that the Mexican government did not want to forfeit its reputation as a refuge for political dissidents. Former President Cárdenas, whom Castro had met and favourably impressed, intervened on his behalf. Within a short while most of the arrested men were released. Those whose presence in Mexico was illegal were given a deadline to leave the country. Those whose papers were in order were told to report regularly to the police. Partly at the request of the US Embassy (acting in turn on behalf of Batista), Castro was kept in detention, together with Che Guevara and Calixto García, until after the conclusion of a Pan-American summit conference in Panama. Batista had said that he would not go to Panama if Castro was at large. It was about this time that *Bohemia* invented a new phrase, the 'fidelista complex', meaning an irrational fear of the large shadow of Fidel Castro.

After the Panama conference, Castro was released, leaving only Che and Calixto in prison. The Mexican police had been given information that Che and Calixto had been involved in subversive activities in Guatemala and other Latin American countries. Che told Fidel that he should not delay the revolution on their account, but Fidel replied sternly: 'I won't abandon you.' After a few more weeks, Che and Calixto were also released.

Occasionally Castro still had time for a private life. He had heard from Naty about her pregnancy, and had asked her to meet him in the United States during his tour. She explained that this was impossible: she already had a daughter to look after and other responsibilities. When Naty gave birth to Fidel's daughter Alina, he asked Lidia to call on Naty and send him a report on the child. He may have felt some doubt whether the child was really his, rather than Naty's husband's. Lidia reported that little Alina was definitely a Castro. Fidel sent the baby some silver earrings, and told Naty that if she joined him in his revolutionary project, he would marry her. She declined the offer, and he was soon looking elsewhere.

Castro was physically attracted to a number of girls he met in Mexico, but usually the relationship did not develop. He went out on several occasions with a Venezuelan poet called Lucila Velásquez, but spent virtually all the time expounding his political ambitions. Lucila caused laughter by asking Hilda, in the presence of Fidel, how she had found an opportunity to persuade Che to marry her. Fidel's brother Raúl, who had a more genial and fun-loving character than Fidel, tried to persuade him not to talk politics when they went out together with young women. Fidel ignored this advice. He not only talked politics, but tended to lose interest when his enthusiasm was not reciprocated.

His only serious affair began when he was under arrest. He was visited in the prison by Teresa Casuso, a distinguished and glamorous Cuban writer living in Mexico, who had read about Castro's fate in the newspapers. She was accompanied by a beautiful young house-guest whom Casuso called 'Lilia' in her memoirs (her real name was evidently Isabel Custodio). Castro adopted the manner which he always adopted when he wanted to impress a stranger. As Casuso described it: 'He gave the impression of being noble, sure, deliberate . . . He gave me a greeting of restrained emotion and a handshake that was warm without being overdone. His voice was quiet, his expression grave, his manner calm, gentle.' While talking to Teresa Casuso, he also shot sidelong glances at her attractive guest.

As soon as Castro was released, he went to Casuso's flat and virtually took up residence, moving many of the weapons which had escaped the police raids into her flat for safe keeping. He talked politics to Teresa, and tried hard to charm the young Isabel. For Isabel's benefit his appearance briefly became uncharacteristically clean and tidy. After a while he proposed marriage to her, having obtained permission to do so from her parents, as traditional good manners required. She accepted, but after a month changed her mind. While Fidel reverted to preparing his revolution, ignoring his fiancée, she reverted to a former suitor with more time on his hands. Like Naty Revuelta before her, she was doubtful about the desirability of joining Castro on an armed invasion of Cuba, which was part of the deal. Castro told her that she had made a wise choice, and that the other man was more suitable. When this affair started, Fidel had just heard that his former wife Mirta was about to marry a wealthy businessman. It is possible that the news had something to do with his precipitate proposal of marriage to Isabel.

In Cuba the students continued to bear the brunt of opposition to Batista. Most confined themselves to more or less peaceful demonstrations. A few tried more extreme methods. A group of *Auténticos* tried to assault a military garrison in Matanzas, on the lines of Castro's Moncada attack, fourteen being killed in the process. In August 1956 the FEU President Echeverría, who had formed a new Revolutionary Directorate (DR), passed through Mexico City and had a meeting with Castro. The aims and methods of the DR and MR-26-7 were similar, with the French Revolution as a common lodestar. The DR had attempted to organise an armed assault on the presidential palace. Echeverría and Castro each wanted to take over the other's organisation, deploying the usual arguments about the desirability of unity and co-operation. Neither was willing to concede leadership. They concluded by signing an ill-defined pact of mutual support.

Apart from personal rivalry, there were some policy differences between Echeverría and Castro. Echeverría favoured assassination as a prime weapon in the struggle against Batista. Castro was more cautious. Without ruling out assassination in exceptional circumstances, he argued that assassination usually meant replacing one individual with another who would follow the same line, while the perpetrators forfeited public sympathy. In planning the attack on Moncada, he had considered seizing the high-ranking officers in their homes, but had rejected this option. 'We wished to avoid scenes of tragedy and fighting in the presence of their families.'

A few weeks after Castro's meeting with Echeverría, their differences over assassination became public. The DR shot dead the new SIM chief, Colonel Antonio Blanco Rico, when he was leaving a nightclub. In the aftermath numerous people were killed, including ten men who had sought asylum in the Haitian Embassy. The Colonel was a questionable target, being a reforming officer who since his appointment had tried to put an end to the practice of torture by SIM interrogators. Castro publicly condemned his killing. 'Such acts must not be indiscriminate . . . From a political and revolutionary standpoint, his assassination was not justified. Blanco Rico was not a Fascist executioner.'

Having lost most of his assets in the June police raids, Castro was again desperate for money. At length he did what he had often sworn not to do: ask for money from his old enemy former President Prío, who had taken millions of ill-gotten gains into exile in Florida, and was willing to finance almost anyone who offered to fight against Batista. Prío had spoken up for Castro when he was under threat of extradition to Cuba. This perhaps enabled Castro to justify to himself a change of attitude. Prío was at first reluctant to meet the man who had so often denounced him for corruption; but he was persuaded by mutual friends, including Teresa Casuso, to do so. Both Prío and Castro had reason to believe that if they left their respective countries of residence legally, they would not be allowed back. Castro therefore swam across the Rio Grande and made an illegal entry into Texas for the rendezvous with Prío, a rare case of a wetback not wanting to prolong his stay. After two long conversations Prío agreed to give Castro US$50,000 almost immediately, with a further US$50,000 to follow.

For the MR-26-7, this was a huge injection of finance. It enabled Castro to restock his weapons arsenal, and to bring more militants from Cuba for military training. He also started to prepare transport for the expedition. After an abortive attempt to purchase a decommissioned naval patrol boat in the United States, he spotted what he thought was a suitable boat for sale in the port of Tuxpan on the Caribbean coast of Mexico. It was a squat, 13-metre wooden motor yacht, which its former American owner had named after his grandmother, the *Granma*. The woodwork and the two small diesel engines needed extensive repairs, and the boat could accommodate comfortably only about twenty people. But Castro was determined to press ahead. He bought the yacht for US$18,000; and made a down-payment on a nearby house, which could be used as an assembly point for men and equipment. The men due to take part were dispersed to areas outside Mexico City, mostly near the location of the *Granma*. Castro increased his personal precautions, sleeping almost every night in a different house.

In October 1956 Castro's sisters Emma and Agustina took Fidelito on what was supposed to be a two-week visit to Fidel in Mexico City. He was delighted and spent a lot of time playing with Fidelito, even when talking business with his fellow conspirators. He then proceeded to renege on a promise which had been given on his behalf to return Fidelito to his mother. He arranged for Fidelito to stay indefinitely with a Mexican couple who were close and trusted friends, and who lived in a villa with a swimming pool in the smart suburb of Pedregal. He justified his action by saying that it was in Fidelito's interest, and that Fidelito would get a better education in Mexico than if he were returned to his 'most ferocious enemies'. Some weeks later, when Fidel's sisters were taking Fidelito for a walk in Chapultepec park, a large black car pulled up, three armed men jumped out and seized Fidelito. Fidelito's Mexican guardians complained to the police that the Cuban Embassy had arranged the kidnapping of Fidelito. But by then Fidelito was already in Cuba, and there was no possibility that the Cuban authorities would return him.

The Cuban government knew that Castro had received financial support from Prío and was planning to take some sort of action before the end of 1956, as he had promised. They even accused him of preparing an invasion of Cuba with help from General Trujillo of the Dominican Republic, triggering another long and indignant rebuttal. The Cuban Embassy renewed pressure on the Mexicans to curb Castro and his gang. As a result he was subjected to closer police surveillance.

Castro was under pressure from many sides to defer plans for an armed invasion. He had tried to enlist the support of the Communist Party for strike action coinciding with his landing. In reply the Communists sent repeated messages that the situation in Cuba was 'not favourable to military action'. Frank Pais travelled to Mexico from Santiago to warn that the support group in Oriente was not ready to launch the planned uprising. Melba Hernández returned from a visit to Cuba with the same message. Castro rejected this advice, arguing that it was vital to maintain the credibility of his promises to take action before the end of the year. The MR-26-7 had even circulated leaflets saying: 'In 1956 we shall return or be martyrs.' Colonel Bayo said that the Cuban government knew of his imminent departure, and that in warfare it was a fatal mistake to let the enemy know your intentions. Castro also rejected this opinion. He said he did not care if everyone knew that he was coming. It was his form of psychological warfare.

In any case, he soon had no choice. The police were closing in, having obtained information that Castro was again preparing armed action, in breach of the conditions of his residence in Mexico. Castro believed that he was betrayed for money by his old university friend Rafael del Pino, who visited from the United States and asked a lot of questions about Castro's plans. The police's information could have come from many other sources. In any event, on 21 November police raided Teresa Casuso's flat and seized weapons belonging to Castro. A friendly policeman warned that he had seventy-two hours to leave the country, or face arrest and prosecution. He ordered the men chosen for the expedition to assemble where the *Granma* was moored on the Tuxpan river. He arranged for a telegram to be sent to Santiago saying: 'The book you ordered is out of print.' It was a coded message for Frank Pais, meaning that the landing would be on 30 November at a beach near Niquero in Oriente. He had calculated that the crossing would take five days.

On 23 November Castro set out from Mexico City by car. Just outside the city, police stopped him. After a large payment he was allowed to proceed, but the police followed him. When he reached Tuxpan, the police informed the Cuban Embassy that he was about to depart by sea. Repairs to the *Granma* had still not been completed, but there was no time to wait. That same evening eighty-two expeditionaries piled into the boat, together with ninety rifles, two hand-held anti-tank guns, three machine guns and about forty pistols. Fuel, food and water had been loaded earlier. Shortly after midnight on 25 November the overloaded boat, with lights extinguished, moved slowly down the river and out into the Caribbean. One man asked when they were going to join the main ship. He had assumed that the *Granma* was merely a lighter. Rain was falling and the wind was picking up.

Conditions on board were extremely crowded and uncomfortable. The mood was a mixture of apprehension and elation. At last the preparations had ended. The hour of liberation was near. Someone began singing the Cuban national anthem. Everyone stood up and joined in. 'To die for the motherland is to live!' As the old vessel chugged out into the darkness, a few friends and well-wishers watched silently from the shore.

8 In the Sierra

For the eighty-two men crowded into the *Granma,* the 1,200-mile voyage from Mexico to the east of Cuba was a nightmare. As soon as they reached the open sea, the boat started to roll in the waves and most of the men suffered severe seasickness. For a while the bilge pump failed to work, and water had to be bailed out by hand. The journey had been expected to take five days at most, but due to bad weather, overloading and a slipping clutch, it took seven days. Supplies of food and water started to run low. On top of these setbacks, a man fell overboard during the night, and in the darkness it took more than an hour to locate and rescue him.

Castro was one of the few men who were not seasick. When the weather improved he tried to keep the men busy with tasks such as the cleaning of weapons. He followed progress impatiently on the navigator's charts. He had no means of warning his people in Oriente that his arrival would be delayed. Just twenty-nine years old, he was already a veteran in revolutionary warfare. He was hardened to setbacks. The enterprise on which he was embarked might look foolhardy to some, but not to him. The revolution he wanted would benefit the people, and would be welcomed by the people. All that was needed was someone with the determination and willpower to make it possible.

At dawn on 30 November 1956, when the *Granma* was supposed to arrive, Frank Pais led his men in the planned uprising. Armed with rifles and dressed in uniforms with red and black MR-26-7 armbands, they launched a series of attacks on government buildings in Santiago. The maritime police station was occupied and set on fire. Similar attacks took place in Manzanillo and other towns. Celia Sánchez took men and vehicles to the beach where Castro should have arrived, and waited for him in vain. The plan was for the expeditionaries to attack a military post in the nearby town of Niquero, coinciding with the uprising in Santiago, before setting off towards the Sierra Maestra. After two days of intermittent action, Pais's men dispersed to their homes, having suffered very few casualties and arrests, but dispirited by

Castro's non-arrival. On the *Granma* Castro listened on a portable radio to news of the attempted uprising.

The Cuban Government had been expecting Castro to land in Oriente, and had reinforced the military presence in the province. Despite this the authorities virtually lost control in Santiago on 30 November. Additional troops were airlifted in. By the time the *Granma* finally arrived, the uprising was over and the military were on heightened alert, with aircraft patrolling the coast looking for Castro.

The *Granma* reached the coast just before dawn on 2 December, but in the darkness the navigator was unable to identify his exact position. 'Are you sure this is Cuba?' asked Castro impatiently. He was afraid they might land by mistake on one of the many small offshore islands. It was already broad daylight when the boat finally went aground in shallow water. It was still several hundred metres from the shore and well short of the intended destination. The men had to wade laboriously through soft mud to the shore, carrying weapons but leaving most of the heavy equipment on the boat, including machine guns, ammunition, radios and medical supplies. The shore turned out to be a mangrove swamp. It took the men another two hours to struggle through it. As Che Guevara recorded in his journal, it was not a landing but a shipwreck.

Finally on dry land, the men found a charcoal burner living in an isolated hut. Castro put his hand on the peasant's shoulder and said: 'I am Fidel Castro. My companions and I have come to liberate Cuba. You have nothing to fear from us, because we have come to help the peasants. We shall give them land to work, markets for their products, schools for their children and decent housing for the whole family. We need something to eat, but we shall pay you for it.' 'All right,' said the peasant, 'but be careful with that gun. Somebody might get shot by mistake.' He said he had some sweet potatoes on the fire, and would kill a pig. Before the pig was cooked, however, they heard gunfire and decided they must move on without more delay. A naval vessel had spotted the *Granma* and was firing on the mangroves where they thought the occupants might be hiding.

For three days they moved slowly towards the foothills of the Sierra Maestra, the rugged, jungle-covered mountain range stretching ninety miles along the south coast of Oriente province. To escape detection they walked mostly by night, hiding up during the day. At daybreak on 5 December, exhausted and hungry, they were resting in a field when they were suddenly attacked by a detachment of the Rural Guard. Castro had failed to post sentries, and was taken completely by surprise. The first the men knew of the Rural Guards' stealthy approach was when volleys of machine gun and rifle fire erupted from several directions. A few were killed or wounded instantly.

There was panic and confusion. Some surrendered; others ran for their lives. Castro was some distance from the main group when the shooting began. He ran with two companions towards a hill with some trees and bushes. They took cover and lay still, listening to the shouts of the soldiers in the distance.

At about midday a light aircraft circling overhead spotted Castro's group and made a low pass. The three ran into a sugar-cane field, and eventually found an area of dense growth where they were completely hidden. Castro's two companions were Universo Sánchez, a burly peasant who acted as Castro's personal bodyguard in Mexico and subsequently, and Faustino Pérez, a thirty-six-year-old pharmacist. Castro was fully dressed and had his rifle with telescopic sights. Sánchez had his rifle but was barefoot, not having had time to put on his boots when the Rural Guard attacked. Pérez had boots but had left behind his rifle. At this stage the Rebel Army consisted of three men and two weapons. They had lost contact with everyone else.

Castro wanted to leave the cane-field that night and continue eastwards to a house in the foothills of the Sierra, which belonged to an MR-26-7 supporter and was their first destination. But for once he allowed himself to be overruled by the other two, who thought it wiser to stay put under the sugar cane until the aircraft and Rural Guard gave up searching for them. They spent four days and three nights hiding in the cane-field, eating little more than the juice of cane-stalks. Castro talked incessantly. The other two mostly kept their thoughts to themselves.

Pérez later recalled:

Fidel discussed continuing on to the Sierra Maestra. He was already convinced that we would meet up with our companions. We would go that same afternoon, he was saying, or the next day in the morning. Personally, I was thinking at that moment that perhaps it would be possible to arrange a truce . . . But Fidel was already talking about the future combat actions which we must undertake in order to keep growing . . . To be able to speak, we had to put our heads together, to talk in whispers, because we were certain that the army surrounded us. And in this whisper, speaking with his usual enthusiasm, Fidel told us his future plans. But not only plans for the future. For the first time I heard him speak a lot about other things, about the meaning of life, about our struggle, about history, about all those things . . . I remember that for the first time I heard him repeat the phrase of Martí that 'all the glory of the world would fit inside a grain of maize'. I'd known the quotation, but not in this context, in the context of what life means for a revolutionary, and how one should not fight for personal ambition, not even for ambition of glory . . . He said that a revolutionary feels an obligation, and gets satisfaction from it at the same time, to fight for others, to fight for his people, to fight for the humble . . . What I'm telling you is what struck me the most, but there were many other things. About organising the country, about the people of Cuba, the history of Cuba, the future. And about the need to launch a revolution, a real revolution. We didn't speak of Marxism and Communism in those days, but of a social revolution, a true revolution . . .'

The recollections of Sánchez, who tended to act Sancho to Castro's Quixote, were more down to earth:

> Fidel started discussing – apparently to give Faustino and me some courage – what would be the revolution and the future. He talked of the revolutionary programme, he raised our spirits. At no time did he consider himself defeated. It was always a thing with him to talk about regrouping our people. I began to believe at one stage that he was crazy. I said to myself, 'Shit, he's gone crazy.' You'll see that my rifle has my name scratched on it with the tip of the bayonet, because I thought that when they killed me, my family would know it was me who was killed, and I wouldn't just disappear.

When they settled down to sleep the first night in the cane-field, Castro said he was determined not to be taken alive. He lay with his rifle on his chest with the barrel under his chin and his finger on the trigger, saying he would shoot himself if the Rural Guard found them. Sánchez said he was crazy. A land crab or some other animal could disturb him, and he would shoot himself for nothing. Castro said: 'You do what you like. I'm sleeping like this.'

With no sign of aircraft or Rural Guard detachments, the group finally set off and arrived at the house of Guillermo García, a friend of Celia Sánchez. He became the first recruit to the Rebel Army. Several other peasants from the area volunteered to help search for survivors from the expedition. A few days later they reached the house of Mongo Pérez, a local bandit living higher up in the hills. Mongo was the brother of Crescencio Pérez, a huge, grey-bearded, patriarchal figure, who was the unofficial chieftain of the local peasantry. Crescencio and his associates were in a state of virtual warfare with the authorities. They therefore regarded Castro's group of rebels as welcome allies.

In Mongo's house Castro received news of another group of survivors. On 18 December, thirteen days after the disastrous encounter with the Rural Guard, he met Raúl Castro and four others, all with their weapons, and later another single survivor. Fidel was overjoyed. The Rebel Army had been more than doubled. Soon there was even better news. They made contact with a group of seven men from the *Granma*, including Che Guevara. Fidel rebuked them for having lost most of their rifles, but the Army was now twenty men (sixteen *Granma* survivors and four local recruits) with twelve weapons. At the end of December a last group of three more *Granma* survivors was found.

By this time the government had called off the special deployments of troops and aircraft. Forty-six men from the *Granma* had been killed or captured. Contrary to press reports, Fidel Castro's body had not been found; but the authorities thought that at worst there could only be a handful of men still at large, and they were confident that sooner or later the Rural Guard would pick up any remnants of the force. Castro's mother Lina, still in mourning for the death of her husband a few weeks earlier, told the local newspaper: 'I suffer as a mother of soldiers and revolutionaries, but if Fidel and Raúl decide to die, I pray that they may die with dignity.'

Castro sent Mongo Pérez to Manzanillo and Santiago to tell the MR-26-7 organisation that he was alive and well, and to ask for supplies. Mongo and a local woman called Eugenia Vardecia returned with weapons and other equipment. Eugenia became an indefatigable supporter, travelling with mules up and down the mountainside, bringing stocks of weapons, food and even books for the rebels. Faustino Pérez was despatched to Havana with instructions to reorganise the MR-26-7 underground militia, and to ensure a continuing supply of recruits, weapons and money to the rebel force in the mountains.

During January 1957 Castro's column moved slowly eastwards into the heart of the Sierra Maestra. From a base here he prepared his first offensive action. The group descended to the narrow coastal strip to attack a small military post near the beach at La Plata. It was vital that this first action should be successful, and to ensure this they needed reliable information about the strength of the garrison. Local peasants said that Chicho Osorio, a *mayoral* (land company overseer), was in close contact with the soldiers. Finding Osorio riding on a mule, Castro's men seized him and took his pistol. Castro pretended to be an army officer searching for rebels. Osorio, who was half drunk, said that he too was looking for rebels. He needed his pistol back because if he found Fidel Castro, he would kill him like a dog. His boots, he said, came from a rebel whom he had caught and killed. That sealed his fate, related Guevara. Using information provided by Osorio, they surrounded the garrison in the middle of the night, fired on it, and called on the soldiers to surrender. When the soldiers refused, they resumed firing and set the garrison on fire. When the post finally surrendered, two soldiers were dead, five wounded and three captured. The rebels carried away the weapons stocked at the post. Guevara was ordered to treat and bandage the soldiers' wounds. Castro congratulated the captured soldiers on their bravery and released them. But on Castro's orders Osorio was executed with a bullet in the head.

The action at La Plata alerted the government and the national army to the fact that Castro was around and dangerous. But the geography of the Sierra Maestra made it difficult to send in a strong force to eliminate him. A small guerrilla group could move faster through the mountains than a large, heavily loaded army unit unfamiliar with the terrain. In the early months of the campaign the army's tactics had two main strands. They forcibly relocated peasants suspected of providing Castro with logistic support; and they tried to obtain intelligence about his location, in order then to bomb and strafe him from the air.

A crucial factor in Castro's ability to survive, and gradually to build up the effectiveness of his tiny army, was the attitude of the Sierra peasants. The peasants received no benefit or protection from the state, and had no reason to respect its representatives. A brief attempt by the government to win them over by offering new housing and other benefits, in return for co-operation against the rebels, was not sustained long enough to have much effect, and was undermined by punitive measures such as forced relocation. Farmers or cattlemen who were fugitives from the law, and who were regarded and treated as bandits, were the natural allies of the rebel guerrillas. Most peasants in the Sierra, even those who had lived there for generations, were technically squatters on someone else's land. They were constantly trying to extend the land they cultivated, but were liable to eviction by the *mayorales* at any time, if the owner wanted to use the land for some other purpose.

It was difficult, however, for Castro to turn the peasants' hostility to the authorities into active support for himself. Like peasants everywhere living in remote areas, they were suspicious of all outsiders, whether soldiers or rebels. Their initial attitude to Castro was not as spontaneously enthusiastic as the regime's later propaganda led people to believe. Some peasants who joined the Rebel Army with the idea of destroying the power of the landowners changed their mind and withdrew when it became apparent that the struggle would be long and hard. Conditions for the rebels in the first months were tough, even by the standards to which the peasants were accustomed. They were constantly on the move, subjected for days on end to the cold rain of the mountains, sleeping on the ground (later they acquired hammocks), wading across streams, and hacking their way through thick, thorny vegetation.

The rebels did not look like a force capable of defeating a professional army. They were unshaven, dirty, smelly and foul-mouthed. Morale in the early months was shaky. Castro maintained an air of total confidence, but had to use draconian methods to enforce discipline. He threatened death for desertion, treachery, disobedience and even 'defeatism'. That was the fate of one peasant who joined the rebels but was caught by the army on a mission in the lowlands. For a large reward he was persuaded to return to the mountain as an army spy. He revealed the location of Castro's well-hidden base camp, which was then subjected to a devastating aerial bombardment. When his treachery was discovered he was immediately shot.

The growth of the Rebel Army was due more to the arrival of urban volunteers than to recruitment from the local peasantry. Guevara was sometimes despondent about the apathetic attitude of the peasants. Despite this, Castro gradually built up a network of peasant support throughout the Sierra Maestra. He took a great deal of trouble to demonstrate that his revolution involved more than promises of land redistribution. People living in the area controlled by the Rebel Army generally received much better treatment than that traditionally meted out by the Rural Guard and other authorities. The rebels usually paid for food and other services, unlike the army who just seized whatever they needed. Castro took an interest in the private lives and personal views of people who were used to being treated as little more than workhorses or beasts of burden. His men helped with the coffee harvest on the mountain slopes, assistance which was especially valuable because at that time many of the peasants had been forcibly relocated. His ruthless treatment of men like Chicho Osorio also earned him a lot of goodwill. The *mayorales* were often the most hated and feared men in the region. Someone who could shoot Osorio and other overseers and get away with it gained respect and admiration.

On 16 February Castro moved down the mountain again for a meeting with leaders of the MR-26-7 in the rest of Cuba, including Frank País, Faustino Pérez, Armando Hart, Haydée Santamaría, Vilma Espin and Celia Sánchez. It was the first time he met Celia, who was to play a crucial role in his life until her death from cancer in 1980. They took to each other immediately. Aged twenty-nine, the daughter of a local doctor, she was slim, dark-haired and good-looking in a slightly severe manner. She was also intelligent, practical and tirelessly efficient. She had already proved one of Fidel's most valuable collaborators, organising an extremely active support group in her home town of Manzanillo.

At this meeting there were the first hints of the tension which would later develop between the Movement in the Sierra and in the Llano (plain, i.e. the rest of Cuba) Castro insisted that he needed more men and more supplies to be sent to the Rebel Army. Fulfilling that task must take priority over all other objectives. He felt that members of the MR-26-7 Directorate in Havana and Santiago were concentrating too much on building up their own sections' membership and capability, including a military capability, instead of focussing on supplying the Rebel Army. He turned down a suggestion from Faustino Pérez that a second front be opened in the Escambray Mountains in the central province of Las Villas.

The visitors brought newspapers with them, so that Castro could catch up on developments in Cuba and the wider world. Batista's relations with the United States seemed to be better than ever. A whole range of sophisticated American military equipment was being supplied. The US Ambassador had personally handed over seven new Sherman tanks and referred to Castro publicly as a 'rabble-rouser'. There was a big US naval visit to Havana. The head of the Cuban Air Force, which had been trying to bomb Castro's camps, was awarded a high US decoration.

However, the tide soon started to turn in the battle for American public sympathy. After his success at La Plata, Castro had sent a man to Havana to ask Faustino Pérez to bring foreign journalists to the Sierra to publicise the Rebel Army's existence and activities. Batista could censor Cuban newspapers, but it was more difficult to keep out news about Cuba appearing in foreign newspapers. Faustino Pérez duly brought a senior American journalist for a clandestine meeting with Castro in the Sierra. This was Herbert Matthews of the *New York Times*. He was given a carefully choreographed reception, designed to give him the impression that the Rebel Army was much bigger than it really was. Fidel talked about operating in 'groups of forty men', and had a man interrupt them with urgent news about a fictitious 'second column'. Raúl led the same line of men back and forth through the trees, at a distance where Matthews would think they were different groups. Castro was at his most charming and persuasive.

The result was a brilliant success for Castro. Matthews's first article started: 'Fidel Castro, the rebel leader of Cuba's youth, is alive and fighting hard and successfully in the rugged, almost impenetrable vastness of the Sierra Maestra . . . General Batista cannot possibly hope to suppress the Castro revolt.' Castro was described as courageous and idealistic, adored by his men and with an overpowering personality. The Cuban Defence Minister then kicked an own goal by claiming that Matthews had written 'a chapter in a fantasy novel', and that he had not in fact interviewed 'the pro-Communist insurgent Fidel Castro'. Matthews then produced photographic evidence to prove that he had indeed interviewed Castro.

To coincide with Matthews's series of articles, Castro issued another Manifesto to the Cuban People. He called for revolutionary action throughout the island, including the burning of sugar-cane fields, the sabotage of public services, the 'summary execution of the thugs who torture and assassinate revolutionaries', civic resistance, and finally a general revolutionary strike.

Castro might issue declarations from his remote mountain fastness calling for revolutionary action in the cities, but many of the most militant revolutionaries were not under his control, and owed him no allegiance. In Havana the man most able to call the shots was José Antonio Echeverría, president of the FEU and head of the DR. The DR was carrying out frequent bombings and acts of sabotage, to which the police responded with mass arrests, the torture of suspects, and occasional exemplary extra-judicial killings. The differences between Castro and Echeverría, which had emerged in their talks in Mexico City, remained unresolved. Castro had bitterly criticised Echeverría and the DR for failing to take action in support of his *Granma* landing, despite the pact of mutual support which they had signed in Mexico. The DR in turn was sceptical and dismissive of Castro's slow guerrilla war in the mountains, believing that the quickest and most effective way to end the dictatorship was by physically eliminating the dictator.

In March 1957 the DR launched an attack on the presidential palace, and came close to achieving their objective. If Batista had not by chance taken a concealed lift from his office to his third-floor private apartment just before the attack, he would probably have been killed. Thirty-five DR militants were killed at the palace before the police regained control. Echeverría himself, after trying to make a broadcast from a radio station which had also been occupied by DR militants, was killed by police in the street shortly afterwards. Fidel Castro once again publicly dissociated himself from the attempted assassination. It was 'a useless spilling of blood. The life of the dictator does not matter. . . . I am against terrorism. I condemn these procedures. Nothing is solved by them.' By a curious symmetry, Batista also opposed the assassination of his principal opponent. When the US Ambassador proposed to him that their respective intelligence services infiltrate an agent to kill Castro, Batista is said to have replied: 'I couldn't approve that. We're Cubans.'

Echeverría's death was fortuitously beneficial to Castro, in that it removed a charismatic potential rival, and made it easier for Castro to assert his leadership over the opposition to Batista. But Castro's criticism of Echeverría's policy of magnicide had its logic, and was not just based on personal rivalry or a fear of being marginalised if Echevarría had succeeded. Castro's constant fear, right up to the moment he took power, was that Batista might be replaced, for example following an assassination or military coup, by someone who would offer a new face, possibly a face more acceptable to the public, but not a fundamental change in the system. This would obstruct and delay the *real* revolution which Castro wanted.

As the year progressed, fortune continued to favour Castro by eliminating potential rivals for leadership of the opposition. In May an armed group financed by ex-President Prío landed on the north coast of Oriente, very much in the style of Castro's *Granma* landing. It was betrayed by a peasant, and then trapped and wiped out by the army. This same month Castro decided that the time was ripe to launch a larger-scale attack than the one at La Plata. The Rebel Army now numbered about 120 men and had been supplied, mainly by Celia Sánchez, with new weapons and ammunition, including machine guns. Castro descended again to the coast, this time with about eighty men, and attacked the military post at El Uvero, twenty miles east of La Plata, in the direction of Santiago. Celia Sánchez took part, becoming the first woman to assume a full active military role in the Rebel Army. Castro fired the first shot in what proved a tough battle lasting several hours, with casualties on both sides. By the time the post fell, six rebels had been killed and nine wounded. In the garrison fourteen soldiers were dead, nineteen wounded and fourteen captured.

Following this action the government withdrew the army from small outposts in the Sierra Maestra region. This deprived Castro of relatively easy targets, but reinforced his practical control of what now came to be called the Liberated Zone in the mountains. The withdrawal of military posts created a perception among the local peasantry that Fidel Castro was indeed the only effective authority. The victory at El Uvero also greatly enhanced Castro's reputation in the country as a whole. He was now the best-known and probably most popular opposition figure in Cuba. He was no longer a wild young man who engaged in quixotic but suicidal attacks. He was a guerrilla leader who had captured a military post defended by fifty well-armed soldiers.

By July the Rebel Army numbered above two hundred, and Castro decided to divide it into three sections, commanded by himself, Raúl Castro and Che Guevara. Raúl and Che both held more radical and overtly Marxist views than Fidel, and in turn indoctrinated their men with Marxist ideas. Fidel remained more cautious and uncommitted, conscious above all of his need for mainstream political support. In Mexico he had broken with the *Ortodoxo* leadership over their insistence on trying to negotiate with Batista. Now the *Ortodoxo* leadership came to him, implicitly recognising that Batista's obduracy had proved him right. In a gesture of support and adhesion four *Ortodoxo* leaders, including Raúl Chibás (brother of the party's founder) and Felipe Pazos, a distinguished banker and economist, travelled to the Sierra for a meeting with Castro. Making the most of their presence, Castro drafted the Sierra Maestra Manifesto, which Chibás and Pazos also signed.

The Sierra Maestra Manifesto was presented as a riposte to Batista's attempts to pit the politicians against the revolutionaries, and to disseminate the notion that the revolutionaries opposed elections. 'We want elections, but with one condition: truly free, democratic, impartial elections.' Such elections would only be possible if Batista had departed and been replaced by a provisional government 'supported by all'. The manifesto rejected mediation by any other country, called on the United States to stop arms supplies to the Batista government, and rejected any proposal for a provisional military junta. It then set out a long list of measures which the proposed civilian provisional government must introduce, including agrarian reform, industrialisation and a national campaign against illiteracy.

Guevara did not like the manifesto. He accepted it as a tactical necessity, but thought it made too many concessions to bourgeois ideology. But in fact Castro had got everything he wanted. The *Ortodoxo* politicians, caught between Batista's repression of normal political activity and Castro's military success and prestige, had in effect signed up to Castro's Moncada programme. Elections yes, but only after the appointment of a provisional civilian government (nominated by whom but Castro?) and the implementation of a political programme (predetermined by Castro).

Castro's powerful personality and persuasive manner enabled him to make both Marxists and democratic politicians believe that he was on their side. But this ambiguity made it difficult to maintain discipline and cohesion among the MR-26-7 members with whom he had no direct contact. He wanted to maintain tight control of a clandestine organisation spread throughout Cuba, and even among the exile community, but without giving it a clear strategy and ideological position. This caused growing uncertainty, confusion and dissension in the ranks of the Movement's activists in the Llano. Some of the men in the cities, daily risking their lives in acts of sabotage, disruption or illegal propaganda, felt that their contribution was undervalued by the leadership in the mountains. Castro was felt to have tendencies to *caudillismo* (dictatorship), to be running the show as a strongman who had to consult no one. Some of the anti-Communist nationalists in the Movement were resentful of the standing and influence of Castro's Argentine friend Guevara, who was known to be a radical Marxist.

The tension between the Rebel Army and the Movement came to a head in July, eight months after Castro's arrival in the *Granma*. Frank Pais, the most prestigious and effective of the Llano leaders, the man who led the abortive uprising in Santiago on the day when the *Granma* was supposed to land, wrote to Fidel Castro to say that he and Armando Hart, the leader of the underground in Havana, had decided to revamp and restructure the MR-26-7 in its entirety, giving each of six regions representation on the National Directorate. He said their aim was to rectify the lack of effective co-ordination, and to provide a clear programme which was 'serious, revolutionary and within the realm of possibility'. They had enlisted a group of intellectuals to work on this programme. Pais added that Castro as leader would of course decide on the proposal, but he asked for an early decision.

Castro recognised Pais's qualities and importance to the Movement, but he did not at all like being bounced. Before a serious breach could develop, however, Pais was caught and killed by police in Santiago. The aftermath showed the enormous sympathy which the MR-26-7, and Pais in particular, enjoyed in Santiago. Thousands defied police intimidation to attend his funeral, and there was a widely supported protest strike by workers. Middle-aged women paraded under a banner reading: 'Stop the murder of our sons!' Castro also expressed outrage and bitterness over Pais's death. But he moved quickly to transfer most of Pais's responsibilities to Celia Sánchez, whom he could trust and direct. His instruction to Celia was clear and simple: 'All guns, all bullets, and all supplies to the Sierra.'

In the months following the attack at El Uvero, there were some small-scale raids and ambushes, but no major military engagements. Castro did not want to risk a setback by venturing too far or too soon from his mountain strongholds. He concentrated on training and improving communications, complaining in a letter to Celia Sánchez that being a commander involved more bureaucracy than fighting. Batista for his part thought that the guer-rillas were contained in the mountains, and that the revolt would wither on the vine. The United States government, aware of the hollowness of Batista's claims to be in full control of the situation, began to hedge its bets. An abortive naval revolt in Cienfuegos in September 1957, part of a wider dissid-ent movement among the military, showed that even the armed forces could not be completely relied on by Batista. The naval conspirators had been in touch with both the US Embassy and the MR-26-7.

The CIA stepped up its efforts to get close to all the significant opposition groups including the MR-26-7. Castro was deeply suspicious of United States intentions, but thought it would be undesirable, as Che Guevara put it, to confront Uncle Sam before the time was ripe. He sent orders to his men in Santiago on how to respond to the first approach from a United States diplomat. This was his first entry on to the stage of international diplomacy, and he drafted instructions with care:

> We can receive any US diplomat, just as we would any Mexican diplomat or a diplomat from any country . . . It is a recognition that a state of belligerence exists, and is therefore one more victory against the tyranny. We should not fear this visit if we are certain that no matter what happens, we will keep the banner of dignity and national sovereignty flying. And if they make demands? We'll reject them. And if they want to know our opinions? We'll explain them without fear. If they wish to have closer ties of friendship with the triumphant democracy of Cuba? Magnificent! This is a sign that they acknowledge the final outcome of the battle. If they propose friendly mediation? We'll tell them that no mediation is possible in this battle . . .

In October a meeting took place in Miami of representatives of seven polit-ical parties and opposition groups, aimed at co-ordinating the struggle against

Batista. The main instigator was ex-President Prío, whose apparently inexhaustible funds remained the principal source of financing for opposition activities. The participants at the meeting created a Liberation Council and signed a document, known as the Miami Pact, calling for united action to put an end to the Batista dictatorship. The main document made no reference to the Rebel Army. It urged the existing armed forces of Cuba to 'unite with us' in support of freedom. A secret annex to the Pact said that once Batista was gone, 'the revolutionary forces will be incorporated into the regular armed forces of the Republic, with their arms'.

The Pact was signed on behalf of the MR-26-7 by Felipe Pazos, one of the signatories with Castro of the Sierra Maestra Manifesto, and by Lester Rodríguez, the Movement's representative in Miami. Their job in Miami was merely to raise money and promote support for the Movement among the exile community. They had no authority to sign agreements or take political decisions. They later claimed to have consulted some members of the MR-26-7 in Cuba about a draft of the Pact, and believed they had authority to accept it. They did not have the time or the means to consult the full National Directorate, or Fidel Castro. They evidently assumed that the Movement would prefer them to sign up to what looked to them an unobjectionable document, rather than stand aloof, with the danger that the MR-26-7 would appear isolated and lacking in solidarity. When the document reached Havana and Santiago, the other leaders of the Movement, notably Armando Hart, expressed serious reservations. The Pact did not recognise the leading role which the MR-26-7 had earned by its actions. It suggested that after Batista the old political parties would simply take over from where they had left off. However, Hart concluded that the least damaging course would be not to repudiate the Pact, but to ride with it as a *fait accompli*. He sent the document up to the Sierra for a final decision.

Fidel passed the Miami Pact to Raúl and Che, who both exploded with indignation. They accused Pazos and Rodríguez of stupidity and incompetence. Worse than that, it was treachery. They had gone along with a calculated ploy by the old politicians to marginalise the Rebel Army. For some weeks Fidel himself expressed no opinion, leading Che to worry that he was accepting Hart's advice to do nothing. In fact there was no likelihood that Castro would do nothing. He was thinking, planning, composing his response. Like his brother and Guevara, he had a clear vision of the future of the Rebel Army: it would not be incorporated in the national army, it would replace the national army; indeed, it would replace the Batista government. But this could not be expressed with brutal frankness. The situation called for finesse and diplomacy. He had to play tough and demonstrate that he could not be bounced into accepting a role for his movement as just one of a number of opposition groups. But he still needed the sympathy and goodwill of a broad spectrum of opinion, and could not afford to appear arrogant and power-hungry.

He composed a long letter repudiating the Miami Pact. The letter had the carefully crafted structure that would become familiar in his speeches. It started in a gentle and even humble tone, then gradually built up to a torrent of indignation and invective against his opponents and rivals, continued with a defiant promise to fight on alone if necessary, concluding with a statesman-like willingness to accept collaboration if all his conditions were met.

Castro wrote that it was a bitter experience for those fighting and dying in Cuba, sustained only by the dignity of a noble cause, to read that the future of their movement had been decided without their knowledge, without the courtesy of any consultation, by a group of people living in the comfort of Miami. The exiled politicians had plenty of money and weapons, but had turned a deaf ear to the pleas for help from the real revolutionaries fighting a desperate battle inside Cuba against the might of Batista's army and police. The Miami Pact contained intolerable omissions. It did not, as minimal patriotism required, reject foreign interference in the affairs of Cuba. It did not reject the notion of a provisional military junta, despite all the evidence that provisional juntas became permanent and were the bane of Latin America. It gave the self-appointed Liberation Council the right to decide the composition of the government which would replace Batista. This was totally unacceptable. The proposal to disarm the revolutionary forces after the departure of Batista would create a situation of anarchy. The MR-26-7 would assume responsibility for public order, since they were the only organisation with the means and integrity to do so. Castro reminded the authors of the Pact that the Sierra Maestra Manifesto had proposed the appointment of a civilian provisional head of government after the fall of Batista. Since after five months no one had put forward a candidate, the MR-26-7 now proposed that the government be formed by Manuel Urrutia, a distinguished judge. In Castro's next sentence the proposal had become an established fact. 'It is not we who propose him, but his own conduct, and we hope that he will not refuse to render this service to the Republic.'

The exiles tried in vain to dissuade Castro from publishing his letter. They offered to accept most of the substantive changes which he wanted. Friends of Prío, the main target of Castro's wrath, pointed out to him that Prío had financed the *Granma*. Castro was unmoved. Batista was as delighted as the exiles were dismayed, and ensured that Castro's letter was widely reported in the censored Cuban media. It showed that the opposition was divided, and that Castro brooked no rivals.

The Liberation Council had their own candidate for provisional President. This was Felipe Pazos, who had earlier been encouraged to believe that he would also be Castro's candidate. But Castro now saw this as a trial of strength, and insisted on Urrutia. Urrutia had earned Castro's goodwill by vigorously defending members of the *Granma* expedition, and of Frank Pais's militia in Santiago, when they were captured and put on trial for rebellion. Castro believed that the amiable judge would provide a good non-partisan front for a government which he in practice controlled from behind the scenes. He would in any case block the path of the various ambitious politicians who had their eye on the job. Urrutia accepted with enthusiasm his nomination by Castro as President-in-Waiting. He travelled to the United States and elsewhere, promising to lead Cuba to democracy, freedom and the rule of law. He added to the pressures which induced the US government to start gradually distancing itself from the Batista government.

While castigating his Cuban rivals, Castro took great trouble to maintain the goodwill of the international media. Following in the footsteps of Herbert Matthews, a succession of Western journalists visited the Sierra Maestra. For their benefit Castro kept up his image as a romantic, idealistic, non-Communist freedom fighter. He even encouraged support and financial contributions from businessmen, saying they would be better off without Batista's corrupt officials and grasping tax-collectors. One visiting American journalist aroused Castro's suspicions. He later recalled: 'He was not asking questions, he was just fooling around, playing a role. I said: "This is a spy. They've sent us a spy." But what were we going to do? We couldn't hold a trial and execute him just on suspicion.' As soon as the suspect left, Castro moved his base camp, and put up additional camouflage. His men also moved a hut which was easily visible from the air, and could be used to locate Castro's position. Sure enough, a few days later an aircraft appeared and, after circling several times, dropped some bombs near the hut.

Enrique Meneses, a Spaniard working for *Paris Match*, spent nearly four months with Castro, participating in the daily life of the guerrillas. Fidel was at times feverishly active. At times he lay slouched in his hammock, reading or planning his next move. Celia Sánchez then as later controlled access to him. She understood his moods and ensured that all his needs were met, whether for a dentist or an intellectual debate. He questioned Meneses at length about his experiences as a journalist in other countries, and his impressions of revolutionary Third World leaders such as Nasser. He also spent many hours of the night expounding to Meneses his own ideas about the new Cuba which would emerge after the Revolution, for example how new agricultural communities might be set up, with free education and medical treatment for all.

Meneses was the only foreign journalist who had the stamina to stay with Castro for more than a few days. The guerrillas had hammocks and other luxuries which they had lacked in the first months in the Sierra, but it was still a tough life. The staple food was yucca or malanga roots, only occasionally supplemented by pork, chicken or snake-meat. Castro usually moved camp every day. He was up at dawn, drinking strong black coffee and lighting his first cigar. While the men packed up the camp, Castro usually listened to the early morning radio news bulletins. He then shouldered his rifle and marched off at the head of the column, setting an exhausting pace. Sometimes the column marched from 6 a.m. to 8 p.m., stopping only if they came to some peasant huts and were offered coffee. Castro usually declined offers of food. When they did stay for a meal, Meneses noticed that Celia Sánchez would thrust a 100–peso note into the hand of one of the peasants before the column moved off. It was not payment; rather an informal exchange of gifts. After a few days of this life on the move, Meneses decided to keep his boots on at night. He could not endure the pain of pulling his boots onto his swollen feet the morning after a day's march.

With outsiders Castro usually talked the language of Utopian Socialism. This was the pleasant, smiling face of the Revolution. But he knew the realities of power. He knew that it would not be an easy or pleasant task to break the power of the dominant economic class in Cuba, which would inevitably oppose the social and economic transformation which he planned. Che Guevara described Fidel in this period as representing the 'bourgeois left'. But for an intellectual fundamentalist like Che, even most Communists were tainted with bourgeois attitudes. The real Castro, as opposed to the image presented by friendly Western journalists, shared and encouraged the Marxist convictions of Che and Raúl. His objection to the Cuban Communist Party was not to its ideology, but to its subservience to the Soviet Union and criticisms of himself. While curbing the role and influence of the Llano moderates, he gave an increasing degree of military and even political autonomy to both Che and Raúl. Towards the end of 1957 Che was appointed *Comandante* (major in a normal army but the top rank in the Rebel Army) and given command of his own column operating in the mountains to the east of Fidel's base.

In March 1958 Armando Hart was arrested and found with documents including correspondence between leading members of the Movement and the Rebel Army. Rafael Díaz-Balart, Under-Secretary for the Interior and Fidel's brother-in-law, read out on the radio extracts from the correspondence which proved, he said, that both Guevara and Raúl Castro were Communists, and that Raúl was an avowed admirer of Stalin. Hearing Díaz-Balart on the radio in his mountain camp, Fidel was furious. He shouted that he would shoot Raúl. As recorded by Meneses, he summoned Raúl for a dressing down and yelled: 'I hate Soviet imperialism as much as Yankee imperialism!' But Fidel's anger was directed more at Raúl's indiscretion than at his beliefs. Very soon after this incident, Fidel appointed Raúl also to the rank of *Comandante,* and allocated to him sixty-five men with which to establish a new front – 'column no. 6' – in the Sierra Cristal on the north coast of Oriente. He told Raúl to burn cane-fields on the family farm at Birán, to make it clear that they were acting on principle and showing no favours to friend or family.

By the spring of 1958 all the mountainous areas of Oriente were outside the government's control. The Rebel Army had its own hospital, schools, printing press, slaughterhouse, land-mine factory and even cigar-making factory. Its radio station (Radio Rebelde) was broadcasting news which was propagandistic but generally more reliable, and therefore more effective, than the absurdly optimistic bulletins of the Batista government. Despite all this, Castro was nowhere near being able to confront Batista's army in a conventional battle in the lowlands. The way forward in his view was now through civil action designed to bring about the internal disintegration of the regime. He was confident that the mass of the people were behind him, and would respond if a clear lead was given. He now started turning his attention to the organisation of the revolutionary general strike which would lead to the collapse of the government.

Batista's position was indeed looking very shaky. In the first months of 1958 he suffered a series of political reverses. In February the Cardinal Primate of Cuba issued a statement in the name of all the bishops, calling for a government of national unity to prepare the way for a return to 'peaceful and normal political life'. Soon afterwards a group of distinguished judges issued a protest at the arbitrary brutality of the police. Still in February the MR-26-7 underground in Havana carried out a spectacular publicity stunt. On the eve of the Grand Prix motor race, with journalists from around the world descending on Havana, three men approached the world champion driver, the Argentine Juan Manuel Fangio, in the bar of the Lincoln Hotel. Two of them drew pistols and, in the best Hollywood style, told Fangio to come quietly. They drove him to a safe house in the smart Vedado district. Police searched for Fangio in vain. The race went ahead without him. Fangio watched it on television. He was then released near the Argentine Embassy, with a letter of apology and explanation from Faustino Pérez. The propaganda impact of this kidnapping, carried out in broad daylight under the noses of Batista's security forces, was enormous. Many people around the world became aware for the first time that there was an active and effective resistance to Batista's rule, even in the big cities.

Batista tried to regain some political initiative, and to restore the wavering support of the US government, by announcing elections in June. To make the elections credible he restored constitutional guarantees outside Oriente province. But the resultant upsurge of press criticism, student agitation and legal demands for the release of political prisoners forced him to suspend the guarantees again and reimpose full censorship. Most worrying of all for Batista, the US government in March suspended a shipment of arms, as a sop to the growing criticism in the American media and Congress of the government's close ties with an unpopular dictator.

The proposed general strike was the main topic of discussion at a meeting which Castro held in mid-March with members of the Movement's National Directorate. The idea was that the strike would trigger a national uprising, led by the MR-26-7 cadres in the cities. Some members of the National Directorate argued that the time was not ripe. The MR-26-7 underground in the cities had very few weapons with which to launch an uprising. Under pressure from Castro, however, the meeting agreed that the strike should go ahead in the near future, the exact date to be decided by the leadership in the cities. Faustino Pérez was given responsibility for co-ordinating the final preparations.

One of the questions which Castro discussed at length in the Sierra was whether the guerrillas should shave off their beards. The plan was that if the national strike took hold, the Rebel Army would occupy the towns in Oriente. Castro wanted his men to look like a smart and disciplined force. Meneses said that beards made the Rebel Army more exotic and therefore newsworthy. Others argued that if the rebels were without their distinctive beards, the army and police would be able to kill innocent civilians and claim that they were rebels. This argument persuaded Castro to leave the beards in place.

In the following weeks, several dates for the national strike were fixed and then postponed. Finally, at a meeting on 8 April with other anti-Batista groups, Faustino Pérez insisted that the strike must go ahead the next day, 9 April. The *Auténticos* and *Ortodoxos* refused to accept this, and withdrew their support. The others decided to go ahead regardless. The MR-26-7 clandestine radio transmitters had been preparing the public for the imminent announcement of a general strike, and it was judged that further delay would damage their credibility.

On 9 April the popular CMQ radio station was interrupted by a voice announcing that the general strike had begun. Listening in his camp in the Sierra Maestra, Castro leapt up in elation. He embraced his colleagues and told a visiting Argentine writer that they would soon be in Havana. He ordered immediate attacks on military posts to support the strikers. However, the rebel announcer on Radio CMQ was quickly silenced. A planned rebel announcement on television failed to materialise. During the rest of the day reports came in that more than fifty people had been killed in Havana and another hundred in Santiago, and that the strike had fizzled out. Intercepted police radio messages indicated that the police chief, under orders from Batista to act with the utmost severity, had told his men he wanted no wounded and no prisoners. Suspected strike organisers were arrested and their bodies later delivered to the morgue.

The strike was not a total failure. In the centre and east of the country, and especially in Oriente, there was generally strong support. But in Havana and other towns in the west, where the majority of workers lived, the response was weak. The date of the strike was disclosed only at the last moment, in order to deprive the government of time to prepare counter-measures. But it was the workers who were inadequately prepared. Some never heard that a strike had been ordered. Others, having been warned to beware false strike calls, hesitated to act. The government by contrast was ready to act with great ferocity. When strikers in Oriente realised that they were getting little backing from Havana, they too gave up the struggle.

The Communists could have given critical support. Over several decades the Communist Party had built up a strong following in the big unions, especially in the sugar industry. But the MR-26-7 organisers in most places had brought the Communists into the planning at a very late stage, or not at all, and this gave the Communists a pretext for sitting on their hands.

Castro was despondent and furious. Having built up expectations with talk of 'total war' and 'the final blow', he felt a devastating sense of failure. Later he would describe the outcome of the strike as 'the hardest blow suffered by the Revolution in its entire history'. He blamed the MR-26-7 leaders in the cities for incompetence, poor co-ordination and factional jealousy. He wrote to Celia Sánchez that he would never trust them again. 'I must take responsibility for the stupidity of others.' The result was that the leadership in the Llano lost more ground to the hard-line Marxists in the Sierra. From this time it would be the Rebel Army which took the political as well as the military decisions.

Batista was elated by the failure of the strike. It gave him the confidence to undertake a course which he had hitherto hesitated to attempt, an all-out military assault on Castro's mountain strongholds. Ten thousand soldiers, commanded by General Eulogio Cantillo and supported by armour, artillery and aviation, surrounded the Sierra Maestra and moved in for the kill, starting with a drive down from the north towards Castro's principal base.

As the campaign developed, however, it became apparent that geography, inexperience and low morale more than offset Cantillo's advantage in numbers and weaponry. Castro had only about 300 men, but he moved them rapidly to achieve a local superiority. He had marched back and forth through the Sierra during more than a year, and knew the terrain much better than his adversaries. He was constantly on the move, issuing orders, urging his men to dig trenches and above all not to waste ammunition. When confronted by a large force he withdrew, laying mines and preparing ambushes. For a few tense days he was worried that his radio transmitter and ammunition dump would be overrun. But his tactics slowed and eventually halted the offensive.

At the point of the army's greatest advances, the rebels were confined to the highest parts of the central spine of the mountains. But the approaches to the crest were, as Castro said, like the pass of Thermopylae. A few well-armed men on high ground, protected by trees and rocks, could hold off hundreds struggling up the slopes. The army suffered heavy losses of men and equipment. In July 1958 a whole battalion was trapped in a narrow valley, surrounded, and forced to surrender. Two hundred and twenty soldiers were captured, disarmed and handed over, with demoralising publicity, to the Red Cross. In August more than a hundred more suffered the same fate.

During the eleven weeks of the campaign Castro wrote several letters to the officers commanding the forces opposing him, always in a chivalrous tone. 'After all,' he informed General Cantillo, 'we are your compatriots, not your enemies . . . Perhaps when the offensive is over, if we are still alive, I will write to you again to clarify my thinking, and to tell you what I think we, you, and the army can do for the benefit of Cuba.' To a battalion commander whom Castro had known at Havana University, he wrote:

> It would have been hard to imagine when we were together at the university, that one day we would be fighting against each other, even though we perhaps do not even have different feelings about our country . . . I have often wondered about you and the comrades who studied with you. I said to myself: 'Where are they? Have they been arrested in one of the many conspiracies?' What a surprise to learn that you are here! And although the circumstances are difficult, I shall always be glad to hear from you. I write these lines on the spur of the moment, without asking you for anything, only to greet you and to wish you, very sincerely, good luck.

This was the officer whose battalion was subsequently surrounded and cut off. Castro then wrote to him again: 'I offer you an honourable, dignified surrender. All your men will be treated with the greatest respect and consideration. The officers will be permitted to keep their weapons.' When they eventually did surrender, after several unsuccessful attempts to break out of the encirclement, Castro ordered Guevara to prepare lunch for the prisoners, before they were released to the Red Cross.

Guevara disapproved strongly of the tone of Castro's letters to the enemy. In his view, old-fashioned courtly chivalry had no place in the implacable class war of the twentieth century. But Castro had been made into a Spanish gentleman at his boarding schools, and this could not easily be eradicated. At another level Castro understood that it was not good for morale, for a soldier about to enter battle, to be confronted with the thought that perhaps after all the enemy were not such bad people. He had a much more acute sense of psychological warfare than did the austere Guevara.

During the offensive there was heavy aerial bombardment, not only of Castro's positions but also of the houses of farmers and peasants who lived in the area and provided logistic support. This stoked the fires of Castro's feelings about the United States. The aircraft and other equipment had been supplied by the United States under programmes which in theory allowed for their use only in external defence. Moreover, Castro heard that the bombers were being armed and fuelled at the US naval base at Guantánamo on the south-east coast of Oriente, and that 300 rockets had just been handed over in Guantánamo to the Cuban Air Force. No new arms sales had been approved since March, but the US government took the view that contracts signed before March must be honoured.

The Americans faced a dilemma. They did not like the systematic use of torture and murder by Batista's police, but at the same time they were appalled at the possibility of a Castro victory. While much of the American media took at face value Castro's bland assurances of goodwill towards private property and foreign investment, the government had intelligence about the Communist sympathies of some of his closest associates. In a remark which later became famous, the head of the Caribbean desk in the State Department said that many people thought Batista was a son of a bitch, but American interests came first: 'At least he is our son of a bitch.'

Castro was well informed, through an agent in the Cuban Embassy in Washington, about American official thinking. He wrote to Celia Sánchez: 'When I saw the rockets being fired at Mario's house, I swore to myself that the Americans would pay dearly for what they are doing. When this war is over a much wider and bigger war will begin for me: the war that I am going to wage against them. I know that this is my real destiny.'

Raúl Castro, who had been relatively inactive in the north-east of Oriente during the fighting in the Sierra Maestra, now proceeded to 'arrest' Americans as a lever to persuade the US government to stop the use of the Guantánamo base to support Batista's bombers. He seized a total of forty-nine Americans, twenty-five civilians working at an American nickel mine and in a sugar mill, and twenty-four marines travelling in a bus near the Guantánamo base. This mass kidnapping caused outrage, and demands for retaliation, in the

American media and Congress. Communications between Fidel and Raúl were difficult, and it is uncertain whether Fidel had authorised Raúl's action. In any event Fidel claimed not to know about the kidnappings and to be making investigations. After three weeks, during which there was no bombing, the kidnapped Americans were released.

Some time later, with the embargo on new arms contracts confirmed in the United States, the British government spotted an opportunity to boost its exports. Egged on by the General Manager in Cuba of the Shell Oil Company, an ardent supporter of General Batista, Britain signed an agreement to supply Cuba with seventeen Sea Fury aircraft and fifteen Comet tanks. Castro sent a message to British Prime Minister Harold Macmillan urging him not to approve the supply to a dictator of weapons which would be used to kill innocent civilians. He recalled the suffering of the British people under aerial bombardment during the Second World War. The message went unanswered and unheeded.

The motives for the contract at the British end were commercial rather than political. 'Export or die!' was the watchword. Fidel Castro, however, unaware that Britain's situation was quite so desperate, was tipped by news that the deal had gone ahead into another explosive rage. He announced that when Batista fell, the new Cuban government would boycott all British products, confiscate all British assets in Cuba, and arrest all British nationals in Cuba (no less). Meanwhile Revolutionary Law no. 4 introduced these measures in the territory controlled by the Rebel Army. The law was never applied rigorously, not least because the first British nationals with whom the rebels had contact were people providing moral and financial support. But Castro was not a man who readily forgot and forgave.

The Rebel Army's success in holding off Batista's army greatly strengthened Castro's position as the dominant force in the political opposition. Representatives of eight opposition organisations (including the MR-26-7 but excluding the Communists) met in Caracas and issued a 'unity manifesto', drafted by Castro, which endorsed the policy of armed resistance and, while recognising the contribution of other armed groups such as the *Auténtico* and DR guerrillas in the Escambray Mountains, gave clear pride of place to the columns of the Rebel Army. The exclusion of the Communists did not mean that Communist influence had declined. On the contrary, the Communists buried their old disagreements with Castro, and now actively sought a closer relationship. Castro welcomed their support. Disillusioned with the MR-26-7 organisation in the cities, he looked to the Communist Party to provide a disciplined mass organisation supporting the revolutionary measures which he planned to introduce post-Batista. Carlos Rafael Rodríguez visited Castro in the Sierra, and set up a permanent liaison.

Some of the more anti-Communist members of the Movement, notably Faustino Pérez and Carlos Franqui (the journalist running Radio Rebelde), objected to Rodríguez's prolonged presence at the Rebel Army headquarters, and tried to persuade Castro to send him packing. Rodríguez had made himself at home even to the extent of following the Rebel Army's norm of growing a beard. Castro answered the critics by saying that it would be unkind to throw out Rodríguez just when he was beginning to look like Lenin. Castro in fact greatly admired Rodríguez's sharp intellect, and would give him an important role during many decades.

With morale at rock bottom after the failure of the summer offensive, the Batista army began to disintegrate. Some soldiers defected, and others refused to fight. Castro could switch from defensive to offensive tactics. Columns led by Camilo Cienfuegos and Che Guevara, with 82 and 148 men respectively, broke out of the mountains and moved West. Choosing difficult terrain which the army preferred to avoid, they pressed on to the central province of Las Villas, sidelining the efforts of the four guerrilla groups which had earlier established themselves in the Escambray mountains.

In mid-September 1958 Fidel himself moved with his main force into the lowlands of western Oriente, to begin the process of surrounding the main army concentration in Santiago. He moved forward slowly, capturing some army posts and bypassing others. He told Melba Hernández that his military tactics were the same as in ping-pong: always return the ball where your opponent least expects it. Further east, columns led by Raúl Castro and Juan Almeida formed the other side of the pincer movement. To keep up the psychological pressure, Radio Rebelde broadcast a string of communiqués, proclamations and ultimata, all played back by a powerful transmitter in Venezuela. By November most of Oriente and Las Villas provinces were under rebel control. Only the capitals, Santiago and Santa Clara, remained in government hands, and their fall looked imminent. In December Manuel Urrutia, the Provisional President-Designate, flew into the Liberated Zone with a consignment of weapons donated by Admiral Larrazábal, the President of Venezuela. He met Castro and found him cool and offhand. This was Castro's way of nipping in the bud any illusion that, as Provisional President, Urrutia would exercise real power.

On Christmas Eve Castro allowed himself the luxury of taking Celia Sánchez to a family dinner in Birán. His mother Lina and older brother Ramón laid on a sumptuous meal and the best cigars for the conquering hero. The burning of cane-fields by Fidel's rebels was forgiven and forgotten. Lina asked if Fidel wanted to shave. He said he had no time. (The beard was now a badge of honour.) In this happy atmosphere he might have talked all night, but he stood up obediently when Celia told him it was time to go.

With the situation in Cuba deteriorating by the hour, the United States government was now on red alert. President Eisenhower was advised that although Fidel Castro was probably not himself a Communist, his movement had been penetrated by Communists, and if he formed a government it would probably include Communists. US Ambassador Smith, with the support of prominent American businessmen, had been urging his government to give Batista enough military and other assistance to enable him to survive. But in consultations in Washington the Ambassador was persuaded that Batista was now a lost cause, and that the best way to keep out Castro would be for Batista to go into exile and be replaced by a military junta with wider support and a cleaner reputation. The best man to head the junta would be General Cantillo, who had been removed from command in Oriente after the failure of the summer offensive. Cantillo was widely seen as an honourable professional officer who had been unfairly treated by Batista. The State Department also favoured the inclusion of Colonel Barquin, a capable and prestigious officer in jail in the Isle of Pines for plotting against Batista.

A special emissary of President Eisenhower went to Havana to persuade Batista to leave. Batista tried to argue that his position was stronger than the Americans thought, but accepted that he could not survive without their support. He reappointed Cantillo as commander in Oriente. Cantillo, in close consultation with the US Embassy, began sounding out potential junta members. He hoped to bring Castro on board by presenting his manoeuvres as a plot to oust Batista (he was in fact in close touch with Batista) and by offering participation in a provisional government to Urrutia and other civilians to be nominated by Castro. On 28 December he flew to a meeting with Castro in Oriente.

Castro had been in occasional contact with Cantillo since the time of the summer offensive. When Cantillo was removed from command in Oriente, Castro wrote to him urging him to do his patriotic duty and come out openly against Batista. Now that Cantillo had been reappointed as commander in Oriente, Castro was suspicious of the motives for Cantillo's visit to him. He told his colleagues that to bring about a rapid and bloodless end to Batista's government, he was willing to consider giving Cantillo a job, perhaps as Defence Minister, in a post-Batista government. But Cantillo would have to accept the Rebel Army's terms rather than the other way round.

The meeting between Castro and Cantillo lasted four hours. Cantillo said that most of the army, including the troops in Santiago, were willing to join forces with the Rebel Army to get rid of Batista. Castro said he would not accept a coup or the formation of a military junta in Havana. Cantillo said he could arrange for the garrison in Santiago to surrender to Castro and to join the rebellion. They would then march together to Havana, precipitating the collapse of Batista's government. Castro insisted that Batista should not be allowed to escape. He must be put on trial as a war criminal. Cantillo accepted this plan of action, but said he could not prevent Batista from flying out of Havana. It was agreed that the army rising in Santiago should take place at 3 p.m. on 31 December.

The sand was running out rapidly for the old order. On 30 December Che Guevara's column took control of most of Santa Clara, the capital of Las Villas province. Cantillo urged Batista to leave while he could. He sent a message to Castro saying that circumstances had changed and that action would now be taken at the national level. Shortly after midnight on 31 December, Batista wrote a letter of resignation, urging the armed forces to obey the new government 'of which General Cantillo has taken charge'. He then took his family and closest associates to the military airfield, gave some final words of advice to Cantillo, and flew into exile. In the morning General Cantillo went to the presidential palace with Carlos Piedra, who as the senior judge of the Supreme Court was now under the Constitution the nominal Head of State. Watched by Cantillo, Piedra announced a ceasefire and signed decrees appointing the members of Cantillo's new government.

In his headquarters in Oriente, Castro reacted furiously to the first report of Cantillo's action. 'This is a betrayal, a cowardly betrayal!' Brushing aside suggestions that they wait for confirmation of the news from Havana, he ordered his men to prepare for an immediate advance on Santiago. He spoke personally on Radio Rebelde, ordering his troops to move forward on all fronts, and to enter into talks only if the enemy offered to surrender. 'Revolution, *yes!* Military coup, *no!* Coup d'état behind the backs of the people, *no!* Coup d'état in agreement with Batista, *no!* Taking victory away from the people, *no!*' He asked the people to prepare for a general strike to force the unconditional surrender of Batista's army.

Events in Havana moved fast. Cantillo barely had time to receive congratulations from a diplomatic delegation, including the Papal Nuncio and US Ambassador, before the junta collapsed. Cantillo was placed under house arrest by Colonel Barquin, acting on behalf of the MR-26-7. Barquin had been released from prison in the Isle of Pines, and had just flown in to Havana.

During this momentous New Year's Day, the streets of Havana had for some hours been eerily silent and expectant. Then, as the realisation spread that Batista had gone, the city erupted into noisy celebration. There was some vandalism and attacks on the property of Batista supporters, including the Shell manager, but on the whole the mood was joyful rather than vengeful. Castro made a second broadcast on Radio Rebelde, ordering the MR-26-7 underground to assume the role of police and to maintain order. He urged everyone to refrain from acts of vengeance, promising that war criminals would be arrested, tried and punished.

Castro was determined to prevent the anarchic violence and looting which he had witnessed in Bogotá in 1948, and which had occurred in Havana after the fall of Machado in 1933. It was the explosion of uncontrolled violence following the departure of the dictator Machado which had created the conditions for Batista's original rise to power. Now the MR-26-7 militants emerged from hiding, displaying their red and black armbands, and quickly put a stop to the activities of individuals smashing parking meters and other symbols of Batista's rule.

In the early hours of 2 January, Cienfuegos and Guevara led their men into Havana, and took over Camp Columbia and La Cabaña military base. The previous day Colonel Barquin had taken command of Camp Columbia, on behalf of the MR-26-7. Accompanied by Armando Hart, the MR-26-7 leader who had also just been released from prison in the Isle of Pines, Barquin telephoned Castro's headquarters and said: 'Put Fidel Castro on the line.' But Barquin had months earlier turned down a proposal that he join forces with the Rebel Army. Castro now refused to speak to him, or even to Hart. 'Tell him I'll speak only to Camilo.' Justifying himself later, Castro said: 'Why the hell should I talk to a man who had spurned the Revolution?'

Castro now moved into Santiago, and received from Colonel Rego the surrender of the Moncada barracks. He then went to the main square where a huge crowd was gathering. He told them that he had heard that he was expected that day in the capital of the Republic. He was already in the capital of the Republic. *Santiago* was the capital of Cuba. It was the first decision of the Revolution. (It would be quietly forgotten when the practical difficulties sank in, but it suited the moment.)

Castro recalled 1898. Then General Calixto García, the leader of the independence forces fighting against Spanish rule, led his column to the Heroic City of Santiago, but was not allowed to enter or to raise the Cuban flag. Instead the United States expeditionary force, already in Santiago, raised the Stars and Stripes over the Governor's palace. With the exuberant crowd cheering him on, Castro announced: 'The Revolution begins now . . . This time it will not be like 1898, when the North Americans intervened at the last moment and took over our country.'

Castro told the crowd about his dealings with General Cantillo, and why the assumption of power by a new military junta was unacceptable. He said most men in the armed forces were decent and honourable. Only a small minority had committed crimes against unarmed civilians, but they must be brought to justice. He spoke about the role played by women in the Rebel

Army, and said that discrimination against women would now end. On and on he talked. Dawn was approaching, but Castro was not tired, and the crowd was certainly not tired. More and more Castro became the people and the people became Castro:

When I landed with 82 men on the beaches of Cuba, and people said we were mad, and asked us why we thought we could win the war, we replied: 'Because we have the people behind us!' And when we were defeated for the first time, and only a handful of men were left and yet we persisted in the struggle, we knew that this would be the outcome, because we had faith in the people. When they dispersed us five times in forty-five days, and we met up together again and renewed the struggle, it was because we had faith in the people. Today is the proof that our faith was justified.

Castro was not only the people, he was the embodiment of the history of Cuba. He recalled the frustrated dreams of the independence fighters. He said that, after having dinner with his mother a few days earlier, he had stopped during the night at the monument to the Protest of Baraguá. At Baraguá Maceo, defeated and powerless, nevertheless refused to accept the terms imposed by the victorious Spanish general, because they did not include independence and the abolition of slavery.

At that late hour, we were the only people present in that place. We thought of the daring feats of our wars of independence, and how those men fought for thirty years and in the end did not see their dream come true, but witnessed only one more frustration. Yet they had a presentiment that soon the revolution of which they dreamed, the nation of which they dreamed, would become reality . . . In my mind's eye I saw these men relive their sacrifices, I felt their dreams and their aspirations. The men who fell in our three wars of independence now join their efforts to those of the men who fell in this war, in the struggle for freedom. We can tell them that their dreams are about to be fulfilled, and that the time has finally come when you, our people, our noble people, our people who are so enthusiastic and have so much faith, our people who demand nothing in return for their affection, who demand nothing in return for their trust, the time has come, I say, when you will have everything you need . . .

9 Power

Bliss was it in that dawn to be alive. And indeed, the dawn of 1959 in Cuba was one of the most comprehensively blissful moments in any country's history. Six months earlier quite a few middle-class Cubans had viewed the prospect of a Castro victory with trepidation. Six months later quite a few would already be worried at the direction the country was taking. But at the start of 1959 the overwhelming majority of the Cuban population, of all classes and races, were caught up in the mood of exhilaration and euphoria. The war was over. The years of fear and impotence were over. Suddenly everything seemed possible.

The atmosphere in Havana was thick with religious symbolism, which the materialistic and hedonistic values of many *habaneros* (people of Havana) did nothing to diminish. Castro was seen by many, especially women, as a Christ-like figure, the pure one descending from the mountains to clean away the dirt and corruption of the cities. Even the sinful and unworthy could now redeem themselves by demonstrating their support for the Revolution. Castro himself, now aged thirty-three, was a Marxist and atheist, but he knew how to exploit the religious feelings of others. A medallion of the Virgin of Cobre, Cuba's most revered image, was visible around his neck. He encouraged the legend that the Movement had started with twelve men. The temptation to create a parallel with Christ's apostles was too great to be resisted.

When the first rebel columns entered Havana, Guevara kept a discreetly low profile in La Cabaña fort, leaving the limelight to Camilo Cienfuegos. Camilo's austere figure, black beard and gentle, dignified manner gave him an even more Christ-like appearance than Castro. And the *barbudos*, the bearded soldiers of the Rebel Army, far from looting and raping as some had feared, turned out to be models of discipline and good behaviour. Meanwhile, the Maximum Leader himself approached slowly, allowing the excitement and expectation to build up. His triumphal progress from Santiago to Havana took five days. He travelled sometimes by jeep, sometimes by helicopter, and finally on the turret of a tank, greeted everywhere by adoring and grateful crowds.

Jules Dubois was a reporter for the *Chicago Tribune*. His testimony is typical of many:

> 'I must see him! I've got to see him!' one hysterical woman said to me, tears flowing from her eyes. 'He has saved us! He has liberated us from a monster and from gangsters and assassins!'
>
> That was not the isolated opinion of a lady filled with emotion at the arrival of Castro. It was a general opinion that thousands of Cubans volunteered without the asking. In all my years of reporting in Latin America never had I seen a similar tribute to one man.

At the numerous stops on the way to Havana, Castro gave speeches, press conferences and interviews. It was already apparent what would make the Cuban Revolution different from all previous revolutions. This was a revolution on television. Most people in the towns had access to a television. Day after day they watched him, Castro the tall, bearded warrior in a creased uniform, with his cigar and thick horn-rimmed glasses, Castro the philosopher king, Castro mobbed by crowds, Castro embracing the humble, Castro above all talking, explaining, teaching, justifying. Fired up with adrenaline, he slept two or three hours most days, but did not appear tired.

Military victory and public adulation had put almost unlimited power into Castro's hands. He had no intention of relinquishing it. But he kept his intentions concealed. For the time being he thought he could operate more effectively behind the facade of a moderate, reformist government. He used his unchallengeable position to get everyone to accept, even if reluctantly in some cases, that Manuel Urrutia was now the President, chosen by the people (Castro or the people, what was the difference?). Castro's right to interpret the people's will was the more unquestioned because he was disclaiming any personal ambition for himself. He said modestly that he had been asked by the President to serve as his military assistant, and that he would fulfil this role for as long as the President wished him to do so.

Urrutia was President, but it was Castro who took presidential decisions, often on the spur of the moment, consulting no one. He bumped into Carlos Franqui, the director of Radio Rebelde, shortly after Franqui had broadcast on Castro's orders a call for a general strike to thwart any attempt by the military to form a junta. Castro had been favourably impressed by Franqui's performance, and offered him the job of Labour Minister in the new government. At first Franqui thought he was joking. When Castro insisted, Franqui declined the offer, saying he had no knowledge of trade unions or labour management. Castro said that in that case he could be Finance Minister. Franqui said he knew nothing about finance. Castro was irritated. He had already offered the Finance Ministry job to Raúl Chibás, the *Ortodoxo* leader, who had turned it down for the same reason. 'Around here it seems no one knows anything,' he said. 'Do what you want and sort it out with Urrutia. I can't stand around waiting for a government to be formed.' Franqui said he wanted to start a revolution in Cuban culture. He had lots of contacts in Europe and Latin America – writers, artists, philosophers, scientists, film-makers – and wanted to invite them to Cuba to start a cultural revival. Castro looked grim. The last thing he wanted now was foreign intellectuals telling him how to run the Revolution. 'No, no, no! Franqui, you're crazy. Anything but that.' And without more explanation he jumped into his jeep and drove off to mix again with the adoring crowds.

Castro's boundless confidence in his own judgement often led him to swim against the current. At his moments of defeat and failure he exuded optimism and faith in ultimate victory. Now, in his greatest moment of triumph, he was more than usually alert to pitfalls and dangers. The Cantillo–Piedra junta proved stillborn, but Castro in his first public speeches was still preoccupied by the threat of a last-minute attempt by the military to cling to power. He used for the first time his technique of crowd manipulation, 'direct democ-racy', to beat down any such attempt. He asked his audience if they wanted a military government. 'No!' yelled the crowd. Did they want Mr Piedra as President? 'No! No! No!'

His many stops on the way to Havana were not only to bask in public acclamation, but also to receive reports on the situation of military units in the area, and to satisfy himself that local garrisons and government buildings were firmly in the hands of trusted MR-26-7 cadres. In fact by this time any threat from the army had melted away. Cienfuegos and his *barbudos* entered the great military base of Camp Columbia in Havana on 2 January 1959 with no opposition. This was where in 1933 Sergeant Batista had organised the 'sergeants' revolt' which first put national power into his hands. It was where General Batista had seized power again in 1952. It was where, two days earlier, President Batista had said farewell to his friends and collaborators. Now the officers and soldiers of Batista's army humbly stood to attention and saluted as the bearded youths of the Rebel Army walked in purposefully to take command.

The most immediate problem for Castro came from the Revolutionary Directorate. Despite the costly failure of the DR's attempt to assassinate Batista the previous year, and the death of their leader José Antonio Echev-erría, they retained strong support especially among students in Havana. They had also established a guerrilla front in the central Escambray Mountains, and fought alongside Guevara's troops in the final phase of the war in central Cuba. With the collapse of Batista's army, the DR demanded their place in the sun. DR militants fraternised and co-operated with the MR-26-7 in maintaining public order in Havana and elsewhere. But Castro wanted no one to take a share in the Rebel Army's glory. Che was ordered not to allow the DR guerrilla soldiers to march with his own column into Havana.

The DR leadership were upset at Castro's attitude. They were also unhappy at the way he had announced, without consultation, that Urrutia was the people's choice as President. They were even more annoyed when President Urrutia, acting naturally on Castro's advice, appointed a government of liberal technocrats and supporters of the MR-26-7. None of the other opposition groups were offered ministerial posts, Castro arguing that the situation called for a homogeneous government. Again, to deflect any charge of personal ambition, Castro could point to the fact that he himself and his closest associates (Che, Camilo, Raúl) were also outside the government, with only a military role.

The DR, flexing their own muscles, seized a large stock of weapons from a Cuban Air Force base, occupied the presidential palace in Havana, and took weapons, including even some tanks and armoured cars, to the university campus. Guevara and Cienfuegos had to use a lot of moral pressure to persuade the DR to evacuate the Presidential Palace in favour of President Urrutia. Even when this pressure was successful, Castro remained worried about the DR's accumulation of weaponry.

As he passed through Varadero on the final stage of the journey to Havana, Castro called on the parents of José Antonio Echeverría, the DR's former leader. As Fidel embraced Echeverría's tearful mother, she thanked him for what he had done. Due to Fidel, she told the press, the sacrifice of her son had not been in vain. Later, on the outskirts of Havana, Castro was reunited with his nine-year-old son Fidelito, whom he had not seen for more than two years. Once again the invincible warrior showed that he was capable of gentler emotions. Mirta, bowing to the inevitable, had agreed that Fidelito should be brought back from school in New York to rejoin his father.

Entering Havana at last on 9 January, Castro was greeted with church bells, factory whistles, ship sirens and naval gun salutes. He called at the presidential palace and addressed the public briefly from the balcony, but kept his big speech for Camp Columbia. Hitherto access to the great military base had been strictly controlled. Now, in another symbolic gesture, thousands of civilians were allowed to pour in to hear his speech. As he spoke, white doves symbolising peace were released, and one of them settled on his shoulder. This was almost certainly a prepared stunt, but it convinced many Cubans that Castro was indeed a man favoured by God, or the saints, or the Afro-Caribbean spirits.

In this first big set-piece speech in Havana, Castro displayed all his oratorical skills, later to become so familiar. His voice was surprisingly high-pitched in a man of so macho an appearance; he started slowly and hesitantly, as if needing the audience to help him, then gathered pace and volume, winding them up, building the tension, then suddenly releasing it in the least expected manner. After a thunderous passage he turned to Cienfuegos and said, like a schoolboy anxious for approval: 'Am I doing all right, Camilo?' 'You're doing all right, Fidel,' said Cienfuegos.

Despite this jocular exchange, the tone in this speech was sombre rather than triumphal. He said the future would not be easy. The danger came from divisions within the Revolution. The newly formed government were not geniuses, but were honest and would do their best. The MR-26-7 had played the major role in defeating the Batista dictatorship, and it was right that they should have a dominant role in the government. If the government did not perform well, the people would vote them out. Then, without naming the DR, Castro started to whip up the crowd against them. He said some people had seized weapons from a military base which was under the command of the Rebel Army. The weapons should be returned to the barracks where they belonged. Why had these weapons been taken? For what were they needed? Against whom were they to be used? The crowd shouted their indignation. Once again, Fidel's magic worked. The pressure of public opinion, strengthened by a demonstration by 'mothers' calling for the handing in of weapons, enabled Castro to bring the DR to heel without resorting to overt force.

Castro set up his principal office and home in the penthouse of the Havana Hilton Hotel, soon to be renamed the Havana Libre (Free Havana). There he held court to a stream of Ministers, journalists and foreign visitors, with Celia Sánchez as usual controlling access. He liked to visit the hotel kitchens unannounced, or to exchange banter and repartee with the journalists who lay in wait in the hotel lobby. He was often on the move. He travelled around Havana in a jeep, visiting factories and offices, receiving more adulation, listening to complaints and making notes to be passed to the government for action. He made lightning visits to outlying provinces, and a longer tour of Oriente. While working in the capital he would sometimes sleep in the Hilton, sometimes in the flat of Celia Sánchez in the prosperous suburb of Vedado, sometimes in a house in the seaside town of Cojímar east of Havana, sometimes in Che Guevara's house near the Tarara beach. He seemed at times disconcerted and unsure of his new role. Recalling this period in old age, he said that he had spent most of his life fighting against authority. Suddenly everything was changed. The skills and abilities which he had developed as a guerrilla leader were no longer relevant.

In Cojímar and Tarara Fidel could still play the role of conspirator, planning battles against his domestic and foreign enemies, discussing tactics with his closest intimates, such as Che Guevara, Raúl Castro, Camilo Cienfuegos and

Ramiro Valdés. Unknown to the official government, this government in the shadows was where the real power was concentrated. Raúl had already, during the war in Oriente, set up the G-2 security network. It was now expanded and gradually converted into the all-embracing intelligence and security apparatus which would always keep Fidel one step ahead of those plotting against him.

In locations outside Havana Fidel held secret meetings with the leadership of the Cuban Communist Party. He saw little long-term future in his own MR-26-7. It had the advantages and drawbacks of a broad church with no clear ideology. It had served its purpose in securing for him mass support from a wide range of opinion. In the weeks before and after his victory, thousands had jumped on the band wagon, without having any real revolutionary convictions. What he would need for the next stage, the shift to a more radical left-wing position, was a well-organised and disciplined elite, which only the Communists could offer. As he later explained: 'They had men who were truly revolutionary, loyal, honest and trained. I needed them.' The Communists for their part had mixed feelings about being courted by Castro. They liked the smell of power, but sensed that Castro's aim was to use them for his own purposes. The meetings with the Communists were highly secret. Castro did not at this stage want to alienate the moderate liberals who were supporting him. Nor did he want to give the Americans a pretext for direct intervention, as had happened a few years earlier in Guatemala. He said to Blas Roca, the Secretary-General of the Communist Party: 'Shit, we are the government now, and yet we still have to meet illegally!'

Castro's family life was also part public and part private. Fidelito could often be seen and even photographed with his loving father. But those who knew of Fidel's visits to the flat of Naty Revuelta understood that a heavy weight would fall on them if they talked about it too openly. In Naty's flat Fidel spent a lot of time playing with Alina, his three-year-old daughter. She enjoyed playing with him, but did not like the present he gave her of a bearded guerrilla doll. Nor did she like the smell and ash of cigars which he left everywhere, or the burly bodyguards who made themselves at home in the flat during his visits. She was told that Fidel was a relative. It was not until several years later that she learnt that Fidel was her father.

Castro knew that public knowledge of his affair with Naty would damage his image. At the same time he felt a moral obligation to acknowledge his paternity of Alina. He promised Naty that he would ask the Minister of Justice to introduce a new law which would make it possible for Alina to take his name. Meanwhile she was Alina Fernández, Naty's husband having magnanimously agreed to treat her as if she were his own child. When eventually, many years later, Alina was offered the possibility of being officially a Castro, she rejected the offer, preferring to remain a Fernández.

For Naty the problem was not the legal position of Alina, but her own relationship with Fidel. Now separated from her husband, and cold-shouldered by many of her upper-class former friends, she did everything possible to ingratiate herself with Fidel after his arrival back in Havana. From the Sierra Maestra he had sent her a bullet as a token of his affection. She was still as attractive as ever, and very much in love with him. She hoped now to marry him, despite having turned down the offer of marriage made when Alina was born and Fidel was in Mexico. She tried to dress and act like a revolutionary, and expressed enthusiastic agreement with Fidel's plans and ideas. She was given some tasks which showed that she was still in favour, such as finding a suitable school in Havana for Fidelito. But as far as marriage was concerned she had, as Castro himself put it, missed the bus. The old passionate relationship never really returned. Fidel's visits became more infrequent and then stopped. Naty thought she had a big enemy in the form of Celia Sánchez. This was probably unjust, since Celia merely understood and acted on Fidel's wishes. Celia did not mind Fidel sleeping with other women, and indeed she acted as procuress on top of all her other roles. Meeting Fidel's physical needs did not involve trespassing on Celia's territory as principal confidante and companion. But there was no room for Naty. When she went to Celia's flat to ask to see Fidel, she was kept waiting and then told that a meeting would not be possible.

Why did Fidel not marry Celia? She was clearly devoted to him, and was spending more time with him than either Mirta or Naty had ever done. Perhaps Celia was, as many suspected, a lesbian. But this need not have ruled out marriage. She could the more easily tolerate his infidelities. Fidel's need for sex was strictly physical. He was, on the evidence of a model who claimed to have slept with him, 'the worst lover in the West'. A quick coupling, and then get on with more important matters. There were rumours among Castro's entourage that he had sounded out some trusted colleagues about the possibility of his marrying Celia. The head of the Communist Party was said to have advised that it would be bad for the Revolution for Fidel to marry a girl of bourgeois background (and with anti-Communist prejudices). Perhaps Fidel was glad to have this advice, preferring to avoid any closer personal ties.

In these early weeks in Havana, Castro certainly had little time for his private life. The first big issue was retribution. There was mass euphoria over Batista's fall, but also anger and a desire for revenge. As Batista's grip had weakened, the brutality of his henchmen had increased. Many people had relatives or loved ones who had been killed or ill-treated by soldiers or police, or by unofficial thugs such as the 'tigers' who operated in Oriente. New revelations in the press kept emotions on the boil. Only a week before Batista's departure, four Catholic students carrying supplies for the MR-26-7 had been arrested, tortured over several days in an army post, and then hanged. The priest who found the bodies also found the remains of dozens more victims buried in shallow graves.

The anger directed at Batista's thugs was inevitably extended to Batista's foreign friends and supporters, and especially the US government. The Cuban press was now laying bare the extensive aid and training given to Batista's armed forces and police by US military missions over many years. The US Embassy was revealed to have maintained very close links with the hated SIM military police. *Bohemia* carried a photograph of the US Ambassador under a caption which said: 'Smith laughed and partied while Cuba drowned in blood and horror.'

Castro had not forgotten Britain's supply of aircraft and tanks to Batista in the last months of the war. Within a few days of his arrival in Havana, he raised the issue with the British Ambassador. He said he wanted good relations with Britain, but feelings were running strong. Some gesture from Britain was needed to enable him to cancel the law imposing a boycott of British goods. He suggested the British government issue a statement expressing regret over the supply of weapons to Batista, and offer to pay for a thousand houses for peasants in areas that had been subjected to bombing attacks. The Foreign Office toyed with the idea of a statement expressing goodwill towards the new government, but ruled out any apology or act of atonement. Frustrated by British officialdom, Castro turned to the Shell Oil Company, whose former manager had been instrumental in arranging the arms deal, and who were now anxious to undo the damage. Addressing the workers at the Shell oil refinery, Castro said the company was willing to give all its employees a large wage increase, and to contribute US$250,000 to build peasant houses. In view of this, and despite the absence of any expression of regret from the British government, he would recommend, if the workers agreed, that the boycott of British goods be lifted.

Castro had repeatedly told the people not to take justice into their own hands, but had also repeatedly promised that those responsible for killings and torture would be punished. In the Free Territory a Revolutionary Law had been promulgated prescribing death by firing squad for war criminals. Che Guevara and Raúl Castro, as well as Fidel, had presided over executions during the war. In the town of Camaguey, on the road from Santiago to Havana, Castro had, in response to public pressure, ordered his military commanders to prepare new special tribunals, and to execute by firing squad those guilty of killing unarmed civilians.

The special tribunals, composed mainly of officers in the Rebel Army with little or no legal training, went to work rapidly. The type of justice dealt out was popular among most Cubans, but went down badly abroad, and especially in the United States. Judgements were reached, and sentences carried out, with what seemed to many foreign observers to be unseemly speed. In Santiago, where Raúl Castro had been left as military commander, seventy-one members of Batista's armed forces were sentenced to death, and executed. Film of a condemned man being gunned down by a firing squad caused a wave of international shock and condemnation. Some US Congressmen and sections of the American media described the executions as a bloodbath, accused the new government of seeking vengeance rather than justice, and talked of possible reprisals such as cutting imports of Cuban sugar.

Castro reacted to this criticism with indignation and outrage, creating a vicious circle. Asked by a journalist in the lobby of the Hilton Hotel what he thought of the possibility of American intervention, he replied that if the US Marines invaded, 'two hundred thousand gringos will die'. This typical piece of off-the-cuff histrionics was viewed by many in the United States as gratuitously offensive. And the more he whipped up public support for the executions inside Cuba, with crowds shouting *'Al paredón!'* ('To the wall!'), the more negative the reaction abroad. At a huge rally in Havana on 22 January he asked those who thought that the war criminals should be executed to raise their hands. When they all duly did so, Castro said: 'Gentlemen of the diplomatic corps, gentlemen of the press of the whole continent, the jury of a million Cubans of all opinions and classes has voted!'

In another deliberate act of defiance towards his foreign critics, he staged the first Havana trial before a mass audience at the Sports Palace. The defence counsels appeared to do their best, but the crowd frequently shouted insults at the defendants, and the outcome was never in doubt. The principal and most notorious defendant, Major Sosa Blanco, was certainly guilty of many atrocities; but in the trial he conducted himself with dignity and even humour, describing the proceedings as a Roman circus. Most of the international press shared this judgement. Later, in a final gesture of contempt for conventional due process, Castro angrily rejected the acquittal of a group of aviators (charged with bombing civilian targets) and ordered a retrial, at which they were found guilty and given long prison sentences. He explained himself in a sentence which to many people merely confirmed that legality had been superseded by arbitrary power: 'Revolutionary justice is not based on legal precepts, but on moral conviction.'

On television Castro expanded on the reasons for contesting the court's acquittal of the airmen. He said that just as a war criminal had the right to appeal against a verdict, so the prosecution, representing the Revolution and therefore the people, had the right to appeal against an unjust verdict. Champions of the principle of double jeopardy were appalled. But there were not many such people in Cuba. Most Cubans accepted and indeed welcomed

Castro's position. It increased their sense of liberation. He was liberating them not only from the tyranny of Batista, but from the tyranny of a legal system which had rules and codes and procedures, but did not deliver justice. Under the old system money, influence and clever lawyers would enable a man to get away with murder, while the poor found no redress. For years the American mafia had run huge gambling and prostitution rackets, in collaboration with corrupt Cuban police officers, and had enjoyed impunity from the law. Most Cubans had more confidence in Fidel's moral conviction.

The US government faced a dilemma. They were under domestic pressure to condemn the trials and executions, but realised that official public criticism would merely stimulate anti-American sentiment. Some members of the Administration already favoured a hard public line against Castro, accompanied by covert preparations to overthrow him. The majority, however, wanted to keep their options open. They hoped that after a period of letting off steam the Cuban government might, if not provoked, gradually settle back into a more moderate and responsible attitude. The State Department therefore kept a prudent silence about the trials, and sent repeated messages expressing a wish for good relations. After a speech in which Castro attacked his American critics, the US chargé d'affaires (Ambassador Smith had resigned and left) told Castro in person that the United States wanted good relations. Castro replied politely that he was glad to hear it, and that he too hoped for good relations. But his actions did not change. It did not suit him to distinguish between a privately friendly US government and a publicly hostile US Congress and media. He may have believed that, despite their assurances, the State Department were encouraging and orchestrating a media campaign against him. In any event he adopted the principle that the best means of defence was attack.

He was especially infuriated by Americans who referred to the condemned men as 'Batista supporters', implying that support for Batista was their only crime. 'We are not executing innocent people or political opponents. We are executing murderers.' He accused the Americans of hypocrisy, saying that Batista did not give his opponents any sort of trial: he just had them killed, and there were no protests in the United States. 'They did not write against the dictator, because the dictator was nothing more than the servant of their economic interests. Who are they to protest, who had war criminals in their service?'

Deliberately widening the argument, he railed against United States support for other brutal dictators such as Somoza in Nicaragua and Trujillo in the Dominican Republic. He attacked the use of nuclear weapons by the United States in Japan. He said the total number of war criminals executed in Cuba was four hundred, 'one for every thousand men, women and children murdered in Hiroshima and Nagasaki'. In another speech he said: 'When Cuba was governed by thieves, there were no campaigns in the United States. When Cubans were being killed every night, when young men were found murdered with a bullet in the head, when barracks were heaped with corpses, when women were violated, there were no campaigns. Nor did Congress, with rare exceptions, speak out to condemn the dictator.'

All this emotion was genuine enough. But Castro had the ability to be passionate and calculating at the same time. Having a foreign enemy was useful in consolidating support and national unity. Castro also had a more specific reason for stirring up feeling against the United States. He was preparing the ground for a much more fundamental conflict, which he knew was inevitable. The government formed by Urrutia would be an interim government. It was to start the revolutionary programme, but only the relatively easy and uncontroversial parts, like replacing corrupt officials and starting a national campaign against illiteracy, while Castro consolidated his power base and prepared for the more difficult stages.

He had not worked out in detail the whole revolutionary process, but he intended to transform totally the system of ownership of land and industry. The egalitarian society which he planned to create would necessitate a degree of expropriation and state intervention which was bound to bring him into conflict with two powerful forces, the United States and the Cuban middle class. Therefore, to push through his programme successfully he would first have to weaken both the internal and external opposition, and above all their ability to reinforce each other. Any nationalistic conflict with the United States would help to drive a wedge between the United States and its Cuban natural allies. He did not stage public executions in order to provoke a conflict with the United States, but when American criticisms began, he exploited to the full the resentments which they aroused within Cuba.

The Ministers in Urrutia's government were mostly middle-class social moderates, some strongly anti-Communist. But they were all nationalists and therefore 'anti-imperialist'. They were at one with Castro in wanting to diminish the political, economic and cultural dominance of the United States in Cuba. They went along without too much crisis of conscience with both the executions and Castro's angry rejection of American criticism. Roberto Agramonte, the former *Ortodoxo* leader and now Foreign Minister in Urrutia's government, defended the executions with foreign diplomats by saying that they were the only means to prevent enraged victims of the Batista era from taking justice into their own hands. This was the sort of pragmatic argument which did indeed help to assuage foreign opinion. Men like Agromonte did not contest the basic political values and beliefs which the United States shared with most of the Western world. Constitutions should be respected. Political parties should be allowed to compete freely. Governments should be formed by the victors of a free election. The judiciary should be independent of the executive, and should act in accordance with due process. These were the values that had been implanted in Cuba in 1898, and to which many Cubans continued to pay at least lip service.

Castro's position was different. He certainly did not want to appear apologetic or defensive about the revolutionary trials. His objective was not to win approval abroad, but rather to wean Cuban public opinion away from the assumption that their great and successful northern neighbour was the model to be copied, and was anyway too strong to defy. What right had the Americans to give Cuba lectures in justice and democracy?

Castro was not yet openly rejecting the central features of Western democracy, but he was moving in that direction, and the seeds of such a rejection, based on 'moral conviction', had been sown at an early age. At school he had learnt moral and spiritual values. Some things were good and some things were bad. Stealing was bad. Helping the poor was good. When he grew to maturity and looked at his country, what did he see? As individuals, Cubans were no more wicked than other people. Indeed many had admirable qualities of kindness and generosity. Yet their governments, whether elected or not, had almost invariably been characterised by corruption, theft, graft, cynicism and self-indulgence. Why was this? What had the democratic constitution and the independent judiciary done but protect and consolidate social division and social injustice? What did political parties do but make false promises and squabble over the spoils of power? A political system which enabled a few to increase their huge wealth, while keeping a majority in squalor and misery, must be wrong. When had the crimes of the rich and powerful ever been punished? What was the use of penal codes and 'due process' if they produced the wrong results?

Some of the worst of Batista's cronies had taken refuge in the United States, which was refusing to extradite them. This was another stick with which he could beat the Americans. But he assured the crowds that these traitors would not go without punishment:

> There can be no worse penalty for the traitors [shouts of 'To the wall!'] – no, a punishment worse than the firing squad – than the penalty of being unable to feel this pride and this dignity, this feeling of generosity and unselfishness, this feeling of infinite love and hope with which our country rewards those who know how to be its true sons! And being deprived of this happiness, of this satisfaction and this pride, being deprived of this feeling, having to live in envy and despair, having to weep when the people laugh, having to laugh when the people weep, this is a worse punishment

than the firing squad. Having to live with the eternal shame of having no homeland, having to live in the cold without a people and a country, this is a worse penalty, because it is the moral firing squad for traitors!

Early in January, all political parties in Cuba were abolished for the time being. Other decrees dissolved the Congress elected under Batista, banned from political life everyone who had participated in the rigged elections of 1954 and 1958, froze the bank accounts of officials suspected of corruption, and appointed new people to numerous posts in the executive and judiciary, including thirty-six out of forty Supreme Court judges. Further decrees revised the Constitution to make it compatible with what the revolutionary government was doing. Urrutia's Prime Minister, Miró Cardona, suggested that only a Constituent Assembly could properly produce a new constitution, but this objection was brushed aside. Fidel wanted it, and that was enough.

Castro said that in the first months of liberation it would be a crime to thrust people into politics. Most people, including foreign observers, assumed that he envisaged only a pause before normal political life was resumed and elections held, as he had often promised. But if they had looked more closely at his words, they might have foreseen the actual course of events. Electoral politics, in the sense understood by Castro, was not a valued right of which people had been deprived during the Batista era, but something unpleasant and discreditable, which it would be a crime to 'thrust' on the people. The newspaper *Revolución,* the mouthpiece of the MR-26-7, celebrated the abolition of political parties with enthusiasm. It said the Revolution was doing away with 'the views of the past, all the old political games. Party politicians should not be allowed to undermine the Revolution with their opportunism and hypocrisy.' As for elections, Castro said they would be held in fifteen months, 'more or less'. Shortly afterwards, it was 'not before eighteen months'. Then a new slogan started being heard: 'Revolution first, elections afterwards.' Finally it was said that elections should be held when the Revolution was complete, and the people literate.

The MR-26-7 did not need to be abolished, since it was not a party but a 'movement'. Castro had earlier considered converting the MR-26-7 into a political party, which would participate in elections. He had envisaged that there would be a phase of traditional party politics before he had built up enough support to move to a one-party or no-party state. Now, however, he decided that the massive popularity which he enjoyed enabled him to move faster. He talked of the MR-26-7 only in the context of its historical role and achievements, not as an organisation with a future. He was no longer the leader of a mere movement, still less of a political party, but of the whole people. He represented the Revolution, and the Revolution represented the people. Everyone could and should support the Revolution. Those who did not, the counter-revolutionaries, were against the people, almost by definition servants of some anti-Cuban interest. Again, many Cubans happily accepted Castro's dismissive views on political parties and elections. There had been elections under Batista, and the result was always a foregone conclusion. In 1959, with Castro's public support so clear and so overwhelming, what need was there to test it in elections?

At a big rally, Castro said that enemies of Cuba might think they could destroy the Revolution by assassinating him. They would not succeed. If he were killed, leadership of the Revolution would be taken over by men more radical than he. To avoid any doubts over the future, he would propose that his brother Raúl be named as his deputy and successor. He said he would have preferred to nominate someone who was not a relative, to avoid charges of nepotism, but Raúl was the man best qualified to assume the task.

Having named his successor (everyone knew that what Castro 'proposed' was a done deed), Fidel set off on his first visit abroad. He invited himself to Caracas to attend the first anniversary of the overthrow of the dictator Pérez Jiménez, and to thank the Venezuelans for the moral and military aid which they had given to the Rebel Army in the final stages of the war in the Sierra Maestra. He was greeted at all his public appearances in Caracas by huge cheering crowds. President-Elect Rómulo Betancourt said that, if Fidel were running for office in Venezuela, he would win by a landslide. He made numerous public speeches, calling for close ties between Cuba and Venezuela and implying, discreetly by his standards, that the United States and its business interests were the main threat to progress in Latin America. In a private conversation with Betancourt he asked if Venezuela would be able to supply Cuba with oil and a loan of US$300 million, since Cuba could become embroiled in 'a game with the gringos'. Betancourt was alarmed by this request, and avoided any commitment.

As a schoolboy, under the influence of his Spanish teachers, Castro had dreamed of a strong and united Latin America, which would be able to stand up to the all-powerful United States. He always believed that his destiny was to act on a wider stage than Cuba. When the war in Cuba was nearly over he told the Communist Carlos Rafael Rodríguez that after the fall of Batista, he intended to devote his energies to the overthrow of the dictators in Guatemala and the Dominican Republic. Rodríguez took this as meaning that Castro had no ambition to govern Cuba. He was mistaken. Castro aimed to rule Cuba, but also to promote revolution throughout the region.

On his return from Venezuela, Castro was forced to recognise that he could not continue to run a government to which he technically did not belong. President Urrutia, with his Prime Minister and cabinet, tried to act always in accordance with Castro's wishes. Ministers who were relatively close to Castro, such as Education Minister Armando Hart and Defence Minister Augusto Martínez Sánchez, visited the Hilton Hotel quite frequently to discuss plans and programmes with Castro. But Castro seldom turned up at meetings of the cabinet in the presidential palace. No one paid much attention to government decisions unless they knew that Castro had personally endorsed them. Celia Sánchez, ever the efficient administrator, expressed the view that having two centres of authority would not work, and that Castro should run the government directly and openly.

The crunch came over a relatively minor issue. It was the accepted view of all the revolutionaries that gambling and prostitution were among the most degrading and demeaning features of Batista's Cuba. The government therefore foresaw no difficulty when they ended the national lottery, and closed the casinos and brothels. However, hundreds of people who were affected – waiters, croupiers, prostitutes, etc. – protested to Castro about the loss of their livelihood. Castro told the government to reverse the decision, arguing that the workers involved should be retrained or found alternative employment before the establishments where they worked were closed down. Moreover, Castro wanted to use the national lottery as a source of government revenue. Upset at being repudiated in this way, Prime Minister Miró Cardona proposed that he should resign, and that his post be taken by Castro himself. With some show of reluctance Castro agreed to become Prime Minister. At the same time the role of the President was greatly reduced. He no longer presided over cabinet meetings, and became a largely ceremonial figure. The post of Prime Minister, which when Miró Cardona held it involved little more than bureaucratic co-ordination, became with Castro the absolute and exclusive centre of power.

Bringing power and responsibility together did not, however, mean that government business was now conducted smoothly and efficiently. Castro's temperament was a major obstacle. He was often several hours late for appointments, including cabinet meetings and public events where tens of thousands of people were waiting for him. He seemed indifferent both to the inconvenience and to the waste of resources which his unpunctuality caused. Although consistent and unyielding in his strategic objectives, he underwent disconcerting changes of mood and tactics, to the extent that amateur psychologists sometimes speculated about symptoms of manic depression. Ministers could find him at times impatient and offhand, but then at the next meeting, as if to make amends, warm and interested. After ignoring for several weeks the requests of the new US Ambassador for a meeting, to demonstrate that the Ambassador was no longer the most important man in Cuba, he attended an intimate dinner with him at short notice and listened politely and responsively to the Ambassador's lengthy explanations of American policy.

As head of government Castro took little interest in day-to-day economic management. But from the start he showed a fatal attraction to gigantic schemes to conquer nature and change the landscape, the sort of projects that appealed to other modern pharaohs such as Mussolini and Stalin. Having no great rivers to dam or divert, he devoted his energy and enthusiasm to a project to drain a huge swamp, the Ciénaga de Zapata, which stretched many miles inland from the Bay of Pigs on the south coast of Central Cuba. He planned to convert this virtually unpopulated region, infested with mosquitoes and crocodiles, into a rich area for rice-growing and tourism. He paid frequent visits to the swamp. On one occasion his motorboat was snagged and sank beneath him. He leapt onto a spit of dry land and sat there patiently reading a book, while colleagues organised a rescue. On another occasion his helicopter pilot, Air Force Commander Díaz Lanz, set off to fetch more petrol, leaving Castro on the beach of the desolate Bay of Pigs. Díaz Lanz crash-landed in the swamp and failed to return. Castro and his companions had to walk more than ten miles to find a telephone to summon help. By this time a huge search was in progress, in the course of which Raúl Castro in turn crashed in a light aircraft. Raúl's aircraft was found half-buried in mud, but it was several hours later before Raúl himself was found alive and well. Despite these setbacks Fidel proceeded to build a floating house on a lagoon in the middle of the swamp, which he used as a retreat and place to entertain special guests.

Castro now turned his mind to another heroic and ultimately impossible task: to win over North American public opinion, while maintaining his defiant and antagonistic attitude towards the US government and towards American economic interests in Cuba. He prepared the ground by softening his line on war crimes. At a special congress of the MR-26-7, several delegates argued in favour of ending the execution of war criminals. Hardliner Raúl said these opinions were 'shit'. Fidel, now playing the role of moderate, called Raúl to order, and told him to apologise. The congress approved a telegram to military commanders ordering an end to executions. Raúl later reported that the telegram arrived too late, since the last criminals sentenced to death had already been executed. As with other apparent disagreements between Fidel and Raúl, it was difficult to know whether this display of dissension was for real. Probably it was theatre, designed to make both the hawks and the doves believe that they had got their way, and for good measure to create the impression that the alternative to Fidel would be even tougher.

In April Castro visited the United States, in response to an invitation from the Society of Newspaper Editors. He had hesitated over whether to accept the invitation, expressing to colleagues the worry that if he were received by President Eisenhower he would look like just another Latin American stooge fawning on the superpower. However, he decided that he had sufficiently demonstrated his anti-imperialist credentials. He had broken with tradition by paying his first overseas visit to a Latin American country. His visit to the United States was in any event unofficial, and he would treat the people rather than the government as his main interlocutor.

He went with a large delegation, which included some prominent businessmen and excluded all Communists and other extreme left-wingers. He made a big impact, attracting crowds everywhere and engaging in debate and repartee with everyone he met. Following the advice of an American public-relations company, he remained polite and good-humoured even when subjected to hostile questioning. Students and other liberal elements gave him a warm and even enthusiastic reception. But any good feeling towards the United States which this might have fostered in Fidel was offset by irritation at the patronising tone adopted by many of his interlocutors, and by the aggressively persistent questioning from the press about his Communist links. And indeed most Americans, like their government, viewed the bearded revolutionary with deep misgivings, and in some cases with fear and loathing. The previous month the National Security Council and the CIA had been authorised to plan means of removing Castro.

President Eisenhower arranged to be out of Washington during the five days when Castro was there, and Secretary of State Dulles had just resigned on health grounds. The government did not want to snub Castro openly, thereby giving a pretext for more anti-American rhetoric, but nor did they want to give him the seal of approval which a meeting with the President might have implied. Officials in the State Department were relatively well disposed and willing to talk about possible aid projects. But Castro wanted no discussion of aid. He was determined to demonstrate that he was not like all the Latin American leaders who went to Washington with a humble begging-bowl. The many economic experts in his delegation began to wonder why they had been asked to come.

So what did Castro want to achieve during this visit? Partly his objective was to 'know your enemy'. Partly it was to encourage and strengthen the small but vociferous pro-Castro lobby inside the United States. Partly it was just to make a splash on the world stage, and to challenge publicly the American assumption that the Caribbean was their natural sphere of influence. Even his jokes were often barbed. Introduced to the man in the State Department who was in charge of Cuban affairs, he said: 'I thought I was in charge of Cuban affairs.' Above all, he wanted to impress a new and difficult audience. He was a great performer, and like a great actor or musician he *enjoyed* performing. In New York he set out to show that he was a man of the people, performing antics in front of animals in the zoo and eating a large meal in a cheap Chinese restaurant. He brushed aside the efforts of Carlos Franqui and others to interest him in a more intellectual agenda, such as seeing the paintings by Picasso and Lam in the Museum of Modern Art.

His PR skills at public gatherings in the United States were indeed so effective that Raúl Castro telephoned to express anxiety that media coverage was giving the impression of a sell-out to the imperialists. Castro was also successful in winning friends in his confidential meetings. He had a long session with a CIA expert on Latin America, Dr Bender, to whom he explained that he was allowing the Communists to show their heads so that he could later deal with them more effectively. Bender was persuaded that Castro was not only not a Communist, but was anti-Communist. He and Castro agreed to exchange secret intelligence on Communist infiltration.

Bender was easier to charm than Vice-President Nixon. Castro's long meeting with Nixon served only to deepen mutual mistrust and antagonism. Nixon confronted him with evidence of growing Communist influence in Cuba. Castro brushed this aside, saying there was no need to be so frightened of the Communists. He talked about the government's plans in health, education and agrarian reform. Nixon raised the executions and the failure to set a date for elections. When Castro said that the people supported the revolutionary trials, and had no interest in early elections, Nixon replied that a leader should do what was right, and not just follow the crowd. Clearly unimpressed by Castro's ideas of economic reform, Nixon advised that he should learn from the economic success of Puerto Rico. He suggested that Castro send an adviser to study the Puerto Rican example.

Castro felt that he was being patronised and humiliated. When Nixon later gave his version of the meeting to the press, Castro's body language was clear to those who knew him. On the surface he remained courteous and correct, but he was struggling to contain his anger and resentment. Nixon, for his part, was grandly condescending. In a confidential note for President Eisenhower he reported: 'He is either incredibly naive about Communism or under Communist discipline. My guess is the former.' Nixon also commented that Castro was more ignorant about economics than any leader he had ever met, and that Castro's anti-Americanism was 'virtually incurable'. Nixon's only concern about his own handling of the meeting was that perhaps he might be criticised for giving Castro too much time.

From the United States, Castro went on to pay a successful and trouble-free visit to Canada. But by now Raúl was agitating for him to return to Cuba. Raúl wanted Fidel to make a big anti-imperialist speech on May Day, to demonstrate that he had not gone soft on the capitalists. But Fidel thought he had a subtler way of making trouble for Uncle Sam. He flew on to Trinidad, Brazil, Argentina and Uruguay, mainly in order to attend a Latin American economic conference in Buenos Aires. There he proposed a regional common market and an ambitious development plan, to which the United States would be invited to contribute US$30 billion. He argued that such a 'Marshall Plan' for Latin America would ultimately benefit the donors as well as the recipients. The Americans dismissed the proposal as unrealistic. Castro also failed to get the support that he had hoped for from his fellow Latin Americans. Most Latin American leaders (even if not their peoples) felt comfortable under the protective wing of the United States, and had no desire to follow Castro's provocative line. A few years later President Kennedy would put forward the Alliance for Progress, involving almost as huge an amount of American aid as that proposed by Castro. By one of the ironies of history, the undeclared purpose of Kennedy's action would be to immunise Latin America from the threat of Castroism.

Castro's star performance during his foreign tour made him even more attractive to the numerous women inside and outside Cuba who wanted to conquer the conquering hero. In the United States he had met a beautiful Argentine psychiatrist, Dr Lidia Vexel-Robertson. She followed him to Cuba, apparently with the aim of marrying him, but was annoyed to find that a German girl, Marita Lorenz, was in residence next to Castro's apartment in the Hilton Hotel. Marita was the daughter of the captain of a German cruise ship that had visited Havana in February. Fidel went on board, took a liking to Marita, and tried to persuade her to stay in Cuba as his secretary and interpreter. At the time she declined, but Fidel was persistent. He sent an aide to talk to her again when the cruise ship was docked in New York. This time she accepted the offer and moved to Havana. However, Lidia Vexel-Robertson managed to ensure that Marita was, as the latter put it, placed under virtual house arrest. While aggrieved over this treatment, Marita met and became friendly with Frank Sturgis, head of security in the Cuban Air Force and later famous as a CIA operative and Watergate burglar. Meanwhile, Celia Sánchez saw off the threat from Vexel-Robertson.

Castro usually refused to answer questions from journalists about his private life. This was partly to protect his image; but there was also some truth in his frequent assertions that his private life was not important. He had normal fatherly feelings towards his children, but seldom allowed them to distract him from the business of government. When Fidelito, who liked riding around Havana in an army jeep, was involved in a serious accident, Fidel refused to be diverted from the interview which he was giving at the time on television. He was told that Fidelito was in hospital with internal injuries which would require a major surgical operation. Raúl, who was with him in the television studio, said he should go to the hospital, since the surgeon would need his permission to operate. Despite this, Fidel persisted with the interview. Only when members of the studio audience ('the people') interrupted to insist that he go to Fidelito, did he relent. Fidelito's mother Mirta was at the hospital, increasingly angry at Fidel's delay. When he finally arrived she told him coldly: 'You haven't changed. You are as irresponsible as ever.'

In a sense, Mirta was right. Castro often acknowledged his failings as a parent, but he did not change. He had numerous affairs, but accepted no commitments. The only great passion in his life was making revolution. He had little interest in routine administration. He complained about the number of people who constantly pestered him for decisions. It was the big fundamental revolutionary changes which absorbed his attention. During the summer of 1959 he was stepping up the pace of economic reform. He had little knowledge of economics, but this did not prevent him from having clear and strong opinions. He had little respect for those American-trained economic advisers who told him that market forces could be channelled but not suppressed. For Castro, market forces were the negation of both morality and rationality. For him the market was the law of the jungle, the law that allowed the strong to prey on the weak, keeping countries like Cuba in a state of dependency, exporting cheap raw materials and importing expensive manufactured goods. How absurd to assume that the unplanned results of market forces could be more beneficial than the results of rational planning and centralised direction! Had not the Soviet Union demonstrated that state control and state planning, with strong and determined leadership, could in a single generation convert a backward agricultural country into an industrial superpower? Were not the shibboleths of free enterprise merely a pretext enabling large companies in Cuba, often foreign-owned, to make huge profits from the toil of Cuban workers who continued to live in abject poverty?

Firm in these convictions, Castro issued a series of decrees designed to redress the social injustices and inequalities which prevailed in Cuba. Public utilities, including the US-owned national telephone company, were ordered to reduce their charges, the first step on the road to nationalisation. Rents for low-cost accommodation were halved. Low salaries were raised. Above all, the project closest to Castro's heart, agrarian reform, was finally enacted. The law was signed by every member of the cabinet, most of whom were given scarcely enough time to read it. In May he announced it to the world in melo-dramatic fashion from his old headquarters high up in the Sierra Maestra. The big estates, with some exceptions where large units were necessary (notably for sugar production), were broken up and converted into co-operatives or smallholdings. Some 200,000 peasants would receive title deeds to the land they worked. Castro made himself President of the National Institute of Agrarian Reform (INRA), which was responsible not only for the reorganisation of land holdings, but also for housing, electrification, health and education in rural areas. INRA constituted virtually a separate government, which ensured that national resources would be diverted away from privileged urban areas to the hitherto neglected countryside.

Some radicals, and even some foreign observers, thought the reform was moderate, since the maximum individual holding of 1000 acres was larger than many had foreseen. But private ownership of the redistributed land was something of a fiction. The land could not be sold and the extent of INRA control of co-operatives made them more like state farms than real co-operatives. Land owned by Batista, or *batistianos* (followers of Batista) who had fled or were dead or in jail, was directly taken over by the state. Where compensation was payable for expropriated land, it took the form of twenty-year bonds. The amount was determined in relation to the declared value of the land for taxation purposes. This was Castro's way of punishing those landowners, probably the majority, who had by persuasion or bribery obtained a low valuation of their land, in order to pay as little tax as possible. In any case the reform was radical enough to provoke protests from most landowners affected, including Fidel's older brother Ramón, who later in the year told the press that the reform would be disastrous for agricultural production. Fidel went to the offices of *Revolución* and shouted to the editorial staff that they should attack his brother without hesitation.

In practice, the implementation of the agrarian reform soon became less a matter of the letter of the law than of 'moral conviction', and of Castro's determination to break the power of the landowning class. He told the staff of INRA that the Revolution had ceased to be something romantic. It was now only for genuine revolutionaries, for those willing to say: 'Leave all that you have, and follow me.' In an even more explicit comparison with the first Christians, he told a Catholic congress that Christ's teachings had met a lot of opposition. 'They did not prosper in high society, but germinated in the hearts of the humble people of Palestine.'

So indeed it was. The economic measures alienated many wealthy Cubans who had at first hoped that Castro would restore democracy without undermining the economic status quo. At the same time they made Castro even more popular among most sections of the population. In the short term all except the very rich found themselves better off. Most workers, whether urban or rural, had more income and lower expenses. The disastrous macro-economic effects would take time to manifest themselves. The moderates in the government were, however, increasingly worried at the direction Castro was taking, and especially at the growing influence exerted by Communists within the administration. Communists were given control of a School of Revolutionary Instruction, where young officials and military officers were indoctrinated in Marxism. More and more policies were drawn up not within the relevant Ministry but in the Office of Revolutionary Plans and Co-Ordination, a sort of Marxist think-tank and kitchen cabinet.

The US Embassy formally conveyed the US government's 'concern' on behalf of US citizens affected by the economic reforms, and sought an assurance that compensation would be prompt and adequate. This was the start of a long and increasingly acrimonious exchange of notes thinly dressed in polite diplomatic language. American pressure made it harder for Cuban moderates to oppose the reforms without appearing to be in cahoots with the imperialists. *Revolución,* the mouthpiece of the MR-26-7, was instructed by Castro to stop attacking the Communist Party, on the grounds that it was essential to maintain national unity in the face of foreign pressure. Ministers who criticised the sometimes arbitrary and heavy-handed implementation of the agrarian reform were replaced. The Minister of Agriculture, who had not been consulted during the preparation of the agrarian reform law, was replaced by Pedro Miret, Castro's unconditionally faithful comrade-in-arms from the time of Moncada and the *Granma.*

Some anti-Communists started to jump ship. In late June the commander of the Air Force, Díaz Lanz, defected to the United States, and publicly denounced the growth of Communism in the armed forces, encouraged by Raúl Castro. He testified before the Internal Security Sub-Committee of the US Senate, implying (at least in the eyes of most Cubans) that what happened in Cuba was viewed as an *internal* matter for the United States. Díaz Lanz took with him several other air force officers, including his chief of security, Frank Sturgis, who in turn smuggled the disgruntled Marita Lorenz out of Cuba. She was quickly recruited by the CIA and later returned to Cuba. She went to the Hilton Hotel dressed in her Rebel Army uniform and used the keys she still held to steal documents from Castro's rooms.

President Urrutia denounced Díaz Lanz for his defection to the United States, but angered Castro by himself making a lengthy public attack on Communism, thereby implying that Díaz Lanz had a legitimate cause for concern. In private Urrutia was even more outspoken. He confided to his secretary that if the drift towards Communism continued, he might have to resign. The security apparatus built up by Raúl Castro and Ramiro Valdés ensured that Urrutia's private worries quickly reached Fidel Castro. Díaz Lanz's defection had made Castro extremely sensitive to such indications of disloyalty. He summoned the editor of *Revolución,* Carlos Franqui, and told him to prepare in strict secrecy, for publication the next day, 17 July, an especially large edition with huge headlines announcing Castro's resignation.

Neither Franqui nor the shocked nation reading the news were given an explanation of why Castro had resigned.

Castro then went on television to explain that he had been obliged to resign by the attitude of President Urrutia, who had shown no interest in promoting social improvements for the people. He had delayed or obstructed reforms proposed by the government. He had set a bad example by accepting a large salary and living in luxury. Instead of defending the Revolution against the attacks of Díaz Lanz, he had made himself another champion of anti-Communism. His attitude was close to treason. He was moreover planning actual treason. He evidently shared the same ideas as Díaz Lanz. With Castro out of the way, Urrutia would no doubt find plenty of American agents to serve in his government.

As soon as Castro stopped speaking, the news presenter started reading messages from the public furiously demanding Urrutia's resignation. Urrutia had watched Castro's broadcast on television with growing dismay. At first he asked to be allowed to speak on television himself, and was told that he could do so. But he abandoned any attempt to defend himself when an angry crowd started to gather outside the presidential palace. Instead he wrote a letter of resignation, slipped out of the palace through a side door, and later sought refuge in the Venezuelan Embassy. Osvaldo Dorticós, Minister of Revolutionary Laws and the Minister most in tune with the new and more radical direction of the Revolution, was appointed President of the Republic in place of Urrutia.

Castro said he would allow his own future to be decided at a mass public meeting in the Plaza Civica (later Revolution Square) on 26 July, the anniversary of Moncada. Tens of thousands of peasants travelled by their own means to Havana for the occasion. Thousands more were bussed in by government agencies. More than half a million people had assembled in the square before Castro arrived. When he finally appeared, the crowd cheered for ten minutes before he could start to speak. During his four-hour speech they frequently interrupted with roars of approval and support. At their insistence he agreed to resume the post of Prime Minister (which he had never in practice relinquished). At his invitation the peasants raised their machetes in the air and thundered their determination to strike down anyone who threatened the Revolution.

Urrutia, well-meaning but vain and self-important, was an easy target for Castro to destroy. A more serious challenge to the trend towards Communism came from Húber Matos, who was not a member of the old establishment but one of the most successful and popular officers in the Rebel Army. A former teacher and farmer, Matos had proved a brilliant military leader. Promoted to *Comandante* and given command of his own column, after the fall of Batista he was appointed governor and military commander of the central province of Camaguey. He complained to Castro about the rise in Communist influence in the armed forces. Reflecting the views of the ranch-owners in Camaguey, Matos also criticised the way the agrarian reform was being implemented. Castro did not like being lectured by Matos, but for some months chose to ignore him. The problem came to a head when Raúl Castro was appointed Minister of the Armed Forces. Matos viewed Raúl as the principal promoter of Communism within the government. He sent Fidel a letter conveying the irrevocable resignation of himself and fourteen fellow officers in Camaguey.

Had Matos merely resigned, he would probably have been allowed to go quietly. But his letter of resignation contained criticisms of Castro that were bound to ignite his blackest fury. After complaining of the increasingly arbitrary actions of the government, Matos said that great men became smaller when they started to be unjust. 'Now, Fidel, you are destroying your own work. You are burying the Revolution. Perhaps there is still time . . .' Castro wrote back immediately saying that Matos's allegations were false and libellous and that he was siding with Díaz Lanz and Urrutia. 'I am under no obligation to account to you for my actions, and you have no right to stand in judgement over me. Reading your letter I realised that you were unable to appreciate the tolerance and generosity with which I have treated you.' He said that since Matos had resigned irrevocably, he was sending Camilo Cienfuegos to take over command of the armed forces in Camaguey.

The challenge from Matos came at an extremely awkward moment. Castro had spent a great deal of time and money organising a huge tourist congress in Havana. Two thousand tourist agents from around the world, mainly from the United States, had been invited and lavishly entertained, in the hope of attracting millions of additional tourists to Cuba. Castro was warmly applauded when he told the delegates that Cuba was peaceful, friendly and welcoming to foreign tourists. It was immediately after this address that he received the letter of resignation from Matos. After receiving Castro's reply Matos planned to go on radio and television in Camaguey to defend his position. He was prevented from doing so, and Cienfuegos was sent to Camaguey to arrest Matos and his fellow officers. Later the same day Castro flew to Camaguey and spoke to a crowd of peasants who had been brought in from the surrounding countryside. His speech was carried live on national television. He accused Matos of being ambitious, ungrateful and treacherous towards the Revolution. Like Díaz Lanz and Urrutia he had tried to gain the support of reactionaries by peddling propaganda that the government was Communist. He had timed his barracks revolt to disrupt the tourist congress designed to bring hundreds of millions of dollars to Cuba.

Castro returned to Havana where he was due to address the tourist congress again. When he was on the seafront near the Hotel Nacional, a B-26 bomber flew overhead dropping leaflets signed by Díaz Lanz, calling on Castro to sack the Communists in his government. The aircraft, piloted by Díaz Lanz himself, made several passes over the city before flying back to the United States. Anti-aircraft guns fired at it but failed to make contact. Explosions were heard in various parts of the town. The press reported that two people had been killed and fifty wounded in the bomb attack. Díaz Lanz denied dropping any bombs, and it is possible that the casualties were caused by anti-aircraft shells. In any event public fury was vented against the United States. Angry crowds demonstrated outside the US Embassy and the Hilton Hotel. Castro on television denounced the role of the US government, saying they either deliberately connived in the bombing raid or did not know that their territory was being used for this purpose. Which was worse?

All this excitement totally wrecked Castro's earlier efforts to persuade the tourist congress and the world that Cuba was a peaceful and friendly place for tourists to visit. It deepened his anger against Húber Matos and strengthened the position of the hard-liners who argued that Matos's action was part of a conspiracy to bring down the government. When the government met to discuss what to do about Matos, Raúl Castro said he was a traitor and should be shot. A few moderates, notably Faustino Pérez, the man who had hidden with Castro under the sugar cane after the landing of the *Granma,* argued that Matos had committed no crime. But most shared Castro's view that Matos posed a serious threat. Matos was duly charged with counter-revolutionary activities. After an ugly show trial, in which Castro himself intervened at great length in support of the prosecution, Matos was sentenced to twenty years in jail. The message was clear. Anyone who opposed Castro's line was an enemy. Being anti-Communist was now synonymous with being counter-revolutionary.

Shortly after Matos's arrest, Camilo Cienfuegos took off from Camaguey in a light aircraft with an inexperienced pilot. The aircraft never arrived at its destination. A massive search failed to find any trace of either aircraft or passengers. Many of Castro's enemies, including Matos himself, believed that Castro organised Cienfuegos's death, due to his alleged reluctance to act against Matos. But there is no convincing evidence to support this supposition. At about the time of Cienfuegos' flight a Sea Fury was despatched to shoot down a light aircraft, presumed to have flown from Florida, which was reported to be dropping incendiary devices on cane-fields in central Cuba. The pilot reported that he had successfully carried out his mission. He may in fact have shot down Cienfuegos in error. But a normal flight path from

Camaguey would have taken Cienfuegos across a long stretch of sea, and a simple accident is another possible explanation of his disappearance.

What is certain is that Castro was now determined to assert his control over every institution in the country which could conceivably constitute a focus of opposition. Havana University, for generations a centre of dissent and agitation, was slowly but surely converted into a stronghold of conformism. Troublesome academics were expelled or neutralised. Among the students, the three strongest factions were the DR, the MR-26-7 and the Communists. Before the annual union elections Castro went to the university to address the students. Still immensely popular and therefore difficult to oppose, he argued that the Revolution faced both internal and external enemies. Divisions within the Revolution would play into the hands of its enemies. Unity was essential. If different factions tore each other apart, all would lose. In elections for office there should be an agreed candidate for each post, and everyone should rally behind the unity candidate. Anyone who tried to stand against the unity candidate was branded as a counter-revolutionary. The choice was between patriotism and treachery. Soon all offices were held by Castro's nominees.

In the trade unions, the anti-Communist majority, most of whom had rallied to the MR-26-7, were forced to share power with their Communist opponents, always in the name of unity. The Communists used tactics familiar in trade unions in other parts of the world. They packed meetings with their supporters and exploited the apathy and confusion of their opponents to gain disproportionate representation in union committees. But they knew that without Castro's protection they could quickly be crushed. They therefore acted exactly as Castro intended, as a disciplined and loyal elite imposing his line of 'revolutionary unity'.

The printers' trade union was the main instrument which Castro used to bring the media under his control. During his first months in power, Castro often talked about the virtues of a free press. He was so overwhelmingly popular that little appeared in the media which displeased him. But the sharp move leftwards in the second half of 1959 changed all that. Conservative editors and journalists became more hostile. Print workers in turn started to harass and disrupt editorial staff who persisted in attacking the government. The right-wing newspapers were vulnerable to attack, since they had mostly supported Batista, and many of the editors and journalists were known to have received undeclared subventions from the Batista government. In January 1960 Castro introduced a requirement that newspapers should print a 'clarification' by the printers' union to articles which they considered inaccurate or tendentious. This *coletilla* (tailpiece) was the beginning of the end of press freedom. Opposition newspapers struggled on for some months more, but a combination of political and financial pressures, and occasional exemplary arrests of outspoken journalists, eventually induced all the hostile papers, and television and radio stations, to conform or close down.

For those holding office in the government, the choice was even more stark. Those unwilling to work with Communists, like Faustino Pérez, resigned. In October 1959 Che Guevara, having spent two months during the summer visiting Third World countries mainly in Asia, replaced Felipe Pazos, the distinguished economist and co-signatory of the Sierra Maestra Manifesto, as Governor of the National Bank. According to a popular joke, Castro filled the post by asking his followers if any of them was an *economista*. Che Guevara raised his hand in the mistaken belief that Castro had asked for a *comunista*. The anecdote certainly conveys a sense of Che's qualifications for the job. Not surprisingly the announcement of his appointment caused panic in financial circles and a run on the banks.

10 Invasion

After nine months in power, Castro had made a lot of enemies. He went everywhere with a team of bodyguards. Even his closest associates seldom knew where he intended to spend the night. His security services were receiving numerous reports of plots to kill him. Groups of anti-Communist rebels, some supported by the CIA, had established guerrilla bases in the mountains of central Cuba. Thousands of middle-class people, including much-needed doctors, engineers and other professionals, were moving to Florida, hoping and expecting to return when the disastrous Castro government collapsed. The most militant exile groups were trying to speed up Castro's fall by sending boats and light aircraft to carry out sabotage. Factories were bombed, and cane-fields set on fire.

Castro had also alienated most members of his own family. The agrarian reform had provoked a public feud with his older brother Ramón. His youngest sister Juanita was outspoken in denouncing Fidel's leftist policies and hostility to the Church. She was especially furious when Fidel tried to stop their sister Emma from getting married in Havana Cathedral. Fidel and Raúl disliked the idea of an ostentatious middle-class wedding. They tried to persuade Emma, who had always supported Fidel in his youthful political escapades, to hold the wedding in a small, modest church. Juanita refused to accept Fidel's moral blackmail and shouted: 'It's Emma's wedding, not yours!' Fidel relented, and agreed to attend the ceremony in the cathedral. But he made his point by arriving a hour late and covered in mud. He had spent the morning setting an example by doing manual work on a farm.

Castro had not only alienated the Cuban middle class. He had also provoked the hostility of several other governments in the Caribbean. From the start he had openly promised to give 'hospitality' to refugees from right-wing dictatorships in the region. Groups of exiles undertook training in Cuba for armed action against Panama, Nicaragua and the Dominican republic. Castro denied any involvement in such activities, but few took his denials seriously.

General Trujillo of the Dominican Republic decided to hit back. He made contact with a group of anti-Castro conspirators in Central Cuba, mainly cattle-breeders and other landowners. The plotters thought that they had co-opted two of Castro's *Comandantes,* who then acted as a bait to draw Trujillo into a trap. On Castro's instructions, the false rebels sent a radio message to Ciudad Trujillo, saying that they had captured the town of Trinidad and asking for weapons to be sent to a nearby airfield. Castro and his bodyguards hid near the airfield. They watched as an aircraft arrived and unloaded munitions before flying back to the Dominican Republic. A second aircraft brought more weapons and nine Batista supporters, who went to a house which had been designated as a secret rendezvous. Castro in person then walked through the front door to carry out the arrests. More than a thousand alleged plotters in other parts of Cuba were later also arrested.

Castro believed that his main defence against plots to overthrow him was the support of ordinary Cubans. He still had the enthusiastic backing of most workers, peasants and students. He kept this alive by constant public speeches and television appearances. Nearly everyone watched television; and every day the television reminded them of how much they had benefited from the Revolution, and how much they would lose if the treacherous counter-revolutionaries, supported by the CIA, were to succeed in bringing the Revolution down.

In January 1960, however, Castro was upstaged on television, for the first and only time in his life. In the course of a long interview with a team of journalists, he was asked about two defectors from the air force. He said every revolution had a few traitors. These two had been helped and encouraged by the American and Spanish Embassies. He maintained courteous relations with the Spanish Ambassador, but was well informed about the sort of activities which his Embassy engaged in. The Spanish Ambassador, the Marqués de Vellisca, was watching the television at home and decided that Fidel had insulted him once too often. He drove to the television studios and marched purposefully to the room where Castro was talking. Officials and bodyguards, recognising who he was and uncertain whether he was expected, did nothing to stop him. Castro was in the middle of an exposition on capital investment in industry when the Ambassador burst onto the screen. Castro stopped in astonishment, half rose from his chair, and said: 'What do you want?' Ignoring Castro, the Ambassador turned to the moderator of the programme and asked for permission to make a statement. 'You should also ask permission from the Prime Minister of the Republic,' interjected Castro. The Ambassador said that he would gladly do so; he was sure that the Prime Minister, being a democrat, would not refuse his request. With millions of Cubans watching in amazement, a shouting match developed.

CASTRO: If they allow this sort of thing in Spain, I will allow you to do it in Cuba.

VELLISCA: In Spain they do not allow anyone . . .

CASTRO: I categorically refuse . . .

VELLISCA: I have been slandered . . .

ARMY COMMANDER ALMEIDA: Gentlemen, would you please take it easy

. . .

VELLISCA: He has not been invited . . .

At last someone thought to pull the plug. The picture disappeared from screens and the shouting was replaced by the solemn notes of the 26 July anthem. When the picture was restored, the Ambassador had been taken by the arm by the army commander and other dignitaries, and bundled out of the studio. Castro was lecturing the studio audience on the need for diplomats to show a minimum of dignity and respect to their hosts. Warming to his theme, he ridiculed Vellisca as a Falangist serving a ruler who went everywhere surrounded by Moorish guards. Didn't he know that Cuba was no longer a Spanish colony? Were these the diplomatic standards of Fascism? The studio audience, sensing that it was time for them to join in, started shouting: 'Throw out the bum!' Castro, quickly resorting to his favoured method of direct democracy, said his opinion also was that the Ambassador should be expelled. President Dorticós, Castro's tame head of state, announced pompously that as President he endorsed the Prime Minister's recommendation, which was therefore an official decision. The Ambassador was given twenty-four hours to leave the country. When he reached Madrid, General Franco is said to have told him: 'As a Spaniard, you did well; as a diplomat, very badly.'

Castro never doubted that his main shield against his enemies, internal and external, was 'the people'. But the people were helpless without weapons. In opposition he had often denounced the amount of money spent on the military. Now that his own power was threatened, he started looking urgently for sources from which to re-equip his armed forces, and to arm a national militia. The militia served a triple purpose. It constituted an armed political police, able to monitor and repress any anti-government movement among the population. It provided a first line of defence against an invasion, whether by anti-Castro Cuban exiles or by US Marines. Finally, the militia formed an armed support organisation independent of the regular armed forces. It thus reduced any risk that the Rebel Army might become a political force in its own right, and a potential threat to Castro's supremacy.

In the early months of the Revolution Castro bought large quantities of rifles and ammunition from Belgium. But as American hostility grew, the US government put pressure on its friends and allies not to supply arms to Cuba. Denied aircraft by the United States, Castro tried to buy seventeen British Hawker Hunter fighters to replace the seventeen Sea Furies which Britain had supplied to Batista. Under pressure from the US government, Britain refused to allow the sale. Foreign Minister Selwyn Lloyd told Parliament that such a sale would 'introduce a new factor into a still very delicate situation'. Castro responded to Britain's rejection with a public display of defiance, and a strong hint that he would look to the East for support. He told a mass rally: 'If we cannot buy aircraft, we shall fight on the land, if the time comes when we have to fight. If they don't sell us aircraft in England, we shall buy them from anyone willing to sell to us . . .'

Even Communist and neutral Yugoslavia decided not to put its good relations with the United States at risk by providing weapons to Castro. In the Cold War situation prevailing in 1959, the only industrialised countries securely outside United States influence were the Soviet Union and its Warsaw Pact allies. Castro had engaged in elaborate deception in an attempt to disguise the closeness of his relations with the leaders of the pro-Soviet Cuban Communist Party. He now needed the Communists not only to provide disciplined administrators, but also to facilitate an opening to the Soviet Union. He realised that only the Russians could enable him to escape the economic and military stranglehold of the United States. It was not the Russians but Castro who took the initiative in proposing closer relations. Indeed, the Soviet authorities were at first wary of a man who had for years been denounced by the local Communist Party as a dangerous adventurer. But when Castro began to attack anti-Communism as a threat to the Revolution, the Russians decided that he was someone with whom they could do business.

In October 1959 Castro set up the first of a series of meetings with the only available Soviet interlocutor in Havana, the Tass news agency representative Alexander Alexayev, who was a senior undercover officer of the KGB intelligence service. Alexayev was surprised to receive a message that the Prime Minister wished to have a 'friendly meeting' with him in his office in the INRA headquarters. Alexayev arrived with a gift of Russian vodka and caviar. Castro received him accompanied only by INRA Director Nuñez Jiménez. Following instructions from Moscow, Alexayev said the Soviet government and people felt great admiration for the Cuban leader, and for the work he was doing to achieve social progress for the Cuban people. This was more than an empty expression of diplomatic politeness. It was the first clear signal that the Soviet government accepted Castro as the leader of an authentic Revolution, and were not hung up on his many past public repudiations of Communism.

During the introductory pleasantries, Castro saw that Alexayev had noticed the medallion of the Virgin of Cobre which Castro wore round his neck. 'Don't worry,' said Castro, 'it's the image of a Christian saint which a little girl in Santiago sent me when I was in the Sierra Maestra.' Having made clear that the medallion did not indicate any allegiance to the Catholic Church, Castro suggested that they taste Alexayev's present of vodka and caviar. A secretary brought crackers, and the three men tucked in. 'What good vodka!' said Castro, 'what good caviar! Nuñez, I think it's worth establishing trade relations with the Soviet Union! What do you think?' Nuñez said he had recently visited a Soviet industrial and scientific exhibition in New York. It had been opened by Deputy Prime Minister Mikoyan. Why not bring the exhibition to Havana? Castro agreed, and asked Alexayev to support the idea. Alexayev said he believed the Soviet government would be glad to set up trade relations with Cuba. But surely the first step was for Castro to re-establish the diplomatic relations which had been broken off by Batista? Once embassies had been set up in Moscow and Havana, they could negotiate trade agreements. Castro argued that it would be prudent to start only with commercial links. It would be unwise to frighten the Americans by setting up embassies too quickly.

In subsequent meetings it was agreed that the Soviet industrial fair would come to Havana in February 1960, and that it would be formally opened by Deputy Prime Minister Mikoyan. Castro and Che Guevara negotiated through Alexayev a trade agreement which was ready for signature during Mikoyan's visit. The agreement offered Castro a lifeline against the threat of a US-led economic blockade. The Soviet Union undertook to import 425,000 tons of Cuban sugar in 1960 and a further 1 million tons in each of the following four years. They would pay for it mainly in oil, fertilisers and other industrial goods, as well as through the provision of technicians.

Castro accompanied Mikoyan on a tour of Cuba, travelling in a Soviet helicopter. He later recalled that during this tour he was nearly responsible for the world's first air hijack. The Soviet pilot took off with only enough fuel for twenty minutes flying. He then proceeded to fly in the wrong direction. The pilot refused to change course when Castro insisted that there was nothing but open sea on the route the helicopter was taking. 'I was in a difficult dilemma. I was about to drown out of courtesy. Either I drowned out of courtesy, or I had to hijack the helicopter.' Eventually he persuaded Mikoyan to instruct the pilot to turn back.

Castro was delighted with the agreement he signed with Mikoyan. Like many other people in that era, he and Guevara greatly overestimated the quality of Soviet technology. Dazzled by Soviet achievements in space and military rocketry, they saw no drawback in receiving payment in Soviet goods and services, rather than in convertible currency. They believed Khrushchev's boasts that the 'Socialist camp' was catching up the West, and would soon overtake it. It would be many years before the Cubans realised the crippling cost of tying their economy to the Soviet system.

Even if Castro *had* foreseen the economic drawbacks, he would still have gone ahead. He was willing to pay almost any price to be able to defy 'imperialism'. He saw himself as engaged in a race against time. Sooner or later, the United States would try to crush the Cuban Revolution. He could not hope to defeat an all-out US invasion. But by making the cost of such an invasion high, in both military and diplomatic terms, he could induce the Americans to choose other methods. The national militia could not stop the US Marines; but if the militia were sufficiently numerous, well-armed and motivated to inflict high casualties on an invading force, this would consti-tute an effective deterrent. Similarly, the trade agreement with the Soviet Union fell far short of a security guarantee, but it represented a gesture of political as well as economic support. It therefore raised the potential diplo-matic costs and risks of any American action against Cuba. The CIA would not be able to snuff out the Cuban Revolution, as it had snuffed out the Guatemalan Revolution, without any international repercussions.

In March 1960 a French ship blew up in Havana harbour. It had brought a cargo of Belgian arms and ammunition. Two massive explosions killed eighty-one people and injured hundreds more, including many Cuban dock-workers and firemen. Everyone in Havana heard the explosions and saw the great mushroom-shaped cloud of smoke rising slowly over the harbour. It was a disaster, but in every disaster Castro always looked for an opportunity. He saw the explosion as proof of the implacable and merciless hostility of the enemies of the Revolution, and especially of the Americans. There was no real evidence of American complicity. But who else had the means and the desire to weaken the Revolution's defences? Castro denounced the alleged American atrocity with every weapon in his oratorical armoury. He invented a new slogan, which for many years would be repeated at the end of every speech: '*Patria o muerte, venceremos!*' ('Homeland or Death, We Shall Prevail!') Was history repeating itself? In 1898 the US battleship *Maine* also blew up in Havana harbour. The Americans then assumed, also without evidence, that the Spaniards were responsible. They too invented a good slogan with which to rally public opinion: 'Remember the *Maine*!' They went to war and 'liber-ated' most of what remained of the Spanish Empire, including the Philip-pines and Cuba.

Castro's accusations of American sabotage and murder were the last straw for the US Administration. On 17 March 1960 President Eisenhower finally signed an authorisation for covert action to overthrow Castro. The plans had been prepared over the course of the previous year. A paramilitary force of Cuban exiles would be trained and equipped to invade the island. Meanwhile support would be stepped up for armed opposition groups inside Cuba, and for pinprick attacks by small groups of exiles.

A few months later the CIA received authorisation to work with the Mafia to assassinate the Castro brothers and Che Guevara. The Mafia were aggrieved at the loss of their gambling and prostitution rackets in Cuba, so official involvement in a hit against Castro could be plausibly denied, even if the direct perpetrators were identified. The Technical Services Division of the CIA considered various exotic possibilities, such as the famous exploding cigars and the powder designed to cause Castro's beard to fall out. But the technique actually tried was old-fashioned poison. Agents paid and trained by the CIA made several attempts to introduce poison pills into Castro's food; but they all failed.

In the spring of 1960 deliveries of Soviet crude oil started to arrive in Cuba. The government ordered the three major oil companies with refineries in Cuba (Shell, Esso and Standard Oil) to process the Soviet crude. They were reluctant to do so, since the refineries were geared to process the companies' own crude, normally imported from Venezuela. At the same time the companies wanted to avoid a head-on clash with the government. Left to themselves, they would probably have agreed to accept the Cuban demand. But following a strong steer from Washington, they refused. So the spiral of action and reaction continued. Castro seized control of the refineries and put in Soviet technicians to operate them. The US government cancelled Cuba's quota for sugar imports into the American market. Castro nationalised more American assets in Cuba, including banks and sugar mills.

He also tried to exploit the rapidly worsening relationship between the United States and the Soviet Union, following the shooting down over Russia of an American U-2 spy plane. Prompted by an appeal from Castro, Soviet leader Nikita Khrushchev said that in the modern age distance did not guarantee impunity. 'In a figurative sense, if it were necessary, Soviet artillerymen could support the Cuban people with rocket weapons.' This cautious and obscure statement was nothing like the explicit commitment of military support which Castro wanted, but it further alarmed and infuriated the Americans, especially when Khrushchev added that the Monroe Doctrine was dead. Under the Monroe Doctrine the United States gave itself the right to prevent any Old World country from interfering in the Americas. 'The only thing to do with something dead,' said Khrushchev wittily, 'is to bury it, so that it does not poison the atmosphere.'

Castro raised the temperature further by exaggerating the significance of Khrushchev's bluster. He was ill at the time, but insisted on giving a television interview from his sick-bed. He said that Cuba had the firm backing of the Soviet Union, and that Soviet missiles were real, not figurative. The Catholic bishops of Cuba, already aggrieved over increasingly virulent attacks on the Church by pro-Castro journalists, now publicly denounced Castro's government for seeking the support of the bastion of atheist tyranny. Thousands of Catholic students gathered in Castro's old school in Santiago and shouted: 'Cuba yes, Communism no!' Castro hit back with more attacks on the Church. Several Spanish priests were arrested and expelled. Left-wing students from other Latin American countries attended a big anti-imperialist congress in Cuba, after which some of them stayed on to undergo guerrilla training.

The Foreign Ministers of the Organisation of American States, meeting in Costa Rica, issued the San Jose Declaration, condemning the interference of 'totalitarian states' in the affairs of the hemisphere. US Secretary of State Herter had wanted the Declaration to condemn Cuba and Castro explicitly by name, but the Latin American Ministers, uneasily conscious of Castro's popularity in their own countries, preferred a vaguer wording. Castro replied that Cuba was being punished for breaking the chains which tied it to the United States. He issued a 'Havana Declaration', calling on the peoples of Latin America to break their chains also.

Such was the charged atmosphere in September 1960 when heads of government from around the world flew to New York for the General Assembly of the United Nations. Castro's mother Lina was among those seeing him off at Havana airport. She was worried that the Americans would try to kill him. Fidel became irritated by her fussing, saying that he had undertaken much more dangerous journeys without coming to harm. 'What about the *Granma*?' Once in the air, however, Fidel also began to worry about the dangers. He turned to his chief of security, Ramiro Valdés, and asked if they would have an escort plane. Valdés said no. Castro looked grim. 'What a mistake! If I were running the CIA, I'd shoot down the aircraft at sea and report it as an accident.' Valdés and the rest of the entourage went silent and looked nervous. They looked even more nervous when a group of US jet fighters streaked into view and flew close to them. But now Castro was relaxed. They were approaching the United States mainland. Castro was confident that the Americans would not shoot him down over their own territory.

The Shelburne Hotel in New York was persuaded by the State Department to put up the large and unruly Cuban delegation, but insisted on a cash deposit when they arrived. Castro took offence and stormed out. He went to the United Nations headquarters and told Secretary-General Dag Hammarskjold that he would remain there until hotel accommodation was offered to his delegation on reasonable terms. He threatened to bed down in Central Park, saying that his men were used to sleeping in the open. Finally the Cubans went to a cheap, run-down hotel in Harlem. As prostitutes and their clients came and went, Castro played host to sympathetic journalists and to an array of anti-establishment activists including Malcolm X.

When Khrushchev arrived in New York, he immediately proposed to call on Castro. Castro offered to call on Khrushchev first, as a mark of respect for the Soviet leader's seniority and for the Soviet Union's superpower status. But Khrushchev saw the propaganda benefits of a meeting in Harlem. It would draw media attention to American ill-treatment of both Cuba and their own black minority. With cameras flashing, the squat, portly, sixty-six-year-old Khrushchev embraced the tall, bearded thirty-four-year-old Castro.

The logistics of the embrace were difficult, as Khrushchev acknowledged many years later in his memoirs. Castro bent forward rather awkwardly over Khrushchev's bald pate, allowing the grinning Soviet leader to give him an enthusiastic bear-hug. The scene was a mixture of high drama and comedy. Khrushchev told journalists assembled outside the hotel that Castro was an heroic man who was leading the Cuban people in their struggle for freedom and independence. Asked by a journalist if he regarded Castro as a Communist, he replied that he didn't know if Castro was a Communist, but that he, Khrushchev, was certainly a *fidelista* ('believer in Fidel').

The next day Khrushchev staged a further photo-opportunity, walking the length of the General Assembly to give Castro another effusive greeting. Later each of the two men stood to lead the applause for the other's speech, even though Castro had broken the General Assembly's records, and most delegates' patience, by talking for four and a half hours. The Cuban delegation were invited to a dinner at the Soviet legation, where numerous toasts were drunk to undying friendship. During the dinner Khrushchev played the role of jovial buffoon, making jokes in dubious taste mainly at the expense of his glum-faced Foreign Minister, Andrey Gromyko. He blamed Gromyko for having established diplomatic relations with Batista's government. As a result, said Khrushchev, Gromyko should be tried for treason by one of Cuba's revolutionary tribunals. As for Castro's unwillingness to be called a Communist, Khrushchev related that when Castro died and went to heaven, St Peter ordered all Communists to take one step forward. When Castro did not move, St Peter shouted: 'You there! Are you deaf?' In this atmosphere, Castro had little opportunity to raise serious matters. But in a short private talk between the two leaders, Castro explained his need for weapons, including tanks and aircraft, to defend the country against an American-backed invasion.

Castro was probably not amused by Khrushchev's joke about his reluctance to be called a Communist. At this period he was still maintaining the public image of a nationalist and social reformer, not of a Communist or even Socialist. When the French philosopher Jean-Paul Sartre had visited Cuba earlier in the year, and praised Castro for introducing Socialism, Castro had quickly interjected that it would be best not to describe the Revolution as Socialist. Sartre promised not to use the word when he wrote about his visit. The Russians were also happy to go along with Castro's game-plan. Khrushchev assumed in any case that Castro's overtures towards the Soviet Union were opportunistic rather than ideological. Nevertheless, by the time Khrushchev met Castro in New York he was already confident, as he privately told his entourage, that Castro would become 'a beacon of Socialism in Latin America'. He believed that American hostility would drive Castro towards the Soviet Union 'like an iron filing to a magnet'.

Castro returned to Havana still nursing his anger and resentment over his treatment in New York. He had to fly back in a borrowed Soviet aircraft, his own aircraft having been impounded by the US authorities on the grounds that the Cuban airline owed money to American companies. He described the United States as a 'cold and hostile nation', and New York as a 'city of persecution'. Blacks and Cubans were routinely ill-treated. Newspapers served the interests of their big business owners, constantly duping and misleading their readers. How could it be otherwise in a country where everything and everybody was motivated by material interests, by money?

Castro now assumed that an American-backed attempt to overthrow the Revolution by force was inevitable and probably imminent. Following his initial approach to Khrushchev, Cuban officials started to negotiate secret contracts for the supply of tanks and other weapons from the Soviet Union and Czechoslovakia. To strengthen internal security Castro set up a new layer of protection, the Committees for the Defence of the Revolution (CDRs). In every village, every street, every city block, a committee was formed of trusted residents to keep an eye on other local residents, and to report to the authorities any sign of disaffection or unusual activity. In time, 80 per cent of the entire population would be part of the CDR system. It was a more comprehensive system of surveillance than even Stalin had created.

Castro also began to lose his scruples about the interrogation methods which he had so often denounced in the era of Batista. A reporter from *Revolución* obtained evidence that an officer in State Security called Escalona was engaging in 'apple ducking', pushing a prisoner's head repeatedly into a barrel of water to extract information. Carlos Franqui, the editor of *Revolución*, showed the evidence to Castro, believing he would be shocked and indignant. Instead, Castro produced the argument used by most governments which sanction torture. He said that a group of suspected saboteurs had been released for lack of evidence. Then they were arrested again and questioned by Escalona. He 'put the fear of God in them' and they confessed. As a result, a whole network was picked up and many lives saved. Franqui pointed out that this was exactly the argument used by Batista and his cronies. Castro was uneasy. He said that using 'a bit of pressure' could be justified, but that the Revolution would never use torture. He promised to ensure that Escalona did not go beyond acceptable methods. But when did 'pressure' become 'torture?' The crude physical tortures commonplace under Batista did not return. But rough treatment, darkness, solitary confinement, hunger, threats and other forms of psychological torture were used in this period in the cause of state security.

In October 1960 the US government prohibited most exports to Cuba. This was the beginning of the economic embargo or 'blockade'. The effect on the Cuban economy was devastating. Factories and assembly plants that depended on American imports were forced to close. The artificial boom created in the previous year came to an abrupt end. As usual, however, Castro turned hardship to his political advantage. The anger and resentment of Cubans affected by lay-offs and shortages was turned against the Americans. Castro said on television that the Cuban people would face months, possibly years, of hardship; but Cuba would not starve, and would not surrender. 1961, he said, would be the Year of Education. A massive programme of investment would make the Cubans the most highly trained and educated people in Latin America. This would enable them to diversify their economy and break out of the prison of dependence and underdevelopment.

Propaganda started to take some fairly grotesque forms. At Christmas 1960 a large marquee was illuminated with a novel version of the nativity scene. The guiding star was José Martí. The Three Wise Men, Fidel Castro, Che Guevara and Juan Almeida (a black member of the leadership) were bringing to the Cuban people the gifts of Agrarian Reform, Urban Reform and the Year of Education.

The CIA was in a hurry to get rid of Castro before he became more deeply entrenched. There were rumours, press stories and intelligence reports about the impending arrival in Cuba of Soviet weapons, including aircraft. By early 1961 it was known that Cuban pilots had been sent to Russia to train on MiG fighters. The Americans' main problem was that the anti-Castro exiles were extremely diverse, factious and quarrelsome. Every little group had its own leaders and its own programme. The CIA had a tough job forcing them to set aside their differences and accept incorporation in a broad-based Democratic Revolutionary Front (FRD). Young men judged to have suitable qualities and motivation were taken to military training camps in Guatemala. There the CIA created Brigade 2506, named after the identity number of a soldier who died in training. Many officers in the Brigade were former professional officers in Batista's army. But the CIA did not want to appear to be backing a restoration of the old dictatorship. The men chosen to provide the political leadership of the FRD were mostly democrats and disillusioned former supporters of Castro. The 'President' was Miró Cardona, the lawyer who briefly served as Prime Minister in the first government after Castro's seizure of power.

The CIA also stepped up military and other assistance to rebel groups already inside Cuba. In January Castro complained that 80 per cent of the 300 people in the US Embassy were spies. He ordered the Embassy to reduce its size to that of the Cuban Embassy in Washington. In response the United States broke off diplomatic relations completely, and withdrew all its staff. Heavily armed detachments of Cuban exiles in fast launches fired on ships trading with Cuba, and staged hit-and-run attacks on factories, sugar mills and other installations situated on the coast. The stage was set for what CIA Director Allen Dulles expected to be the last act in Castro's turbulent political career.

Castro had spies in all the main exile groups and was kept closely informed of their activities, including the military training in Guatemala. But the CIA kept a tight control of planning. The Cuban leadership of the FRD was kept in the dark about military preparations. Even the commanders of the Brigade were not told until the last moment when and where the invasion would take place. Some exile leaders were angry at being excluded from the inner circle of CIA planners. Others accepted the reasons for this tight security. Castro expected an invasion, and warned the population frequently that it was imminent; but he too had no foreknowledge of the time and place of the attack. He divided his army and militia into three sectors, covering the east, centre and west of the island. He expected a feinting attack at one end of the island, designed to draw away his forces, before the main invasion went ahead at the other end.

J. F. Kennedy, sworn in as President in January 1961, inherited from his predecessor the secret plan for the overthrow of Fidel Castro. He had doubts about whether it would work; but he was assured by the Chiefs of Staff and CIA, with all the strength of their professionalism and experience, that it would succeed, as had the similar project in Guatemala. It would have been disastrous for Kennedy to begin his presidency by appearing to lack the nerve to take tough action in defence of American interests. What would happen to the thousands of Cuban exiles in Central America, trained and prepared for action? Embittered and disillusioned, they would become a walking advertisement of Kennedy's weakness and inability to check Communist expansion. There was therefore never any realistic chance that Kennedy would cancel the operation. He made some minor changes, designed to reduce the visibility of United States involvement, and went ahead.

The Brigade undertaking the invasion numbered some 1,400 men, divided into five infantry battalions and one battalion of paratroops, supported by artillery and five tanks. In early April 1961 it was transported from Guatemala to Puerto Cabezas on the Caribbean coast of Nicaragua. The ruler of Nicaragua, General Somoza, was as keen as his Guatemalan counterpart to help the CIA and the Cuban exiles to get rid of Castro. Somoza went to Puerto Cabezas to wish the Brigade good luck. He jovially asked them to bring back some hairs from Castro's beard. On 13 April the Brigade set sail in seven ships, with US naval vessels providing an escort at a discreet distance. The ships were from various countries, several having been borrowed by the CIA from the United Fruit Company. The fleet had been preceded by a single ship which had the task of providing a diversion. Another ship set sail from Florida, with a small force whose job was to stage a diversionary landing in the easternmost part of Cuba.

Late on Friday 14 April Castro was in his military command post in Havana when a message arrived that a suspicious ship had been sighted close to land not far from Guantánamo. Castro and his army commanders had already concluded that a landing in Oriente was probably imminent. He now ordered twelve militia battalions in Oriente to move to positions on the coast. He remained at the command post all night, awaiting news of an attack. In the event the intended diversionary landing in Oriente never took place. All the possible landing sites were so heavily guarded by militia that the officer in charge of the operation decided not to go ahead.

In the early hours of Saturday, two days before the main fleet was due to arrive in Cuban waters, eight B-26 bombers, painted in the insignia of the Cuban Air Force, took off from a base in Nicaragua and flew the 750 miles to Cuba. At dawn six of them, operating in pairs, bombed and strafed the three Cuban military airfields. Their crucial task was to destroy the tiny Cuban air force on the ground, so that the invasion force would have command of the air during the landing. They damaged the runways and destroyed several of Castro's aircraft, before flying back to Nicaragua. Anti-aircraft fire failed to hit any of the attacking aircraft. Seven men in the bases were killed and fifty-two wounded. However, the raid was only partially successful. Some of the targets hit were decoys or aircraft already out of service. Some Cuban aircraft had been hidden. A few escaped damage by taking to the air. In particular, all four of Castro's operational Sea Furies remained serviceable.

It was announced in Miami that the bombing of Cuban airfields had been done by Castro's own air force. To support this story one B-26 flew direct from Nicaragua to Florida. The aircraft had been carefully prepared, with bullet-holes in the wings, to look like a Cuban aircraft which had escaped after a fight. The pilot said that he had bombed his own base before flying to Miami to join the exiles. Another bomber which had developed engine trouble also flew on to Florida.

Castro was soon able to confirm that none of his pilots was missing and that the story about defections was completely false. At first he assumed that the bombing raids were the start of the long-expected invasion. With the army already on maximum alert, he now ordered the police to arrest en masse everyone suspected of counter-revolutionary links or sympathies. However, hours passed and there were no reports of landings by exile forces anywhere on the coast. He concluded that the raids must have been just another stage in the softening-up process designed to weaken and demoralise his forces. He turned his attention to the psychological battlefield. He went on television to ridicule the announcement of defections, producing photographs and other evidence to prove that the raids had been carried out by American aircraft painted in Cuban colours. He recalled the outrage and indignation of the Americans over the Japanese attack at Pearl Harbor. The American sneak attack on Cuba was 'twice as treacherous as Pearl Harbor and a thousand times more cowardly'.

The next day the funeral of men killed in the raids provided a platform for more fiery rhetoric. 'What the imperialists cannot forgive us,' he roared, 'is that we have made a Socialist revolution under their noses.' This was the first occasion on which Castro publicly described the Revolution as being Socialist, 'a revolution of the humble, with the humble, for the humble, democratic and Socialist'. After years of denial and deception, this was the moment to reveal that Cuba under Castro was, after all, Socialist. He had planned to make the announcement on May Day, but could not resist the temptation to make an immediate defiant response to the air raids. It made the adoption of Socialism look like an act of retaliation. The crowds cheered the news as if it were indeed a smack in the face for the American aggressors. So Socialism slipped in as the official doctrine of the state on a wave of nationalist fervour.

The fleet carrying Brigade 2506 reached the southern coast of central Cuba without being detected by Castro's forces. Under cover of a moonless night, landing craft started ferrying troops to beaches in and near the Bay of Pigs, a narrow inlet stretching some ten miles into the Zapata peninsula. There were delays and minor mishaps in bringing the landing-craft ashore. Coral reefs in shallow water added to the difficulties of a night-time landing. But there was little armed opposition. A jeep-load of militiamen fired on the first arrivals, but were quickly silenced by heavy fire from the landing-craft. The landing sites had been chosen, in last-minute consultations with President Kennedy, because the area was very sparsely inhabited. A narrow strip of dry land along

1. Castro, aged eighteen, in a photograph from his school year-book

2. The young revolutionary: Castro in his early twenties

3. Castro, leader of the guerrilla forces against President Batista, in the Sierra Maestra Mountains, March 1958

4. Castro, the rebel leader, with his son Fidelito, in Havana, February 1959

5. Castro watches as Cuba's President, Manuel Urrutia, signs the document appointing him prime minister, 16 February 1959

6. Castro (first on left) and government colleagues at the March 1960 funeral procession for victims of the La Coubre explosion, attributed to a US attack on the Cuban ship of that name in Havana harbour. Third from left is Ernesto 'Che' Guevara.

7. The prime minister as manual worker, sugar-cane cutting with other volunteers, February 1961

8. Castro, frequently photographed on the sports field, takes a swing at the opening game of the Cuban inter-provincial baseball championships, February 1977

9. On a visit to the Soviet Union in May 1963, Castro and Nikita Khrushchev demonstrate their solidarity

10. Castro and his brother Raul, Cuba's defence minister, mark May Day in 1993

11. Castro welcomes Pope John Paul II on arrival in Havana for a five-day visit to Cuba, January 1998

12. Ramon Castro (right), Fidel's elder brother, and the British Ambassador with Baroness (Janet) Young, leader of a British business delegation, in 1991

13. Castro and United Nations Secretary-General Kofi Annan on a visit to Havana in April 2000

14. Fidel Castro with Leycester Coltman

the coast was separated from the rest of Cuba by the huge Ciénaga de Zapata swamp. Kennedy wanted the operation to look more like an infiltration than a frontal assault. It was hoped that the geography of the region would give the Brigade time to establish a strong beachhead before serious fighting could occur. Intelligence agencies had correctly indicated that this stretch of coast was much more thinly defended than more obvious sites for a landing. A small militia outpost which saw troops disembarking during the night took more than an hour to get to a radio telephone to raise the alarm.

Castro was spending the night at Celia Sánchez's flat in Havana. At 3.15 a.m. the telephone rang with news that troops were disembarking at Playa Larga in the Bay of Pigs and at Playa Girón ten miles further east. Later reports indicated that paratroops had been dropped a few miles inland, evidently to take control of the three roads that passed through the swamp. This was not what Castro had expected. His strongest military units were in the east and west of the island, and were deployed mainly to protect centres of population.

Was this the real thing or a feint? Castro checked that there were no reports of landings in other parts of the country. He then telephoned Captain José Ramón Fernández, the commander of the militia officers school located south of Havana. He ordered Fernández to take charge of the militia units nearest to the Zapata peninsula and to attack the beachhead as soon as possible. Castro said he would bring tanks and artillery to support him, but that it was vital to put the invaders under pressure immediately, before they had time to organise and consolidate the beachhead. Castro's fear was that the invaders would announce the formation of a provisional government, which would then be recognised by the United States. In this scenario the new government would call for external help, providing a pretext for open American military intervention

Castro next started to organise the remnants of his tiny airforce, which consisted of eight serviceable combat aircraft. Nothing could be done before dawn, by which time all or most of the invading troops would be on land. But he saw it as vital to sink or put out of action the ships which had brought the invading force and which would continue to play a key role in supporting and supplying the beachhead.

At 4.30 a.m. the senior pilot at the air base outside Havana was already in the cockpit of his Sea Fury when he was told that Fidel wanted to speak to him. Castro explained the situation and said: 'Lad, you've got to destroy those ships for me.' At dawn the three available aircraft at the base, two Sea Furies and one B-26 bomber, took off and soon sighted two ships in the Bay of Pigs, with others further offshore. On their first run their rockets missed the target. On the second run they hit and damaged both the ships in the bay. A large freighter, the *Houston*, had disembarked one battalion and its equipment during the night, but still had a second battalion on board when it was struck. It went aground on rocks several miles from the intended landing site. Some men were drowned when struggling to get ashore, and a lot of equipment was lost. The second vessel in the bay, the *Barbara J*, contained the American 'advisers' who constituted the CIA command post. After being struck by a rocket the vessel started to take water. To escape further damage it steamed out of the bay and headed south.

The Cuban aircraft then returned to base to refuel and rearm. By 9.30 a.m. they were launching a second attack, this time on the ships offshore from Playa Girón. They hit another big freighter, the *Rio Escondido*, which had disembarked all its troops but was still unloading supplies. It exploded in a huge fireball and sank soon afterwards, taking down a large quantity of food, ammunition, medical supplies and aviation fuel. Following this further blow the remaining ships called a halt to the unloading of supplies and set off for the open sea, promising the troops on land that they would return under cover of night.

The invasion force was supported by some fifteen B-26 bombers. These aircraft took more than three hours to reach Cuba from their bases in Central America. The plan was that they should use an airstrip near the village of Girón. The battalions which landed at Playa Girón quickly captured both the village and the airstrip; but the loss of aviation fuel and other supplies meant that the airstrip never became operational. The B-26s could therefore operate for only some forty minutes over the beachhead before they had to undertake the long journey back to Central America to refuel. Their rear machine-guns had been taken out to make space for additional fuel, but this made them vulnerable to attack. Four B-26s were shot down by Castro's three T-33 jet trainers, which were faster and more manoeuvrable. The CIA planners had assumed that the T-33 trainers could not be used as combat aircraft, but the Cubans had made space to mount a machine-gun, and this makeshift arrangement proved very effective against the lumbering B-26s.

By 8 a.m. Captain Fernández had assembled two battalions of militia at the Australia sugar mill on the northern edge of the Zapata swamp, which was also the base of a unit of the Rebel Army. Castro kept ringing Fernández, impatiently asking for news and urging offensive action. As part of Castro's plan for developing the Zapata region, a road had been built from the sugar mill through the swamp to Playa Larga. The road passed through a village called Palpite. Castro told Fernández to occupy Palpite, which he proceeded to do. Some of the Brigade's paratroops were supposed to have captured Palpite, but they had landed in swamp several miles from their target and failed to reach the village.

Hearing that 500 militia had taken Palpite without opposition, Castro ordered them to advance further down the road towards Playa Larga. They soon made contact with the Brigade's second battalion, which had landed at Playa Larga. and taken up positions along the road to Palpite. The militia immediately launched an attack. However, the swamp on both sides of the road meant that they had to advance on a very narrow front. The attack was repelled, the militia suffering heavy casualties. It looked like a disastrous start for Castro. But the militia's suicidal action was not altogether welcome to the invaders. A member of the Brigade later recorded in his memoirs the conster-nation caused by this first action of the militia. The Brigade had been told that the militia were ill-trained and reluctant conscripts, who would offer little resistance to a well-armed and disciplined force. Instead, they kept charging forward even when their comrades were being gunned down by the Brigade's machine-guns. It was not going to be a walkover.

Castro now decided to take direct command. Judging that a helicopter flight would be too dangerous, he drove at breakneck speed along the road east of Havana and after three hours reached the Australia mill. He set up his headquarters in the manager's office. During the course of the day troops and militia from Cienfuegos, a large port east of Girón, approached along the coast and made contact with the battalions which had landed at Playa Girón. Howitzers and mortars arrived and began to bombard the Brigade's forward positions. Some newly delivered Soviet tanks were transported along the road from Havana, the crews learning to use the equipment on the journey. The sight of Stalin tanks greatly raised the morale of the militia. However, the Brigade's tanks also proved highly effective, directing their fire down the roads which were the only routes by which Castro's forces could approach. Both sides fought tenaciously, and for two days there was a virtual deadlock. Castro did not know how many troops were in the beachhead, and did not want to risk another all-out onslaught.

During these two days, however, Castro's forces were receiving a contin-uous stream of reinforcements of men and equipment. The Brigade, by contrast, was cut off from its supporting ships and began to run short of ammunition and even food. There was no sign of the internal uprising in Cuba which the Brigade's arrival was intended to trigger. The Brigade's B-26 aircraft made repeated bomb attacks on Castro's positions, but with limited effect. The pilots had no fighter protection and became so exhausted with the long flights to and from Central America that on the second day four Amer-ican volunteers took over at the controls. The CIA tried to keep up the morale of the Brigade by hinting that direct American intervention might be immi-nent. Troops cheered when a group of US Sabre jets flew low overhead. But the aircraft merely took photographs and did not attack Castro's positions.

A powerful US aircraft carrier was now positioned offshore, but President Kennedy turned down a request from US naval chiefs to use the carrier's aircraft to knock out Castro's tanks and to provide air cover for the Brigade's ships to land more supplies.

The end was inevitable. The Brigade's commander, Pepe San Román, told the CIA command post by radio that the only remaining option was an evacuation. But even to get the Brigade back onto the ships would be impossible without American air cover. After more fruitless consultations, a voice from the CIA post told San Román: 'Sorry Pepe, you've done everything you could. You've fought well. Break off and scatter. Good luck. Don't call me again.' San Román picked up the microphone and shouted: 'We don't need any pats on the back, you bastard. What we need are your jets!' It was not to be. A few men tried to save themselves by wading through the swamp, with the idea of eventually joining up with rebels in the Escambray Mountains. A few took to the sea in small boats. But escape was impossible. Three days after the landing, 1189 men of Brigade 2506 surrendered to Castro's forces. About thirty had been killed in the disembarkation and a further eighty in the subsequent fighting. Among Castro's men there were about two hundred dead, possibly more.

Castro milked his victory for all it was worth. He took journalists on a conducted tour of the battlefield. On 20 April he spent four hours on television, in his most pedagogic style. With maps, charts and other exhibits he explained how the victory had been won. He read from captured CIA documents which claimed that the Cuban military were ill-equipped and ill-trained. The imperialists, he said, made the mistake of considering only material factors such as logistics and firepower. The revolutionaries, by contrast, knew the importance of moral factors: the people, their motivation, their desire for freedom and justice. What right had the United States to rule Cuba? They had a completely different culture. The Cubans did not speak English and did not chew gum. The United States had great military might, but Cuba had something more important – honour, dignity, courage, and a determination to resist aggression. Cuba was not just another sardine to be swallowed by the American shark. It was a spiny sea urchin, which the shark could not digest.

Over the following four days the interrogation of prisoners was shown live on television, with a panel of journalists putting the questions. Castro calculated that whatever the prisoners said was likely, in its overall effect, to reflect well on himself. Some prisoners remained defiant, criticising Castro for failing to hold elections. But this at least indicated that they had not been ill-treated or intimidated. Some were confused and easily led into contradicting themselves, or appearing to be tools of the Americans. A few tried to ingratiate themselves by admitting that they had been misled about the situation in Cuba and that the invasion was unjustified. On 25 April Castro himself took over the questioning, walking among the prisoners with a microphone like a talk-show host. 'Be honest,' he said to one prisoner. 'Surely you recognise that you are the first prisoners in history who are allowed to argue with the head of the government you came to overthrow, in front of the whole country and of the whole world!'

When President Kennedy warned that the Cuban government should not overstretch American tolerance, Castro responded with a mixture of humour, historical distortion and Marxist pedagogy:

> Kennedy's speeches are like Hitler's. Hitler threatened small neighbouring countries, and Kennedy is threatening Cuba and saying he will intervene. He says his patience is coming to an end. Well, what about our patience, with all the things we have had to endure? The imperialist powers use the method of surprise attacks, the same method of Hitler and Mussolini. We wish they would reconsider things, take a cold shower or a hot shower, anything. Let humanity, let history end a system which is now outdated. Imperialism must pass, just as feudalism did, just as slavery did.

In the warm glow of his victory, Castro could afford to be reasonably magnanimous towards the Brigade 2506 prisoners. Fourteen were put on trial for crimes allegedly committed before the Revolution. All the rest were offered to the United States in return for 500 tractors and an apology. Negotiations over the ransom dragged on for eighteen months. Finally the prisoners were flown to the United States in exchange for medicine and food valued at about US$52 million.

On the beach at Girón a huge billboard was erected, proclaiming: 'GIRON – THE FIRST IMPERIALIST DEFEAT IN THE AMERICAS!' And indeed, the events at Girón and the Bay of Pigs sent shock waves around the world, and especially through Latin America. Suddenly the prospects for revolutionary change in the continent seemed transformed. In most of Latin America there was rural poverty, migration to crime-ridden shanty towns, mass unemployment, hyperinflation and gross inequalities of wealth. Even where formal democracy existed, power seemed to be firmly entrenched in the hands of a small, wealthy elite, often backed by corrupt military officers. How could all this be ended? Soviet Communism had little appeal, being seen as a grey and alien ideology. But Castro was different. He combined socialism with nationalism and the romantic Latin American tradition of armed rebellion. It was a potent cocktail. At the Bay of Pigs it had proved powerful enough to withstand an assault prepared and backed by the might of the United States. For millions of people in Latin America, especially students, the Cuban Revolution became a beacon of hope, as Khrushchev had predicted. By the same token, those upholding the existing political order were alarmed and deeply worried.

Inside Cuba, the enthusiasm of Castro's many supporters reached new heights. The Bay of Pigs was a dream come true. For decades Cuba had been treated by its great northern neighbour with a mixture of contempt and patronising benevolence. Now it had to be taken seriously. The Cuban David had stood up to Goliath and won a famous victory.

But there was a darker side to the picture. In the days before the invasion at least 20,000 people (considerably more by some accounts) had been arrested, mostly in Havana. The prisons could not contain such large numbers, so theatres and sports arenas were used as detention centres. Castro saw the arrests as a practical and necessary precaution, but they served also as an act of mass intimidation against his critics and opponents. A few hundred of those arrested may have belonged to the opposition networks set up by the CIA. Many more thousands were merely middle-class people who did not like the government's expropriations and land seizures, or its anti-Catholic and pro-Communist propaganda. Most of those arrested were released within a day or two of Castro's victory at the Bay of Pigs. But it was an unpleasant experience to find that one was on a police list of suspected counter-revolutionaries. It encouraged yet more people to pack their bags and join the stream of those departing for exile in Florida.

11 The Missile Crisis

The Soviet leaders watched the events at the Bay of Pigs with a mixture of satisfaction and anxiety. Nikita Khrushchev had made a big public show of support for Castro in New York, even describing himself as a *fidelista*. The overthrow of Castro would therefore have represented a personal humiliation for Khrushchev and a setback for Soviet prestige. Despite their very different backgrounds, moreover, Castro and Khrushchev had established a genuine personal rapport. They were both self-confident, ebullient, passionate, and contemptuous of formality and protocol. Both felt deep resentment over what they saw as American arrogance. Both were inclined to express their resentment through bluster and threats.

One important difference between the two men was that whereas Castro had concentrated all power in his own hands, Khrushchev was still part of a collective leadership. Khrushchev could be more freewheeling abroad than at home. When Carlos Franqui went to interview Khrushchev in Moscow, he found him much more constrained than he had seemed in New York. The more cautious and conservative members of the Politburo argued that the Soviet Union should not become too deeply committed to a man as unpredictable and uncontrollable as Castro. Khrushchev himself recognised the problem. He commented that Castro was 'a young horse that hasn't yet been broken. He's very spirited. He needs some training. We'll have to be careful.'

During the Bay of Pigs fighting, Khrushchev sent a message to President Kennedy saying that the Soviet Union would give the Cubans 'all necessary help' in beating back the invasion. This was an attempt to impress Third World countries and to deter the United States from direct intervention. But the threat was empty. Khrushchev had no intention of starting an all-out nuclear war. Short of that, there was very little the Soviet Union could do in practice to help the Cubans against an American attack. They had no significant naval or military forces in the Caribbean region.

Khrushchev was delighted when Castro emerged victorious, but was concerned that Castro should not push his luck too far. If the Americans sent their own forces to attack Cuba, Khrushchev's bluff would be called. The best course was now for Castro to cool things down and avoid provoking the Americans further. This was the clear message which the Russians conveyed to Castro.

In this situation, Castro's declaration that the Cuban Revolution was Socialist, another kick at the Americans, did not go down at all well in Moscow. The Russians could scarcely condemn a declaration of support for Socialism, but they pointedly refrained from welcoming it. The Soviet government sent a message of congratulation to Castro on the occasion of May Day, but completely ignored his declaration that Cuba was Socialist. It suited the Russians that Cuba should be a 'progressive' Third World country, like Egypt under Nasser or Algeria under Ben Bella, but not a fully fledged member of the Socialist (i.e. Communist) camp. It was established dogma in the Soviet Union that once Socialism was built, it could not be reversed. History could not go backwards. If the government of Nasser or Ben Bella were overthrown and replaced by a more right-wing government, that would be a setback for the Soviet Union but not a disaster. The fall of a full-blown Communist regime would by contrast be so serious that the Soviet Union would feel obliged to go to almost any lengths to prevent it, as it had done in Hungary in 1956. But whereas the Soviet armed forces could intervene rapidly and effectively in Eastern Europe, they had no means of intervening effectively in the Caribbean.

For a year, therefore, the love affair between Castro and Khrushchev went through a cooler phase. Castro did not want to be a second-class associate of the Socialist camp, but an equal partner inside the camp. He tried hard to show that he was a good Marxist, willing to follow Soviet economic methods. He flattered and promoted the leaders of the old Cuban Communist party, who remained the most trusted interlocutors of the Soviet Embassy. He sent his thirteen-year-old son Fidelito to school in Moscow. He gave the Communists a dominant position in a new integrated political organisation, the ORI, which brought together the MR-26-7, the Communists and the Revolutionary Directorate. He sided with the Soviet Union in the increasingly bitter quarrel which was developing between the Soviet Union and Communist China.

Castro also tried to imitate the control and regimentation of society characteristic of the Soviet Union. The authorities started to persecute not only political opponents, but also social deviants. An official was sent to Moscow to study how to deal with prostitution. (He was told that under Socialism prostitution did not exist.) Police swooped on the still relatively lively red-light districts of Havana and made mass arrests of prostitutes, pimps and homosexuals. Some of the more liberal-minded members of the government protested to Castro over these police actions, especially the arrest of homosexuals. They pointed out that some of those arrested as homosexuals were intellectuals who had given loyal support to Castro's Revolution. In reply to these complaints, Castro said that only pimps who made a living from prostitution would be tried and punished. Prostitutes would be sent to re-education centres and then found alternative work. Homosexuals would not be punished, but would be excluded from any role in education, or in the artistic and cultural life of the new Cuba. In fact a number of homosexuals *were* punished. They were forcibly enrolled, together with various categories of common criminals, into the notorious Military Units for the Support of Production (UMAP), a forced-labour organisation.

In old age Castro came to regret the homophobic zeal of his early years in power. He even became quite politically correct. But in the 1960s he was under the influence of both Soviet puritanism and Cuban *machismo* (glorification of masculinity). Brother Raúl was even more macho and homophobic, perhaps partly to compensate for his own extremely effeminate appearance. The Castro brothers loved guns and other symbols of masculinity. They admired the great generals and great rebels of history. They despised men who were soft and gentle. They tended to associate artists, poets and dancers with femininity. One contemporary writer whom Fidel admired and praised was Ernest Hemingway. Not only was Hemingway a Yankee who liked Cuba and had supported the Revolution; he also wore a beard, smoked cigars, loved guns and wrote about men who waged a solitary and heroic struggle against overwhelming odds.

Castro had no use for intellectuals who were non-political, or who simply followed their own inclinations. To get his views across he organised a series of meetings in the National Library with writers, journalists, artists and film and theatre directors. The ostensible reason for the meetings was to discuss a decision by the official Film Institute to refuse support for an avant-garde documentary film which gave a warts-and-all picture of Cuban low life. The film had been praised by prominent intellectuals, but it was not the sort of optimistic and uplifting material that Castro wanted. As usual he packed the meeting with his supporters. It soon became apparent that the intellectuals were virtually in the dock. Even the seating plan reinforced this impression, with Castro and government representatives lined up on a dais facing the intellectuals below. He ostentatiously placed his pistol on the table in front of him.

For two days Castro left the talking to others, notably his old Communist friend Alfredo Guevara. Like a Stalinist prosecutor, Guevara berated those writers, artists and film directors who produced decadent, elitist and subversive work, gratifying their personal whims rather than serving society. When

Castro himself finally spoke, he seemed at first moderate and conciliatory. He said the government did not claim to be infallible. The Revolution would never oppose freedom. But the Revolution was under attack, and no honourable person could ignore the impact of his work on the Revolution. 'People here have expressed the fear that the Revolution will drown freedom of expression, and suffocate the creative spirit of writers and artists . . . But the revolutionary should place the interests of the Revolution above even his own creative spirit.' He produced a slogan which he would repeat *ad nauseam*: 'Within the Revolution, everything; against the Revolution, nothing.' When Franqui later argued with Fidel that people should be able to put forward different opinions without being considered enemies, Castro said: 'You're a stubborn fool, Franqui. All opposition is counter-revolutionary.'

In December 1961 Castro announced that he and the Revolution were not just Socialist, but fully committed to Communism. In a television interview he described his intellectual development. If he was a Communist, why had he not revealed this earlier? Had he changed his mind, or were his frequent previous repudiations of Communism false? He answered this question in language very similar to that which he had used eight years earlier in a letter written from prison to Naty Revuelta. Lenin could not have achieved anything if he had been born in the eighteenth century. Every revolution had to wait for the right historical conditions to develop. 'I believe absolutely in Marxism . . . Did I understand it at the time of Moncada as I understand it today after ten years' struggle? No. Did I have prejudices about Communism? Yes. Was I influenced by the propaganda of imperialism and reaction against Communism? Yes. Did I think Communists were thieves? No, never. I always thought Communists were honourable, decent people.'

A month later Castro made a speech committing himself even more emphatically to Communism. 'I am a Marxist–Leninist and shall be a Marxist–Leninist until the day I die.' The Soviet government was still not impressed. It knew that part of Castro's purpose was to drag them into guaranteeing the security of Cuba. The Russians also gave a very cool response to the 'Second Declaration of Havana', in which Castro urged the peoples of Latin America to rise up in armed rebellion against their governments. This was Castro's defiant reaction to a decision by the Organisation of American States, at United States instigation, to expel Cuba from the organisation and to break all relations with Cuba. Castro's incitement to armed rebellion was viewed by the Russians as provocative and irresponsible. It only made life more difficult for local Communist parties, and gave a pretext for repression. In public the Russians remained politely supportive towards Castro; but privately they made their displeasure clear. 'You cannot imagine the tremendous reprimand we received from the Soviets,' said Castro many years later.

'They were totally opposed to our support for the revolutionary movement
. . . The only thing we got from the Soviet Union was worries.'

The Soviet authorities made it clear, even in their public statements, that
in their view Cuba was still not part of the Communist community. It was
the Republic of Cuba, not Socialist Cuba. To be accepted Castro would have
to get on message, and follow the line decided in Moscow. And indeed, in
personality Castro could scarcely be more different from the sort of steady
and reliable stooges that the Soviet government liked inside the Socialist
camp. He was, as José Meneses accurately described him: 'undisciplined,
independent, excitable, bohemian, visionary, temperamental, disobedient
and proud'.

In February 1962 Castro virtually disappeared from public view for several
weeks. His elation over the victory at the Bay of Pigs had worn off. He
became depressed and irritable. He had nailed his colours to the Soviet mast,
yet the Russians seemed to be leaving him in the lurch. The economy, despite
his grandiloquent promises and predictions, was in steep decline. 'Agrarian
reform works,' was a slogan endlessly repeated; yet some state-run dairy farms
ceased to produce anything, since the cattle had all been eaten. In the town
of Cárdenas there was a serious riot over food shortages. Some expropriated
small farmers joined the anti-Castro guerrillas in the Escambray Mountains.
Rationing was introduced and extended to more and more products. President Dorticós added insult to injury by saying that oranges, in short supply
for the first time ever, were a 'bourgeois' fruit. Industry was also in disarray.
The CIA's continuing efforts to cripple the economy through sabotage,
directed by 'Task Force W', had less impact than the incompetence and inexperience of the new Cuban economic managers.

Even the literacy programme, the centrepiece of the Year of Education, had
some negative side-effects. Students were dispatched to the villages to teach
peasants to read and write, with textbooks praising the heroes of the Revolution and the benefits of agrarian reform, and urban schoolchildren were
taught the virtues of manual labour by being sent during vacations to work
in the countryside. These young people spent months in mixed-sex camps, far
away from parental control, as a result of which there was an explosion of
unplanned teenage pregnancies.

Beset by economic and social problems, Fidel was also suffering the
loneliness of power. He was surrounded by bodyguards and obsequious
bureaucrats, who obeyed his every word but provided no real companionship.
Even Celia Sánchez found her role and influence diminished. Fidel sensed that
his relations with Che Guevara were no longer as intimate and trusting as they
had been in the past. Che continued to work hard, as Governor of the Central
Bank and later as Minister of Industry, trying to bring order into the chaotic

economy. His task was made more difficult by Castro's off-the-cuff initiatives and sudden changes of tack. Che had earlier been much more pro-Soviet than Fidel, but he was now visibly unenthusiastic about Castro's efforts to turn Cuba into a tropical copy of the Soviet Union. Unlike Fidel, he refused to echo Moscow's attacks on Communist China. He even shocked his colleagues by remarking in his quiet, sardonic manner that he was 'pro-Chinese'. In earlier years Fidel and Che had spent long nights discussing politics. Che was the companion whose intellect he most admired. Che's semi-detachment from the pro-Soviet drive increased Fidel's sense of emotional isolation.

But once again Castro showed his resilience. He recovered his spirits and returned to the political fray. He now adopted a new approach. He blamed himself for giving the pro-Soviet 'Old Communists' too much rope. They had become too big for their boots, and were virtually taking control of the machinery of government. Security reports said that many ordinary people associated the Communists with austerity, shortages, humourlessness, persecution and the undermining of parental authority. In March 1962 Castro showed who was the boss by removing the most prominent Old Communists from positions of power, and publicly criticising their 'sectarian' excesses.

One of the heroes of the Revolution, José Antonio Echeverría, had said in a speech shortly before his death that he hoped the actions of the revolutionaries would 'find favour with God'. In reproducing this speech the Communists expunged the reference to God. Castro ridiculed and castigated the 'sectarians' for trying to rewrite the history of the Revolution to suit their own orthodoxies. He started to allow greater cultural diversity. Non-Communist members of the government felt renewed hope that the Revolution would after all promote freedom rather than a different form of dictatorship.

When Castro was trying hard to draw close to the Soviet Union, the Russians were cautiously aloof and unresponsive, unwilling to be dragged into expensive and dangerous commitments. But by a curious accident of timing, when he lost patience and turned against the pro-Soviet Communists, the Russians suddenly became much more positive and forthcoming. This was because the Soviet government, at Khrushchev's instigation, had approved a secret plan designed to strengthen dramatically the Soviet Union's international influence and prestige. It was a plan which would bring the world to the very brink of nuclear war.

Since the foundation of the Soviet Union, its leaders felt surrounded and threatened by Western hostility. Western countries intervened in 1919 in an attempt to destroy the new Communist state. In the Second World War, Hitler's armies reached the outskirts of Moscow, and were beaten back only after massive devastation and the loss of 20 million Soviet lives. After the war Stalin imposed his iron grip on the countries of Eastern Europe which the

Red Army had occupied; but the West, under the leadership of the United States, organised a string of alliances to contain the Soviet threat. The NATO (North Atlantic Treaty Organisation) alliance stretched from Norway on the Soviet Union's north-western frontier to Turkey on its south-western frontier. To the south were CENTO (Central Treaty Organisation) and SEATO (South East Asian Treaty Organisation). The circle was closed by the huge American military deployments in Japan and the Pacific.

Feeling insecure and vulnerable, successive Soviet governments devoted huge resources to developing new military weapons, especially nuclear weapons and rockets. They achieved considerable success. Khrushchev tried to enhance Soviet influence and security by parading ever-larger rockets through Red Square and boasting of their terrifying capabilities. This impressed his friends and alarmed his enemies. Some Americans were worried about a 'bomber gap' and a 'missile gap'. But in reality the Soviet Union was never able to match American technology and American military and industrial might. The US government knew through their U-2 spy planes and other intelligence sources that there was no bomber gap and no missile gap. For four years the Soviet authorities watched impotently as US spy planes flew the length and breadth of the Soviet Union, photographing everything. The Russians had no aircraft capable of reaching the altitude at which the U-2s flew, and no missile capable of shooting them down.

Even when the Soviet Union finally managed, in 1960, to shoot down a U-2, and to achieve a measure of aerial espionage parity through satellites, they remained at a major strategic disadvantage. The Americans had missiles with nuclear warheads targeted on the Soviet Union in Western Europe and Turkey, right on the Soviet borders, as well as a huge superiority in submarines and bombers. While Russia was surrounded, the United States was relatively secure, protected by the Atlantic, Pacific and Arctic Oceans.

Then came Castro. Unexpectedly the Soviet Union found itself with a friend and potential ally just ninety miles from the United States mainland. Also unexpectedly, Castro survived the first attempt by the United States to overthrow him. The thought gradually crystallised in Khrushchev's mind that if he could secretly install in Cuba nuclear missiles capable of striking American territory, this would alter the balance of power in the Soviet Union's favour. Apart from deterring an American attack on Cuba, missiles on Cuban soil would give Khrushchev a powerful lever with which to extract concessions elsewhere, such as in West Berlin, which the Russians saw as a hostile enclave in their sphere of influence. Khrushchev later described his thinking. 'If we installed the missiles secretly, and then if the United States discovered the missiles when they were already poised and ready to strike, the Americans would think twice before trying to liquidate our installations by military means . . . It was high time America learned what it feels like to have her own land and her own people threatened.'

Some Soviet generals were unhappy at the proposal to deploy forces so far from home and in a region so vulnerable to American pressure. But most of the Politburo supported Khrushchev and by April 1962 he had won the internal argument. The task now was to win over Castro. The Soviet newspaper *Pravda* came out with strong praise for Castro, even endorsing his criticism of the Old Communist 'sectarians'. The Soviet Ambassador in Cuba, a narrow-minded bureaucrat who had always distrusted Castro as an unreliable maverick, was replaced by Castro's old friend, the 'journalist' Alexander Alexayev.

Khrushchev now sent two senior personal representatives, Marshal Byriusov and Uzbek Party Secretary Rashidov, to talk to Castro. Byriusov said the Soviet government was worried about the possibility that the United States, frustrated by their inability to destabilise Castro's government, might look for a pretext for direct military action. At a meeting in Vienna President Kennedy had told Khrushchev pointedly that the United States had shown restraint in not intervening in 1956 when Soviet forces moved into Hungary. Khrushchev took this as a warning that the Soviet Union should similarly keep out if the Americans invaded Cuba. What could be done to avert the danger of an American attack?

Castro agreed that the Americans would not let their failure at the Bay of Pigs be the last word. The best deterrent would be for the Soviet Union to state publicly that any attack on Cuba would be considered an attack on the Soviet Union. Byriusov said it would be unwise to make such a commitment without having the means to carry it out. It might even provoke the action which they wanted to avoid. He then set out Khrushchev's proposal to deploy secretly in Cuba a strong Soviet military force, including forty-two medium and intermediate-range missiles with nuclear warheads, Ilyushin 28 bombers, and anti-aircraft batteries. Would this be acceptable?

Castro said he would need to consult his colleagues. At first he was uneasy. It was made clear that the Soviet military would retain complete control of the missiles that they proposed to install in Cuba. Castro had often criticised small countries which allowed their territory to be used by the armed forces of the great powers, thereby becoming mere pawns in the superpower chess game. He would now be doing just that. But other considerations soon made him decide to approve the proposal. First, he saw the plan as representing in practice the security guarantee which he had long sought. Once the Russians had troops and missiles in Cuba, they could not fail to resist actively an American invasion. Second, as part of the deal the Soviet Union offered to supply, for Cuba's own use, a wide range of sophisticated military equipment, including MiG fighter aircraft and anti-aircraft guns. Third, he would be helping to shift the balance of power in favour of the Socialist camp.

For Castro, this last point was the most important. He was intensely conscious of the magnitude of what was at stake. By strengthening the international position of the Soviet Union, he would strengthen the cause of Socialism everywhere, even if Cuba's role looked undignified. Reminiscing many years later, Castro said that the Soviet proposal had 'political inconveniences'; but he had repeatedly asked the Soviet Union for help in defending Cuba against an American invasion. 'It would have been morally wrong to expect a country to support us, even to the point of going to war, while failing to do what was convenient for them, for political reasons or for reasons of prestige.'

In May 1962 work began on preparing sites to receive the Soviet missiles, warheads and aircraft. In July Raúl Castro was invited to Moscow by Soviet Defence Minister Malinovsky to work out the complex logistics of the operation and the details of supplies for the Cuban armed forces. Raúl was given red-carpet treatment, including a dinner in his honour attended by Khrushchev and almost the entire Soviet leadership. He was invited to give an address on television. Most of his requests for equipment for the Cuban armed forces were met. He was shown secret military factories and installations, and encouraged to believe that the Soviet Union was overtaking the United States in military hardware. Since his student days Raúl had been an enthusiastic admirer of the Soviet Union, and of Stalin. He returned to Havana even more convinced that Soviet Communism represented the wave of the future. The following month Che Guevara went to Moscow, ostensibly to discuss the modernisation of Cuban steel plants, but in fact mainly to tie up the loose ends of the missile agreement.

The strictest secrecy was maintained. Inevitably many Cubans soon became aware that large numbers of Soviet personnel were arriving in Cuba, and that secret installations were being built. But a complex plan of disinformation was put into operation, designed to mislead hostile observers about the purpose of the activity. Troops arrived in civilian clothes and were described as technical advisers in everything from soil erosion to metallurgy. Only five Cubans were supposed to know the full picture of what was happening: Fidel and Raúl Castro, Che Guevara, President Dorticós and security chief Ramiro Valdés.

A year earlier Khrushchev had talked publicly of defending Cuba with rockets. Che Guevara had announced that Cuba was protected by one of the world's most powerful states. Fidel had talked of accepting 'the Soviet offer of missiles'. At that time it was all empty bluster. When it started to become a reality, all the protagonists maintained a scrupulous silence. To the extent that the presence of Soviet military personnel was too obvious to be denied, it was presented as a training programme. After the visits of Raúl and Che to Moscow, a bland communiqué was issued, saying that in view of imperialist threats, the Cuban government had requested the supply of arms and technicians to train Cuban servicemen.

However, the Americans had numerous intelligence sources on Cuba, including U-2 aircraft regularly flying over the island. By August the CIA had observed surface-to-air missiles (SAMs) under construction, as well as anti-ship cruise missile emplacements. Castro knew from his own intelligence sources, and from news reports, that the US military were becoming very agitated at the evidence of a Soviet missile build-up. By September President Kennedy was being accused by right-wing politicians and commentators of being weak and ineffectual over Cuba. He responded by calling up 150,000 reservists, a signal that the Soviet build-up would not go unanswered.

On 16 October 1962 CIA photo-analysts gave President Kennedy conclusive proof that offensive weapons were being installed in Cuba. Some medium-range ballistic missiles (with a range of 1,100 miles) were already in place, and it appeared that sites were being prepared for intermediate-range missiles (with a range of 2,200 miles, i.e. able to reach all of the United States except the north-west corner). US forces around the world were placed on heightened alert. The Chiefs of Staff unanimously urged the President to authorise a massive air strike on Cuba, without warning, targeting all missile sites, all airfields, all military camps and even all buildings large enough to be possibly concealing a missile, such as sugar refineries and warehouses. The strike would be immediately followed by an invasion. General Curtis LeMay, Chief of the US Air Force, was the most gung-ho. 'If there is to be war, there's no time like the present. We're ready and the bear is not.' However, Kennedy had learnt from the Bay of Pigs not to rely on the judgement of his professional military advisers. He ordered that preparations be made for an air strike and invasion, but decided to impose a naval blockade first, to give the Russians an opportunity to step back from the brink. He believed that a surprise attack on Cuba, causing heavy Soviet casualties, would inevitably cause Khrushchev to make a military response elsewhere, probably in Berlin, and that this would lead to global nuclear war.

On Saturday 20 October rumours swept Havana that the US military were mobilising and that an attack was imminent. Troops and aircraft were assembling in Florida in huge numbers. The editor of *Revolución* desperately sought instructions on what to say. Should he raise the alarm or would that be counter-productive? Fidel was busy ensuring that his troops were on maximum alert. In his absence no one was willing to give a steer to the media. On Monday 22 October *Revolución* appeared with the headline: 'US prepares invasion of Cuba.' Despite this there was not much sign of panic or alarm in Havana. The Bay of Pigs had encouraged people to believe that Fidel would somehow come out on top. Official propaganda insisted that Cuba was 'not alone'. There was almost a festive atmosphere, as Cubans hid their fear beneath a façade of bravado and cheerful fatalism.

That evening President Kennedy went on television. He displayed the photographic evidence that offensive Soviet missiles were being installed in Cuba. He said that such a threat to US security could not be accepted. The Russians must withdraw the missiles. The United States was imposing a strict quarantine. Soviet ships approaching Cuba would be stopped and searched, and not allowed to proceed if they were carrying military supplies.

Castro responded to Kennedy's broadcast with a much longer television broadcast of his own. He outlined the history of American threats and aggressions against Cuba, culminating in the 'total blockade' announced by Kennedy. Cuba had the right to defend itself, and to acquire whatever weapons it needed, without asking for permission from the imperialists. He ridiculed Kennedy's assertion that the missiles in Cuba were offensive. No sane person could imagine that Cuba wanted to attack the United States. The rifles used by the invaders at the Bay of Pigs were offensive. All the weapons in Cuba were defensive. Their sole purpose was to defend the island from attack. 'What have we done? We have defended ourselves. That is all. Were the imperialists expecting that after their first hostile act, our people would surrender, that the Revolution would raise the white flag?'

Castro was uneasily aware that Kennedy had shifted the focus of the crisis from Cuba to the mid-Atlantic. How it now developed was outside the control of the Cuban government. It would depend exclusively on the decisions and determination of the Soviet authorities. However, Castro was at first confident that the Soviet Union would not submit to the American demands. It seemed to him unthinkable that a major country should allow itself to be humiliated in this way. After all, the Russians were merely deploying the sort of weapons which the Americans had already deployed in Britain, Italy, Turkey and elsewhere, in all cases with the consent of the receiving countries. Castro did what he could to stiffen the Russians' resolve. He urged them to give an explicit warning that they would respond immediately with nuclear weapons if Cuba was attacked. He suggested that the Russians raise the stakes by putting their forces in Europe on maximum alert and by moving the Soviet government to their underground wartime stations. The Russians in fact did none of these things. Khrushchev was looking for ways to lower rather than heighten tension.

It was clear that if nuclear war did come, Cuba would be devastated. But there was still no collapse of morale among the Cuban population. Most people seemed to accept Castro's assumption that they would fight to the death if necessary, but never surrender.

The story of the missile crisis has been told in many books and indeed films. For several days Kennedy and Khrushchev conducted a desperately tense process of negotiation, made more complex by the pressures to which both the main protagonists were being subjected in their own countries. Castro was now in the margin. He sent lengthy messages to Khrushchev, to the Secretary-General of the United Nations (the Burmese U Thant) and to other world statesmen. But this was now a life-and-death confrontation between the two superpowers. There was little Castro could do to influence the outcome.

Kennedy's quarantine looked fraught with danger. But it proved to hold the key to a solution. U Thant and a group of neutral countries sent an appeal to Khrushchev not to challenge the quarantine, so as to allow time for negotiations. This enabled the Russians to step back from the brink, 'in the interests of world peace', without appearing to make any concession of principle. On 24 October, to the relief of the whole world, the ships in the Atlantic carrying military supplies slowed or halted, and in some cases turned round and headed home.

But tension soon built up again. The Americans sent not only U-2 aircraft at high altitude over Cuba, but also fast reconnaissance aircraft flying at very low level. Castro had no control over the Soviet missiles, but he did have lots of conventional light anti-aircraft guns, some deployed to protect Soviet missile sites. He ordered them to fire on the low-level American aircraft. None was shot down. But on 27 October a Soviet SAM shot down a U-2, killing the pilot. According to one account, first circulated by Carlos Franqui, Castro was responsible. In this version of events Castro was visiting a Soviet SAM installation when the radar picked up the flight of a U-2. Castro asked how the Soviet battery would shoot down the aircraft. The Russian commander told him which button would have to be pressed, whereupon Castro pressed it, firing the missile.

This dramatic story is almost certainly apocryphal. Castro himself has admitted that he had no say in the use of Soviet missiles. But he believed that it was the Cuban example which induced the Russians to act. Decades later he said: 'What is my opinion? They are soldiers, we are together, the enemy is there, and the firing begins. I believe is was a simple spirit of solidarity which made the Soviets decide to fire as well.' On another occasion he seemed less certain. 'For me it is still a mystery. I don't know whether the Soviet battery commander caught the spirit of our men and fired too, or whether he received an order. This is something we don't know ourselves and at the time we didn't want to ask too much about it.' The most plausible version is that

General Statsenko, the commander of Soviet forces in Cuba, gave the order to fire, believing that the decision lay within his discretion.

Such discretion can be dangerous. Under standing orders in the United States, the US Air Force could immediately and without consultation attack any SAM site which fired on an American aircraft. General LeMay had a powerful group of bombers ready for precisely this contingency and was about to launch an attack when a telephone call from the White House ordered him to hold back. LeMay was disgusted at what he saw as Kennedy's weakness and indecision. 'The Russian bear has always wanted to stick his paw in Latin American waters. Now we've got him in a trap, let's take his leg off right up to the testicles. On second thought, let's take off his testicles too.' LeMay was not aware that at precisely this moment the President's brother, Attorney General Robert Kennedy, was putting to the Russians a new proposal for a comprehensive settlement.

The next day, the deal was done. The Russians agreed to withdraw the missiles from Cuba, and to allow United Nations inspectors to verify the withdrawal. The United States gave an informal undertaking not to invade Cuba. The US government would not acknowledge publicly any link with Turkey, but also let it be known privately to the Russians that it was their intention to withdraw the Jupiter missiles in Turkey within a few months.

Khrushchev believed that he had got enough to have made his Cuban adventure worthwhile: an assurance that Cuba would not be attacked; a promise that missiles would be withdrawn from Turkey; and an enhanced reputation as a man of peace and good sense. But that was not how most people saw the outcome. In the eyes of most observers, including some in the Soviet Union itself, the Americans were the clear winners. They had taken a tough line and forced the Russians to back down. Kennedy more than recovered the prestige which he had lost at the Bay of Pigs. Khrushchev appeared to have talked big and acted small.

On Sunday 28 October Celia Sanchéz received a telephone call with news of the deal which was being announced by the news agencies. She passed the telephone to Castro. He could scarcely believe it. He then exploded in uncontrollable rage. He felt totally betrayed by Khrushchev. For the sake of Socialism and the Soviet Union, he had been prepared to sacrifice himself and his country. Now, without even consulting or informing him, Khrushchev had surrendered to the enemy. It was total humiliation. He shouted every insult and obscenity he could think of. He kicked the wall in his office. A large mirror crashed to the floor, showering glass everywhere. He finally summed up again his view of Khrushchev: 'Maricón!' ('Faggot!')

When he calmed down, Castro began to prepare a statement of the Cuban position. Cuba would accept the deal negotiated between the United States and the Soviet Union provided five conditions were fulfilled: an end to the economic embargo on Cuba; an end to sabotage, assassinations and other subversive activities organised by US agencies; an end to hit-and-run military attacks by exile groups based in Florida; an end to the violation of Cuban territorial waters and air-space by US ships and aircraft; and the withdrawal of the US naval base at Guantánamo in Eastern Cuba.

This statement looked a rather futile exercise, since there was no chance that the Americans would accede to any of Castro's demands. The statement seemed merely to highlight Castro's humiliation and impotence. But there was one point on which he could show that he and Cuba could not be taken for granted. He would not accept international inspection of the withdrawal of missiles, unless his conditions were met. The Soviet and US governments had already agreed that such inspection should take place. But they had not consulted the Cuban government, and Cuba was an independent, sovereign nation. Here at least was an issue on which Castro could salvage his honour and dignity, and Cuba's honour and dignity.

Castro also told the Russians that, regardless of their agreement with the Americans, he would not accept low-level American overflights. If such flights continued, he would try to shoot the aircraft down. Castro later said:

> I am certain that if the low-level flights had been resumed, we would have shot down one, two or three of these planes . . . With so many batteries firing, we must have shot down some planes . . . I was at the San Antonio air base, where we had some batteries, and that was where at 10 a.m. American planes had flown over. I went there and waited for the planes. I knew there would be a counter-strike if we fired, and possibly we would have many casualties. I thought it was my duty to be there, in a place that would be attacked, but the planes did not come that day.

A temporary suspension of low-level flights had been ordered by Kennedy at the request of the United Nations Secretary-General, who was due to travel to Havana and who realised that his chances of getting Cuban co-operation would be nullified if American aircraft were roaring overhead. On 30 October U Thant flew to Havana with a large delegation whose job would be to inspect the Soviet missile sites. To gain Cuban acceptance U Thant had insisted that all the inspectors should be from neutral countries. At a meeting with Castro, U Thant explained that he had come as a friend, with the task of facilitating peace.

However, Castro's frame of mind was well described as being that of a wounded bull, ready to attack anyone approaching him. He told U Thant grimly that the Cubans wanted peace as much as anyone, and that peace could be achieved if the Americans agreed to put an end to unlawful aggression by accepting his five points. If they declined to do so, he would not allow inspections. U Thant said that the Russians had agreed to United Nations inspections of their missile sites and of incoming and departing Soviet ships, up to the time when they could confirm that all missiles had been removed. Castro said that unless his conditions were met, there would be no inspections before, during or after the removal of the missiles. He added that U Thant was acting as a lackey of the great powers. Did he not realise what harm he was doing to the rights of small countries like his own? U Thant said the duties he had to perform were sometimes distasteful. Castro would not be moved. He said that Cuba would fight for its rights and independence, alone if necessary.

U Thant returned to New York empty-handed. The Americans were exasperated. General LeMay told General Taylor, President Kennedy's military consultant: 'I told you that yellow bandy-legged bastard would fuck up the works.' He pressed for the United States to station a powerful naval force off Havana and a fleet of bombers overhead. Castro should then be asked to allow US forces to inspect the missile sites themselves. If Castro refused, the bombing of Havana would begin immediately.

The Russians were also infuriated by Castro's intransigence. They had given their word over United Nations inspections, and now Castro was making them break their word. They had to bring him round, and quickly. However, Castro's rage against what he saw as the Soviet betrayal was such that he refused to see or even speak to the Soviet Ambassador. Alexayev warned Moscow that Castro was in a dangerous mood, and suggested they send a high-level special emissary to mollify him. Deputy Prime Minister Mikoyan was given this difficult task.

The day before Mikoyan's arrival, Castro said on television:

We have not violated anyone's rights. We have not attacked anyone. All our actions have been based on international law. We are the victims of an embargo, which is an illegal act, and of an attack by another country . . . The United States has repeatedly violated our air space. This business of inspections is just another attempt to humiliate our country. Therefore, we will not accept it.

He went to the airport to meet Mikoyan, but gave him an ostentatiously cold and formal reception. He reiterated to Mikoyan his arguments against any sort of international inspection of Cuban territory.

Mikoyan had hoped that after Castro had let off steam, he would become more amenable to pressure. He expected to have a fuller discussion the following day. Instead he was sent on a tour of farms and factories outside Havana. It was weeks before Castro agreed to see him again. During this time

Mikoyan's wife died, but he decided that keeping Castro in play had to take precedence over attending his wife's funeral in Moscow. The Soviet government, under increasing pressure from the Americans to fulfil their side of the agreement, and seeing that Mikoyan was making no progress with Castro, agreed to an even more humiliating form of inspection. The missiles were loaded on the decks on Soviet ships, which took to sea and then removed the covers to allow US helicopters and ships 'close alongside' to inspect them.

When Mikoyan eventually did get to see Castro, he was patient but firm. He pointed out that the Soviet Union was giving Cuba massive amounts of aid. It had obtained a commitment that the United States would not invade Cuba. If this was negated, due to Cuban obstruction, the Cubans could find themselves confronting the United States on their own. Notwithstanding that, the Soviet Union stood ready to provide additional aid and co-operation. He invited Castro to visit Moscow for a full discussion of how to strengthen the bilateral relationship.

Castro responded calmly and constructively. He realised he could not go on biting the hand that fed him. He recognised also that nothing would delight his enemies more than a continuing public dispute between the Soviet Union and Cuba. For a fortnight the Cuban media had been full of indignation over Soviet behaviour. Now Castro telephoned Carlos Franqui: 'Lay off the Soviets, okay? Eleven articles against them is more than enough.'

Over the years Castro came to accept grudgingly that the Russians had to pull out the missiles, due to their military and naval inferiority to the United States. He told one visitor that Khrushchev was 'older and wiser' than himself, and that his own harder line could have resulted in a catastrophic war. But he continued to believe that Khrushchev should never have put the missiles into Cuba in the first place unless he was prepared to keep them there. The Cubans had been misled by Soviet propaganda about the strength of their armed forces. 'I never foresaw the possibility of withdrawal. Perhaps it was because of the revolutionary fervour, passion and fever of those days. Once the missiles were established, we never even considered that they might be withdrawn.'

12 Revolution and More Revolution

It took time for Castro to recognise Khrushchev's wisdom in withdrawing the missiles. For some months he felt it as a personal humiliation. The outcome of the crisis plunged him again into a period of introspection and depression. He smoked a lot of cigars, and drank a lot of coffee and brandy, but he lost his usual voracious appetite. Visitors noticed his changed appearance. He lost weight, and looked tense and gaunt. With his intimates he kept chewing over the folly and injustice of Khrushchev's decision to pull back without consulting him. Far from strengthening international socialism, Khrushchev had given the Americans an undeserved triumph. After all, it was not Castro who had asked for the missiles in the first place. Why on earth had Khrushchev been so keen to bring the missiles to Cuba if he was going to scuttle at the first show of American displeasure?

As Castro saw it, the Russians had made other serious errors. Why had they insisted on secrecy? Surely the whole point of deterrence was that the enemy should be aware of the deterrent. They were doing nothing illegal. Cuba had every right to receive weapons from a friend. Secrecy merely made them look underhand and deceitful. It was also an error to give misleading information about the type of missiles being installed. Castro himself had loyally followed the Russians in arguing that all the weapons in Cuba were defensive, because their purpose was to defend Cuba. But he would never have denied, as the Russians did, that the intermediate-range missiles arriving in Cuba were strategic weapons, capable of offensive use if necessary. Lying about this had played into Kennedy's hand, giving him the moral high ground. The only missiles which the Russians did not withdraw were some surface-to-air missile batteries. They left these in Cuba only after Castro accepted the humiliating condition that he could not use them to shoot down the American U-2 aircraft which were continuing to fly over Cuban territory.

What made the situation even more galling for Castro was that the European and Latin American Communist Parties, and most independent left-wing intellectuals, were praising Khrushchev for his statesman-like conduct, and for supposedly saving world peace. Only the Chinese had given wholehearted support to the Cuban position. They at least understood that those representing the poor, the oppressed, the exploited, had to make a stand sooner or later. Concessions for the sake of preserving peace only increased the appetite and determination of the imperialists. It was tempting to throw Cuba's weight firmly on to the Chinese side in support of world revolution. But China simply did not have the industrial and military strength to sustain Cuba against an American blockade. With Soviet aid many new industrial projects had been started, but meantime industrial production in Cuba was declining across the board. Cuba was not even able to meet its supply commitments to the Soviet Union. If the Russians in response cut oil supplies, Cuba would return to a pre-industrial subsistence economy. Perhaps, Castro sometimes hinted, he should leave Cuba and hand over to someone able to work more harmoniously with the Russians.

When Castro talked of resignation, he was only expressing frustration, or testing reactions. He had no serious intention of relinquishing power. In December 1962 he spent some days in his old haunts in the Sierra Maestra, reliving the heroic struggle against Batista. The experience helped to restore his self-confidence and morale. Then in February 1963 he received a thirty-one-page personal letter from Khrushchev. It had been written during a long train journey and was an emotional, eloquent and, in Castro's word, poetical document, justifying the sacrifices made by the Soviet Union in the cause of peace. The letter invited Castro to set aside past differences and to pay a visit to the Soviet Union, where he would be given a very warm reception. Castro was deeply touched by the letter. He decided to accept the invitation. After all, Cuba was in desperate need of Soviet aid, for defence as well as the economy. And Cuba could still provide valuable services for the Soviet Union, being as it was an outpost of Socialism in the heart of the Americans' sphere of influence.

To prepare the ground for his visit, Castro started once more to praise the Soviet Union. He claimed to have been misreported when *Le Monde* published an earlier interview in which he had been critical of the Russians. But he was careful not to close off any options completely, and to keep his friends as well as his enemies guessing. His renewed enthusiasm for the Soviet Union was not so unqualified that they could take him for granted. Nor was his hostility to the United States so absolute as to cause the Americans to give up hope of extracting him from the Soviet embrace. A few days before leaving Cuba he gave two long interviews to an attractive American woman journalist, Lisa Howard, in which he spoke positively about some recent measures taken by President Kennedy, in particular a decision to stop hit-and-run attacks on Cuba by exile groups based in Florida. Howard reported to the CIA that Castro wanted a rapprochement with the United States.

On 26 April 1963 Castro flew out of Havana in a huge, lumbering Soviet aircraft. After a bone-shaking sixteen-hour flight, the aircraft reached Murmansk in thick fog. Castro went to the cockpit to watch the landing; but after two failed approaches to the airport he withdrew, not wanting to make the pilot nervous.

He had intended to stay a few days in the Soviet Union, but ended up staying five weeks. He visited fourteen cities, was fêted and honoured everywhere, and made numerous speeches. The Russians pulled out all the stops to gratify him. Wherever he appeared, crowds cheered and shouted his name. When he took a fancy to a blonde Ukrainian girl, the Soviet Ambassador to Cuba obligingly drove her to a discreet late-evening assignment in Castro's hotel. He reviewed the May Day parade from the Kremlin wall, addressed a special rally in Red Square, was made a hero of the Soviet Union and was awarded the order of Lenin. No foreigner had ever received such honours in the Soviet Union. Yet this was not the veteran leader of a great power. Castro was officially thirty-six years old (in fact thirty-five), the leader of an island with a mere eight million people.

The Soviet Government also promised more economic and military aid. With typical bravado, Khrushchev promised that Soviet engineers would design and manufacture a machine to cut and process Cuban sugar cane. Castro undertook to make better use of Soviet aid, by imposing Soviet-style working methods and discipline. But discipline and restraint never came easily to Castro. He puffed his cigars unconcernedly at formal ceremonies where smoking was prohibited for lesser mortals. He threw the Soviet security system into confusion by insisting on going for a walk in Red Square in the middle of the night.

The Russians' extravagant display of goodwill towards Castro did not make him forget his bitterness over the withdrawal of the missiles. His anger was now dissipated, but he was still mystified by what seemed to him inexplicable errors in the Soviet handling of the crisis. He tried without success to get an explanation. Many years later he recalled: 'I put a lot of questions to all the Politburo members I met. I asked them one by one:

> Tell me, how was that decision made? What were the arguments used?' I couldn't get a single word out of them. They wouldn't answer the question. Of course, you can't be impertinent and say: 'Listen, answer me!' For all my questions, I couldn't get an answer.

Even after nearly a month of the official visit, Castro had not had enough. He spent a further week on a 'private' holiday with Khrushchev. The atmosphere in Khrushchev's dacha was very relaxed and friendly, but even now Khrushchev felt unable to be completely frank about the missile crisis. For him, a crucial element in the deal with Kennedy was the secret American promise to remove their Jupiter missiles from Turkey. But he knew this was another sore point with Castro. The Russians had told Castro that the missiles in Cuba were needed to defend Cuba. If that was true, what was the relevance of American missiles in Turkey or Italy? Offering to withdraw the missiles in Cuba in return for American withdrawals elsewhere made it appear that Cuba was merely a pawn in a larger game. Khrushchev was aware of Castro's sensitivities on this point; but in reading out to Castro the text of an exchange of messages with Kennedy during the crisis, he let slip a reference to Turkey and Italy. Castro interrupted, as he later related. 'I said: "Nikita, would you please read that part again about the missiles in Turkey and Italy?" He laughed that mischievous laugh of his. He laughed, but that was it. I could see that he was not going to repeat it. As the saying goes, you don't talk about nooses in the house of a man who has been hanged.'

When Castro returned to Cuba, he praised everything he had seen in the Soviet Union so effusively that his comments were published in full in Moscow, over two days, in both *Pravda* and *Isvestia*. His adulation of all things Soviet killed off the tentative moves which had been under way in Washington to explore the possibility of improving relations with Cuba. Instead, the economic embargo was tightened, and the CIA was authorised to embark on a new and more aggressive programme of sabotage and disruption.

With trusted intimates, such as Che Guevara, Castro criticised Khrushchev's policy of 'peaceful co-existence' and his reluctance to support violent revolution in Latin America. Fidel said that Khrushchev had betrayed Cuba once and could do so again. He allowed Che to publish a long article on rural guerrilla warfare which was seen as an oblique endorsement of the Chinese hard line. But in front of the television cameras Castro had only glowing praise for Khrushchev and his policies. More importantly, he inaugurated a long period of ever-closer integration with the Soviet economy, the centrepiece of which was to produce more sugar in return for Soviet oil. At the start of the Revolution, Castro had wanted to diversify the economy, reducing the importance of sugar. But the Russians had no use for Cuban cement or chemicals. They wanted sugar. So the dream of diversification away from sugar was abandoned.

With the economy already in deep trouble, Hurricane Flora devastated much of the Cuban countryside. But challenges brought out the best in Castro. He personally directed rescue operations, appearing everywhere, raising morale, inspiring confidence in the Revolution's future. If Castro was expected to visit a factory or farm, the workers would work day and night to ensure that he was favourably impressed. Once he had been and gone, however, life would usually return to the new normality of low output, low motivation and torpid state management.

With investment now concentrated in the countryside, the capital city became increasingly shabby and run down. The revolutionary élite were normally expected to set an example of austerity by living in small flats. The many big houses of the former middle class were mostly either abandoned and decaying, or occupied by groups of impoverished internal migrants from Oriente. Sometimes Castro rewarded an official by allowing him to take over a large house abandoned by its former owners. But the new occupants tended to start behaving like the wealthy owners of the bad old days, chasing away small boys who climbed over the garden wall to steal fruit. Castro and Guevara preached that the Revolution would produce a New Man, motivated not by greed and ambition but by a desire to serve the community. Castro stuck doggedly to this belief, but was forced to recognise that it would be a slow process. The Cuban media, now totally subservient to the government, campaigned against the shirkers and loafers who were supposedly to blame for the continuing failure to achieve economic targets. Compulsory military service was introduced, not only to strengthen still further Cuba's large and well-equipped armed forces, but also to indoctrinate young men in the habits of discipline and hard work which so many seemed to lack.

On 26 July 1963 Castro addressed a rally to mark the tenth anniversary of his attack on the Moncada barracks. Among the thousands dutifully listening was Fidel's mother Lina. A few days later she died. Fidel attended the funeral with other members of the family including his younger brother Raúl, the hard-line Minister of the Revolutionary Armed Forces. But while Raúl wept copiously, Fidel showed no emotion at all. Was this an inability to express feeling, or just self-control? No doubt something of both. He had behaved the same way when he heard of his father's death while in exile in Mexico. On that occasion bystanders had been struck by the very un-Cuban lack of emotion with which Fidel received the news. The only sign of any inward reaction was that for a while he became more silent and introspective than usual.

Castro also showed little emotion later in the year when he heard the news of President Kennedy's assassination. His reactions were observed by a French journalist, Jean Daniel, who had come to Cuba after a meeting with Kennedy in Washington, and who wanted to act as an unofficial honest broker between the two governments. In the past, Castro had usually spoken of Kennedy with his full repertory of mockery and abuse, as an arrogant playboy. During the missile crisis he described Kennedy as behaving like the pirate Henry Morgan. He was not even up to the standard of Francis Drake, who 'had undoubted qualities'. But by the time of Daniel's visit, Castro's view of Kennedy had mellowed. Talking to Daniel he acknowledged that Kennedy had begun to show some realism and moderation. He commented that at least Kennedy was better than his Republican opponent, Senator Goldwater. 'I am willing to say I am a friend of Goldwater,' quipped Castro, 'if that will help Kennedy to defeat him.'

Castro was having lunch with Daniel when they were interrupted by an urgent telephone call for Castro from President Dorticós. According to Daniel, Castro looked sombre as he listened to Dorticós's report. 'A shooting? . . . Wounded? . . . Very seriously? . . .' When he returned to the table, he said: 'It's bad news.' An aide switched on a radio, and the group listened to the bulletins on Kennedy's condition. When Kennedy's death was announced, Castro stood up and said to Daniel: 'Well, that's the end of your peace mission. Everything is changed.' He searched for something positive to say about Kennedy which would nevertheless not be insincere. Eventually he said to Daniel: 'I'll tell you one thing: At least Kennedy was an enemy that we had got used to. This is a serious matter, an extremely serious matter.' He asked Daniel what he knew about Lyndon Johnson, the Vice-President who was swiftly sworn in as the new President. What was Johnson's relationship with the CIA? Daniel knew very little about Johnson.

When an American radio reporter described Jackie Kennedy's blood-stained stockings, this prompted an outburst from Castro about the bad taste and sensationalism of the American media. 'What sort of mind is this? There is a difference in our civilisations after all. Are you like this in Europe? For us Latin Americans, death is a sacred matter. Not only does it mark the close of hostilities, it also imposes decency, dignity, respect . . .' When details emerged about the assassin, Lee Harvey Oswald, who had been a member of the Fair Play for Cuba Committee, Castro said: 'They'll try to put the blame for this on us.' Defensively, he pointed out that he had always been against assassination, even during the struggle against Batista. Speaking on television the following day, Castro said the Cubans had nothing to do with the assassination and knew nothing about Oswald. No leftist would have committed such a crime. It was more likely that the assassination was the work of the extreme right, of people who opposed Kennedy because they wanted a more aggressive and belligerent policy.

Facing an election in less than a year, President Johnson was not going to risk appearing soft on Castro. Tightening the economic and diplomatic squeeze on Cuba became an even higher priority for the new Administration. Castro's question about Johnson's relations with the CIA proved foresighted. Johnson evidently had fewer scruples than the Kennedy brothers about using assassination as a political weapon. An employee of the Havana Libre cafeteria was recruited by the CIA and tried to place a cyanide capsule in a milk-shake drunk by Castro. But the capsule had been frozen and broke before it could be delivered.

The American economic squeeze increased Cuba's dependence on the Soviet Union. Castro was under pressure from Khrushchev to reduce the huge cost of Soviet support. Khrushchev wanted Castro to sign up unreservedly to his doctrine of peaceful co-existence, and to try to restore normal relations with the United States. During a second and briefer visit by Castro to the Soviet Union, the two leaders approved a five-year trade agreement, in which the Soviet Government committed itself to taking most of Cuba's sugar production at favourable prices. In return, Castro endorsed peaceful co-existence, and assured his hosts that he had no desire to provoke the Americans.

However, events soon produced another dangerous crisis. The US Coast Guard arrested four Cuban fishing boats for allegedly fishing in US waters. Since the boats were found to have breached no Federal law, the US government ordered their release. At this point the state authorities in Florida claimed jurisdiction. The crews of the four boats were taken to Key West and put in prison. For all his promises of restraint, this was more than Castro could stomach. He went on television to denounce the American action. He said that US warships violated Cuban territorial waters every day. A spy-ship was permanently stationed offshore from Havana. Spy-planes regularly violated Cuban airspace. Yet here were thirty-six innocent Cuban fishermen, in international waters, arrested, imprisoned and subjected to every indignity in an attempt to force them to defect. His response was to cut off the supply of water to the US naval base in Guantánamo. Raising the stakes further, the Americans dismissed most of the Cuban workers at the base. At a crisis meeting of the Cuban government, Castro and his ministers joked about the panic which Khrushchev must be undergoing.

But Khrushchev did not have to worry. A Florida judge gave the four boat captains suspended jail sentences of six months, and fined them US$500 each. The fines were paid immediately and the crews returned in their boats to a heroes' welcome in Havana. Castro greeted them as examples of the New Man produced by the Revolution. 'Your dignity and morale must have impressed the enemy. This is a new generation of Cubans.' Playing partly to the gallery in Moscow, Castro went on with a show of moderation. He said that the Guantánamo naval base should be returned some day to Cuba, but there was no hurry; meantime, now that the Cuban fishermen had been released, he was willing to resume water supplies. However, the Americans were not willing to be beaten with that stick more than once. They decided to supply the base by tanker until desalinisation plants had been installed.

For all his frequent talk of Communist discipline, Castro remained a maverick and a magpie, hopping from one enthusiasm to another. In 1964 his obsessive focus of interest was agriculture. He spent little time in his office with government papers. He travelled frequently around the countryside, visiting the remotest villages, often driving his own jeep, questioning farm workers, listening to complaints, above all giving everyone the benefit of his seemingly encyclopaedic knowledge of agronomy, mostly acquired from books and magazines. With his exceptional memory, he impressed even experts with his detailed knowledge of their particular disciplines. He had total confidence in his own abilities and intuitions. Reading an article in a technical journal would be enough for him to impose a new agricultural policy throughout the country.

The sugar harvest, Castro announced, would more than double over the next five years to reach 10 million tons by 1970. The Revolution would produce 'a sugar atomic bomb', enabling it to dominate the world market. He took personal charge of experiments to measure the growth of sugar cane under different conditions. He said there would also be massive increases in meat and dairy production. Hundreds of special breeder bulls were imported from Canada to raise the quality of Cuban cattle. He launched a grandiose scheme to grow coffee in a belt of land around Havana, and ordered the planting of massive new citrus orchards.

Feeling a twinge of remorse about the situation of his old mistress Naty Revuelta, Castro had found her a job as a Science Attaché in the Cuban Embassy in Paris. Despite having no qualifications for the job, the beautiful Naty proved very effective in persuading some distinguished French scientists to take an interest in Cuba. In particular she made contact with a French agronomist called André Voisin, who specialised in the use of grasses as cattle-feed. Castro read a book by Voisin, and decided that his ideas on pasture for cattle should be put into practice throughout the island. He ordered 2,000 copies of every one of Voisin's many books, for distribution to schools and experimental farms, and invited the Frenchman to visit Cuba to lecture. When Voisin and his wife arrived, they were treated like visiting heads of state. At a dinner Castro insisted that Voisin taste some 'Cuban Camembert'. Voisin conceded that it was 'not bad' and 'in the French style'. Castro doggedly persisted in trying to get Voisin to admit that Cuban Camembert was better than French Camembert. Voisin could not be pushed that far. He reached for one of Castro's cigars, and asked if Cuban cigars were not the best in the world. 'You can't beat tradition. My cheese and your cigars have centuries of experience behind them.'

That was the problem for Castro's new agriculture. He brushed aside the accumulated wisdom of traditional Cuban farmers. The dramatic improvements which he expected did not materialise. Voisin, perhaps overexcited by the attentions of his domineering and demanding disciple, died of a heart attack while still in Cuba.

In October 1964 Khrushchev was suddenly ousted from power. His colleagues accused him of harebrained schemes, over-hasty decisions, boastfulness and numerous other defects. All these faults had been demonstrated, according to the new Soviet leaders Brezhnev and Kosygin, in Khrushchev's handling of the Cuban missile crisis of 1962, when he had 'invited defeat' at the hands of the imperialists, and gravely damaged Soviet prestige.

After his initial shock, Castro was left with mixed feelings over Khrushchev's fall. He had never completely forgiven Khrushchev for having withdrawn the missiles from Cuba without consulting him. He remained scornful of Khrushchev's unwillingness to support violent revolution in Latin America. But despite these political differences, Castro felt genuine admiration and affection for Khrushchev as a man: his sharp, peasant intellect and warm, ebullient personality. Castro saw in Khrushchev something of his own mercurial temperament. He had often praised Khrushchev to the skies. His speeches extolling Khrushchev's virtues had usually been published inside the Soviet Union. He could not afford to alienate the new Soviet leadership by appearing to defend his old friend; but he judged it would be opportunistic and undignified to join in the criticism. He therefore kept silent.

Castro hoped that the new leadership in Moscow would be more positive towards his efforts to foment the spread of revolution. Despite Soviet disapproval, he had continued to channel weapons and other assistance to guerrilla organisations in various Latin American countries. He scrupulously avoided any interference in Mexico, since the Mexican government had not broken relations with Cuba. But other Latin American governments had followed the lead of the United States in breaking diplomatic and economic ties with Cuba. If slapped in the face, Castro was not a man to turn the other cheek. If the governments of Colombia and Venezuela joined the United States in trying to destroy the Cuban Revolution, he in turn would help the Marxist guerrilla groups that were trying to overthrow those governments. Che Guevara was given a free hand to launch the 'Andean project', an unsuccessful attempt to ignite a guerrilla insurrection in the mountainous regions of Argentina, Bolivia and Peru.

Castro's government had also established contacts with revolutionary movements in other parts of the world, including Zanzibar, South Yemen, Palestine and Vietnam. The Cubans provided some training and equipment. Even revolutionaries from the United States, mostly blacks, were invited to spend time on Jibacoa beach, east of Havana, where they could meet fellow revolutionaries such as visiting members of the Vietcong. Castro took a particular interest in pro-Cuban Americans. He arranged for Bunny Hearn to receive a lettuce every day for her pet rabbit.

In 1964, however, the region of the world which seemed most ripe for revolutionary change was Africa. Black Africa was backward, turbulent and only partially free of European rule; and most backward and turbulent of all was Congo Kinshasa, the former Belgian Congo. The United States was spending a lot of resources to ensure that this huge country, with its vast mineral resources, remained under a pro-Western government. What a coup it would be if Castro could act as a catalyst for revolutionary change in the Congo!

The man to spearhead Cuba's first major incursion into Africa was Che Guevara. Guevara's departure did not, as some believed, mark a serious split with Castro. Fidel and Che always had some ideological differences and arguments, but their friendship and mutual admiration was never impaired for long. It sometimes suited them to play a double act, with Castro as moderate and Guevara as the extreme radical. During the war against Batista, when some anti-Communists complained to Castro about Guevara's Marxist views, Castro said that after victory he would send Guevara on a foreign mission to get him out of the way. And indeed, a few months after victory he sent Guevara on a tour of Africa, Asia and Eastern Europe, lasting more than two months. Asked by a colleague why Castro had sent him on this long and seemingly rather pointless mission, Guevara replied: 'Because I annoyed him too much.' But Guevara was being playful. From the start Castro was determined to play a major role on the world stage, and he saw Guevara as having the intellect and vision to prepare the ground.

By the end of 1964 Guevara had run out of steam as Minister of Industry. The new emphasis on agriculture had downgraded the importance of industrialisation. Guevara was also embroiled in a prolonged and fruitless ideological argument with most of his fellow Ministers. He wanted to move straight to a Utopian Communism in which everyone was paid according to his needs, with only moral incentives to work hard. The more orthodox Communists in the government insisted that in the early stages of Socialism it was essential to have material incentives, i.e. pay differentials. Castro for once stood on the fence, sympathising with Guevara but not wanting to support in public an anti-Soviet line. At this point it suited both Castro and Guevara that Che should leave Cuba and devote himself entirely to the spread of revolution. In February 1965 Guevara made a speech in Algiers, in the course of another African tour, setting out the case for worldwide revolutionary action against imperialism. He criticised the Soviet Union for timidity, and for acting like imperialists, giving insufficient aid and tying political strings to it. On his return to Havana, he was greeted by Castro, but then disappeared from public view. Was he in disgrace? Was he in prison or dead? Where was he? Castro refused to say.

In fact Guevara had embarked on a new quixotic adventure. He told his mother: 'Once again I feel the ribs of Rocinante under my heels . . . I return to the road with my lance under my arm.' He flew with a team of élite Cuban volunteers to Brazzaville in Central Africa. The left-wing President of Congo Brazzaville wanted Cuban military and security help, both to consolidate his own position and to engineer revolution in the much larger neighbouring Congo Kinshasa. Guevara set about the task of organising a Marxist guerrilla movement in Congo Kinshasa. It was an uphill struggle. Tribalism was strong, political awareness virtually non-existent. Most of the potential Congolese recruits were unimpressed by the Cuban revolutionaries and mystified by Guevara's Marxist rhetoric.

Back in Cuba, economic conditions remained difficult. Most people still supported the Revolution, and many believed Castro's promises of a prosperous future under Communism. But the present involved hard work with little reward. Those who showed the wrong attitude were hounded by the Committees for the Defence of the Revolution. Not surprisingly, there were still people who wanted to leave, especially those who had relatives among the exile community in Florida. But direct links with the United States had been broken, and it was difficult and expensive to get on a flight to Mexico or Spain. Some therefore took the desperate course of trying to travel the ninety miles to Florida in flimsy homemade boats or rafts. Those who succeeded were greeted as heroes and seen as evidence of the terrible conditions in Castro's Communist dungeon.

The boat people were bad propaganda for Castro. But he thought he could turn the situation to his advantage. He suddenly announced that anyone who wanted to join relatives in the United States was free to do so. The government would help to arrange their departure from the fishing port of Camarioca. Thousands took up his offer. Castro was content to get rid of disaffected people, but the numbers were greater than he had wanted or expected. He announced that young men between fifteen and twenty-six would not be allowed to leave. 'We are not prepared to provide cannon fodder for Vietnam.' The Americans were also worried at the prospect of an uncontrolled mass migration. For the first time in years the two sides had a common interest in negotiating a deal. Soon two flights a day were departing from Cuba for Miami with a list of passengers agreed between the two governments.

Economic difficulties and public disaffection were not going to make Castro backtrack from his Marxist–Leninist commitment. In October 1965 the ruling party, whose name had changed several times, always implying a loose coalition of revolutionary groups, was reconstituted and given a new and simpler title: the Cuban Communist Party. The membership of the Central Committee was published. Che Guevara's name was not on the list. Was this confirmation that Che had fallen from grace? It was probably to avoid this impression that Castro finally decided to give at least a partial explanation of Guevara's mysterious disappearance. In melodramatic style he read out in public a letter which Che had written to him before his departure from Cuba six months earlier. The letter was long and emotional. 'Other nations call for my modest efforts. I can do what you are unable to do because of your position as the leader of Cuba. The time has come for us to part . . . If my final hour finds me under other skies, my first thought will be of this people and especially of you . . . I embrace you with all my revolutionary fervour, Che.'

Che's letter did not reveal his intended destination. And it was not long after Fidel published it that Che gave up the hopeless task of organising a revolution in the Congo. He returned secretly to Cuba, planning to start again in the more familiar and congenial environment of South America. His appearance was heavily disguised. Fidel Castro invited his most intimate colleagues to a meal to meet a foreign businessman. At first none of them realised that the plump, balding, middle-aged foreigner was none other than The Che. After a period of rest and recuperation in Cuba, Guevara flew secretly to Prague. From there he and seventeen Cubans travelled to Bolivia, resolved to light a revolutionary flame in the heart of the South American continent.

While Castro's secret agents were providing weapons and training to revolutionary movements around the world, he himself was trying to build the broadest possible international coalition of Third World governments and movements opposed to 'imperialism, colonialism and neo-colonialism'. In 1966 he staged in Havana the First Tri-Continental Conference of Africa, Asia and Latin America. There were already plenty of left-wing Afro-Asian organisations and movements. The novelty in Castro's approach was to bring Latin America into the circle. This was a head-on challenge to one of the most central tenets of US foreign policy: that the Western hemisphere was an area of special interest, under US tutelage and protection. In American eyes the Tri-Continental Conference increased even further the danger and malevolence of Castro's international role.

A master of publicity and rhetoric, Castro was now a significant actor on the world stage. But he could not hide the fact that he presided over a weak and dependent economy. The planned growth in sugar production was still proving elusive. Castro had enthusiastically ordered large numbers of the specially designed Soviet combine harvester, but it proved inefficient on rough land, and no substitute for manual labour. To set an example, Castro spent hours and days being photographed cutting cane with a machete, sweating profusely. Thousands of urban workers were drafted to the countryside to help with the harvest.

In 1966 Castro had hoped to conclude a deal with China to exchange sugar for rice. Such a deal would have increased his room for manoeuvre, making him less dependent on the Soviet Union. But at the last minute the Chinese pulled out. They could not spare the rice and did not need Cuba's sugar. Meanwhile Castro had converted rice-fields in Cuba to sugar cane. As a result even rice, a staple of the Cuban diet, was in short supply. The Chinese Embassy in Havana further infuriated Castro by assiduously circulating their crudely self-serving anti-Soviet propaganda. Castro felt exasperated and betrayed. In a series of speeches he lashed into the Chinese with all the fury and rancour of a rejected suitor.

Later in the year Castro went through another of his periods of apparent depression and withdrawal, speaking little and appearing distraught and frustrated. Possibly he was ill, or had a minor operation. But as on previous occasions, he recovered his spirits and returned to the fray in an even more militant frame of mind. His quarrel with the Chinese had not made him any better disposed to the Soviet Union. He launched a scathing attack on the pro-Soviet Communist Party of Venezuela. The Venezuelan Communists had criticised Cuba for meddling in Venezuelan affairs, and for supporting a Venezuelan 'faction' which favoured armed insurgency rather than political action. Castro would take lessons from no one. No country, he insisted truculently, had achieved Communism, not even the Soviet Union. Since the road to Communism was in uncharted territory, every revolution had the right to seek its own route. Cuba would continue to support the Marxists who were ready and willing to fight, rather than those who just wanted to talk.

Castro found an eloquent spokesman for his ideas in the shape of the left-wing French intellectual Régis Debray. After long hours of discussion with Castro, Debray published his book *Revolution within the Revolution,* setting out with passionate conviction Castro's case for creating ever more hot-points of rural guerrilla insurgency in the Third World. The book gave hope and inspiration to thousands of young Latin American radicals. From his secret camp in the Bolivian jungle, Che Guevara fanned the flames in a long message calling for 'two, three, many Vietnams' to sap and eventually destroy the strength of US imperialism. Castro in turn talked up the progress of the Bolivian insurgency. He said the Americans were sending more and more 'advisers' to prop up the repressive Bolivian government, but, as in Vietnam, they would fail to stop the revolutionary tide. Castro's intelligence chief in Paris contacted Debray and transported him secretly to the Bolivian jungle, so that a distinguished writer would be able to give a first-hand account of the Triumph of the Revolution.

But a gap was opening up between Castro's predictions and the reality of Che's meagre progress. Weakened by illness, and demoralised by the harsh terrain and relentless rainfall, Guevara's little band were on the run. Castro sent some trusted high-level agents to reinforce the group, but the Cubans were cold-shouldered by the Bolivian Communist Party, and viewed with suspicion by many of the peasants they had come to liberate. In October 1967 Guevara was captured by a detachment of the Bolivian army. On orders from the Bolivian High Command the prisoner was shot. Photographs of his naked corpse, his head propped up to facilitate recognition, were sent round the world. The Empire had struck back.

Fidel Castro was deeply upset by the news, and for once he showed his feelings. According to Celia Sánchez, he locked himself in his room and punched and kicked the walls. His emotion was not only for the death of a friend. It was a major setback to his own hopes and ambitions. How could he explain away Che's failure? In public, Castro praised him as a great and selfless revolutionary, but it now also suited him to point out that Che had a fault. He was too modest, too unconcerned about his safety. Castro said that even in the Sierra Maestra, Guevara had shown an impetuous disregard for danger. His colleagues had had to intervene to prevent him from putting his life at risk unnecessarily. This criticism was not a betrayal of Che. Castro was merely trying to minimise the damage to the revolutionary cause. Guevara was captured and killed because he was too unconcerned about his personal safety. Other revolutionary leaders, Castro implied, would not have this weakness, and wound not fail. Bolivia was not, for the time being, a second Vietnam. But the imperialists should not rub their hands with glee. Other Vietnams would certainly emerge.

It was not only the imperialists who were pleased to see the end of Che Guevara. Pro-Soviet journalists around the world wrote articles drawing lessons from Guevara's failure. It showed, they argued, that in Latin America armed insurgency would fail; that the way forward lay through patient, non-violent political work against a background of peaceful co-existence. Castro had no difficulty recognising this line as an indirect criticism of himself. His irritability was worsened when he learnt that some prominent Cuban 'Old Communists', especially those close to the Soviet Embassy, were plugging the same line.

Castro's security services had received a lot of advice and equipment from the Soviet KGB. This did not prevent the KGB from running its own network of informants and agents of influence inside Cuba. Nor did it prevent Castro from keeping tabs on the KGB. On Castro's orders Manuel Piñeiro, 'Redbeard', a security officer fanatically loyal to Fidel, organised a surveillance operation, with bugs, directional microphones and secret cameras, against Cuban officials suspected of being more loyal to the Soviet Union than to Cuba. Some were arrested and confronted with the evidence

of their disloyalty, to the fury and indignation of the KGB. The most prominent 'Old Communist', Aníbal Escalante, showed his admiration for Stalinist
methods by making an abject public confession of his faults, requesting that
the full weight of revolutionary justice be used against him.

In a further attempt to offset the public demoralisation caused by Che's
death, Castro ordered a Great Revolutionary Offensive, in the style of Mao's
Great Leap Forward. Almost all that had survived of private enterprise – small
shops, bars, restaurants, repair centres – were nationalised. These places, said
Castro, were centres of profiteering, corruption, idleness and immorality.
They were offensive to honest, hard-working people in the fields and factories. Later he tried to crack down on displays of Western popular culture. The
'Swinging Sixties' had arrived even in revolutionary Cuba, producing a crop
of long-haired boys and mini-skirted girls addicted to Beatles music. Parents
were pressurised to stamp on such symptoms of counter-revolutionary
degeneracy.

Castro's immediate reactions to Che's death were tactical and political. He
tried to explain away Che's failures, while at the same time using his
martyrdom to inspire revolutionary enthusiasm. Che became an icon of
purity, idealism and commitment. But Che's death had a more long-term and
profound effect on Castro's own outlook and state of mind. With Castro, Che
had always served as a revolutionary conscience, constantly prodding him to
stick to principled, radical positions and to eschew cautious pragmatism.
With Che's death, Castro was freed from this sometimes troublesome
conscience. He was emotionally tired. He seemed to be permanently at war
on all fronts, not only against the imperialist enemy but also against Soviet
timidity and duplicity, against Chinese divisiveness, against the lack of mili-
tancy of Latin American Communists, against the laziness and shoddy work
of many Cubans, against the dead hand of incompetent Cuban bureaucrats.
He began to hanker for a more stable and comfortable relationship with the
Soviet Union. Perhaps his rejection of Soviet advice had sometimes been
over-hasty. Perhaps Guevara's failure did show that the road to worldwide
revolution would be longer than he had hoped. He began to feel, and to
express, more gratitude for the Soviet aid which he had previously accepted
as no more than his due.

The culmination of Castro's return to the Soviet fold came in 1968, when
the Soviet Union and several Warsaw Pact allies invaded Czechoslovakia to
crush the reformist government of Alexander Dubcek. Many left-wing intellectuals expected Castro to condemn the invasion. Important Communist
Parties in the West, notably the French and Italian, had publicly deplored the
Soviet action. How could a champion of national independence like Castro
fail to denounce a blatantly illegal act of superpower aggression? But Castro

saw things very differently. For him Dubcek's 'Socialism with a human face' was not socialism at all. It was a cover for a drift to Western liberalism. Dubcek was allowing the false freedom to chip away and undermine all the basic tenets of the Marxist state. Consciously or unconsciously, he was trying to reverse the progress of Communism. Above all, he was giving aid and comfort to the West, and especially to the United States.

It therefore did not take Castro long to decide to come down firmly in support of the Soviet action. It was painful to have to use military force, but necessary and right to do so when Socialism was under threat. Castro described the invasion as an act of comradely solidarity. He was privately grat-ified to see that the Soviet Union still had the nerve to take decisive and controversial action to uphold the strength and unity of the Socialist camp. On a visit to Moscow he even suggested to his hosts that he might engage in an act of public self-criticism for the many anti-Soviet comments he had made since the time of the missile crisis. The Russians advised him not to make any such self-criticism. They had invested a lot of capital in building up the image and prestige of Castro, and saw no benefit in his admitting to mistakes, even the mistake of having criticised the Soviet Union.

Like Margaret Thatcher, Castro always viewed a particular event in the context of the wider conflict between ideologies. Whom would it benefit? The Western camp or the Socialist camp? Us or them? His view of the Soviet invasion of Czechoslovakia was similar to the view taken by Thatcher, two decades later, of the invasion of Panama ordered by the first President Bush. The liberals might complain. The lawyers might say that it was contrary to international law. But it clearly benefited the forces for good in the world, and therefore deserved unqualified support. As Castro said when justifying the execution of Batista soldiers, justice was not a question of legal technicalities, but of moral conviction.

13 The Private Man

As far as the Cuban public knew, Castro had no private life. His working hours, his admirers assumed, were all devoted to the Revolution. And in fact, this image was not far from the truth. He resembled Margaret Thatcher not only in his assessment of invasions, but in temperament. He had a mission to change his country and the world. His obsessive desire to fulfil this mission kept the adrenaline running and gave him seemingly inexhaustible energy. Like Thatcher, he often worked or talked until 3 a.m. or 4 a.m., showing no sympathy for weary aides who wanted to go to bed. Relaxation with no political purpose, such as reading fiction, had little appeal. If he read Shakespeare's *Julius Caesar*, it was to study what the play had to reveal about the mechanics of the historical process. Even when fishing at a holiday resort, he usually spent much of his time expounding his plans and ideas to his entourage. He would often devote many hours or even days to entertaining foreign visitors, but only because they had influence or prestige, or something practical to offer, such as a favourable press article. To the limited extent that he did have a private life, it was increasingly shrouded in secrecy.

In the first years of the Revolution, people knew at least something about Fidel's family life and personal interests. He was occasionally photographed playing games such as baseball, even fooling around on a golf course. His son Fidelito was seen travelling with him. Nothing appeared in print about his sex life, but in private he was called 'The Horse', a tribute to his supposed sexual prowess. Rumours, gossip and jokes circulated about his liaisons with various attractive women. People wondered whether he slept with Celia Sánchez, and whether there was any truth in the stories that Celia was a lesbian. Would he marry Naty Revuelta? Or perhaps Teresa Casuso, the glamorous friend whom he met when in exile in Mexico? Castro disliked and discouraged such gossip. By the late 1960s the barriers had become completely sealed. Everything related to his private life was treated as a state secret. This was one aspect of the Soviet system which Castro adopted without any reservation. He despised and vilified what he saw as the Western obsession with the private lives and tastes of famous people.

The curtain of secrecy covered even innocuous activities. By the age of forty Castro had settled down into a virtually monogamous long-term relationship. Yet it was not until near the end of the century that anyone outside his closest circle even knew of the existence of the woman with whom he spent the greater part of his adult life. She was Dalia Soto del Valle, a woman some twenty years younger than Castro. She came from a well-off family in the cigar business in Trinidad. Castro first met her when she was working as a secretary in the Sugar Workers' Union. From the time that she started living with Castro, she was cut off from almost all contact with her family and former friends. Her mother reportedly said that she had 'lost a daughter', and that Dalia was a virtual prisoner. She lived with Castro in a house on the western outskirts of Havana which became his main home. The only nearby buildings were occupied by military officers or security officials. The house had a large garden, but so many mature mango and ceiba trees that nothing happening in the garden would be visible from an overflying aircraft or satellite. Castro's fleet of cars disappeared into underground garages, and a heavily protected bunker was built under the house.

Dalia has been described as tall, fair and handsome, with a finely chiselled nose, and a thick mass of hair. She often wore black leather boots. In view of the tropical heat in Havana, the boots must have been for Castro's benefit. Dalia accepted with good grace that her role in Fidel's life was limited. Over breakfast she would pamper him with his favourite dishes, such as honey, buffalo yoghurt or grilled snapper. But as soon as Castro's aides appeared to discuss his programme for the day, Dalia quietly disappeared into the background.

By the time Fidel and Dalia had lived together for twenty years, they had acquired the routines and language of a typical middle-aged married couple, calling each other 'old thing' ('viejo' and 'vieja'). Dalia bore Fidel five sons. All were given names beginning with A, including Alex, Alexander and Alexis. Alexander was also Castro's *nom de guerre* in the Sierra Maestra. The obsession with Alexander must be significant. The Greek Alexander came from remote Macedonia, a long way from the sophistication of Athens. Yet he conquered most of the known world. Fidel came from remote Oriente, a long way from the political hub of Havana. But with better luck, and a bit more backbone in Moscow, might he not have gone down in history as a modern Alexander? That was certainly his ambition.

Castro clearly thought that alongside the modern Alexander there was no place for a First Lady. To the extent that anyone played that role, it was shared between Celia Sánchez and Vilma Espin, the President of the Cuban Federation of Women and wife (later divorced) of Raúl Castro. It is possible that Fidel had a brief sexual relationship with Vilma before she became attached to Raúl. An aide claims to have entered Fidel's tent in the Sierra Maestra during the war against Batista, only to find Fidel with his trousers down. A woman, whom he thought he recognised as Vilma, was crouching in the shadows. Fidel did not seem greatly embarrassed. He said: 'I won't be a moment. Don't go far. And keep Celia away.'

Whether or not this story is true, Vilma developed into the most presentable public face of Cuban revolutionary womanhood: pretty, lively, gracious and totally loyal to Fidel and to Communism. As for Raúl, he was Fidel's declared deputy and successor, and the guarantor of the loyalty of the armed forces. But he had none of Fidel's charisma and strength of character. He often drank to excess (usually the best Scotch whisky) and showed the effect by becoming either aggressive or maudlin. Despite his position and relationship to Fidel, Raúl was always somewhat in awe of the Maximum Leader. He hesitated to raise problems with Fidel if he thought Fidel would be annoyed.

Raúl's self-confidence may have been affected by the rumours about his parentage. His mother Lina had produced two sons, Ramón and Fidel, who looked very similar, both being tall and strong, with handsome, classical features; and then several years later she produced a third son, Raúl, who was short, effeminate-looking, and with slanted oriental eyes. By the time Raúl was born, Lina's husband Don Angel was already in his late fifties. Surely, people speculated, Raúl's father must have been someone other than the elderly Angel Castro. The favoured candidate was Felipe Miraval Miraval, the sergeant in charge of the local Rural Guard detachment. Miraval later became a colonel. After the Revolution he was given a long prison sentence for his involvement in the murder of a left-wing politician during the rule of Batista. He never openly claimed to be the father of Defence Minister Raúl, but gave encouraging winks and nods when fellow-prisoners questioned him about the rumours.

No one ever doubted the parentage of Ramón Castro. His appearance and gestures were so similar to Fidel's that people sometimes mistook him for the Commander-in-Chief. He gently stroked his beard and nose in exactly the manner of Fidel. He was also as garrulous as Fidel, becoming even more so with the passing of the years. But in contrast to Raúl, Ramón never even approached Fidel's politics. After the Revolution he had little contact with Fidel, and when talking to members of the government used expressions like 'you Communists'. As for Fidel's other siblings, Emma and Lidia remained generally well-disposed and supportive. The others drifted away from him. Juana became fiercely hostile, defecting to the United States and denouncing him as a dictatorial monster.

By the time Fidelito reached his teens, he was going to school under an assumed name, and was kept completely out of public view. Fidelito's mother

Mirta had departed for Spain in 1965 with her second husband. She was allowed to visit Cuba to see Fidelito only on condition that she said nothing to the media about her life or relationship with Fidel. Fidel's illegitimate children had little contact with him. All the boys were packed off in their early teens to Moscow, to study science and Marxism. The most troublesome child proved to be Naty Revuelta's daughter Alina. At the age of ten Alina was told that her father was not Naty's former husband, but Fidel Castro. The little girl was delighted. It gave her a good riposte to the children at her school who boasted about having important fathers. She also assumed that her all-powerful father would now solve all her problems and all the problems of her friends, such as shortages of food and inadequate housing. Complete strangers threw letters into Alina's garden, asking her to intervene with Fidel, for example on behalf of an unjustly imprisoned relative. She duly wrote to her father with a list of requests, but received no reply. Instead she was invited to a private viewing of Fidel playing basketball with the Cuban national team. She was not impressed. Whenever Fidel got the ball a path opened up in front of him. The professionals in the opposing team made only a poor pretence of trying to block his advance.

As a teenager Alina showed symptoms of being rebellious and emotionally disturbed. She joined a group of gilded youth, children of the government elite who exploited their position to drink, party and make love like the privileged youth of the old regime. When just seventeen she accepted a proposal of marriage from a secret police officer called Yoyi, who was considerably older than herself. He separated from his wife, a black entertainer, in order to marry Alina. Shortly before the planned wedding Alina received a summons to see her father in the Palace of the Revolution. The officials who called at the house where Alina and her mother lived were brusque and insulting, an indication that Fidel was not pleased. When Alina was ushered into Fidel's office, he looked serious but not hostile. They embraced. After some small talk, Fidel came to the point. She was too young to get married. In any case, the man she proposed to marry was completely unsuitable. It was outrageous that she should propose to marry at her age without even consulting him. In reply, she asked how she could have consulted him. She had had no contact for years and did not even know his telephone number. He acknowledged that he had been a bad father and had not devoted enough time and attention to her. But now it was his duty to stop her making a bad mistake. Did she know that Yoyi had been married to a cabaret singer? Alina asked if he was suggesting that Yoyi was unsuitable because he had married a black woman. Fidel told her not to be disrespectful. The point was that Yoyi wanted to marry her for self-interested reasons, because she was his daughter. How could that be? she asked. She had received no benefit at all from being his daughter, so why should Yoyi imagine he would gain any benefit from marrying her?

Eventually Fidel became impatient and laid down his terms. Alina should cancel the planned wedding. If after a further six months she still wanted to marry Yoyi, she could go ahead. He would attend the wedding, and pay for a wedding reception. But if she went ahead without the delay he proposed, he would have no further contact with her for the rest of his life. She decided to accept his conditions. After six months she had not changed her mind, and Fidel fulfilled his side of the bargain. The wedding reception reflected the obsessive secrecy which by now surrounded all Fidel's private activities. The only guests were bodyguards, security officers and Interior Ministry officials. The marriage, as Fidel had feared, lasted only a few months. Alina had two more marriages, and numerous affairs. She worked for a time as a model in a state enterprise which sold clothes and staged fashion shows for foreign tourists and diplomats. She sometimes embarrassed her loyal and long-suffering mother Naty. On one occasion she was arrested for prostitution. She became a much sought-after target for visiting western journalists who wanted a sensational 'scoop' about an encounter with Castro's rebellious daughter. Finally she escaped to Spain with a borrowed passport.

Fidel spent little time with his children and other relatives, even with his brother and deputy Raúl. Nor did his children by different mothers have much contact with each other. Alina was thirteen when she first met Fidelito, in the flat of Uncle Raúl. Fidel himself was seldom alone. He was usually surrounded by senior officials as well as bodyguards. His entourage usually also included a few personal friends such as Pepin Naranjo, his personal secretary, and Rene Vallejo, his personal doctor. With them he would play chess or chat about whatever topic was at the front of his mind. But visitors were often struck by the invisible barriers created by his position. Even in private he seemed something of a one-man band. His entourage laughed at his jokes, and provided just enough interjections to keep up the flow of conversation. But they never put up more than token opposition to his views on any subject. Ministers who in other situations were self-confident and assertive, in Castro's presence became silent or obsequious. When Castro was touring a factory or farm, he would often engage in banter with anyone from the manager to the cleaning lady. He would seem tolerant and relaxed even if someone shouted complaints at him. But ministers and generals knew that they should not imagine that they were free to raise awkward matters with him. They knew that in his presence they were expected to listen and support, not to be protagonists.

Castro had a keen enjoyment of food and drink. As a child he took a close interest in the work of his parents' Spanish cook, and never forgot how to prepare some typical Iberian dishes such as *bacalao* (salted cod). As a young man he often did his own cooking, and considered himself an expert in preparing spaghetti. Later, when he had professionals to do his cooking, he sometimes walked into the kitchen to chat about how dishes should be prepared. At diplomatic meals he liked to show his expertise by discussing the food with his hostess. He appreciated good whisky and good wine, learning a lot about French wine from Georges Marchais, the leader of the French Communist Party. He was on one occasion so intrigued by the quality of a bottle of rare vintage port served by the Portuguese Ambassador that he had the empty bottle broken open, so that he could examine the crust.

Until the age of forty-eight, he was a heavy smoker of cigars. In October 1985 he gave up smoking, on medical advice and to set an example. He always attached importance to keeping fit. In his thirties and forties he still took vigorous exercise, including an occasional game of basketball. In later years his main form of exercise and physical relaxation was swimming. He sometimes swam underwater, with a fish harpoon, or snorkelled on the surface. He swam slowly, but could cover three or four kilometres. His interest in swimming encouraged the CIA to believe that this might provide a means of getting close to him. One plan was to place an unusually large and colourful shell on the sea-bed where Castro often swam. If Castro touched the shell, it would explode. When the Cuban counter-intelligence services learnt about these plots to assassinate him while he was swimming, he always swam with bodyguards in close attendance.

Despite the many reports of assassination plots, Castro only rarely wore special body protection. Press speculation about body armour was made plausible by Castro's physical build. His trunk was rather stout in comparison with his long, thin legs. He once boasted that his only bullet-proof vest was a moral one. In the same vein, he compared himself to a lion-trainer facing down a lion. 'The lion-trainer turns his back, and the lion stays calm. Sometimes I just turn my back and I am at ease.'

He had no ear for music, and listened to it only as a public duty. He also had little interest in the plastic arts. By contrast he loved books, and read voraciously throughout his life. He chose books mainly for their factual content and practical usefulness. But sometimes he read books which were unlikely to have relevance to his work, such as Hawking's *A Brief History of Time* and biographies of the great military leaders of antiquity. He claimed to have read *Don Quijote* six times. He was himself a literary perfectionist, spending hours polishing the text of letters to foreign heads of government.

When Castro met a delegation of Cuban journalists, he apologised for not seeing much of their work:

I rarely have time to watch television. Sometimes I see a three-minute summary of what has happened over the weekend. I often have meetings, commitments at all hours. For this reason I also read the press very quickly. You know that there are very few newspapers. Since there is a paper shortage, they can be read quickly. I have little time to listen to the radio. But I do read many despatches. I read many reports to find out what is happening in the world, and that takes time . . . I rely very much on books, because one learns a lot from them . . .

Totally absorbed by the exercise of power, Castro never seriously regretted devoting his life to politics. But he sometimes claimed to be the victim of duty:

I would like to be like García Márquez, who goes from one place to the other, wherever he wants to go, and doing whatever he wants. I would like to be a painter, or a scientist who does research. I can tell you that I chose the hardest job, and that what I am doing now is fulfilling my duty. If those who want to see the back of me can make this possible, but with honour and dignity, I shall be very grateful.

At a lunch with some European diplomats, Castro was asked whether he had any private hobbies, and how he spent his spare time. As usual, he said he had little spare time, and talked about his interest in swimming and reading. Then he added, with an innocent expression: 'To tell the truth, I especially like reading the reports sent by embassies in Havana to their governments.' He looked round to see the reaction of his audience to this apparent indiscretion. If a Cuban intelligence officer talked openly about spying on foreign embassies, he would no doubt be arrested for treason. But Castro made the rules, and he could give himself the pleasure of ignoring them.

'Well, we aren't as well informed as the Americans,' he went on:

Do you realise that every radio message, every telephone call going in or out of Cuba, is intercepted and recorded by the National Security Agency? And it's not only Cuba. Most of the world, especially Latin America, gets blanket coverage. They bug and tape their friends as well as their enemies. If the President of Venezuela picks up the telephone to talk to the President of Mexico, within hours a translation of the verbatim text of the conversation will be circulating in Washington . . .

This led on to a discussion of security. Castro commented that journalists in Washington often got hold of confidential information. This was because diplomatic reports and even secret intelligence were copied to so many people in so many different government departments. Because of that, leaks could easily occur. And when that happened, it was usually difficult or impossible to track down the source. 'We try to avoid that problem. We circulate confidential documents only on a strict need-to-know basis. Copies usually go only to a few named officials. Sometimes one of our Ambassadors sends me a report marked "To be read only by the Commander in Chief in person." The trouble is, after I've read it, I don't know what to do with it without breaching the rules . . .'

14 The Economy, a Poet and Chile

On 2 January 1969, the tenth anniversary of the Triumph of the Revolution, Castro asked a huge crowd in Revolution Square whether they would agree to have their sugar ration reduced. It was not the question they had wanted to be asked on this momentous anniversary. Life for most Cubans was already extremely difficult. Making ends meet was, in the common euphemism, 'complicated'. People still recognised and appreciated the most obvious and well-publicised benefits of the Revolution. Everyone could at least get a job, and they were not unduly bothered if this sometimes meant having three people doing the work previously done by one. Even in the remotest villages children went to school, dressed in smart uniforms, and received free school meals. The textbooks taught them about the heroic deeds of Fidel and Che, but also that all Cubans were now equal, with no white masters and black servants. The sick had access to free medical treatment of a standard previously available only to the well-off. Where the Revolution seemed constantly to fail was in production and distribution. Cuba was an island, yet the fish once on offer from street-vendors was nowhere to be found. Fruit continued to grow in the island's benign tropical climate, but why did so much of it rot on the trees, or in state warehouses?

Private shops had been closed in the Great Revolutionary Offensive of 1968. The state shops had plenty of attendants, but very few goods on the shelves. Castro had paraded detailed evidence to prove that 95 per cent of the private hot-dog vendors had been profiteers and counter-revolutionaries. The new state restaurants had no profiteers but usually also no hot dogs, and the waiters showed little interest in serving their clients. Rations were constantly being cut, and supplies running out. René Dumont, a sympathetic foreign adviser, summed up the situation: 'There was nothing to buy, and for that reason no incentive to work.' Now Castro was proposing that the ration of sugar, of all things, should be cut.

Earnestly, cajolingly, Castro explained the problem. The weather had been adverse. There had been drought when rain was needed, and then too much rain. Cuba had an obligation to send large amounts of sugar to the Soviet Union and East European countries, which had given valuable help to Cuba. When Cuba was faced with the threat of an invasion, they had provided sophisticated and expensive military equipment, without charge. When the imperialists imposed an economic blockade, they had agreed to purchase the sugar previously exported to the United States. They supplied oil and other vital commodities on terms much more favourable than were available elsewhere. But Cuba had to honour its side of the bargain. Difficulties in the sugar industry meant that Cuba was in danger of falling short in its supply commitments. Every ounce of sugar was desperately needed to fulfil Cuba's obligations. Until the production problems had been overcome, he proposed that the Cubans should accept a reduced sugar ration of two and a half kilos a month. Did the people agree? The cheer-leaders dutifully shouted their approval. But the response was not the clear mandate which Castro wanted, so he went over the arguments again. In the end, the volume of support was sufficient to enable Castro to conclude that the people themselves had freely and decisively resolved to accept further sacrifices.

While sugar remained the linchpin of the economy, Castro's time and energy were increasingly concentrated on the dairy industry. The death of the French agronomist André Voisin had in no way diminished Castro's determination to revolutionise milk production. Free milk for all schoolchildren was one of the revered and genuinely popular achievements of the Revolution. Castro had boasted that in a few years time Cuba would export dairy products to the Netherlands. But that goal was receding rather than approaching. The difficulty was that cattle breeds adapted to tropical conditions, such as the zebu, were low milk producers. European breeds were much more productive, but tended to wilt or die during a tropical drought.

Castro was convinced that science and technology could solve the problem. He read numerous books and technical articles about animal husbandry. He consulted more foreign experts. Some advised that he should forget about milk production, and concentrate on producing beef for export. With the money earned, it was argued, Cuba could import all the dairy products it needed. Castro rejected that advice as defeatist. He wanted Cuba to be a major producer of both milk and beef. There were some European and Canadian experts who accepted the challenge and agreed to come to Cuba, both to advise the government and to train Cuban technicians. At Castro's insistence the academic content of university courses was reduced and more emphasis was put on practical technology. The universities started to turn out thousands of engineers, agronomists, soil technicians and animal geneticists. Numerous experimental farms were set up, with Castro taking the closest interest in their programmes and results. He talked for hours on television about the advantages and drawbacks of different hybrid breeds. Every Cuban got to know the names of individual cows and bulls who were outstandingly productive. The most famous of all was *Ubre Blanca* ('White Udder'). When she died, she was mummified and put on display in a museum, a strange new heroine of the Revolution.

Sadly for Castro, the huge effort and enthusiasm which he expended on the dairy industry bore meagre results. High producers like White Udder needed special conditions and feedstock which it was difficult and expensive to replicate on a massive scale. Many of the cattle imported to raise standards failed to adapt to Cuban conditions. The quality of dogged persistence which had served Castro so well in the guerrilla war against Batista was now counter-productive. He persisted with radical and unorthodox experiments long after the evidence suggested that they would prove futile. Foreign experts were frustrated by Castro's constant interference in their work, and rejection of their advice.

In 1970 Castro faced what he himself recognised as the biggest challenge of his career. Since 1965 he had been promising that the 1970 sugar crop would reach 10 million tons for the first time in the island's history. All the resources of the state were harnessed to achieve this result. The goal was much more than an economic necessity. It was a political imperative. Castro had put the entire credibility of his government on the line. The 1969 crop, hampered by hurricane damage and transport bottlenecks, had been a mere 4.5 million tons. But Castro did not make this a pretext for reducing or postponing the target for 1970. On the contrary, he had ordered that steps which might have increased the 1969 crop should be abandoned in order to concentrate all efforts on preparations for the titanic struggle to produce 10 million tons in 1970. Falling short of this target by even one pound, said Castro, would represent a colossal failure.

The 1969/70 Christmas and New Year holidays were postponed to July 1970 in order to avoid any interruption to harvesting. Most of the armed forces, and thousands of urban and factory workers, were drafted to the fields and refineries, under military discipline. Detailed monthly targets were set for every province and every mill, starting in November 1969 and ending in mid-July 1970. Special committees were formed with the task of rooting out absenteeism and idleness. The media urged the people on, as if the survival of the nation depended on it. They were warned to be on the look out for attempts to disrupt the harvest organised by exiles in Florida, or the 'worms' at home who supported them. Everyone was in military mode. It was a battle for survival in which every weapon must be used.

In February the 3 million ton target was reached only one day behind schedule. But from then on the gap lengthened. The main problem was the breakdown of equipment in the grinding mills. Repairs could be made, but while sugar cane was lying on the ground or in lorries, it lost sucrose and the final product was reduced. In May, just when Castro was having to face the inevitability of failure, the anti-Castro exiles in Florida provided a distraction. Alpha 66, an exile military group, sank two Cuban fishing boats and seized the eleven crew members, offering to release them in exchange for Alpha 66 members held in prison in Cuba. Other exile commando groups stepped up their attacks. Castro organised a massive demonstration against the office in Havana where American diplomats worked. The building was formerly the US Embassy, but since diplomatic relations had been broken it was now technically the US Interests Section of the Swiss Embassy. The crowd threatened to invade the building unless the fishermen were released. Both the Swiss and US governments protested. But the US State Department also put pressure on Alpha 66 to release the fishermen. The fishermen were duly handed over to the International Red Cross, and allowed to return to Cuba.

Castro used the return of the fishermen to claim a victory. But he also took the opportunity to admit for the first time publicly a bigger defeat: the 10 million ton harvest would not be achieved. He described the setback as the worst event in the whole revolutionary struggle, worse even than the catastrophic failure of the assault on the Moncada barracks. He told his disappointed audience that he shared their pain. The final total for the harvest, announced on 24 July, was 8,531,688 tons. To achieve even this figure had necessitated a massive diversion of resources from other sectors of the economy. In a speech two days later, on the anniversary of Moncada, he acknowledged that there had been production shortfalls not only in sugar but in a whole range of other goods, including even dairy products. He listed sector after sector where targets had been missed. Who was to blame? The inefficiency of those in leadership positions could not be excluded. Then, with the huge crowd more subdued and sombre than usual, he suddenly and dramatically offered to resign. Most of the crowd seemed at first too startled to respond. A few shouted 'No!' This was not enough to deflect Castro. He would resign there and then, that very day, if that was the people's will. The shouting grew louder and more general. 'No! No! No!' Then came the chanting which usually greeted his triumphs. 'Fidel! Fidel! Fidel!'

Of course, Castro did not want to resign, and did not plan to resign. He had 'resigned' once before, more than ten years earlier. That had been merely a device to get rid of President Urrutia. Urrutia had been chosen by Castro himself, but had then become troublesome and unwanted. On that earlier occasion Castro had every reason to be confident that the overwhelming majority of the people would want him to stay. Could he be so confident in 1970, after he had presided over more than ten years of economic setbacks and failures, culminating in the disaster of the abortive 10 million ton sugar crop? For eight months most Cubans had worked like slaves, including Saturdays and Sundays, harried, chivvied and threatened, only to learn that all their efforts had failed to achieve the triumph which their leader had so often and so confidently predicted.

The state of the economy is usually a critical factor in the survival of any government, even an authoritarian government. Given the grim state of the Cuban economy in 1970, acknowledged in 1970 even by Castro himself, how and why did he survive? When he offered to resign, why did so many people shout for him to stay? Why did they not just keep quiet?

Part of the answer lay in the 'Achievements of the Revolution', the new schools, new roads, new hospitals. But more important was Castro's own personality. He seldom stopped talking, teaching, arguing, discussing. His 'direct democracy' might look like crude manipulation in the eyes of foreign observers, but it undoubtedly made millions of Cubans feel involved and consulted in a way that had never happened under previous governments, even those which had been elected in relatively free elections. Castro desperately wanted the people to understand what he was trying to achieve, to share his enthusiasms and resentments. As a result, most Cubans felt that his failures were also their own failures. And despite the failures, he had given them something to be proud of. Cuba might be the target of American hostility, even hatred, but it was no longer a target of contempt. Cuba was the David who had defied Goliath. When times were hard, should they make concessions, surrender, ask for American aid and investment? Never!

After the traumatic failure of the 10 million ton harvest, Castro remained as resolutely opposed as ever to the notion of multi-party elections and other features of 'bourgeois democracy'. But he became even more determined to extend his own notion of democracy and public consultation. At hundreds of mass meetings, workers were encouraged to put questions and suggestions to factory managers and party officials. Usually the suggestions from the grass roots were closely in tune with whatever Castro had been saying on television. But the orchestration was sufficiently light and indirect to give millions of Cubans the impression that they were indeed involved in decisions about how their factory or farm or hospital should be run. New laws were ostensibly introduced not at the initiative of Castro or the government, but as a consequence of pressure from public opinion conveyed at mass meetings. Repressive laws, for example establishing new punishments for persistent absenteeism, were genuinely popular. Castro's road to socialism was proving steep and stony, but most Cubans still preferred to stick to it. Only a minority, constantly reduced by emigration, were sufficiently disillusioned to want to bury the revolutionary project.

It was relatively easy for Castro to sustain the support and enthusiasm of farm and factory workers, teachers and bureaucrats. The intellectuals were more difficult. They had received a warning shot in 1961 when Castro had bluntly set out his doctrine of 'Within the Revolution everything, against the Revolution nothing.' But the hand of state control on the arts was light by the standards of other Communist countries. Castro made no attempt to follow the Soviet Union in imposing Social Realism. Abstract art and experimental writing were encouraged. In 1971 Cuba still had a relatively lively and diverse cultural life. Under the surface, however, tensions were mounting. Castro's support for the Soviet invasion of Czechoslovakia, and his growing acceptance of Soviet economic methods and direction, had shocked and disillusioned many previously well-disposed intellectuals both inside Cuba and abroad. A few prominent Cuban writers began to test the limits of the government's tolerance.

The crunch came in April 1971 with 'the Padilla affair'. The poet Heberto Padilla never attempted open defiance or public criticism of Castro. But his poems were politically disengaged, and full of enigmatic signals of disillusion. Cuban state security, which kept tabs on Padilla and his foreign friends, knew that in private his attitude to Castro was disrespectful and mocking. For the Cuban authorities the problem was made more serious when Padilla began to acquire an international reputation. An international jury, left-wing but outside Cuban control, awarded him a major literary prize, in preference to two stoutly pro-Castro candidates. The authorities feared that Padilla would become more openly disaffected in the belief that his international fame and connections would provide protection against harassment. Surely Castro would not risk an international outcry by acting against one of the country's most acclaimed writers?

When Castro ordered Padilla's arrest, he knew that there would indeed be an adverse international reaction. He was willing to pay the price. He told his Ministers that it would show who were the true friends of Cuba. Padilla was a corrosive counter-revolutionary influence which must be nipped in the bud. If the likes of Sartre and Octavio Paz and Mario Vargas Llosa ran to his defence, their friendship was not worth having.

Like scores of other dissidents before him, Padilla now faced the ordeal of a prolonged interrogation. Security officials played to him tape recordings of his private conversations. Even when visiting Mexico, the long arm of Cuban State Security had managed to bug his private meetings. There were also tape recordings of his wife, equally compromising. Under the strain Padilla fell ill and was hospitalised. In his hospital bed he received a visit from none other than Fidel Castro. Castro dismissed his bodyguards and stayed alone with Padilla. He said they had a lot to discuss, and plenty of time to do it. He played the aggrieved party. He was not the oppressor but the victim. Abroad, he said, people were speaking against the Revolution, and Padilla was responsible. When had the intellectuals ever done anything constructive for Cuba? They were always criticising, always finding fault. If Padilla still had any decency, any patriotism, it was not too late to show it.

Faced with the prospect of a long prison sentence, Padilla decided to do what Castro wanted. He prepared a long confession of his guilt, incriminating also some of his friends. He hoped that his abject self-criticism, in the grovelling language of Stalinist show trials, would be easily recognised as false and induced only by fear. The confession earned him immediate release. He repeated it, at even greater length, at a specially convened meeting of the Cuban Union of Writers and Artists. Most of those present probably had no difficulty in recognising Padilla's insincerity, but they kept their thoughts to themselves. Castro was well pleased. The loyalists were encouraged and the secret dissidents intimidated. Abroad, Padilla's confession made a predictably bad impression, but sympathy for Padilla himself evaporated. He was seen as a coward who had saved his own skin by incriminating his colleagues.

Castro went onto the offensive. In a speech he denounced the foreign intellectuals who showed more concern for a few renegade writers than for millions of Cuban children who now, thanks to the Revolution, had schools and health care. Cuba had no need for such pseudo-leftists and cultural imperialists. Cuba did not want the freedom to spread counter-revolutionary poison. It had no need for 'false intellectuals who plan to convert snobbery, extravagance, homosexuality and other social aberrations into expressions of revolutionary art'. Later he announced the establishment of a National Cultural Council which would ensure that Cuban writers and artists worked for the benefit of society, not just to gratify their own egos.

In November 1971 Castro felt secure enough to embark on his first trip abroad since 1964. He had demonstrated his total control on the domestic front, and had received new assurances of Soviet support during a visit to Cuba by Prime Minister Kosygin. After a decade of being the only 'beacon of Socialism' in Latin America, he now had a friend and ally in Salvador Allende, elected President of Chile a year earlier at the head of a shaky left-wing coalition ranging from revolutionary Marxist–Leninists to democratic Socialists. Castro had usually been scornful of those who believed that socialism could be achieved through peaceful elections rather than armed revolution. But Allende had taken some radical socialist measures, including the nationalisation of the big mining companies. Castro wanted to consolidate his friendship with Allende, thereby breaking out of the diplomatic isolation which the United States had succeeded in imposing on him in the Western hemisphere.

The Chileans initially expected Castro to stay about a week. In the event he stayed for twenty-three days, and every day was packed with activity. He visited all parts of the country, made speeches, gave press conferences, toured factories, went down mines and talked to everyone, from well-wishers in the street to hecklers at public meetings. Confident of his oratorical abilities, Castro thought he could strengthen support in Chile for Allende and for socialism. Allende in turn knew that Castro had an enthusiastic following among many on the left in Chile, especially students. He wanted to exploit Castro's popularity to his own advantage. At the same time he was slightly worried that Castro might embarrass him by going over the top and saying something outrageously provocative.

On the whole Castro tried to exercise restraint. In private he urged the most extreme and radical groups to show moderation and to avoid alienating the middle class and the military. He called for a 'strategic alliance' between Marxists and left-wing Catholics. He vigorously denied that in Cuba Catholics were persecuted for their beliefs. As in the early years of the Revolution in Cuba, Castro's constant message was the need for unity: if the left squabbled among themselves, this would open a path for the return of the reactionary right.

In his public speeches Castro generally refrained from commenting on the specifics of Chilean domestic politics. He did not want to give ammunition to those who were accusing him of meddling in Chile's internal affairs. Instead he talked at length about the history and experience of Cuba, about the cruelty and injustice of capitalism and above all about the ruthless and self-interested manipulation of Cuba and of Latin America by the United States. The conservative Chilean media naturally did their best to debunk and ridicule him. Here was a man, they said, who survived only thanks to Soviet aid and who had never won a free election, giving lessons to the Chileans on economics and democracy.

Stung by these criticisms, Castro said repeatedly that he had not come to give anyone lessons, but to bring friendship and solidarity. He was not claiming that Cuba should be a model. Cuba had made many mistakes. He hoped that by talking about these mistakes he would help the Chileans to avoid them. But Castro was never able to keep up a self-deprecating tone for long. He soon reverted to propaganda for Cuban achievements and strident attacks on US imperialism. He said that the US-controlled media had for years been spreading lies about Cuba. He therefore had the right to set the record straight. As usual he enjoyed displaying his knowledge. He talked to miners about new mining techniques developed in Cuba's nickel mines, and described how the United States had banned the import of any product or alloy which contained even a tiny amount of Cuban nickel, thereby destroying most of Cuba's markets. He told a gathering of fishermen about the activities of the Cuban fishing fleet; and workers at a fish canning plant about the best type of steel for manufacturing tin cans. He talked about women's rights to a stadium-full of cheering Socialist women. He accepted with good grace a proffered bottle of Coca-Cola, saying this showed he had 'no prejudices'.

Towards the end of his visit, Castro started to get rattled both by the hostile press coverage and by hecklers interrupting his speeches. He suspected the hand of the CIA. In a speech made in Allende's presence, he complained about the lack of courtesy shown to him. Even the Queen of England, he said, had not been subjected to such insults when she visited Chile. And although he remained publicly upbeat and optimistic about Chile's future, he expressed worries to his own entourage about Allende's prospects. The right-wing opposition and the far-left radicals were both becoming increasingly militant and aggressive. During Castro's visit an opposition demonstration in Santiago degenerated into widespread violence, with some of the protestors shouting for Castro to get out of Chile. Events seemed to be slipping out of Allende's control. Castro refused to accept that his own prolonged presence was only aggravating the country's internal divisions. Allende, in Castro's view, was too passive, failing to rally and unite his own supporters and to take the offensive against the opposition. Above all, Allende had failed to purge the armed forces, which remained solidly anti-Communist, ready to intervene if and when they judged that Allende's Socialist experiment had gone too far.

Castro's first encounter with a representative of the Chilean armed forces had taken place earlier in the year, when the Chilean Navy's training ship *Esmeralda* paid a goodwill visit to Havana. The captain gave a reception on board, which Castro attended. As a mark of respect to the Prime Minister, the captain invited him to have a private drink in his cabin. President Allende's sister and some other dignitaries were also invited. When Castro entered the captain's cabin he was closely followed by his usual half-dozen bodyguards, which made the small room uncomfortably crowded. The captain said to the bodyguards that this was a private occasion, and asked if they would kindly wait outside. The bodyguards stared straight ahead and made no move. They took instructions only from Castro. The captain repeated his request. He was the captain of the ship and could categorically guarantee the Prime Minister's safety in his cabin. After another awkward silence, Castro himself at last intervened, telling the bodyguards to leave.

Later, after some amiable small talk, Castro asked the captain what he wanted to do in Havana the following day, a Saturday. The captain said he would like to play golf. Allende's sister was shocked and embarrassed by this suggestion. After all, golf was the most individualistic and bourgeois of games, certain to be frowned on in Cuba. She proposed instead that the captain visit a new hospital or scientific centre. Once again, the captain was polite but firm. He said he had been a long time at sea, working hard, and felt he deserved a break at the weekend. The Prime Minister had very kindly asked what he wanted to do. What he wanted to do was play golf.

So golf it would be. The only golf course in Havana had once been a prestigious place, graced by the Duke of Windsor and Mafia boss Lucky Luciano. Now it was run-down and untended. A portrait of Queen Elizabeth the Second still stared down from the club-house wall, but only a few European and Japanese diplomats still played golf in Socialist Cuba.

As Castro left the *Esmeralda,* he was conscious that he had perhaps not made the best impression. The Chilean captain, with his courtly superior ways modelled on the British Navy, no doubt thought that the behaviour of Castro's bodyguards, and indirectly of Castro himself, had been boorish. So what? Why should the all-powerful ruler of Cuba care about the views and feelings of a relatively obscure visiting Chilean officer? But it was typical of Castro that he did care. If a person was Castro's enemy, he would oppose him relentlessly and implacably. But until that person became an enemy, Castro's instinct was to go to great lengths to win him over, to gain his respect and admiration. He wanted to show the Chilean that the Cuban revolutionaries were not boors, but civilised people who treated their guests with courtesy and goodwill.

On Saturday morning, as the captain drove off uphill from the second tee, he noticed a tall figure striding towards him over the crest of the hill. It was Fidel Castro, and this time he was followed by only one bodyguard. He accompanied the captain during his round of golf. He declined to try driving, but putted enthusiastically and skilfully (for a novice). At a suitable opportunity he mentioned that he had often been the target of assassination attempts. Both the CIA and various exile groups had tried to kill him. He therefore had to have rather elaborate personal security. His bodyguards were trained to expect the worst, and never to be diverted from their task. He hoped the captain would understand the need for these arrangements, and would not misunderstand the incident in his cabin.

Would Castro's day on the golf course help to sweeten the Chilean Navy? Would Allende find a way to buy off or neutralise the hostility of the Chilean military? Time would tell. After his long visit to Chile, Castro was pessimistic.

15 Leader of the Third World

In the Sierra Maestra, fighting his guerrilla war against Batista, Castro had told Celia Sánchez that after victory he would start a bigger and more important war, against US imperialism. Despite all the distractions of the home front, the battle for milk production, the battle for the 10 million ton sugar harvest, he never for a moment lost sight of the wider war. Imperialism for Castro meant the law of the jungle, where the strong were free to dominate and exploit the weak. Socialism meant creating a society based on human rationality, justice and dignity. He was confident (wrongly) that where socialism had been firmly established, where the working class was in power, as in the Soviet Union and Eastern Europe, the clock of history would never be turned back. But he also recognised (rightly) that 'bourgeois democracy' was deeply entrenched in North America and Western Europe. In those regions, as he saw it, the middle class had become a majority. Their comfort and prosperity was based on exploitation of the developing countries. But if the developing countries could break out of their subservience to the West, then the strongholds of capitalism would indeed come under pressure. The poor countries of Asia, Africa and Latin America would provide the decisive battleground in the war of ideas between the two rival systems. Already in 1966, when he hosted the Tri-Continental Conference, he had set out to establish a position of leadership in the Third World.

Not long after returning from Chile, Castro embarked on an even longer foreign tour. His absence would demonstrate, he said, that the imperialists were mistaken in claiming that he was the only person in Cuba who could take decisions. A Soviet delegation was about to arrive in Havana for important economic talks, but he would leave President Dorticós to lead the Cuban side in the discussions. Put another way, Cuba was now flying securely on autopilot. Castro could turn his full attention to a wider stage, the world stage. He boarded a large Ilyushin airliner and set off for West Africa.

The nearest equivalent to Castro in Africa was Sékou Touré, President of Guinea. When the French colonial territories in Africa obtained their independence, most opted to retain close links with the metropolitan power, France providing aid in return for influence. But Sékou Touré rejected French tutelage. An ardent socialist and nationalist, and a fiery orator, he was immensely popular among his own people. Castro saw him as a natural and valuable ally. He spent the long hours of his journey to Conakry studying books and statistics on Guinea, wanting as usual to impress his hosts with his detailed knowledge of their country. Sékou Touré was duly impressed and grateful. Castro told the cheering crowds that their President was the greatest leader on the African continent. If the imperialists attacked Guinea, he said, the Cubans would fight shoulder to shoulder alongside the Guineans.

After a week in Guinea, Castro spent a further seven weeks visiting other friends and allies: Algeria, Bulgaria, Romania, Hungary, Poland, East Germany, Czechoslovakia and finally the Soviet Union. Never seeming to tire, he carried out every engagement in his programmes, showed enthusiastic interest in every factory or farm, heaped praise and flattery on his various hosts, and talked and joked with ordinary people whenever an opportunity arose. Most ordinary East Europeans were impressed with what they saw of Castro. Compared with their own grey and humourless leaders, Castro seemed lively, human, spontaneous.

All the countries he visited were committed in principle to supporting the worldwide triumph of socialism; but none was as committed as Cuba. That was the problem, in Castro's view. Cuba was small, weak and threatened by the United States. But it did its internationalist duty: it gave moral and material help to revolutionaries fighting against repressive right-wing governments; it sent doctors, teachers and engineers to friendly countries which had need of them; it had even sent troops to Algeria when that country was embroiled in a frontier war with Morocco. The East Europeans were relatively rich, and secure under the Soviet umbrella. But what were they doing to help defeat imperialism, for example in Vietnam? Not much, certainly not enough. Even the Russians were showing a worrying inclination to negotiate deals with Nixon and Kissinger, instead of concentrating on aiding the Communists in South East Asia. So Castro played the polite and respectful visitor, but also, in private, the goad, constantly talking about the need to do more for Vietnam. Like other travelling heads of government, he also played to the home audience. He was away from Cuba for a full two months, but the Cuban media ensured that he was seen and heard as much as ever, embracing foreign heads of state, receiving awards and decorations, demonstrating that Cuba was no longer a backwater but a significant player on the world stage.

In September 1973 Castro travelled again to Algiers, this time to attend the Fourth Summit Conference of the Non-Aligned Movement. En route he stopped in Georgetown, capital of Guyana, and picked up two left-leaning Prime Ministers of the English-speaking Caribbean, Forbes Burnham of Guyana and Michael Manley of Jamaica. But what was a close ally of the Soviet Union like Castro doing at a meeting of the 'Non-Aligned?' The Non-Aligned Movement had been founded by countries which wanted to show that there was a third way, a path of independence, the choice not to line up with either of the two great military power-blocks, NATO in the West and the Warsaw Pact in the East. As Cuba became more and more closely tied to the Soviet bloc, some members of the Non-Aligned Movement began to question whether Cuba was any longer a suitable member. At the summit in Algiers, President Bourguiba of Tunisia attacked 'Soviet imperialism', and interrupted when Castro embarked on a speech praising the Soviet Union. Castro was not to be deflected. In the Sierra Maestra he had once shouted at his brother Raúl: 'I hate Soviet imperialism as much as Yankee imperialism!' But now in Algiers he denounced 'the theory of two imperialisms'. The Soviet Union did not attack, or dominate, or exploit any other country, and was not imperialist. Genuine non-alignment, Castro argued, meant supporting the self-determination and independence of all countries, and opposing imperialist exploitation.

Colonel Qaddafi was sharply ironical about Castro's performance. 'There is no difference between Cuba and an East European country, just as there is no difference between the Soviet Union and Uzbekistan. The difference between me and Castro is that he is a Communist, and I am a Socialist. He is aligned, and I am not.' With the conference about to end, a Brazilian observer made a speech obliquely but clearly criticising Cuba for interfering in the affairs of other countries. Qaddafi applauded the Brazilian loudly. But now Castro played his trump card. He had once been well disposed to Israel, and an admirer of its military prowess. But Israel's treatment of the Palestinians, and its ever-closer alliance with the United States, had led him to change his mind. He now stood up and announced that Cuba was breaking diplomatic relations with Israel. It was a dramatic gesture of solidarity with the Arab countries. Qaddafi rose and embraced Castro warmly. From then on they were friends. No East European country had broken relations with Israel. So perhaps, Qaddafi no doubt thought, Castro was non-aligned after all.

In justifying his condemnation of Israel, Castro would always start by emphasising that he felt no hostility towards the Jewish people:

> We repudiate with all our strength the ruthless persecution and genocide that Nazism unleashed in its time against the Jewish people. But there is nothing more similar in contemporary history than the eviction, persecution and genocide being carried out by imperialism and Zionism against

the Palestinian people . . . Piece by piece the Palestinian lands, and territories belonging to neighbouring Arab countries, have been seized by the aggressors, who are armed to the teeth with the most sophisticated weapons of the United States arsenal . . . United Nations resolutions have been contemptuously ignored or rejected by the aggressors and their imperialist allies . . . Can anyone doubt that the United States plays a fundamental role in preventing a just settlement in the region, by aligning itself with Israel, by supporting it, by working towards partial solutions that favour Zionist objectives, and by safeguarding the fruits of Israeli aggression at the expense of the Palestinian people?

Castro's change of position on Israel looked to many people in the West like cynical opportunism. But most Arabs, like Qaddafi, welcomed the change without worrying too much about Castro's reasons or motives. Castro made the most of his new popularity in the Arab world. He flew from Algiers to Baghdad, before continuing to India and Vietnam. In New Delhi he heard that in Chile Allende had been overthrown and killed in a military coup. It was on 11 September, a date which later would become even more notorious, that the conspirators struck. 'The problem in Chile was not Allende,' said CIA Director Colby, 'it was Fidel Castro.'

Although not greatly surprised by Allende's fall, Castro was deeply angered and shaken. He had lost his only real ally in Latin America. The setback was so serious that he decided to restrict his visit to Vietnam to only four days, and to return to Havana earlier than planned. He told the press that the Fascist coup in Chile had succeeded because the people had no weapons with which to defend themselves. He said that Allende had met a heroic death, and that his example would inspire others in Latin America to take up the struggle. (Allende reportedly died wielding a gun given to him by Castro.) Castro felt vindicated in his view that to achieve socialism in Latin America without an armed revolution was virtually impossible. The military caste, trained in the United States and backed by the CIA, would always act to bring down a socialist government, however popular and legitimate it might be.

In contrast to the turmoil in Chile, Castro's position in Cuba was more secure and unchallenged than it had ever been. In 1974 the economy picked up strongly, helped by high international prices for sugar. Soviet aid and advice was at last bearing fruit. Canada, Argentina and various West European countries started providing new trade credits. After fifteen years in power, with the economic and political tide apparently running in his favour, Castro decided that the time was ripe to formalise his position. For the first time, a National Congress of the Cuban Communist Party was held. It adopted a new Constitution, on the Soviet model. The posts of President and Prime

Minister were abolished. Castro was unanimously elected as First Secretary of the Communist Party, President of the Council of Ministers and of the Council of State, and Commander in Chief of the Armed Forces. In the street people continued to refer to Castro simply as 'Fidel'. But all official publications, such as the daily newspaper *Granma*, started the practice of always introducing reports or articles about Castro by giving him his name and titles in full, as if readers needed to be reminded who he was. It did not worry Castro how many tons of newsprint would be required, over the years, just to print his name.

The new Constitution enabled Castro to tell the world that Cuba had democracy and elections. Of course, it was not 'bourgeois democracy', and the elections were not the bad old elections in which corrupt politicians competed to buy votes. Instead, there was People's Power, at municipal, provincial and national levels. In theory anyone, Communist or not, could stand for election to their Municipal Assembly of People's Power. The various Municipal Assemblies in turn elected Provincial Assemblies, which then elected the National Assembly. In practice there were tried and tested instruments, notably the all-pervasive Committees for the Defence of the Revolution, to ensure that no one hostile to the Revolution was elected. The National Assembly met only for a few days every year, usually in the intimidating presence of the Commander in Chief himself, and never challenged the policies of the government. But the system of People's Power provided at least a much-needed structure of local administration. People could complain to their Municipal Assembly about the state of a local school or road, and by responding the Assembly could show that it served a useful purpose.

With Castro consolidated in power, and the economy growing, many Americans began to question whether there was any point in maintaining the trade embargo against Cuba. After all, the United States had normal trade relations with the Soviet Union and other Communist countries, despite all the tensions and conflicts of the Cold War. Some American businessmen thought that Cuba was again becoming an attractive market. The Latin American countries which had followed the United States lead in breaking links with Cuba fifteen years earlier had mostly restored at least commercial ties. President Nixon said: 'There'll be no change towards that bastard while I'm President.' But Nixon was forced to resign over the Watergate scandal. The more pragmatic President Ford, and later President Carter, were willing to look at the possibility of normalising relations with Cuba. Middle-level diplomats of the two countries held secret 'talks about talks' in New York over several months. As usual in his dealings with the United States, Castro played a double game. He tried to charm visiting American Congressmen and journalists, sounding moderate and hinting at his desire for better relations. But in public speeches he denounced US imperialism with as much vigour and passion as ever. He felt that he had no need to make significant concessions. He insisted that the trade embargo must be lifted before formal negotiations could begin. Finally, American interest faded in the face of Castro's renewed and alarming involvement in Africa.

It was in Angola that Castro fought his second war. In 1974 left-wing military officers seized power in Portugal and moved rapidly to grant independence to Portugal's overseas territories. In Angola three rival independence movements contended for power. The Marxist MPLA held the capital, Luanda, and the allegiance of most educated Angolans. But the MPLA faced the prospect of being crushed by a massive pincer movement. The FNLA, headed by Roberto Holden and backed by Zaire and the CIA, moved troops from the north towards Luanda. South Africa moved troops into the south of Angola, in tactical alliance with Jonah Savimbi's UNITA. The Soviet Union gave the MPLA moral and some material help, but was unwilling to risk sending troops. The head of the MPLA, Agostinho Neto, had met Castro in Havana in 1966 at the Tri-Continental Conference. He appealed to Castro for help.

Angola was a far-away country about which the Cubans knew little. But Castro had travelled the world preaching the need for revolutionaries to show solidarity and mutual support. Now forty-eight years old, he had lost none of his ambition and determination. How could he reject an appeal from a fellow revolutionary threatened by both the United States and the apartheid regime of South Africa? He did not hesitate for long. On 7 November 1975, four days before Angola formally became independent, the first two ships secretly set sail from Cuba. Each small ship was crowded with nearly 4,000 troops, as well as tanks and other heavy equipment, causing Castro to joke that conditions had been worse on the *Granma*. Later, as the MPLA's position became desperate, he mounted an airlift, using borrowed Soviet aircraft. He gave a pep talk to every departing contingent, urging them not to fail in their historic mission. About half the soldiers were black, and especially sensitive to the message that Cuba's duty was to save a black African country from the claws of the South African racists and American white supremacists.

By January 1976 Castro had established a force of some 15,000 Cubans in and around Luanda. He devoted almost all his time and energy to the Angolan expedition, poring over maps in his office and personally ordering every deployment and every action. Gabriel García Márquez, the Colombian writer and friend of Castro, would later write:

> He had a deep sense of envy for those going off to a war in which he could not participate. There was no spot on the map of Angola that he couldn't

identify, or a physical feature that he hadn't memorised . . . He could quote any statistic about Angola as if it were Cuba, and he spoke of Angolan cities, customs and people as if he had lived there his entire life.

The Cuban expeditionary force saved the MPLA from destruction. Roberto Holden's FNLA was defeated, and withdrew to the north. The US Congress, fearful of getting bogged down in another Vietnam, ordered a reduction in US involvement. The rapid advance northwards of the South African forces was halted, destroying the myth of South African invincibility. Elated by his success, Castro flew to Moscow, where he tried to quell Soviet anxieties over the dangerous adventure into which Castro had plunged them. Michael Manley, the Prime Minister of Jamaica, later wrote:

> Fidel told me privately that he judged the Russians couldn't do anything after he moved into Angola . . . When the Cuban soldiers were set to fly across the Atlantic, Raúl was on a plane to Moscow. He found the Soviets so infuriated at what he had done that it took two days to calm them down.

From Moscow Castro flew to Conakry, where he conferred with Sékou Touré of Guinea, Agostinho Neto of Angola and Luis Cabral, President of the newly independent Guinea-Bissau. The four leaders promised to maintain their mutual support and also to send aid to Samora Machel, President of Mozambique, another former Portuguese territory, this time under threat from the white regime of Ian Smith in Rhodesia. Back in Havana, Castro continued to direct closely his troops in Angola, as well as sending considerable numbers of doctors, teachers and construction workers. Visitors to Cuba in later decades would find few Cubans who had ever visited Europe or South America, but many who had spent time in Angola, doing their internationalist duty. Castro hoped and believed that the experience would reinforce their revolutionary zeal.

By February 1977 the situation in Angola seemed sufficiently stable for Castro to feel that he could embark on another long foreign tour. In South America the cause of socialism and revolution was making little progress, with repressive military regimes firmly in control of the most important countries. But in Africa and the Middle East the tide of history seemed to be flowing in Castro's direction. He wanted to encourage and stimulate his old and new friends. Africa, in Castro's judgement, was 'the weakest link in the imperialist chain'. The crimes of European colonial rule had created conditions in which the continent could move straight from tribalism to socialism.

After starting in Algiers, Castro spent ten days in Libya with Qaddafi, who once had mocked his lack of non-alignment but was now a firm ally. From

Tripoli he flew to Aden for talks with the Marxist government of South Yemen. Thence to Somalia, where he met Cuban advisers who had been sent to help and support the pro-Soviet government of President Barre. Somalia was engaged in a border dispute with neighbouring Ethiopia, laying claim to the huge Ogaden region of Ethiopia, which was mainly inhabited by Somalis. But Ethiopia now also had a pro-Soviet Marxist government, headed by Colonel Mengistu, which in Castro's view deserved support. Castro's plan was that South Yemen, Somalia and Ethiopia, whose governments all professed to be socialist and internationalist, should unite in an anti-imperialist federation. However, Barre would not be deflected by Castro from his ambition to create a greater Somalia. Castro left angry and frustrated. In Tanzania, Mozambique and Angola he got a warmer reception. He was greeted by the African crowds as a conquering hero, and gladly played the role. In Angola he reviewed his victorious troops, and urged them to yet greater achievements.

President Barre's army meanwhile proceeded to carry out an ill-disguised mass infiltration of Ethiopian territory (in effect an invasion); defeated the badly equipped and demoralised Ethiopian army; and took control of the Ogaden. On the brink of collapse, Mengistu appealed for help to the Soviet Union and Cuba. The Somali government quickly learned that Castro was not a man to be crossed. He blamed them publicly for the conflict with Ethiopia, saying they were 'irredentists, not internationalists'. Soon Cuban troops and Soviet tanks were pouring into Ethiopia. Castro chose one of his toughest and most successful officers, General Arnaldo Ochoa, to command the Cuban troops. In a rapid and brilliant campaign Ochoa drove the Somalis out of the Ogaden.

Castro's ever-deeper involvement in Africa outraged some Western governments, and especially the US government. Castro responded by accusing the Americans of hypocrisy and racism. He blamed the CIA for a bomb which destroyed a Cuban airliner near Barbados, killing everyone on board. Republican candidates for the coming Presidential elections competed in anti-Castro rhetoric. But the American public, scarred by Vietnam, chose a Democrat deeply committed to peace and human rights, Jimmy Carter. Castro kept Carter in play by hinting at a readiness to withdraw his troops from Africa, and reminding the Americans that they had troops deployed in numerous parts of the world. How, asked Castro, could a man devoted to human rights condemn Cuba for helping an independent country to defend itself against an unprovoked attack by racist South Africa? Carter kept protesting at Castro's actions in Africa, but did not pass from words to deeds. As for the United States' neighbours, they had even less inclination to get tough with Castro. President Echeverría of Mexico, on a visit to Cuba, gratified his host by attacking the American claim to have a 'Manifest Destiny' to expand south and west, to the detriment of countries like Mexico and Cuba. Mexico and Cuba must work together, said Echeverría, to protect their interests, their culture and their independence. As for Canada, Prime Minister Trudeau also visited Cuba, and shouted 'Viva Castro!'

Castro's role in Angola, especially his military victory over the South Africans, earned him enormous prestige in Africa, and grudging admiration even among many anti-Communists. His involvement in Ethiopia was more controversial. He angrily rebutted his critics, saying that Ethiopia had clearly been the victim of Somali aggression, and deserved to be helped. But the Ethiopian operation was conducted in close concert with the Soviet Union, and caused renewed allegations that Castro was merely a cat's-paw of the Soviet Union. President Tito of Yugoslavia, who had hosted the First Conference of Non-Aligned Nations in 1961, questioned whether Cuba was a suitable member of the Non-Aligned Movement. However, a majority of members accepted Castro's offer to host the 1979 conference in Havana. Cuba duly assumed the Presidency of the Movement for the period 1979–82. It was a glittering prize in Castro's long struggle to turn his island into a leader of the Third World.

Flushed with his international successes, Castro decided to attend in person, for the first time in many years, the October 1979 session of the United Nations General Assembly. He was no longer the young guerrilla leader who had stormed through New York in 1960. He was a dignified statesman of fifty-two, his beard now greying, who had been the supreme leader of his country for more than twenty years. As he addressed the Assembly he made it clear that he spoke not only for Cuba, but also for the Non-Aligned Movement of which Cuba held the Presidency, and indeed for people in every part of the world.

> There is often talk of human rights, but it is also necessary to talk of the rights of humanity. Why should some people walk barefoot, so that others can travel in luxurious cars? Why should some live for thirty-five years, so that others can live for seventy years? Why should some be miserably poor, so that others can be hugely rich? I speak on behalf of the children in the world who do not have even a piece of bread. I speak on behalf of the sick who have no medicine, of those whose rights to life and human dignity have been denied . . .'

Castro said that some countries in the world had plentiful resources, others had very few.

> What is the destiny of the latter? To starve to death? To be eternally poor? What use then is civilisation? What's the use of man's conscience? What's

the use of the United Nations? What's the use of the world? We can't speak of peace when tens of millions of human beings die every year of hunger, or of curable diseases . . . Enough of words and abstractions. Actions are needed. I ask the rich countries to contribute. I ask the poor countries to distribute what they have. I have not come as a prophet of revolution. I don't want violent upheaval. I am here to ask for peace and co-operation among nations. I am here to warn that either injustice and inequalities are resolved peacefully and wisely, or the future will be apocalyptic. The sound of weapons, and of threatening words, must cease. The world's problems cannot be solved with nuclear weapons. Bombs can kill the hungry, the sick and the ignorant, but they cannot kill hunger, disease, ignorance or the people's just rebellion. In a holocaust, the rich will also die. They have the most to lose. Let us try to solve the world's problems in a civilised way. That is our responsibility, and the indispensable requirement for mankind's survival.

As Castro spoke he was frequently interrupted by applause and shouts of approval. Outside the building a small crowd of protestors carried anti-Communist placards and shouted for Castro to go home. On a US radio station Fidel's sister Juana denounced him as a brutal despot. But Castro was well pleased with the outcome of his visit. In a sense, all publicity was good publicity. When had a small country like Cuba ever before been such a centre of world attention? 'It was the United States which made us an important country,' he told a group of American journalists. 'You taught us to defend ourselves.'

16 The Old Order Changes

Castro had successfully defied and outlived the hostility and threats of five successive US Presidents, from Eisenhower to Ford. Like nationalists elsewhere, he knew how to extract political benefit from having a foreign enemy. The more threatening and bullying the Americans sounded, the more Castro could beat his chest in front of the cheering multitudes in Revolution Square.

However, the mild and amiable President Carter presented a different and in many ways more difficult problem. He kept up the pressure on Cuba over human rights, but he did so in a more respectful tone than had been habitual under previous Administrations. If Castro's government and political system enjoyed public support, why did he need to keep so many individuals in prison for their political beliefs? If he stood for freedom, why were Cubans not allowed to leave their own country? Why were Cuban exiles not permitted to visit their relatives in Cuba? Castro had the standard Marxist answers to these criticisms. Individual freedoms had to be limited in order to protect collective rights and freedoms, the right to work, the right to education, the right to health care. But Castro was uncomfortable being on the defensive. He liked to occupy the moral high ground. While acknowledging that Carter was guided by Christian moral principles, he tried to argue that Carter was also ignorant of the world and surrounded by ill-informed and ill-intentioned advisers.

Carter's foreign policy was criticised inside the United States as weak and ineffectual. Right-wingers argued that Castro was a man who respected only strength. But Carter was in fact the first American President to exercise at least some influence on Castro. Despite having broken with most of the beliefs and attitudes of his social class, Castro had not completely escaped the influence of his Spanish background and education. He was proud and prickly, but also quixotic. If treated with contempt, he responded with implacable hostility. But if treated with respect, his instinct was to respond with friendship and co-operation. The Carter government remonstrated with Castro over his interventions in Africa, but in moderate and reasoned language which in turn forced Castro to go to great lengths, in deeds as well as words, to demonstrate that he was acting in a reasonable and responsible way. On one unprecedented occasion, the State Department confidentially asked for Cuban help in resolving a political crisis in the Zairean province of Katanga. On Castro's orders, the Cuban Foreign Ministry gave a constructive and positive reply. However, the exchanges were leaked to the press, and in the ensuing outcry both sides felt obliged to retreat to their habitual public positions of mutual hostility.

Despite Carter's tiresome pressure over human rights, Castro recognised that his adversary was at least sincere and well-meaning. The Cuban security services had noted that under Carter the CIA had reduced its offensive measures against Cuba, such as the sabotage of industrial installations. Castro decided that he had more to gain from seeking agreements with the Carter Administration than from maintaining a position of defiant confrontation. If he could secure American trade and American tourists, without conceding anything vital, why not go for it? He therefore embarked on a period of quiet negotiation. He freed some political prisoners, adopted a new and more positive attitude towards the exile community in Florida, and talked about permitting family reunions. Soon exiles were being allowed to travel to Cuba to visit their relatives, and some Cubans on the island were allowed to visit Florida. Castro denied that these gestures were a response to pressure on human rights, but he said publicly that Cuba was responding to the ending of American 'terrorism'. He hoped that other criminal activities against Cuba, including the economic blockade, would also be ended.

However, the thaw did not last long. As Carter prepared to seek re-election for a second term, he came under the usual pressures to show that he was tough on Communism in general and Castro in particular. A press campaign started over the presence in Cuba of MiG-23 aircraft, described as a new and dangerous development, threatening US security. Castro said that the aircraft were purely defensive, and that they had been in Cuba for more than a year, as the US intelligence agencies must have known. An even more artificial row blew up over the presence in Cuba of Soviet soldiers. The Soviet Union had maintained a brigade of troops in Cuba since the time of the missile crisis, but now the US media and Congressmen started referring to it as a 'combat brigade', and played it up as another new and threatening development. The Russians and Cubans insisted that the size and role of the Soviet brigade had not changed in seventeen years. Castro ridiculed the notion that it represented a threat to the United States. 'How can Cuba constitute a threat to the United States in any way? We have no nuclear weapons, we have no strategic weapons. The idea is ridiculous. It is the Cuban people who should be worried, having a powerful neighbour armed to the teeth with thousands of nuclear weapons.'

Since tension continued to mount, with Carter still calling for the withdrawal of the Soviet brigade, Castro invited a number of American journalists to a press conference. He repeated that 'Training Centre no. 12', the Soviet name for the brigade, had not changed its location or role since 1962. He challenged Carter to say how long the installation had been in Cuba. 'All US Presidents knew about this installation. The CIA knew about it; President Kennedy knew about it; Johnson knew about it; Nixon knew about it; Ford knew about it; and Carter must know about it . . . It has never been a secret. I ask Carter: Was this installation established in 1976, or 1970, or 1965, or in October 1962 at the end of the missile crisis?' Carter chose not to answer the question. Both he and his Secretary of State insisted that the presence in Cuba of the Soviet brigade was 'unacceptable'. To show the electorate how tough it was, the US government stepped up aerial surveillance of Cuba; established a naval task force in Florida; and staged a theatrical landing of the Marines at the Guantánamo naval base.

The Soviet brigade was much less of a threat to US interests than the Cubans' own meddling in other parts of the hemisphere. During the years of action in Africa, Castro continued to maintain close secret links with guerrilla movements in Latin America, providing training, weapons and communications. Many Marxist revolutionaries regarded Castro as an almost God-like figure. He had carried out a successful revolution against overwhelming odds, defied the Colossus of the North, and defeated the forces of imperialism from the Bay of Pigs to the plains of Angola. This reputation gave Castro enormous influence. Travelling to Cuba for a secret meeting with Fidel was the dream of many would-be Latin American revolutionaries. Few chose to ignore the great man's advice.

Among other initiatives, Castro persuaded three mutually hostile Marxist groups in Nicaragua to join forces in the struggle to overthrow the dictatorship of Anastasio Somoza. The resulting Sandinista National Liberation Front grew steadily in strength, while support for Somoza started to disintegrate. In July 1979 the Sandinistas triumphed, Somoza fleeing into exile. Numerous Cuban military and security advisers and civilian technicians moved in to help the Sandinistas to consolidate their power. Within days of their victory, a large Sandinista delegation visited Cuba to participate in the 26 July celebrations. Castro promised to send hundreds of teachers and doctors to meet the needs of the new Nicaragua. When Castro himself visited Nicaragua, he reminded his audience that twenty years earlier the CIA's Brigade 2506 had set sail from Nicaragua to overthrow the Cuban Revolution. The dictator Luis Somoza, father of Anastasio, had asked the Brigade to bring back for him a hair from Castro's beard. The beard was still intact, said Castro triumphantly, and now it was in Managua!

Later in 1979, the left-wing New Jewel Movement overthrew the government of Sir Eric Gairy in the Caribbean island of Grenada. This time Castro
had no hand in the action. But he quickly established friendly relations with
the new government. In November 1979 he sent 300 construction workers
to help build an enlarged airport on the island. Alarm bells were ringing
louder than ever in Washington. Would the new airport be a base for Soviet
deployments and interventions in the Americas? Was there no limit to
Castro's insidious mischief-making? How and when would the Cuban mega-
lomaniac be brought to heel?

In the event it was again the economy, rather than American military
power, which threatened to bring Cuba to its knees. The relative prosperity
of the mid 1970s proved short-lived. The open market price of sugar
declined. In the years of high prices, Castro had launched numerous
grandiose investments, which could not be sustained. He had always been
contemptuous of money. As a young lawyer, he had frequently not troubled
to collect a fee from his clients. If he had funds, he spent them freely. When
he had none, he borrowed from anyone who was available, without much
serious intention of repaying the money. He retained these lordly attitudes as
head of the Cuban government. In one of only two comments which have
earned him a place in the *Oxford Book of Quotations*, he said: 'Capitalism is
using its money; we socialists throw it away.' He assumed that his Soviet
friends would not in practice insist on the repayment of loans. He talked of
the need for prudent housekeeping, but seldom practised it. Visitors whom
he wished to impress would receive the most lavish entertainment, the best
hotel accommodation at the state's expense, lobster dinners, boxes of the best
cigars. His entourage tended to follow suit. It never occurred to Raúl Castro
to drink any other Scotch whisky than the most expensive brands, such as
Royal Salute.

The huge expense of maintaining a Cuban army in Africa was met mainly
by the Soviet Union, and by Angolan oil revenues. But the drain on Cuban
resources was also large, as was the cost of helping revolutionary movements
in Central America and elsewhere. In 1979 bad weather and plant infesta-
tions seriously reduced the sugar and tobacco crops. All these factors
combined to produce another economic crisis. Just as Cubans had begun to
think that their standard of living was at last improving, it nose-dived. In a
speech to the National Assembly Castro acknowledged the gravity of the
economic situation. 'We are sailing on a sea of difficulties, and we shall
continue on this sea, sometimes stormy, sometimes more calm, towards the
distant shore. We shall not reach it soon.'

The political impact of renewed austerity and shortages was exacerbated by
Castro's earlier decision to allow contact with the exile community. Visitors

from Florida wore expensive clothes, talked about their big American cars, and brought presents for their poor cousins on the island. As disillusion and discontent grew, people once more started using desperate means to leave the country. Some again took to the sea in homemade rafts. Boats were hijacked and forced to sail to Florida. Another escape route was to seek asylum in a Latin American embassy. There was a well-established tradition that Latin American governments accepted refugees from other Latin American countries. Embassies in Havana were guarded by Cuban soldiers, and it was not easy for would-be asylum seekers to gain access. But the location of the Venezuelan and Peruvian Embassies, mansions surrounded by large gardens bordering a wide avenue, made them relatively easy targets for gatecrashers. Groups of people in cars or larger vehicles made several attempts, some successful, to drive at speed into the safe haven of these embassies. On 1 April 1980 a Cuban soldier was killed trying to prevent a commandeered bus from crashing through the gates of the Peruvian Embassy.

When this incident was reported to Fidel Castro, he was already in a disconsolate and irritable mood. He was exasperated by the continuing failure of his Ministers to meet their economic targets. Celia Sánchez, his inseparable friend over more than twenty years, had died of cancer in January, making him more conscious than ever of the loneliness of power. He reacted explosively to news of the Cuban soldier's death. As reported by an eye witness, he went red with anger. He demanded that the Peruvians hand over the six asylum seekers, to stand trial for homicide. The Peruvians refused. After a few tense days, the Cuban government made an unexpected announcement. The guards would be removed from embassies which refused to co-operate in their own security.

As word spread that there were no soldiers outside the Peruvian Embassy, and that anyone could enter the grounds without obstruction, the number of asylum seekers snowballed. More than 10,000 people crowded into the Embassy buildings and camped down in the gardens. The situation embarrassed the Peruvians, as Castro had intended, but the sheer number and visibility of people wanting to leave Cuba was also becoming a public relations disaster for Castro. He tried to bring the situation under control, first by allowing an airlift to Costa Rica of people wanting to leave, and second by whipping up public hostility towards the 'scum' who were disloyal to Cuba. He blamed American propaganda for stirring up disaffection and for misleading 'weak minds'.

The US authorities made the most of Castro's difficulties, but did not want to accept an unlimited flood of refugees. They announced that they would accept 3,500 Cubans, and urged other countries in the hemisphere to accept a similar number. Castro was determined that the Americans should not get off so lightly. He cancelled the airlift to Costa Rica, and announced that exiles in Florida could come by boat to the port of Mariel to collect any relatives or friends who wanted to leave Cuba. Hundreds of boats duly arrived, and a mass exodus began. President Carter said at first that the United States would never turn away refugees from Communist tyranny; but as the flow continued he was forced to change his tune, ordering the Coast Guard to arrest the boat-owners who were bringing refugees. The Cuban authorities added to the Americans' problems by rounding up criminals, lunatics and psychiatric patients, and taking them to Mariel for shipment to Florida. Dishonour was shared. Carter was made to look hypocritical and inconsistent. Castro was humiliated by the public spectacle of Cubans fleeing from his Revolution. But as usual he tried to turn the setback to his advantage, using the safety valve of emigration to rid his country of some 120,000 discontented or unwanted people.

Carter's mishandling of the Mariel exodus contributed to his electoral defeat in 1980 by the conservative Republican Ronald Reagan. During the electoral campaign the Reagan team had promised an ultra-hard line against Castro, not excluding military measures. Elected to office, they continued to breathe fire against the Caribbean dictator. Congress approved the establishment of a propaganda radio station, Radio Martí, beamed at Cuba from a large balloon in southern Florida. Secretary of State Haig promised to deal with the problem of Communist subversion in Central America 'at the source', meaning by action against Cuba.

But in handling American threats Castro was on familiar ground. He rallied nationalist feeling with another show of defiance. He updated plans to resist an American military attack, including even a nuclear attack. He claimed (and almost certainly believed) that the CIA had started to conduct biological warfare against the island. Foreign experts were invited to examine the evidence: during 1981 outbreaks of sugar and tobacco diseases, and of African swine fever, spread suddenly from several different locations on the island. Castro even blamed the CIA for a disastrous epidemic of dengue fever. Whatever the truth, most Cubans believed Castro's version of events. Anger and bitterness against the United States, which had faded during the Carter years, was brought back to fever pitch. Despite the efforts of Radio Martí and continuing economic deprivations, there were now few signs of divisions or weaknesses on Castro's home front. And he defiantly continued to channel aid to Marxist guerrilla forces in Central America, especially El Salvador.

The US government found it difficult to strike directly at Cuba, despite Haig's threat to do so; but it was willing to use fair means or foul to ensure that Castro did not achieve another triumph in Central America. It provided equipment, training and military advisers to help the Salvadorean army in its fight against the FMLN guerrillas. The CIA also organised, funded and equipped the 'Contras', a Nicaraguan opposition force fighting against the Sandinista government from bases in neighbouring Honduras. The Americans received little help or sympathy from their European allies. Even the friendly government of Margaret Thatcher was nervous of giving military assistance to Central American armies widely accused of atrocities against the civilian population. The Americans' principal foreign ally in the struggle in Central America was the military regime in Argentina. The Argentine military had crushed the leftist opposition in Argentina in a ruthless campaign of repression, including the systematic use of torture, assassination and 'disappearances'. Argentine officers now travelled to El Salvador to convey their expertise to the Salvadorean military.

Despite Castro's bitter hostility to the Argentine military government, he had always supported Argentina's claim to sovereignty over the Malvinas. When General Galtieri seized the islands from Britain in a surprise military operation, Castro had little choice but to join the chorus of Latin American approval. He stridently opposed Britain's decision to retake the Malvinas, by force if necessary. He even offered to send troops to help the Argentines to defend the islands. However, Britain's victory, and the subsequent collapse of the Galtieri government, led directly to the withdrawal of the Argentine military from Central America. Unwittingly, Europe's most right-wing government had done a valuable service to Castro and his allies.

In October 1983 Castro's friend Maurice Bishop, the Prime Minister of Grenada, was overthrown and killed by an even more radical Marxist faction. Although dismayed at this turn of events, Castro concluded that breaking with the new government would only make a bad situation worse, possibly leading to a return of the old neo-colonial regime. He therefore continued the Cuban aid programme. But whereas the Bishop government had been popular on the island, and enjoyed wide international recognition, the new regime was clearly illegitimate, extreme and violent. The United States seized its opportunity, mounting an invasion spearheaded by marines, paratroops and commandos. Some Grenadan and Cuban soldiers, and armed Cuban construction workers, put up a futile resistance. Twenty-four Cubans were killed before their ammunition ran out. Within hours the Americans were in full control of the tiny island. Seven hundred Cubans were rounded up and packed off home to Cuba with their tails between their legs.

It was not an invasion, said a euphoric President Reagan, but a rescue operation carried out with the support and agreement of Grenada's Caribbean neighbours, who were as eager as the United States to put a stop to Cuban and Soviet subversion. Castro was indeed humiliated. The Soviet Union protested but did not pass from words to deeds. The United Nations General Assembly overwhelmingly condemned the invasion, but in the United States Reagan basked in the glory of a military victory which was rapid and complete, and which cost no American lives. At the funeral of the Cubans killed in Grenada, Castro's anti-American rhetoric had a more than usually bitter edge. He acknowledged that there was enthusiastic public support for the operation in the United States, but compared it to the crowds in Nazi Germany cheering Hitler's victories over weak and helpless neighbours. 'Where is the glory, the greatness, the victory in invading and conquering one of the smallest countries in the world, with no economic or strategic significance? Where is the heroism of fighting against a handful of Cuban workers and civilian technicians?'

Before the invasion of Grenada, Castro had turned down Sandinista requests for the despatch of Cuban troops to Nicaragua to help in the war against the CIA-backed Contras. At secret meetings with President Ortega and other Sandinista leaders, Castro had argued that the arrival of Cuban troops in Nicaragua would only give the Americans a pretext for a full-scale invasion, and indeed possibly also for a military onslaught on Cuba itself. Castro had also advised the Nicaraguans to pursue moderate domestic policies, and to eschew repressive measures against the opposition parties, the private sector and the Catholic Church.

After the invasion of Grenada, Castro wondered bitterly whether this policy of restraint, designed to avoid provoking the Americans, could any longer be justified. There were thousands of Cuban advisers, technicians, engineers and teachers in Nicaragua. Castro did not want to suffer again the humiliation of seeing his men rounded up without a struggle by invading US Marines. He prepared plans to send Cuban troops rapidly if an all-out American invasion seemed imminent. The head of the Cuban military mission in Nicaragua, General Arnaldo Ochoa, helped to reorganise the Sandinista army and drew up contingency plans for counter-attacks in the event of an American invasion. Fidel Castro held a series of meetings with Raúl, and all the leading Cuban military commanders, to discuss the options. The best course, they concluded, would be not to confront the Americans in a conventional battle. The defence of Nicaraguan territory would be left primarily to the Nicaraguan militias, using guerrilla tactics. Elite Sandinista and Cuban regular forces would mount hit-and-run attacks on American bases and other targets in Honduras, El Salvador and even Costa Rica. The longer they could hold out, and the wider the conflict could be spread, the more international political pressure would be brought to bear on the US government to call a halt to the invasion. Castro wanted above all to prevent the Americans from achieving a quick and clear-cut victory, as in Grenada.

To be viable, all these plans needed Soviet support, not necessarily military but at least moral and political support. There was the rub. For Castro, the most worrying and depressing aspect of the international situation was the state of the Soviet Union. The tired and elderly Soviet leaders repeated mechanically the old Marxist–Leninist revolutionary dogmas, but the fire had gone out of their bellies. Unable to meet the economic expectations of the Soviet people, the leadership wanted at all costs to avoid expensive and dangerous foreign commitments. They gave only limited help to Nicaragua, and pressed the Sandinista government to seek a *modus vivendi* with the United States. They made it known that if the Americans attacked Nicaragua, the Russians would not be able to defend it. They also put pressure on Castro to pull in his horns, insisting that the scale and cost of Soviet economic support must be reduced. All this at a time when Cuba itself was providing massive economic assistance to Nicaragua.

Castro was forced to look for increasingly desperate means of shoring up the still struggling Cuban economy, and of financing his 'internationalist solidarity' and interventionist foreign policies. Unemployed Cuban workers were sent to earn a salary in countries like East Germany. Paintings from the Cuban national collections were secretly sold on the international market. The secret services of the Interior Ministry set up clandestine trading channels designed to outflank the American trade embargo. Panama became the main base for secret Cuban commercial activities, in particular the acquisition of American cypher equipment and computers. Almost any commercial deal, however alien to socialist principles, was considered legitimate if it brought financial benefits to the Revolution.

Cuba was not the only country in dire financial straits. There was a growing international debt crisis. The big Western banks had competed in lending huge amounts of money to countries which appeared to have good prospects, like Brazil and Mexico, but when conditions changed for the worse the banks abruptly stopped lending and resisted requests for the rescheduling of repayments. The financial position of the poor countries of Africa was even more desperate. Castro started to focus his attention on this problem. He read books, articles, press reports. He called for special studies by Cuban and foreign experts. In the course of 1985 alone there were five international conferences in Havana on the world debt problem. Castro insisted to anyone who would listen that the repayment of Third World debt was impossible. He produced endless statistics to prove his case. Even if there were a net transfer of funds from the Third World to the First World over generations, the Third World would still not escape the yoke of indebtedness. It was not in the interest of the rich countries to drive the poor countries of the world into even greater misery and desperation. The rich should recognise that their prosperity was largely based on past exploitation; that the international terms of trade were unequal, helping the strong and harming the weak; that the only solution was to write off Third World debt and make a new start on a fairer basis.

Were the Russians listening? In Castro's view the socialist countries should be supporting his case, should be working to create a more just world economic order, should be setting an example by helping poorer countries, without expecting repayment. Instead they were acting increasingly like the Western banks, imposing harsh conditions on their debtors, and dismissing all ethical and political considerations.

In 1985 Konstantin Chernenko, the sick and bumbling Secretary-General of the Soviet Communist Party, died and was replaced by the youthful and dynamic Mikhail Gorbachev. For a short time Castro hoped that Gorbachev might inaugurate a more assertive and self-confident Soviet foreign policy, and a more constructive phase in Soviet relations with Cuba. He was soon disillusioned. Gorbachev's internal reforms, dressed up as being designed to strengthen socialism, seemed to Castro in fact a dangerous betrayal of Marxist–Leninist principles. Economic decentralisation (*perestroika*) was a step back towards the capitalist jungle of rival autonomous enterprises. Openness (*glasnost*) meant opening the floodgates to slander and misinformation. Worst of all, Gorbachev seemed even more intent than his predecessors on seeking accommodations with the West. He wanted Western credits, and an atmosphere in which military expenditure could be reduced. The US government saw its opportunity to exact a price for an improvement in relations. High on the list of American requirements was an end to Soviet support for Fidel Castro.

Castro felt the cold wind from Moscow. Many Western observers, knowing the extent of Cuba's dependence on Soviet aid, assumed that he would have to go at least some way towards supporting and copying the Gorbachev reforms. For a short period he did indeed try to gratify Gorbachev by encouraging more open discussion and criticism of government ministers (not of himself). But the experiment was not taken far. When his friend Gabriel García Márquez tried to argue that Gorbachev's reforms would give socialism a new lease of life, Castro was dismissive: 'Believe me, Gabo, it will be a disaster.' And when in 1986 Castro introduced his own full-blown reform programme, called the Rectification of Errors, it turned out that the errors to be rectified were not the over-centralised rigidity of the economy, nor the stultifying bureaucratic control of information, but the opposite. Castro reversed the small steps towards economic liberalisation that he had authorised a few years earlier, such as free peasants' markets. He went right back to the egalitarian fundamentalism of Che Guevara, saying that too much emphasis had been placed on material incentives and too little on moral incentives. The Revolution was mature, he said, and Cubans had acquired a sense of social solidarity; they would work best not to obtain personal enrichment, but to sustain and strengthen a just society in which everyone had access to education, health care and security.

For decades Castro had heaped praise on the Soviet Union and held it up as a model to be copied. He knew that some of his followers were bound to be attracted by the Soviet reforms. The threat was difficult to counter. So long as Soviet aid continued, even if at a reduced level, he could not publicly attack Soviet policies. But within the government and the armed forces the word was spread that *perestroika* and *glasnost* were not needed in Cuba, and would only undermine the socialist state. Castro joked to Party workers that he now did not know which was more dangerous for the Revolution, the American eagle in front or the Russian bear behind. After a visit in 1987 by the outspokenly reformist Foreign Minister Shevardnadze, Castro ordered that Soviet officials in Cuba, including senior diplomats, should be subjected to technical surveillance (i.e. bugs and hidden cameras), as had long been customary for American and other Western diplomats. Surveillance was a field in which Cuban State Security were extremely expert, thanks in large measure to KGB training.

Differences between Cuba and the Soviet Union were also beginning to affect the long-running civil war in Angola. Under the overall direction of a cautious and unimaginative Soviet general, the Angolan government and Cuban forces suffered a series of setbacks at the hands of UNITA and South African forces. They retreated to the town of Cuito Cuanavale. The President of Angola, Dos Santos, appealed to Castro to send yet more troops, as the only means of averting a disaster. Castro agreed to do so, on the understanding that the Cubans would have overall command. Cuba's most brilliant and successful officer, General Arnaldo Ochoa, the victor of the Ethiopian war of 1977, was soon in command of some 50,000 men. But Fidel Castro personally kept a tight grip on operations. For nearly a year, starting in November 1987, he devoted 80 per cent of his time, by his own account, to the war in Angola, taking an interest in the smallest tactical deployments, and even in the rations and hours of sleep allowed to his troops. He saw Cuito Cuanavale as his Stalingrad, the rock on which the military machine of the South Africans would be broken, paving the way for the fall of the apartheid regime.

No one was better placed than General Ochoa to run a successful campaign despite having Castro as a back-seat driver in Havana. At the age of eighteen Ochoa had joined Castro's guerrillas in the Sierra Maestra during the war against Batista. He was at Fidel's side at the Bay of Pigs. He had played a prominent role in most of Castro's many overseas military interventions, from Syria to Nicaragua. Unlike most of Castro's ministers and generals, he addressed Castro with the familiar '*tu*', and was confident enough to make disrespectful jokes in the Maximum Leader's presence. But even Ochoa became irritated by Castro's constant interference. He shocked his fellow officers by saying that Fidel was 'crazy'. In December 1987 Castro complained that Ochoa's reporting was too cursory and too slow. In January 1988 Ochoa was summoned back to Havana for face-to-face consultations with the Castro brothers on the defence of Cuito Cuanavale. When Ochoa returned to Luanda he continued to receive a flow of detailed written instructions from Castro.

In February 1988 35,000 UNITA and 9,000 South African troops, supported by tanks, artillery and aircraft, launched their expected attack on Cuito Cuanavale. The first lines of defence were overrun; there was intense anxiety in Havana; but the attackers got bogged down, suffering heavy losses from Ochoa's MiG-23 aircraft; and finally they were forced to retreat.

Left to himself, Castro would have held out for total victory. But he could not do so without Soviet support. Gorbachev wanted a negotiated settlement. Quadripartite talks took place during 1988 between the United States, the Soviet Union, Cuba and South Africa. On 22 December 1988 a deal was finally signed in New York, providing for the withdrawal of all foreign troops. The long Cuban adventure in Africa was at an end.

By this time Castro was scarcely trying to disguise his dislike of Soviet policies. He said that détente, 'the peace of the rich', was being pursued at the expense of poor countries like Angola. Cuba would be different – '*dif-er-ent-e*' – steadfast and independent, loyal to its principles. Discussing the state of the world with NBC reporter Maria Shriver, Castro took pride in Cuba's evident isolation. 'We are left with the honour of being one of the few adversaries of the United States . . .' Was it really an honour? interjected Shriver. 'It is an honour for such a small country as Cuba to have such a gigantic country as the United States live so obsessed with this little island. That the United States should no longer consider itself an enemy of the Soviet Union or of China, but still consider itself an enemy of Cuba, that is an honour for us.'

The external pressures were coming not only from the United States and the Soviet Union. Western politicians who had once been sympathetic to the Cuban Revolution, like the Socialists Felipe González of Spain and François Mitterrand of France, insisted that Castro must move with the times and liberalise his regime. He listened politely, but was unmoved. He released a few long-term prisoners, but clamped down hard on newly emerging dissidents. He knew that the only potential challenge to his power would come from the army. He kept tabs more closely than ever on the behaviour and loyalty of key officers.

In the confident 1970s, when the economy looked strong and Cuba was triumphant in Africa, Castro was usually tolerant of petty corruption or sexual misdemeanours among his officials, provided they worked loyally for the Revolution. But in the new atmosphere of encirclement, and fear of ideological contamination, any sort of deviant behaviour came to be viewed with suspicion, as a possible symptom of disaffection. Most Cuban officials had little opportunity for serious corruption, even if they had the inclination. An exception was in the Interior Ministry, and especially the Convertible Currency (MC) Department, whose job was to earn hard currency by unconventional means, in particular by clandestine commercial deals which breached the US trade embargo. The MC Department set up trading companies in Panama and elsewhere, whose links with the Cuban government were concealed. To fulfil their role, officers in the department had to travel abroad frequently, stay in expensive hotels and generally behave like successful private-sector businessmen.

The head of the MC Department was Colonel Tony de la Guardia, a sort of Cuban James Bond who had played a key role in many of Castro's most secret operations. He led Cuba's first unit of Special Forces; he was in the Congo with Che Guevara; he set up a training school for special operations, and coached groups of revolutionaries from Venezuela, Guatemala and other Latin American countries; he infiltrated and exfiltrated secret agents; he planned an operation to kidnap Batista from the Dominican Republic (but Batista died before it could be implemented); he laundered money for the Argentine Montonero guerrillas and for Palestinian groups in the Lebanon; he sent advisers to help Michael Manley set up a counter-intelligence organisation in Jamaica; he organised an arms pipeline to the Sandinistas when they were fighting to overthrow the government of General Somoza in Nicaragua; most sensitive of all, he was tasked by Raúl Castro with carrying out death sentences on individuals who could not be brought to Cuba, such as the Cuban exile living in Puerto Rico who was believed to be responsible for placing a bomb on a Cuban airliner in 1976, killing seventy-three people.

Tony de la Guardia had a twin brother, General Patricio de la Guardia, who was head of Special Forces in Angola. Patricio was the closest friend and colleague of the army commander in Angola, the prestigious General Arnaldo Ochoa. The twins and Ochoa were the core of a circle of friends, 'the group', who considered themselves to be the elite high-fliers of the Cuban Revolution. Castro recognised and admired their skills and achievements. But reports about their lifestyle caused him concern, not least because it was arousing jealousy and resentment among other senior officers. Their womanising had become notorious, and they acquired expensive Western consumer goods for their personal use. Tony de la Guardia had annoyed Castro by distributing a consignment of arms in Nicaragua without waiting for his authorisation. As for General Ochoa, he used his almost vice-regal position in Angola, and his friendship with Tony de la Guardia, to trade in diamonds, ivory and other local products. He indulged his voracious sexual appetite, engaging in group sex with Cuban and Angolan women, one of whom complained that she had been coerced into participating. More seriously, agents reported to Castro that Ochoa was expressing sympathy for Gorbachev's reforms, and casting doubt on Castro's conduct of the war in Angola.

In January 1989 Castro made a number of changes in the armed forces high command, including relieving Ochoa of his post in Angola. He did not bother to consult his brother Raúl. At a dinner in the Ranchón restaurant in Havana, to celebrate the fiftieth birthday of Soviet Ambassador Juri Petrov, Raúl (who had drunk too much vodka) reproached his brother. 'If you move my officers without the courtesy of consulting me, I am not needed as Minister of the Armed Forces. I resign.' Fidel called him to order: 'Raúl, we're with foreigners.'

Back in Cuba, General Ochoa continued to arouse Castro's suspicions. He was indiscreetly contemptuous of some of the politicians around Castro, notably Carlos Aldana. Aldana was the Secretary for Ideology in the Communist Party, but in practice much more important. Castro at this period travelled everywhere with Aldana, who acted as a virtual Prime Minister. General Ochoa, a national hero who had won the biggest tank battle since the Second World War, was not prepared to kow-tow to a jumped-up 'shit' like Aldana. Ochoa's reputation, Castro thought, had gone to his head. Ochoa said he would accept the proffered post of head of the Western Army, provided Fidel would agree to a serious discussion with the army high command about the future of the country. This arrogance offended both the Castro brothers. They also resented Ochoa's frequent complaints that the government was not doing enough to obtain jobs and decent housing for his soldiers now returning from Angola. Many of the officers who had served under Ochoa in Africa were visiting his modest house on the outskirts of Havana. Was he becoming a focus of opposition within the military? Castro ordered that Ochoa and his friends be subjected to close technical surveillance.

In April 1989, while the investigations into the Ochoa group were still a closely guarded secret, Mikhail Gorbachev visited Cuba. He was greeted by a huge banner reading 'Long live Marxism–Leninism!' It was a reproach, a challenge and an appeal for understanding. Castro recognised that Gorbachev's visit could be crucial for the future of Cuba. He assumed that it was probably too late for anyone to persuade Gorbachev to reverse his disastrous reforms. But perhaps he could at least be persuaded to accept and respect Castro's decision to stick to the fundamentals of Marxism–Leninism, which was after all the creed which Gorbachev still professed to follow. Unlike some of the most radical Soviet reformers, Gorbachev had always seemed personally well-disposed and friendly. Castro pulled out all the stops in an attempt to convince him that although Cuba would go its own way, it remained a loyal and valuable ally, deserving of continuing economic and political support. There was a strange reversal of roles. For decades, cautious and conservative Soviet leaders had tried to restrain the exuberant and volatile young Cuban. Now a grey-bearded Castro, aged sixty-two, was trying to persuade a younger man not to rush headlong down the path of change and novelty.

On the surface, the visit went smoothly and harmoniously, with much smiling and friendly joking. But there was little warmth in the smiles. Gorbachev explained that trade between the two countries would in future be 'on a basis of equality', meaning without subsidies or special favours. Soviet enterprises were now autonomous, so the Cubans would have to negotiate commercial deals with individual enterprises, rather than through central planners, as in the past. In their private talks, it became clear that the Soviet Union was planning a massive reduction in both foreign aid and military expenditure. All this confirmed Castro's worst fears about the direction of Gorbachev's reforms. In Castro's view, Gorbachev was unleashing forces that would tear the Soviet Union apart, leaving the United States as the sole super-power, able to impose its will without opposition. Before Gorbachev's departure, the two leaders signed a twenty-five-year friendship agreement. It was an empty gesture.

Gorbachev flew from Havana to London. Prime Minister Thatcher travelled with him by car from the airport to the Soviet Embassy, and asked about his impressions of Castro. Gorbachev said that Castro was an extraordinary personality, still very sharp and very well informed about the international situation. 'I hope you made it clear,' said Thatcher sternly, 'that it's time he introduced some *perestroika* and *glasnost*.' Gorbachev put on his disarming smile. 'If you think we can control Castro, I'm afraid you're wrong. He will take his own route. The amount of influence we have is zero.'

Fidel Castro would have agreed with that. In Cuba the net was closing on the man whose crimes included wanting to follow the Gorbachev route. When Tony de la Guardia received a tip-off that Ochoa's official car was bugged, he was dismayed. Travelling together, the two men had mocked and ridiculed not only Aldana, but Fidel himself. Raúl Castro meanwhile received a report that Ochoa had a private bank account in Panama and that he had purloined US$200,000 that should have been used to obtain equipment for the Sandinistas. This may have been only the tip of an iceberg. When a colleague warned Ochoa that he was suspected of taking US$200,000 of Nicaraguan money, he was stunned. According to a witness of the scene, for a few moments the battle-scarred military hero looked defeated and frightened. 'I'm finished,' he said. Then, recovering his self-confidence, he added with his usual bravado: 'Your friends' deals are small beer. I'm not in for two hundred thousand, or nine hundred thousand, but more like nine hundred million!'

On 29 May Raúl summoned Ochoa to his office, and accused him of scandalous sexual conduct, of insubordination, of abusing the privileges that went with his office, and of engaging in unauthorised commercial deals which brought Cuba into disrepute. Ochoa indignantly denied any wrongdoing. He claimed that his commercial transactions had not been for personal enrichment but to obtain additional supplies for his soldiers. That sort of initiative, he argued, had always been regarded as not only legitimate but meritorious. Raúl was infuriated by Ochoa's bland denials and arrogant demeanour. At a further meeting a few days later Ochoa adopted a more conciliatory tone, and thought that he had managed to clear his name. Far from it: Raúl had meantime obtained much more serious evidence of corruption, as well as incriminating tape-recordings of Ochoa's private conversations.

On 11 June Fidel Castro called a meeting of all his security chiefs, and asked them to set out the evidence against the Ochoa/de la Guardia group. The following day Ochoa and the de la Guardia twins were observed entering a fast motor launch in a small fishing port. When challenged, they offered an innocent explanation. But the possibility that three of Cuba's most distinguished officers might try to defect was enough to make the Castro brothers take immediate action. That evening Ochoa and his associates, fourteen officers in all, were arrested. Their houses were searched. Fidel and Raúl spent hours discussing what should be done. Should the affair be swept under the carpet, to avoid public embarrassment, or should Ochoa and his friends be put on public trial and given exemplary punishment? The best course, Fidel concluded, was a public court martial for corruption. They should avoid giving the impression that the arrests had any political motivation.

A team of special investigators was set to work. The most serious evidence coming to light related to drug-trafficking. It was known and accepted by the Castro brothers that de la Guardia and his men could hardly avoid having contact with drug-traffickers. The men with *lancheros* (fast launches) in Panama or Florida, who smuggled computers or television decoders for the MC Department, were often the same men who smuggled drugs for the Colombian drug barons. In the past Cuban intelligence officers had been authorised to establish contact with the cartels, and on a few occasions Colombian drugs planes were allowed to pass through Cuban airspace unmolested, the deal being that on the return journey they would carry weapons for guerrilla groups in South America supported by Cuba.

Castro suspected, however, that that the Americans had penetrated the drugs cartels and would exploit any evidence of Cuban involvement in drug-trafficking. He had given instructions that no deal should be done which involved bringing drugs on to Cuban soil or into Cuban territorial waters. When drugs arrived in Cuba by accident, there was a problem. On one occasion a boat carrying Colombian drugs to Florida strayed into Cuban waters and was arrested. The Colombians offered US$1 million if it could be quietly released. Cuban officials accepted the offer but then, on Castro's orders, cancelled their acceptance. He suspected an American trap. Raúl Castro was perplexed by his brother's caution. He told a friend who later defected: 'We've got a million dollars of cocaine stored in the Cimeq laboratories. Fidel doesn't want to destroy it. I want to negotiate it, but he says no. He says we mustn't be linked to this business, and shouldn't do a deal. Can you understand it?'

Castro's attitude to drug-trafficking was pragmatic rather than moralistic. His concern was to avoid giving the Americans a weapon to use against him. Normally confident that nothing moved in Cuba without his knowledge, he was genuinely shocked to discover now that de la Guardia's men had been flouting his orders for more than a year by allowing drugs consignments to be flown to Cuba and then shipped on by launch.

Tony de la Guardia had become over-confident. After all, his job was to earn money for the Revolution by clandestine trafficking. He was used to living dangerously, and drugs deals offered the biggest returns. There was no question of distributing drugs in Cuba. If he could obtain a lot of much-needed hard currency, just by allowing an occasional drugs consignment to pass through Cuba, he was confident that his immediate boss, Interior Minister Abrantes, would not ask too many questions. As for General Ochoa, the investigators discovered that his aide-de-camp, Captain Martinez Valdes, had travelled to Colombia for a meeting with none other than Pablo Escobar, boss of the notorious Medellin cartel. Evidently there was no follow-up, but the visit in itself, without Castro's approval, was treasonable. It later transpired that Martinez Valdes had been approached in Panama by representatives of Escobar, who asked him to go to Colombia for a meeting. Ochoa told Martinez Valdes to turn down any proposal which involved bringing drugs into Cuba, but to show interest if the Colombian and Mexican cartels wanted to launder money by investing it in the Cuban hotel industry. In fact Escobar wanted to buy SA-7 ground-to-air missiles to protect his homes and laboratories in Colombia from possible air attack.

Because of his high rank, Ochoa was first tried by a 'military honour court' consisting of Cuba's thirty-five most senior officers. He and the other thirteen defendants then faced a normal court martial presided over by three generals. The proceedings were broadcast on television, day after day. As in most show trials, it was apparent that the defendants had been coached in what to say. They all accepted that they were guilty of corruption; they all expressed contrition and loyalty to Castro and the Revolution. However, unlike in Stalin's show trials, there is no evidence that the defendants were required to admit to actions or crimes which they had not committed. Like the others, Ochoa admitted corruption and expressed contrition; but he refuted the accusation of drug-trafficking. He claimed to have known nothing about the MC Department's involvement with drugs. He admitted that he should not have authorised the meeting with Pablo Escobar, but said his purpose was only to find out what Escobar wanted to propose.

Fidel Castro himself visited Tony de la Guardia in prison, shortly before the start of the court martial, and talked for about three hours, mainly about matters unrelated to the trial. According to de la Guardia's daughter Ileana, Castro promised leniency if her father accepted full responsibility for the MC Department's drug-trafficking, and did not try to implicate his superiors (including Castro himself). But this second-hand account of the meeting is probably misleading, and may have been influenced by de la Guardia's desire to reassure and cheer up his daughter. In any event, de la Guardia and the other defendants were all officers on active service. For the Castro brothers, it was taken for granted that officers should always obey orders, and 'do their duty', even when facing the prospect of a firing squad. As the trial progressed, it must have become obvious to the defendants that leniency was not on the agenda. The prosecution argued that by engaging in drug-trafficking and other illegal activities, the defendants had undermined the credibility of Fidel Castro, and thereby endangered the security of the state and of the Revolution. No crime could be more serious than that.

The court martial sentenced Ochoa, Tony de la Guardia and two other officers to death; the other ten defendants, including General Patricio de la Guardia, received long prison sentences. The sentences were reviewed by the Council of State, twenty-five men and four women including all the most powerful figures in the regime. The members of the Council were all required to give their opinion, one by one, in front of the television cameras. They all endorsed the sentences. Raúl Castro did so with a great show of reluctance and emotion. He said he had not been able to sleep. When he went to the bathroom to brush his teeth, he saw that tears were streaming down his cheeks. Fidel Castro spoke last. He said that public opinion in Cuba thought that all fourteen defendants deserved to be sentenced to death. It was better that the sentences should be perceived as too mild than too harsh. But greater leniency would represent a betrayal of the thousands of Cubans who had died defending their country and the Revolution. He had no alternative but to endorse the views of his colleagues and to confirm the sentences.

Throughout his long speech Castro looked very unhappy, even broken-hearted. Was it a cynical piece of play-acting? In part, of course. It was he himself who had stage-managed the trial, and willed the outcome. But in part his sorrow was genuine. Never before had a group of supporters, some of whom he had known and trusted for decades, proved so disloyal. How could such a situation have developed? Why did others not pick up the signs of the Ochoa group's disaffection? Later the powerful and ambitious Interior Minister, General Abrantes, was arrested and charged with negligence and dereliction of duty. It was alleged that he had earlier received information about Tony de la Guardia's drug-trafficking, but failed to act on it. Abrantes was also given a long prison sentence. There was a purge of the high-living officials in the Interior Ministry. The Ministry was effectively taken over by more austere and unimaginative officers from Raúl Castro's Armed Forces Ministry.

A number of statesmen and intellectuals around the world sent messages appealing to the Cuban government to commute the death sentences. The Papal Nuncio was instructed to seek an urgent meeting with Fidel Castro in person. Castro received him in the middle of the night. The meeting lasted more than two hours. The Nuncio argued at length, on behalf of the Pope, that commuting the death sentences, as a humanitarian gesture, could only benefit the image and reputation of the Cuban government. Castro replied that the Nuncio had made his case very effectively, and could have the satisfaction of knowing that he had fulfilled his mission as well as was humanly possible. But there was no possibility of his acceding to the Pope's request. Even if he were personally persuaded by the Nuncio's arguments, he was not a free agent. Some people abroad thought he had unlimited power, but this was wrong. There existed a Constitution, and established legal processes. The members of the Council of State had been unanimous in their decision. The National Assembly, the Central Committee and the country at large believed that there should be exemplary punishment. The Nuncio countered that Castro had great moral authority. If he asked the members of the Council of State to review their decision, they would do so. Castro acknowledged that his moral authority was greater than his formal authority under the Constitution. But he thought the sentences were just, and was not prepared to ask for reconsideration.

Over the years Castro spent a vast amount of time trying to enhance his international reputation. Why then was he willing to do immense damage to this reputation by staging the ugly spectacle of a show trial, and imposing four death sentences? Why did he brush aside the appeals even of proven friends like Gabriel García Márquez? The answer is that he thought the survival of his Revolution could be at stake. The Soviet Union was withdrawing its support. Cuba would soon have its back to the wall, facing the hostility of its powerful neighbour without any international backing, and in the midst of a severe economic downturn. The exile community in Florida was confidently predicting the imminent collapse of Castro's regime. Any internal schism would immediately be exploited by his foreign enemies, and could quickly get out of control. The execution of Ochoa and de la Guardia sent a signal to everyone in Cuba, but especially to the armed forces. The times called for discipline, unity, obedience. Everyone got the message.

17 Hard Times

In 1957, when Fidel Castro and a handful of followers were hiding in the gullies of the Sierra Maestra, scarcely anyone except himself thought he had a chance of surviving, let alone winning, his war against one of Latin America's largest and best-equipped armies. In 1989–91 the chances of Castro's political survival looked almost as remote. Two decades earlier he had taken a strategic decision to integrate the Cuban economy with the Soviet bloc, which was now in a process of collapse and disintegration. One hammer blow followed another. Hungary, which provided all of Cuba's buses under a barter arrangement weighted in Cuba's favour, renounced Communism and tore up its agreements with Cuba. In Poland the anti-Communist Solidarity movement swept to power. The Berlin Wall started to crumble under the pressure of East Germans wanting to escape to the West. The all-powerful Stalinist ruler of Romania, Ceauşescu, was overthrown and executed. Castro looked like an isolated dinosaur, left stranded by the tide of history. Most outside observers expected his end to come in months rather than years. The only question, many thought, was whether his departure would be gradual and bloodless, as in Czechoslovakia, or sudden and violent, as in Romania.

In the Western hemisphere there were only two governments friendly to Cuba, the Sandinistas in Nicaragua and General Noriega in Panama. The spotlight was now on Panama. For much of his army career, Noriega had been a paid CIA agent, dutifully passing on any information which came his way about Cuban activities in Central America. But as Noriega became more powerful and more corrupt, his relations with the United States went bad. Under American pressure over his involvement in drug-trafficking, Noriega assumed dictatorial powers and tried to bolster his position by whipping up anti-gringo nationalism. On the principle that his enemy's enemy should be his friend, he asked Castro for weapons and troops to deter an American attack. Castro felt only contempt for Noriega as a person, but he needed Panama as a base for Cuba's trading activities, made more vital by the breakdown of trading agreements with Eastern Europe. He sent a huge quantity of arms to Panama, but no troops (except a few secret military advisers). As he had done with the Sandinistas, Castro advised Noriega to rely for the defence of the country on an armed volunteer militia. Castro explained to Noriega's emissaries that if 'the people in arms' could sustain resistance, even if only in the countryside, the Americans would come under international pressure to call off an invasion.

Noriega took the advice, and was full of admiration for Castro's cunning. But as Castro feared, neither Noriega nor his militia were up to the task. On 20 December 1989, when the United States launched its invasion, the Panama Defence Force and the 'Dignity Battalions' of the militia put up little resistance. Noriega fled in disguise, and failed to rally his troops. Finding the Cuban Embassy surrounded by American troops, he sought refuge in the Embassy of the Holy See; but soon gave himself up and was hauled off to face trial in the United States. Once again, Castro was humiliated. The Soviet Union did not move a finger. Castro's only consolation was that his intelligence services were able to provide a few hours' warning of the American invasion. As a result most of the Cuban advisers and technicians in Panama were able to escape before the US Marines had established control of the country.

That left only Nicaragua. Since their victory in 1979 the Sandinistas had generally followed Castro's advice, especially on military matters. But the war against the Contras dragged on, with no end in sight; the economy declined, with hyper-inflation and growing unemployment; and the Soviet Union refused to help. In 1989 the Sandinista government took a decision which gave Castro grave misgivings. They announced that they would accede to the demands of Western countries that they hold free multi-party elections, in the presence of foreign observers. If the Sandinistas won (and they were confident of winning) the West would at last accept their democratic legitimacy, and the Americans would have no grounds for continuing the war.

The Sandinistas considered that they were acting in the spirit of Castro's advice. He had argued that, in an adverse international environment, the Sandinistas should be moderate and conciliatory. The Soviet Union would not protect Nicaragua, and Cuba on its own was incapable of doing so. The Sandinistas must therefore rely on guile and charm to sustain themselves. However, in Castro's view the Sandinista leaders started going too far in their new-found determination to ingratiate themselves with Western opinion. They allowed the right-wing opposition media to reopen, and even started returning nationalised property to its original private owners.

President Ortega thought he might even win over British Prime Minister Margaret Thatcher, the United States' closest ally. She was persuaded by the Foreign Office to see Ortega, in order to insist that the forthcoming elections must be genuinely free. But the next day she mentioned Ortega's visit in a telephone conversation with President Reagan. Reagan said: 'If I were you, I'd give that one a miss.' Always keen to cultivate her special relationship with Reagan, Thatcher cancelled the meeting with Ortega. But a few weeks later, Reagan having been succeeded by President Bush, she reinstated it. She evidently quite liked the idea of giving Ortega a severe handbagging. On the way to London Ortega stopped in Madrid for a meeting with Prime Minister Felipe González. González told Ortega that Thatcher would not like his olive-green military uniform, modelled on that of Fidel Castro. How about putting on a civilian suit?

Ortega did not immediately take up this suggestion, but the thought later enabled him to show an unexpectedly quirky sense of humour. The meeting with Thatcher was predictably tense. He annoyed her by spending more than half an hour enumerating the social achievements of the Sandinista government. She replied with a long catalogue of Sandinista misconduct, not least their friendship with Fidel Castro. But Ortega was determined to present the meeting in a favourable light. He told a press conference that it had been useful and constructive. It had shown that he and Mrs Thatcher had some things in common. What did they have in common, asked a sceptical journalist. 'Well,' said Ortega, 'we both like dressing in green.'

Back in Nicaragua, Ortega did indeed discard his green uniform. He campaigned in jeans and brightly coloured sports shirts. He posed for the cameras shaking hands with the Sandinistas' most implacable opponent, Cardinal Obando. Castro did not criticise these actions in public, but privately he expressed his doubts. Even the change of dress, in Castro's view, made Ortega look unprincipled and opportunistic. After more than a decade dressed as a revolutionary soldier, Ortega was suddenly pretending to be a civilian and a Western-style democrat. Worst of all, the Sandinistas allowed the US government to channel funds directly to the fourteen-party opposition alliance. This was blatant interference in Nicaragua's internal affairs, yet the Sandinistas kept giving in to every American demand.

> Some people think they can save socialism by making concessions. They fail to take account of the voracious mentality of imperialism and of the reactionary forces. If you give them part of a fingernail, they will want part of your finger; if you give them a piece, they will want the whole finger; if you give them the finger, they will ask for the forearm; if you give them the forearm, they will ask for the arm; and when you give them the arm, they will chop off your head.

On 25 February 1990 the Nicaraguan opposition swept to victory with 55 per cent of the popular vote. The Sandinistas were stunned and incredulous, but accepted the outcome. Castro maintained a glum silence for several days. Then *Granma* published an article written by Castro himself, though not attributed to him, explaining the reasons for the Sandinistas' defeat. Under the burden of an ugly war imposed by the Americans, and with little external aid, the Nicaraguan economy was in decline. The government had made a bad situation worse by attempting capitalist solutions, cutting wages and public expenditure and allowing prices to rise. The obligatory military draft, made necessary by Contra attacks, was deeply unpopular. The people were desperate to end the war, and the only way to achieve this was to give the Americans the government they wanted. In a nutshell, US state terrorism had attained its objective.

The anti-Castro Cuban exiles in Florida were jubilant at the news from Panama and Nicaragua. Two down, one to go! And indeed, the current seemed unstoppable. Within weeks of the Sandinistas' fall, Castro suffered another blow. At the United Nations Human Rights Commission in Geneva, the Americans for the first time secured a majority for a resolution condemning human rights violations in Cuba, and calling for a six-nation delegation to go to the island to investigate. Poland, Czechoslovakia, Hungary and Bulgaria, which for decades had stood shoulder-to-shoulder with Cuba, voted with the United States. Latin American countries which had previously opposed such resolutions as unwarranted interference, now abstained, in response to intense American diplomatic pressure. Castro immediately announced that Cuba would not allow the proposed delegation to set foot on Cuban soil. Cuban spokesmen argued that the resolution was just another manifestation of American power. It certainly demonstrated Cuba's international isolation. Castro was pumped up with anger and bitterness over the 'betrayal' of Cuba by its one-time allies. He said that if the United States invaded Cuba, the governments of Czechoslovakia and Poland, which had co-sponsored the resolution against Cuba, would bear responsibility for the blood that would be shed. Cuban blood would be on the hands of those governments which had written so vile a page of history.

All the East European countries were now treating their long-term trade agreements with Cuba as null and void. They insisted that Cuba must pay with hard currency for any goods they supplied. They also demanded that Cuba pay in full for services hitherto provided free, such as transport costs. Castro decided that if Cuba had to use scarce hard currency, it would import from Japan or Western Europe, anywhere rather than from the treacherous East Europeans. He had long known, from secretly conducted opinion polls and other sources of information, that most Cubans felt contempt for Soviet and East European consumer goods. Their cars, televisions and refrigerators were seen as ugly and inefficient compared with Western products. Castro himself had for years defended and praised the technology of his Communist allies. But now was not the time for worrying about consistency. He bitterly mocked the quality of the products which the East Europeans were no longer sending. Good riddance! Who wanted unwieldy and inefficient Bulgarian forklifts? Who wanted the dreadful Hungarian buses which belched filthy black smoke and kept breaking down? The Cuban audience laughed and applauded, delighted to find that their chief had all along felt the same way that they did. Mockery changed to venomous anger when the East Germans reneged on an agreement to supply powdered milk. This was the main source for the milk distributed to all Cuban schoolchildren. What, asked Castro bitterly, did the new converts to capitalism care about the welfare of children?

Castro produced a phrase to describe Cuba's situation. Many years earlier he had drawn up contingency plans to ensure economic survival in the event of an American military attack, including a total naval and air blockade. This eventuality would create a 'Special Period in Time of War'. As yet there was no naval blockade, but the sudden drying-up of supplies from Eastern Europe created a comparable situation. Castro therefore declared that the country was facing a 'Special Period in Time of Peace'. The message for the population was that they should be ready for living conditions to become about as bad as they could be, short of open war. In the worst-case scenario, the Zero Option, no oil supplies at all would reach Cuba. The urban population would have to go to the countryside and live from subsistence farming.

The notion of a hypothetical Zero Option gave Cubans the small comfort of realising that the country's situation could be even worse than it actually was. But the reality was grim enough. Cuba had to pay for almost all imports with hard currency, of which it was earning little. With huge unpaid debts to both East and West, there were no banks willing to lend more money. Numerous basic commodities and consumer goods were in extremely short supply, or non-existent. Above all, Cuba was having to survive on less than half of the 13 million tons a year of oil delivered in earlier years by the Soviet Union. The petrol ration was progressively reduced to the point where virtually any private use of a car became impossible. Thousands of Chinese bicycles were imported as a substitute for vehicles. It was a blessing, Castro assured the people. The bicycles would be healthier and more friendly to the environment. Cuba was following the example of the Dutch, who were also encouraging people to use bicycles rather than cars.

Large numbers of government bureaucrats were laid off. Most construction projects stopped. Factories producing non-essential goods were closed. Oxen were used to replace tractors. Firewood was used for cooking. Electricity cuts began, lasting eight, then twelve, then sixteen hours a day. Times were very hard, said Castro, and would become even harder. But there would be no surrender. 'Resist! Resist! Resist!' Nor would there be any sell-out of socialism. Since the first years of the Revolution Castro had ended his speeches by shouting 'Homeland or death! We will prevail!' Now, as countries around the world were renouncing socialism, Castro inaugurated a new and extended ending to all setpiece speeches. 'Homeland or death! *Socialism or death!* We will prevail!'

Some years earlier, when the prospects for Cuba looked much more favourable, Castro had waged a successful campaign to stage the Pan-American Games in Havana in August 1991. The United States had naturally been opposed, but in the end had reluctantly accepted the majority view among Latin American countries that sport should not be politicised and that Cuba was a deserving candidate to act as host. Like other Communist countries, Cuba had devoted huge resources to sport and especially athletics. As Castro saw it, training for sports encouraged discipline, zeal and determination among young people; and sporting successes gave the whole population a sense of national pride and achievement. When bread was short, circuses were all the more necessary. But by 1991, with the economy still going from bad to worse, the staging of the games in Havana came to look less like a triumph and more like an expensive mistake. The Cubans had to build a large stadium and numerous other Olympic-standard sports facilities, as well as a 'Pan-American Village' for the athletes. With the construction industry virtually crippled, would this be possible? And did it anyway make sense to divert extremely scarce resources to such a costly sporting event?

Castro acknowledged that if he had foreseen how events would develop, he would never have embarked on the course of staging the games. But to back off when preparations were already far advanced would have been, in his eyes, a terrible sign of weakness. He therefore pressed on, and made completing the installations a top priority. Teams of elite construction workers toiled night and day, and Castro in person made frequent visits to inspect progress and encourage the workers. As the date for the games approached, the political stakes grew even higher. It was not just a question of whether socialist Cuba had the capacity to build the facilities, and to organise the games competently. Many people began to wonder whether the games might light the spark that would bring about Castro's downfall.

The fall of Ceauşescu in Romania was fresh in everyone's mind. He had been a dictator whose control over his people seemed even more absolute and ruthless than Castro's. But an applauding crowd had suddenly turned hostile. Television cameras had caught the moment when Ceauşescu's expression changed from confident self-satisfaction to puzzlement, and then to dismay, anger and fear. Could not something similar happen to Castro? He could not now avoid bringing huge crowds of Cubans into the stadiums, and onto the streets, in the presence of hundreds of foreign journalists. If even a small section of a crowd seized the opportunity to demonstrate against Castro, the impact could be devastating. Castro's aura of invincible control would be broken. The end would follow quickly.

It was therefore not only foreign sports correspondents who applied for visas to cover the games. Some 1,300 foreign journalists came to Havana, many hoping and expecting to see some political excitement. But those who hoped to witness Castro's nemesis were disappointed. The facilities were ready, and the organisation of the games went reasonably smoothly. There were no hostile demonstrations, even on a small scale. The crowds in the stadiums cheered Castro and chanted 'Fidel!' with every appearance of spontaneity. Public enthusiasm and high spirits grew steadily as the Cuban athletes put on their best-ever performance. In the end a Cuban boxing victory brought Cuba to the top of the gold medal table. It was the first time that any Latin American country had ever won more gold medals than the United States in an international athletics competition. Castro was quietly euphoric, but he knew how to play the gentleman. As Latin American spectators crowded round to congratulate him, he modestly played down Cuba's successes, talked up the achievements of other Latin American participants, and even spoke warmly and generously about the US athletes whose sporting spirit had greatly contributed to the friendly atmosphere of the games.

On the last evening of the games, Castro attended a dinner with Latin American sports officials and diplomats. During the meal he was called away to take a telephone call from Carlos Aldana. There was astonishing news from the Soviet Union. Gorbachev had been ousted. Power had been assumed by a committee of eight prominent hard-liners. All the members of the committee were conservative Communists known to be well-disposed to Cuba. In other parts of Havana, senior Cuban officials were already celebrating. They assumed that the hectic course of reform, with its disastrous consequences for Cuba, would now be halted, and that close economic ties with Cuba would be restored. It seemed that at a stroke the prospects for Cuba had been transformed.

Fidel Castro himself, however, was much too wily a fox to leap to conclusions. The news was confused, and the definitive outcome still not clear. Nothing could be more damaging for Cuba than to welcome the coup publicly and then find that it had failed. There were contradictory reports about what had happened to Gorbachev. Boris Yeltsin, the reformist President of the Russian Federation, was still at large and busy trying to organise resistance to the coup.

Castro was conscious that the other dinner guests were hanging on his words, and watching his expression. He was excited and nervous, but careful to show no emotion. He stood up, paced about, asked for more information, made some matter-of-fact comments on the individuals named in the news reports. He then said that the news was worrying. If the Soviet Union descended into chaos and anarchy, that would be the worst possible outcome for Cuba. That was all he would say. It aroused no false expectations. It should not offend any of the factions in the Soviet Union. It gave no hostages to fortune.

It was a good holding line, but difficult to sustain for long. Journalists, both Cuban and foreign, were pressing for a more substantive comment. Did Cuba recognise the new government in Moscow? Or did it still recognise Gorbachev? For more than twenty-four hours, the Cuban Government maintained an awkward silence. Meanwhile Iraq and Libya made statements recognising the new Soviet government. Western governments condemned the coup and called for Gorbachev to be reinstated. Finally Castro authorised the publication of an official statement. He had spent hours tinkering with the short and apparently innocuous text. It said that it was not for Cuba to make judgements on internal events in the Soviet Union. However, the Cuban people hoped the Soviet people would be able to overcome their difficulties peacefully. The statement was transparently designed to avoid compromising Cuba's relations with whichever side emerged victorious. However, the statement did refer to 'the authorities', implicitly accepting the status which the new committee were claiming for themselves. This proved a mistake. Soon afterwards the committee collapsed, and a shaken Gorbachev returned to Moscow and was restored to office.

Gorbachev was restored, but the real power in the land was now Boris Yeltsin, who had led the resistance to the coup and defeated the old guard. Yeltsin was very bad news indeed for Castro. He was not only a radical reformer, but an active anti-Communist; and a friend and ally of Castro's bitterest enemies in the Cuban exile community in Florida. Two years earlier, during a private visit to the United States, he had forged a tactical alliance with the hard-line anti-Castro Cuban American National Foundation (CANF). The CANF provided a substantial sum of money to 'sponsor' a visit by Yeltsin to Miami. There they gave him their view of the situation in Cuba, and an account of Castro's stubborn resistance to the sort of reforms favoured by Yeltsin. They undertook to work to improve Yeltsin's image in the United States, and to lobby for American aid to the Russian Federation. They promised also to use their influence with Jeb Bush, the Governor of Florida and son of President George Bush, to obtain an invitation for Yeltsin to pay an official visit to the United States. They asked what would be Yeltsin's policy towards Cuba. Yeltsin said he would end all aid to Castro's government. There was an unwritten deal. The CANF set up an office in Moscow. Russian parliamentarians were invited to visit Disneyland. The CANF now had excellent access not only in Washington, but also in Moscow.

After facing down the coup, Yeltsin moved fast to dismantle the structure of Communist rule. The Soviet Communist Party was dissolved, and its offices taken over by state organisations. Castro did not attempt the impossible task of hiding these staggering events from the Cuban people. On their television sets Cubans saw statues of Lenin being pulled down by exulting crowds. Soon they witnessed an extraordinary event in Cuba itself. The Red Flag flying over the massive tower of the Soviet Embassy, overlooking the sea and visible from miles around, was quietly pulled down and replaced by the red, white and blue of the Russian Federation.

Was this the end of the affair, the end of a long special relationship? Castro hoped that something at least might be salvaged. After all, the relationship had brought some benefits as well as costs to the Soviet Union. When the Chernobyl nuclear disaster struck the Soviet Union, Castro offered to look after children affected by the radiation. In quixotic fashion, he was ready to take any number of children, for any length of time, and to give them the best available medical treatment and nursing care, at no cost. More than 13,000 children came to Cuba, some staying many years. In the tropical sun, and with the loving care of Cuban nurses, the condition of many children improved dramatically. Children who arrived looking thin, haggard and miserable returned to the Ukraine looking healthy and fit.

Castro's goodwill had not been shown only in charitable gestures. At Lourdes near Havana the Russians had their biggest espionage centre outside the Soviet Union, the base from which they conducted all their signals intelligence in the Western hemisphere. They also needed Cuban sugar. By chance there was a quite severe sugar shortage in Russia just at this critical moment. In response to a request from Gorbachev, Castro rushed to send shipments of sugar to Russia before they had been scheduled. But on 11 September 1991 Gorbachev made an announcement which revived all of Castro's dormant rancour against the Russians. At a joint press conference with United States Secretary of State Baker, Gorbachev said that the Soviet brigade in Cuba would be withdrawn. Once again the Russians were currying favour with the Americans at Cuba's expense. Castro had not been consulted or even informed. It was like the deal to withdraw missiles from Cuba in 1962, only worse. Cuba's views and interests had simply been ignored.

Outside Cuba, Castro's enemies seemed everywhere to be triumphant. But inside Cuba his grip was as strong as ever. The CANF thought it had a network of supporters in Cuba, and that the time was ripe for a show of strength. They encouraged their supporters to stage a demonstration against Castro in Havana. The CANF's radio stations in Florida broadcast appeals for a mass turnout. But the demonstration proved a non-event. There were some expectant journalists, and rather more policemen; but barely a dozen demonstrators, who were quickly dispersed. Most of the CANF's supposed supporters were in fact working for Castro's State Security. Most of the genuine dissidents in Cuba rejected the CANF's aggressively hard line. They wanted a peaceful transition to democracy, rather than the bloodbath which would result from an attempt to overthrow Castro by force.

These moderate dissidents were also few in number, but they presented Castro with a thornier problem. They rejected American patronage, and were therefore difficult to denounce as traitors. He was reluctant to make martyrs of them by arresting them. State Security tried to intimidate them by ostentatious surveillance and by organising public 'acts of repudiation', supposedly demonstrations against the dissidents by angry neighbours. But the acts of repudiation made a disastrous impression, especially when a mob used physical violence against the dignified poet Maria Elena Cruz Varela. Castro concluded that the lesser of evils was to arrest the handful of active dissidents and to charge them with relatively minor offences, such as distributing false information. Cruz Varela was given a two-year prison sentence.

In October 1991 the Fourth Congress of the Cuban Communist Party was held in the eastern town of Santiago. Two years earlier, when Castro had set in train preparations for the Congress, he envisaged that it would announce some important decisions. In particular he wanted to prepare for the future by disengaging from the day-to-day running of the government. He would remain in charge of the Communist Party, thereby emphasising the Party's continuing pre-eminence, and Commander in Chief of the armed forces. But a new post of head of government would be created. It would be filled by the man who in Castro's judgement was the ablest and most reliable of the younger generation of senior officials, Carlos Lage. At the same time many of the old guard would be retired, and replaced by younger men. The Congress would introduce economic reforms designed to enable Cuban socialism to survive in a world dominated by market economies. To stimulate agricultural production, free farmers' markets would once again be legalised, as would some very small-scale private enterprises, such as independent plumbers, carpenters and repair workshops. To give the National Assembly greater credibility, both inside and outside Cuba, its members would be directly elected by the people, rather than indirectly through the municipal and provincial assemblies. The changes would be submitted to a national referendum.

These had been Castro's original ideas, and they had been taken up and developed enthusiastically by the group of younger men whom Castro had chosen and trained to take over the reins of power. But Castro did not close any options. He permitted and indeed encouraged prominent Communist

Party conservatives to put the case against reform. Like most absolute rulers, he liked to have supporters on his right and on his left, so that he could play the role of bridge and moderator. And he put in train a process of mass consultation. In factories, state farms, schools and army units, the Communist Party members were encouraged to hold discussions and to put forward proposals for consideration by the Congress. This looked democratic, but in practice enabled Castro to keep tight control. If the grassroots were told which way Fidel wanted to proceed, they would follow, and urge everyone else to follow. The most important rule in Cuba, understood by everyone and taking precedence over any doctrine of Marx or Lenin, was unity behind the leader. Within limits you could criticise anyone and anything, but *never* Fidel himself.

Long before the date for the Congress arrived, Castro had changed his mind about what it should do. The reforms which he had envisaged would not necessarily be abandoned, but their introduction would be delayed and made more gradual. When a fierce storm was raging, Castro thought, the sensible course was not to open up, but to batten down. If major reforms were announced in present conditions, at a time of acute economic difficulty and intense American pressure, they would look like a sign of desperation, a rejection of past policies and beliefs, and an admission of failure. But there had been no internal failure. In Castro's opinion, the crisis facing the country was due entirely to external factors, above all the disintegration of the Soviet Union. And the state of the Soviet Union was in itself a warning of what could happen if reforms were introduced too quickly and without adequate preparation. When Cuba had overcome the immediate economic crisis, and shown that it had the strength to survive the collapse of the Soviet Union, then it might be desirable, from a position of strength and confidence, to introduce the reforms. Meantime, Cuba must stand firm on its fundamental beliefs.

Castro's doubts about the wisdom of going ahead with major reforms had been reinforced earlier in the year when he had taken part in an Ibero-American summit conference in Mexico, attended by Spain, Portugal and the countries of Latin America. Castro had got on well enough with the King of Spain, but a few Latin American Presidents had reproached him with the lack of democracy in Cuba. The ones who talked most about democracy, Castro noted, presided over countries completely in hock to the United States and characterised by corruption, the obscene wealth of a tiny minority, and the grinding poverty of the majority. Yet because they had political parties and elections, they presumed to being more democratic than Cuba. The parties might be controlled by a handful of magnates, and their policies might be indistinguishable, but that was democracy. What contemptible hypocrisy!

Castro returned from Mexico more determined than ever to make no concessions to this concept of democracy. Whatever happened in the rest of the world, in Cuba there would be no return to capitalism, no divisive political pluralism, no dilution of the role of the Communist Party.

When Castro discussed the upcoming Party Congress with his ministers and advisers, he put the case for deferring, at least for a few years, most of the reforms which had been envisaged. As usual there was no dissent. The old guard were quietly satisfied. Some of the young reformers were disappointed, and perhaps felt that an opportunity was being lost; but all accepted Fidel's judgement. After all, he alone had foreseen from the start the ultimate consequences of Gorbachev's reforms.

Having brought his inner circle on board, Castro set about quashing any expectations among the wider public that the Congress would introduce a major political and economic liberalisation. He told journalists that the Congress would involve a free and wide-ranging discussion. There might be some changes. For example, they might end the exclusion from the Party of people practising religion. This exclusion had been introduced when the Catholic Church was working actively against the Revolution. But circumstances had changed, and the Party would be seen to be more broad-based and representative if religious people were allowed to join. However, the need for unity was stronger than ever. There would be no opening for opposition parties, which would inevitably be exploited and manipulated by the United States. The United States preached the virtues of pluralism, because it helped them to divide and rule. If American hostility ceased, the question of political pluralism might be reviewed. He personally would enjoy taking part in a contested election. But the Americans had become even more aggressively hostile to Cuba. In these circumstances there would be no question of allowing them to establish a fifth column inside Cuba. Nor would there be any return of capitalism. Cuba would continue to have a planned economy, based on rationality, not a market economy, based on the law of the jungle.

To many people's surprise, the only senior government figure who was seriously disgruntled over Fidel's change of direction on economic reform was his brother Raúl. Raúl had become a pro-Soviet Communist long before Fidel, and had always been regarded as a pillar of Communist orthodoxy. But he did not much like his image as a man of unimaginative rigidity, in contrast to the creative genius of Fidel. When Fidel launched the preparations for the Fourth Party Congress, and economic reform was on the agenda, Raúl had taken it up with enthusiasm. He argued to colleagues that the transition to a more decentralised economic system should be undertaken while Fidel was still in command and able to ensure that the process was not destabilising. He began to look to Japan as a new model and a new potential partner. Japan had developed a dynamic decentralised economy, but had also retained a strong sense of social responsibility, cohesion and discipline. Raúl wanted farms and factories run by the army to be a testing ground for the new economic ideas. Consequently, when Fidel went into reverse gear, Raúl was left in an awkward situation. Fidel himself was not publicly committed to reform. He had merely encouraged a debate within the Party. He could still, without losing face or credibility, endorse a policy of no change. For Raúl it was more difficult. Everyone could see that he had been overruled.

When the Congress opened in Santiago, Raúl was not present. A rather lame explanation was given. The Americans were conducting military exercises near Guantánamo, and Raúl had to be at his post in the Armed Forces Ministry in case there was a surprise attack or provocation. Few people believed this story. Rumours swept the exile community that Raúl was ill, or in disgrace, or dead. But this was wishful thinking. A few days later Raúl took his seat at the Congress. He had made his point, and now would move on, supportive and loyal as ever.

Fidel meanwhile was painting a very bleak picture of Cuba's economic situation. Of course, the causes were all external. He gave details of all the agreements which Cuba's former trading partners had abrogated, or failed to fulfil. In recent weeks large quantities of Soviet rice and wheat should have been delivered. How much had actually arrived? None. They had sent no fertiliser, no tyres, no soap and detergents, no steel and non-ferrous metals, no butter, no newsprint, no chemicals. Imagine, said Castro, the desperate efforts of the government to find an alternative supplier of sodium carbonate, with which to manufacture bottles for babies' milk, not to mention beer and rum for older people. Of the Cuban order for spare parts for the Soviet lorries, televisions, refrigerators, fans and bicycles supplied in earlier years, just 1 per cent had been delivered.

This was not a reproach, said Castro, just an explanation of the shortages evident throughout Cuba. There was such confusion and anarchy in the Soviet Union that they could not fulfil their commitments to Cuba even if they wanted to. He had warned of the consequences of the Soviet leaders' reforms, but his had been a lone voice. In any event, Cuba would not make the same mistakes. It would not dissolve the Communist Party. It would not adopt political pluralism, *pluriporquería* (multi-rubbish). Cuba needed no lessons in democracy. True democracy could only be achieved under socialism:

How can you talk about democracy to a child abandoned in the street? How can you talk about democracy with a hungry person, an illiterate person, an unemployed person, one who has nothing, one to whom no one pays any attention, whom nobody respects, whom people with money treat like a dog? What democracy can exist in a society of exploiters and exploited?

The Cuban people would rise to the challenge. Would they surrender, and accept a society of millionaires and beggars, with no social housing, no social security, with education and health care only for those with money? Would they become another Puerto Rico? 'No!' shouted the 1,700 delegates to the Congress.

Castro knew that some of his younger supporters were unhappy with his constant emphasis on sacrifice and struggle. Rather than 'Socialism or Death' they would have preferred a more positive and hopeful slogan. Young people, they argued, would accept socialism if it was associated with the good things in life, not only justice and dignity, but also love, prosperity and happiness. Castro had little truck with this way of thinking. He had publicly rebuked Roberto Robaina, the charismatic head of the Union of Young Communists, for 'forgetting' to shout 'Socialism or Death' at the end of a speech he had made in Castro's presence. The rebuke was mild and semi-humourous, but still a rebuke. For Castro, progress was always achieved at a price, often at the price of suffering and bloodshed. He told the Congress in Santiago that the Cuban Revolution was not the work of one man or one generation. It was a historical process, started in the independence struggles of the nineteenth century. Thousands had died fighting for it. It was the duty of the present generation to save the Revolution, however arduous the task. Even in capitalist countries, many people looked to Cuba as a beacon of hope. They admired 'this small island of freedom and dignity'. Cuba would not disappoint them.

And finally, winding up the Congress, Castro made a concession to the young people who wanted less gloom and doom, and less talk of death. He said that for once he would refrain from shouting 'Socialism or Death', because death would not be necessary. But before reaching this conclusion, he went in the opposite direction, offering the prospect of an apocalyptic martyr's death to *everyone* in Cuba, including explicitly Robaina's Union of Young Communists. There were still very hard times ahead, he said, and those carrying the flag of socialism must be ready to sacrifice themselves.

> If all the Politburo have to die, all the Politburo will die! We will not be the weaker for it! If all the Central Committee have to die, we will die, and we will not be the weaker for it! If all the delegates to this Congress have to die, all the delegates to the Congress will die, and we will not be weaker. The example of each one of us will be multiplied. If all the members of the Party have to die, all the members of the Party will die, and still we will not

be weakened! If all members of the Union of Young Communists have to die, all the members of the Union of Young Communists will die!

That was not all. The logic got lost in the intensity of Fidel's emotion, but it was the emotion that mattered.

And if, in order to crush the Revolution, they had to kill all the people, the people would be willing to die in support of their leaders and their party. Even then, we would not be weakened, because after us they would have to kill billions of people who are not willing to be slaves, who are not willing to continue to be exploited, who are not willing to continue to go hungry! Men may die, but examples never die. Men may die, but ideals will never die. And here we are, willing to shed our blood for our ideals! . . . Without honour and dignity, there cannot be life, nor is life worth anything, nor do we want life. So I will change the slogan for this afternoon. Just today, I will not say 'Socialism or Death', because there will be socialism whatever the price! I do not say 'Homeland or Death', because we shall be able to destroy anyone who wants to take away our homeland!

18 The Final Hour?

In 1992 Andres Oppenheimer, the well-informed columnist of the *Miami Herald*, published his best-selling book, *Castro's Final Hour*. The title, allowing for a bit of literary hyperbole, looked like a reasonably safe bet. Communism was in headlong decline. Fidel Castro was sixty-five years old, and looked his age. The grey beard had become scraggy, and his skin blotchy. The bounce had gone out of his step. He sometimes looked tired and drawn. More frequently than in earlier years, he lost his train of thought, and repeated himself. His gestures and oratorical style seemed to have become more mannered and exaggerated.

The state of the economy was now catastrophic. In any country a fall of 5 per cent in gross domestic product would be viewed as a major recession. The Cuban economy had declined by more than 40 per cent in less than two years and was still shrinking. A population accustomed to eating reasonably well was now surviving on the equivalent of one bad meal a day. Meat of any sort was a rarity. The daily bread ration was reduced to one small tasteless roll. There were long queues for the few restaurants still offering food for Cuban currency, and they served little more than pasta. For the many Cubans who attached importance to personal hygiene, it was degrading and depressing to have to manage without soap, detergent, toothpaste and razor-blades. People without a bicycle had to wait often for hours before being packed like sardines into one of the few buses still on the road. Was there a way out? Castro kept calling for fortitude and resistance, but what hope could he offer?

The much-heralded Party Congress of 1991 had not offered a way forward. It was more of the same, if anything a step backwards, a return to the spirit of Moncada. After thirty-two years in power, Castro was still explaining away setbacks and calling for more sacrifices. What could the government's heroic revolutionary rhetoric mean to a generation of Cubans who had never known Batista or the Bay of Pigs, who were bored with politics, often more interested in rock music or youth fashion?

Castro was well aware that he had a problem of public disillusionment and disaffection, especially among young people. Some Western observers thought that he had lost touch with the reality of his country, that he was given only good news, and that he had come to believe his own propaganda. But there was not much truth in this. He was intelligent enough to realise that underlings tended to tell him what they thought he wanted to hear. He took that into account. He had survived so long partly because he was better informed than his enemies. The job of his secret services was not just to identify spies and dissidents, but to ensure that he knew what people really thought. There were several groups of public opinion pollsters producing confidential reports for the government. Most days Castro's personal support staff submitted to him up to a hundred reports. Some were diplomatic or intelligence reports on international developments, some on domestic economic developments, but several also on public attitudes in Cuba.

If Castro had one talent almost to excess, it was his ability to manage Cuban public opinion. To outsiders his speeches might look over-long, rambling and repetitive, but they still gripped the attention of most Cubans. When Castro was asked where he learned his oratorical skills, he said that he had studied famous orators like Demosthenes at school, but found them laboured and unconvincing. His early speeches as a young man were also laboured and unconvincing. 'I discovered that the secret of public speaking was precisely not to give a speech, but rather to talk to the audience.' The most important requirement, he added, was to speak one's mind honestly. People would always recognise sincerity.

Some Western embassies in Havana had the custom of stationing staff at different places among the crowds listening to Castro's speeches, to assess public reactions. At the 26 July celebrations in 1991, Castro shared the platform with Nelson Mandela. Mandela's speech, with the translation, lasted forty minutes. In that relatively short space of time, the crowd's initial noisy enthusiasm turned to polite boredom. Groups of people started talking to each other and wondering aloud how long the old man would go on. Then Castro spoke for more than three hours. For nearly all that time, despite the hot sun, the crowd was attentive and responsive, laughing at his jokes, silent when he became serious. On the few occasions when the crowd's attention started to wander, Castro sensed this and changed tack.

During the Special Period, and especially in 1992, Castro spoke in public even more frequently than in earlier years. Scarcely a day went by without his appearing on television, opening a new recreation centre, visiting a farm or a hospital, never losing the chance to address an audience. Some critics thought that ideology and government had been replaced by an exaggerated cult of the personality. But it had a purpose. On several occasions he talked for more than an hour about the supply of potatoes, explaining why there was a shortage, describing what was being done to increase production, giving detailed statistics of plantings in different provinces, discussing the merits of different potato varieties, analysing how growth had been affected by the weather, and much more. Talking did not help the consumers who could find no potatoes, but at least they could not doubt that Fidel was aware of the situation and doing what he could to rectify it. Similarly, by opening new discothèques and sports facilities, and talking at great length about them, Castro showed that he knew perfectly well that many young people were bored and frustrated.

Naturally, a few more discothèques, and even a few more potatoes, would not convince young people that Cuba's socialist system was superior to the flourishing consumer societies which they saw in Western films and smuggled magazines. The 1991 Party Congress had virtually killed off hopes that Castro would allow a significant loosening of political controls or liberalisation of the economy. But low expectations are a good base from which to convince people that small advances are significant. And in the two years following the Congress, most of the reforms which had apparently been buried at the Congress were dusted off and quietly introduced. In practice Carlos Lage started acting virtually as a Prime Minister, running the day-to-day business of government. Family-scale private enterprise was legalised. Thousands of Cubans registered as 'own account' tradesmen. Since it was virtually impossible to control the black market in foreign currency, dollars were made legal tender, and dollar shops (hitherto accessible only to diplomats, tourists and foreign technicians) were opened to Cubans able to acquire dollars. Workers in the tourism industry were allowed to accept tips. Farmers, who previously could sell only to the state, at prices fixed by the state, were allowed to sell products from their private plots on open markets, at prices fixed by themselves.

Once again, the government resorted to emigration as a means of easing unemployment and discontent. Most restrictions on leaving the country were lifted. Exit visas were usually granted on demand, except to people holding sensitive positions in the government. Cuban artists were actively encouraged to live and work in countries like Mexico, where they could earn more money. The main obstacle to emigration became obtaining a foreign entry visa, rather than a Cuban exit visa.

The government hoped that Cubans who wanted to go to the United States, having for years been encouraged to leave by broadcasts from Miami, would now be allowed to do so. In a bilateral agreement signed a few years earlier, the US government had undertaken to issue 'up to 20,000 visas a year' to facilitate Cuban family reunions. Any Cubans actually arriving on

American soil, even without a visa, were in any case automatically accepted, being viewed as victims of tyranny. But when departure restrictions were lifted in Cuba, the US authorities decided that they did not want to accept a flood of Cubans. Very few visas were issued. Hundreds of Cubans queued for hours every day outside the US Interests Sections, only to have their application for a visa rejected. In an ironical reversal of roles, Cuban applicants claimed to be the victims of political persecution, and straightfaced American visa officers refused to believe them. Certificates from prominent human rights activists were not sufficient. To be accepted as a bona fide victim of persecution, one had to produce documentary evidence of having spent at least two years in jail. Very few people passed the test. The US government had no interest in helping Castro to lower the pressure of political discontent.

President Bush had said that there would soon be a popular explosion in Cuba, and that he looked forward to being the first US President to walk in the streets of a free Havana. Soon afterwards, there was indeed an explosion, but not in Cuba. Riots, arson and looting broke out in the Watts district of Los Angeles. Bush would leave the White House without having set foot in Havana. Why did the Cubans in Cuba not rise in rebellion? Surely the objective reasons for rioting were far greater in Havana than in Los Angeles? Many Americans were genuinely puzzled at the failure of the Cuban people to revolt. Misled by decades of one-sided and inaccurate media coverage, they were still underestimating Castro's political skills. And although American pressure on Cuba was undoubtedly effective, deepening the economic decline and frightening off potential investors, it actually helped to rally political support for Castro among the Cuban population. Many Cubans, even those who disliked Communism, were terrified by the prospect of a return to power of the fat-cat exiles in Florida, led by the right-wing millionaire Mas Canosa. Would the rich exiles claim back their old properties in Havana, throwing a million Cubans onto the street? No doubt they would bring investment and sparkling new consumer goods, but would they also throw out the social security, free education and free health care which most Cubans wanted to keep? Many Cubans felt safer with the devil they knew.

In public, Castro carefully avoided expressing a preference between President Bush and his Democratic opponent in the 1992 Presidential elections, Bill Clinton. But in private he did not hide his preference for Clinton. His information was that Clinton was a liberal-minded pragmatist, with no personal hang-ups about Cuba. But Castro had by now seen eight US Presidents come and go, and he had no illusions that there might be a significant change in US policy. There were no votes to be won by softening the 'blockade' against Cuba. The only state where Cuba was still a high-priority issue was Florida; and the only way to win votes in Florida was by *hardening* the embargo. He knew that both the Republicans and the Democrats received large financial donations from anti-Castro organisations in Florida, notably the CANF.

During the campaign Clinton tried to steal the Republicans' thunder in Florida by supporting yet another extension of the embargo. President Bush had vetoed the Mack Amendment, a piece of legislation which penalised foreign companies which traded with Cuba. Bush's action was not due to any reluctance to tighten the screws on Cuba, but only because his European and Canadian allies objected strongly to the extraterritorial nature of the Mack Amendment, which extended US law to third countries. Canada and Britain even introduced counter-legislation, prohibiting companies operating in their territory from complying with foreign laws. The Cuban lobby in Florida were irritated by Bush's action. Many of them abandoned their traditional backing for the Republicans when Clinton promised to support a legislative proposal similar to the Mack Amendment, put forward by the Democratic Congressman Torricelli.

Despite this development, Castro welcomed Clinton's victory. He said that during his first term Clinton would have to take account of right-wing pressures over Cuba, as had Kennedy. He was maintaining the embargo and was committed to the Torricelli Bill, but at least his language was less aggressive and bellicose that that habitually used by the Republicans. Castro claimed to be encouraged by Clinton's handling of the crisis in Somalia, where American troops had been killed. Instead of reacting with new acts of aggression, said Castro, Clinton acted courageously and with a cool head.

In talking privately to visitors, Castro sometimes seemed more interested in Hillary Clinton than in Bill Clinton. Hillary's views on health care earned Castro's strong approval. So did her physical appearance. She looked a bit like Fidel's wife Mirta, and like some other women in his life. She was the first First Lady since Jackie Kennedy whom Castro fancied.

During the 1962 missile crisis, when the Americans were demanding the right to on-site inspection of Soviet missiles, Castro thought of saying in a speech that he would allow Jackie Kennedy to come to Cuba to carry out the inspections. But he dropped the idea when some advisers said that Cuban women would not appreciate this sort of macho humour. Thirty years later no one stopped Castro from making politically incorrect jokes about Hillary Clinton. When Sir Edward Heath paid one of his periodic visits to Cuba, Fidel was bubbling with enthusiasm about the Democratic victory. 'Bill Clinton may not be especially interesting,' said Castro, 'but Hillary is definitely good news.' Heath was not the best person with whom to share laddish jokes; but he did not want to appear stuffy, so he shook politely with silent laughter.

Elections, Castro knew, were in Western eyes the one real criterion of democracy. He had often defended the Cuban system of Soviet-style indirect elections to the National Assembly. But the Soviet Union had disappeared from the map, and Castro concluded that he would lose nothing by allowing direct elections. The crucial requirement in his opinion was to ensure that counter-revolutionaries were prevented from becoming candidates. So direct elections were duly held to the National Assembly, and some non-Communists (but not dissidents) were allowed to get elected. Liberalisation did not stretch to allowing the expression of anti-government views. Anyone could propose a candidate; but in each district an electoral commission, comprising representatives of trade unions and other 'mass organisations', was empowered to weed out unsuitable candidates. To maintain 'unity,' *all* approved candidates were elected, provided they got more than 50 per cent of the vote. Castro himself campaigned in the streets of Havana for a seat in the Assembly. A visitor from the BBC was astonished by his performance, commenting that Castro looked for all the world as if he was uncertain of victory.

With foreigners, Castro liked to suggest that he would be happy to retire, were it not for the critical situation of the country created by American pressure. He said that there were plenty of younger people capable of steering the ship of state, but a captain did not leave his post in the middle of a storm.

> It would be a mistake to think that the Revolution is one man. We would be in a bad way if that were true. We have trained new men. There are many young men. We try to renew ourselves. You might be asking, why do they not renew me? I would say that it would be wonderful if they could renew me. But if in these difficult times it occurred to me to resign, or propose that they find someone else to carry out my duties, they would say that I was the biggest traitor in the world . . .

Cut off from the supply of Soviet weaponry, the capability of Cuba's armed forces was in steady decline. The air force, short of fuel and spare parts, was barely operational. Would the Americans take advantage of this weakness, knowing that neither Russia nor anyone else would stir a finger to help Castro? Would the most militant exile organisations stage an armed provocation, in the hope of triggering an outright conflict? After discussing these anxieties, Fidel, Raúl and the leading military commanders drew up a new defence strategy, the 'War of All the People'. Instead of confronting an American invasion force with regular military formations, the armed forces would disperse into prepared hiding places, from which to conduct guerrilla warfare. Many of the new unemployed found jobs building a massive network of bunkers and tunnels, even in central Havana. Castro told his officers that what the US government feared was casualties among their own soldiers. If they knew they would face prolonged guerrilla resistance, they would not attack. Castro acknowledged that an invasion was unlikely. The Americans thought it would not be necessary, and that Castro would fall from internal pressures. But it was best to prepare for the worst. If Cuba showed that it was surviving, and even starting an economic recovery, the Americans might become frustrated and even more aggressive.

Castro's hopes for economic recovery rested mainly on two areas: bio-technology and tourism. Huge resources had been spent in earlier years on biological research centres. Scarce foreign currency had been devoted to acquiring the most sophisticated cutting-edge research equipment. Cuban scientists developed some impressive products. In the early 1990s more that US$200 million was earned from medical exports, notably from contracts to supply meningitis B vaccine to Brazil and Argentina. Castro hoped to achieve even greater success with other pharmaceutical products, including a 'miracle' anti-cholesterol drug called PPG, which was said to enhance male virility. But initial hopes were frustrated. Cuba failed to make significant inroads in First World markets, where registration required many years of elaborate testing, and where distribution channels were controlled by giant multinationals.

Tourism was more promising. Cuba had plenty of sun and beaches, and more culture and scenic variety than any other Caribbean destination. New hotels started sprouting in the main tourist resorts. During the Cold War period, Castro had regarded tourism as a minor and rather undesirable sideline. Now that it offered an economic lifeline for the Revolution, he swallowed his misgivings, and posed for the cameras with Spanish, Mexican and Canadian hoteliers.

Cuba needed foreign investment not only in tourism, but in most other sectors of the economy. Castro knew that even if tourism grew in line with the government's plans and hopes, it would be years before the initial invest-ments started to bring significant returns. The one development which could immediately transform Cuba's prospects would be a major oil discovery. Over several decades Cuba had been producing about a tenth of its consumption of crude oil. The road from Havana along the coast towards Varadero passed several groups of ancient nodding donkeys. But the oil that they pumped up was heavy and sulphurous, difficult to extract and expensive to refine. The field was nearing the end of its useful life. Soviet technicians had tried but failed to find new oil-fields. Castro hoped that Western technology would prove more effective. To attract Western oil companies he was willing to offer terms more favourable than those available in any other country in the world. He knew that no company with international connections would want to incur American displeasure. They would not invest in Cuba unless the potential profits were sufficient to offset the risk of American reprisals. In discussions with foreign oil executives, deliberately kept secret, he said there was a unique opportunity, created by Cuba's dire economic circumstances. Once the first major new discovery had been made, the terms of future exploration contracts would inevitably become less generous. Cuba offered exceptional security. There was no danger of a Communist revolution, he added cheerfully, since it had already happened. There would be no strikes and no expropriations.

A few foreign oil companies, such as Total of France and Petrobras of Brazil, seized the opportunity and signed exploration contracts. But the real prize would be to attract one of the Big Seven. The American companies were excluded by American law. Shell was very committed to the US market and was moreover deterred by the memory of the expropriation of its Cuban refinery and other assets after the Revolution. That left BP. Great efforts were made to excite BP's interest, and the company did indeed dip its toe in the water. Some teams of geologists came to assess the prospects. But BP's office in Washington blew the whistle, warning that BP's interests in the United States would be gravely damaged by any involvement in Cuba. Apart from possible US government action against BP, it was feared that Cuban exiles in Florida would sabotage BP's network of petrol stations. BP decided that discretion was the better part of valour, and withdrew.

By this period the United States had normal trade relations with almost every other country in the world, including Communist China and Vietnam. A small and isolated Cuba no longer constituted any conceivable threat to the security of the United States. But Castro was still a bone which stuck in American throats. He had defied and mocked the world's only superpower, and would not be forgiven. The CANF, with its strong links in Washington and formidable lobbying skills, was ready to jump on any politician who wanted to normalise relations with Cuba. Clinton performed a characteristic balancing act. He kept the Cuban lobby happy by endorsing new anti-Castro legislation; but avoided a serious row with his allies by postponing implementation of the most contentiously extraterritorial clauses. American companies were keen to ensure that their foreign competitors did not get into the Cuban market ahead of them. Some therefore took their own steps to warn off foreign rivals. When the Anglo-Dutch Unilever planned to sign a joint-venture contract to manufacture detergent in a green-field site in Cuba, the Chief Executive of Proctor and Gamble wrote to his counterpart in Unilever accusing him of helping to sustain Communist tyranny, and threatening a political campaign against Unilever in the United States. Castro was probably not far from the truth when he claimed that of every ten commercial joint ventures discussed with foreign companies, nine were abandoned as a result of American pressure.

Castro still aroused passion and hatred in the United States, and especially in Florida, but not much in the rest of the world. Canadians and Europeans generally saw no reason to treat Cuba more harshly than they had treated other Communist countries. In any case, trade and investment was surely a way to break down barriers and promote liberalisation. A resolution put forward by Cuba in the United Nations deploring the US trade embargo was overwhelmingly approved, with fifty-nine votes in favour and only three (including the United States) against. Most of the United States' friends and allies abstained, showing that on this issue they could not support American policy. Castro tried hard to build on these relatively benign attitudes, and to seek new foreign friends to offset the loss of his one-time Communist allies. He was willing to meet and glad-hand even quite low-level visiting business delegations. He attended functions at the Canadian and some West European embassies as frequently as he had once done at the Soviet Embassy.

Cuba's desperate need for capital attracted some unlikely characters looking for opportunities for profitable investment. Michael Ashcroft, not yet the Treasurer of the British Conservative Party but already very rich, became a regular visitor. His luxurious yacht dwarfed the other boats at the Marina Hemingway tourist complex outside Havana. His main interlocutor in the Cuban government was Jesús Montané, who as a young accountant with General Motors in the 1950s befriended the young lawyer Fidel Castro and became a founding member of the 26 July Movement. Since *Comandante* Montané spoke good English, Castro still often used him as a trusted intermediary in dealings with people from the English-speaking world. So the secretive capitalist Ashcroft met the secretive revolutionary Montané to discuss whether a deal might be done.

Castro showed a friendly face to almost any Western politician who visited Cuba, whatever their initial motivation for coming. He often seemed to get on better with politicians on the right, who had no need to prove their anti-Communist credentials, than with Social Democrats nervous of appearing too friendly with an old-fashioned Marxist. Manuel Fraga, a former Minister in Franco's government and now President of the conservative regional government of Galicia, had long-standing links with the large Galician community in Cuba. Fidel Castro, himself the son of a Galician immigrant, established a close and warm relationship with Fraga. He accompanied Fraga throughout a visit to Cuba, and was Fraga's guest for several days in the course of a visit to Spain. At Fraga's request, Castro gave back to the Galician Centre one of the most beautiful buildings in Old Havana, which had been expropriated after the Revolution. 'We are brothers and compatriots,' said Castro. Fraga brushed aside complaints from members of his own party that he was too friendly with a die-hard Communist. He had a duty to look after his spiritual constituents in Cuba, whatever their political complexion.

In 1994 Castro turned up late to an evening reception given by the Chinese Ambassador to mark the anniversary of the People's Republic. In jovial mood, he explained that he had spent the whole day fishing with his friend Fraga. He launched into a paean of praise for Fraga's wisdom and intelligence. He and Fraga saw eye to eye on virtually all the issues they had discussed. If Fraga represented the right wing in Europe, Castro thought he would support the right. Ignoring the sensitivities of his Chinese hosts, he proceeded to congratulate any diplomats he noticed who represented right-wing governments. No doubt he would have got on well with Mrs Thatcher, he declared. He was sorry that he had not had an opportunity to meet her. Perhaps in the modern world the concepts of left and right were no longer relevant.

Having to learn to survive in a capitalist world, Castro was genuinely interested in the views and experiences of Western politicians. Even the modest economic reforms that had been introduced meant that the Cuban government had to grapple with concepts which had long disappeared from the Cuban political landscape, such as personal taxation and variable exchange rates. Over lunch with a junior British Trade Minister, he spent hours talking about taxation. The Minister said that the Conservative government had transformed Britain's economic prospects, putting an end to the Socialists' mistaken policy of spending too much and taxing too much. At the end of the lunch, Castro turned to his newly appointed Finance Minister, and said without a glimmer of irony: 'Did you hear all that? We should follow the example of the British Conservative government. Don't make the rates of taxation too high. If you set the rates too high, it will encourage tax evasion and discourage hard work and initiative.'

When Castro went on to talk in the National Assembly about fiscal and monetary reform, he sounded like a doctor explaining to unhappy children that they would have to swallow some nasty medicine. 'Well, this country has got to get used to the idea of taxes.' He said the leadership did not like having to introduce taxation. They would have preferred to abolish money altogether during the Special Period, and simply distribute equitably whatever goods were available. But in a capitalist world, that would not be possible. Meanwhile, too many pesos were in circulation, destroying the value of peso salaries. The price of goods like cigarettes and alcohol must be raised. Individuals with a large income must be taxed.

We do not have a smidgen of capitalism or neo-liberalism. We are facing a world completely ruled by neo-liberalism and capitalism. This does not mean that we are going to surrender. It means that we have to adapt to the reality of that world. That is what we are doing, with great equanimity, without giving up our ideals, our goals. I ask you to have trust in what the government and party are doing. They are defending, to the last atom, socialist ideas, principles and goals . . . The world is in the hands of capitalism, and this will last for quite a long time. A revolution like ours, as firm and committed as ours, has to take these realities into account.

Even with foreign visitors from whom Castro wanted to learn something, he usually did a lot more talking than listening. He never tired of telling Western politicians, and indeed journalists and businessmen, about the merits of the Cuban system. In Cuba, he liked to point out, there were no drug addicts, no criminal gangs, and no race riots. Democracy? In Cuba there was a continuous process of democratic consultation with all the people. Did ordinary working people have a voice in Panama or Grenada, where the US Marines had imposed their idea of democracy by force of arms? Elections? Cuba had elections, and they were genuinely democratic. In most Western countries, candidates for election were chosen by political parties, not by the grassroots. In Cuba it was the ordinary people, meeting in their neighbourhoods, who proposed candidates. In the United States, you had to be very rich to have any chance of electoral success. The cost of one television commercial was enough to rule out most ordinary people. Was this democracy?

But in practice, visitors argued, it was Castro himself who decided who should be elected. He knew what they meant. Was he a dictator? By no means. He had less constitutional power than most other heads of state, and much less than the US President. The US President could declare war without consulting the Congress. Castro could not even appoint a Minister or an Ambassador without obtaining the prior approval of the Council of State, which was elected by the National Assembly. Of course he had moral authority, the informal power which came from the respect and prestige which he had acquired over the years. But that did not make him a dictator. The Constitution ensured that no leader in Cuba could impose decisions against the will of the people.

After thirty-five years in power, a large proportion of it taken up with talking, Castro was never stumped for an answer. But he still took trouble to prepare for meetings with visitors whom he wanted to influence, asking for briefings about their particular interests. When he met a business delegation led by Baroness Janet Young, he had been informed about her involvement in trade with the English-speaking Caribbean, and her efforts to lobby on behalf of Caribbean banana exporters. At the meeting he showed that he was very knowledgeable about the long-running transatlantic dispute over bananas. In the World Trade Organisation the United States and the Latin American countries had claimed that the European Union's banana regime, which protected Europe's traditional suppliers mainly in the Caribbean, was in breach of WTO free-trade rules. The Cuban Foreign Minister had supported the Latin American line. He took the view that on an issue which did not directly affect Cuba, it was sensible to show solidarity with the rest of Latin America. However, when Castro personally looked into the matter, in advance of his meeting with Baroness Young, he reversed Cuba's policy.

When Fidel was a child, his father's farm had been surrounded by one of the huge sugar-cane plantations owned and run by United Fruit. He knew a lot about the activities of the big American multinationals in their 'banana republics'. So he told Baroness Young and her delegation that the European banana regime was perfectly defensible. The Latin Americans who argued against it were being unreasonable and selfish. They already had the whole of the North American market and a large part of the European market. The Caribbean islands were relatively small producers, and it would be disgraceful to drive them out of business. They did not have the space or resources to develop alternative industries; and could not compete on an equal footing with companies in Latin America whose workers were underpaid and exploited. All this was music in the ears of Castro's visitors, who went away muttering that he was much better informed and more sensible than they had expected.

Castro's well-honed skills in presentation certainly helped to avert the popular explosion predicted by President Bush. But they could not avert the frustration and demoralisation caused by long electric power-cuts, by shortages of food and transport, and by seeing foreign tourists with dollars buying goods which most Cubans could not hope to acquire. Cubans might accept that 'dollar apartheid' was, as Castro often explained, an unpleasant but unavoidable means of economic survival. They might accept that American hostility, rather than government incompetence, was the main cause of the country's economic difficulties. But that did not make the hardships much easier to bear. Whenever a light seemed to appear at the end of the tunnel, something happened to extinguish it. Hopes of significantly increasing electric-power generation took a knock in October 1992 when the Russians pulled the plug on a half-completed nuclear power station. In March 1993 a hurricane, known thereafter as the 'Storm of the Century', caused extensive flooding and wrecked crops and buildings across the island. Later there was an epidemic of a rare disease causing loss of vision and eventual blindness. It was found to be probably caused by malnutrition and lack of vitamins. Some victims were women who had given part of their meagre rations to their children.

Surviving during the Special Period was a constant challenge. Scarcely anyone could avoid some sort of dealing on the black market. A highly qualified senior academic would typically try to get a job as a hotel waiter, in order to earn some dollars. For many people there was a reversal of fortune. Those who had relatives in Miami, sending dollars, became the most privileged. Servants of the Revolution, depending only on their modest peso salary, were now near the bottom of the pile. This gave the authorities a degree of protection from public resentment. Carlos Lage, the man in day-to-day control of the government, could often be seen riding his bicycle to work, without any protection and apparently without any governmental privileges. His mother stood in queues for hours, like any other Cuban, waiting to receive her rations.

Many young people, especially students, turned to prostitution. Aircraft from Mexico and Spain disgorged large numbers of middle-aged single men, eager to obtain the services of attractive teenagers in return for a few tins of meat from a dollar shop. Over the years Castro had made numerous speeches about the bad old days when Havana was full of beggars and prostitutes, exploited by American tourists. It was galling for him to see the return of prostitution on such a large scale. From time to time prostitutes were rounded up by the police and given a warning. Parents were urged to keep their children under control. But the authorities realised that prostitution was at least bringing in dollars, and that serious repression would carry a high political price. Castro tried to argue that the new prostitution was different from the old prostitution. In the Batista era poor girls were forced into prostitution by unscrupulous pimps and gangsters. That sort of exploitation would never be permitted. But 'vocational prostitution', where students or nurses chose to sell their bodies for some extra money, was in a different category. It was regrettable, but could not be considered as a serious crime.

Castro was keen to show his compatriots that he disliked as much as anyone the negative side-effects of tourism, such as prostitution and begging. He used an argument which the Jesuit teachers in his school had used to explain why God allowed evil to exist:

> Virtue proves itself when it is exposed to the contamination of vice . . . I once used a metaphor but later had to recant, because it was wrong. I said that virtue could not be preserved in a cloister, in a convent. Several nuns immediately wrote to me and told me the remark was unfair. I agreed with them and no longer talk of cloisters or of convents. I speak of ivory towers . . .

The friendly reference to nuns was another sign of the times. In a period of hardship and anxiety, it was natural that more people should turn to religion. After decades of decline, attendance at Catholic churches started to grow. Increasing numbers of blacks and people of mixed race, and even some whites, took part in the rituals of Afro-Cuban religions, hoping that the spirits of *santería* would solve their problems. The secret police tried to co-opt *santería* priests, offering money and other favours if they would encourage pro-Castro sentiments among their followers. This did not prevent the priests, in their annual predictions of the future, from warning of calamity, trouble and strife. They had to maintain their credibility.

Castro took the view that the revival of religion was fairly innocuous and could be tolerated. In earlier years he had actively persecuted the Catholic Church. He regarded all religion as a product of ignorance and backwardness. But he recognised that the stresses and strains of the Special Period had inevitably made religion more attractive. He wanted to show understanding and sympathy: hence his favourable public references to people with a religious vocation. He even had a half-compliment for Pope John Paul II: 'A brave man, but a fundamentalist.' Raúl, a signed-up Communist since his student days, seemed to have become even more well-disposed to the Catholic Church. He said in a speech that nuns in hospitals generally worked harder and showed greater dedication than state employees. He then added that before going to bed he always had a few minutes of silent reflection, in which he reviewed whether he had behaved correctly or not during the day, and whether he had done his duty. This, he explained, was a custom which he had been taught at his Jesuit school. Some people began to wonder if perhaps the Castro brothers had been captured for the Church after all. But in reality it was only politics. When a Frenchman asked Castro what would happen when he died, Fidel took the question as relating to himself.

> I'll go to hell. The heat will be unbearable. But the pain won't be as bad as expecting too much from heaven, which always breaks its promises. When I arrive in hell, I'll meet Marx, Engels and Lenin. And you too, by the way, because capitalists also go to hell, especially when they enjoy life too much.

Castro hoped and believed that if the economy recovered, people would have less need of spiritual consolation. Meantime there were some aimless young men who had no interest in either religion or politics. They were bored and frustrated. They could be seen in particular hanging about in the crowded centre of old Havana. Their numbers had been increased by the thousands of disbanded soldiers returning from Angola. Some were unemployed or under-employed. Some listened to radio broadcasts from Miami and dreamed of enjoying the good life of the United States. Most had little chance of getting a visa from the US Interests Section. Trying to leave Cuba without a visa was still illegal, and could be punished with prison. But the young malcontents knew that if they could only get across the Florida straits, they would be accepted into the United States and helped by the prosperous Cuban exile community. A few tried the long-established tactic of setting off during the night in a small boat or a homemade raft. But this was risky. If they evaded the Cuban police, they still faced the dangers of shipwreck and sharks.

A few individuals tried to leave by stealing or hijacking a motorboat. A notorious incident occurred in 1992 when a group seized a boat during the night in the Tamara naval base. In the process they overpowered and tied up four guards at the base. But they could not start the engine, and had to abandon the attempt. To cover their tracks they shot the four bound guards in cold blood. But one twenty-three-year-old guard, Rolando Pérez, survived for thirty-seven days in hospital before dying of his wounds. Castro visited Pérez several times in hospital. At the funeral he made one of his most impassioned and bitter speeches. He denounced the hypocritical and inconsistent policy of the United States towards migrants, which encouraged Cubans to try to emigrate by illegal and dangerous means. They built a wall 'higher than the Berlin wall' to keep out Mexicans, and most other migrants. Haitians were sent back to the poverty and misery from which they were fleeing. But illegal Cuban migrants were welcomed as heroes, even if they had committed the most brutal and inhuman crimes.

Castro said that the hospital treating Pérez had needed to administer a medicine manufactured by a US company, but even the company's subsidiary in Europe had refused to supply it to Cuba. They were forced to obtain the medicine through a third party. In the end all efforts to save Rolando's life were in vain. The 'Christian West,' said Castro, rushed to defend the human rights of hardened criminals in Cuba, but sent no message of sympathy or support to Pérez and his family, or to the victims of armed attacks by bandits from Miami.

> When we bury a person we love, we tell a history of his life. Rolando's history is the history of our people. It is the history of our revolution. He was a noble, good, patriotic, revolutionary, self-sacrificing, hard-working, disciplined boy. He might have been any of our students. He might have been any of our young people. It is said that Christ was lying on the cross for six hours. Rolando was about a hundred and fifty times six hours on the cross put up by those merchants of crime and death.

In 1993 and 1994 there were a few more spectacular attempts to escape in stolen or hijacked boats, some successful. One group hijacked a motorboat and successfully reached the United States after killing a policeman and throwing his body overboard. Then on 13 July 1994 a tugboat in Havana harbour was seized during the night and crammed with sixty-three people wanting to leave. It steered through the harbour entrance and out towards the open sea. Three other harbour tugboats gave chase, and shouted to the escaping boat to stop. When it kept going, one of the tugs tried to block its path and another tried to get alongside. In the darkness and rough seas there was a collision. The tugboat, already heavily overloaded, sank. Harbour police reached the scene, and managed to rescue thirty-one people from the sea; but thirty-two others, including many women and children, had drowned.

News of the deaths caused consternation throughout Havana, and even more so in Florida. Much of the American media treated the incident as a major atrocity. President Clinton said it showed 'the brutal nature of the Cuban regime'. It was alleged in some radio broadcasts that Fidel Castro had personally ordered that the tugboat be sunk and the passengers killed, as a deterrent to others wanting to escape. This version of events was ridiculed in Cuba, but some people believed it.

The sinking of the tugboat was a disaster for Castro. He pointed out that the Cuban authorities had no direct involvement with the incident. The tugmen in the harbour had acted on their own, without alerting the police and border guards. Their action might have been unwise and reckless, but the deaths were obviously unintentional and a tragic accident. All this might be true, but it made little impression. Several ordinary families had been killed trying to flee Cuba. However it was explained, it looked bad.

Recognising the harm done by this incident, Castro had new orders issued to police and border guards. They were instructed to take additional measures to guard ferries and other boats, but in no circumstances to take any action which could endanger life. If a boat was stolen or hijacked, the guards should *not* try to stop it, but merely follow at a distance until it left Cuban waters. Over the next few weeks three more boats were hijacked. As instructed, the border guards merely followed at a distance, and did not intervene. Two people on the first boat who did not want to go to Florida were thrown overboard. In the third incident, a naval officer who tried to stop the hijacking was killed.

On 5 August a group of youths tried unsuccessfully to take over a ferry in Regla, on the eastern side of Havana harbour. In the aftermath there was some stone-throwing and broken windows. The following morning rumours spread that there were plans to hijack a ferry in Old Havana. A crowd of some 200 people gathered at the quayside, hoping for a free ride to Miami. Police arrived and told the crowd to disperse. They refused. There were angry shouts, then some stones were thrown. It was the beginning of the most serious riot in the history of the Cuban Revolution. Groups of young men ran through the streets of Old Havana, throwing stones at the few police on duty, shouting anti-Castro slogans, and trying to break into government warehouses.

Since the early days of the Revolution, Castro had supervised the preparation of contingency plans for dealing with street disturbances. Now was the first time in more than thirty years that the plans would be tested. Cubans were used to seeing, on their television screens, massed ranks of armed police charging and beating demonstrators. But these scenes were from the era of Batista, or from countries ruled by repressive right-wing governments. Castro liked to maintain the idea that under the Revolution, the police would never attack 'the people'. If a disturbance had to be suppressed, it was 'the people' themselves who would suppress it. In line with this, there were 'rapid reaction brigades', a sort of part-time militia or police reserves, whose job was to keep order in an emergency.

In Havana the rapid reaction brigades were mostly comprised of workers at hotel construction sites. Now about fifty of these workers, armed with sticks and iron bars, marched into the central area of Old Havana. The demonstrators did not try to confront them. They just ran off in different directions. Behind the workers a bigger crowd marched down the main Prado road, shouting 'Fidel! Fidel!' And sure enough, in the middle of the crowd was the unmistakable figure of Fidel Castro, with Lage and other leaders striding beside him. He had performed a remarkable piece of theatre, turning the country's first anti-Castro demonstration into a much bigger pro-Castro demonstration.

The riots fizzled out slowly. When the broad Prado had been occupied by pro-Castro demonstrators, the rioters tried to reassemble in smaller side streets, running away when confronted by police or groups of workers. Cameramen from Cuban state television were on the scene almost from the start of the riot and shot about three hours of film. Only a few edited extracts were shown on the television news, but the full material confirmed the impression of eye-witnesses that no more than two or three hundred young men were involved, mostly operating in small groups in different places. So far as is known, no one was killed or injured. A Canadian who by chance was present from the start said that the affair was 'chicken-feed compared to a routine hockey riot in Canada'. The uniformed police played a minor role, and were very restrained, trying to talk the rioters into desisting. At one point a police van stopped near a group of stone-throwers; the police jumped out and managed to seize one of the rioters. As they walked him to the van, he asked if he could take his bicycle, since if it were left in the street it might be stolen. Two policemen duly accompanied him to pick up the bicycle and helped him to load it in the back of the van, before the van drove off.

During that day Castro gave a series of impromptu interviews, first in the street, later in a television studio. He started by playing down the significance of the riots. Those involved, he said, were lumpen and antisocial elements, and a few people misled by American propaganda beamed at Cuba from Florida, especially the disgusting lies spread about the sinking of the tugboat. 'I was in my office when I was told that some people were throwing stones at the police. It was my duty to come in person at once, to see what was happening, and above all to promote calm and composure.' Castro said the whole affair was a result of American planning. The Americans were trying to destroy the Cuban economy, tightening the blockade, and using every means to stop foreign companies from coming to Cuba. They refused to grant visas to Cubans to migrate legally and safely, but encouraged them to leave illegally. Radio and television stations in Florida had stepped up their barrage of lies, slander and incitement. 'This is no longer just an instrument of propaganda. It's a plan to create unrest and confrontation in our country . . . The strategy is to build up dissatisfaction, to divide people and to create a conflict, a bloodbath . . .'

Some of Castro's supporters complained that the police had been ineffective. They suggested that if the police had appeared more quickly and acted more vigorously, the riot would have ended much sooner. Castro defended the police strongly:

> The officers behaved well. They did not use violence. They were cool, calm and persuasive. Our enemies want to provoke violence and make us lose our head. I am proud of the way our people behaved . . . We have to exercise great self-control. In that sort of situation it is better that our own side should be the ones suffering casualties. We cannot abuse our power when we are fighting unarmed individuals. I am convinced of this political principle. I realise that some people are more radical and want what they call an iron fist. If we let ourselves be carried away, we are giving the enemy a tool to use against us, to try to isolate us in front of world opinion by presenting us as repressive, murderers and all that . . . A police battalion could easily have handled the incident. Can you imagine how advantageous it would have been for them if a police battalion had dispersed the riots by firing a few shots and killing ten or twelve people? When it is the people themselves who respond, that is different. I have always believed in the importance of letting the masses deal with such challenges. Weapons should be reserved for invaders or mercenaries . . .'

While still talking extempore in the street, Castro said that boat seizures were a direct consequence of US policies. The Americans refused visas to Cubans wanting to migrate legally, but accepted all Cubans who migrated illegally. Unless the United States agreed to co-operate in introducing more orderly and sensible arrangements, Cuba would not continue to police the Americans' borders for them. He promised to explain the situation more fully in the evening.

News of these remarks quickly reached the US Interests Section, and alarm bells rang. The head of the Section, on instructions from Washington, sent an urgent message to the Cuban Foreign Ministry. The United States would not accept another 'Mariel exodus'. If Castro confirmed the comments which he had been reported as making during the afternoon, there would be serious consequences.

This intervention did not deflect Castro. A Yankee 'threat' only provided additional mood music. In the evening he gave a long account of the history of migration from Cuba to the United States, listing the number of visas issued by the United States in each year (small), the number of Cubans prevented by the Cuban authorities from travelling illegally (large), and the number who had arrived in the United States illegally and been accepted (quite large). If the Americans simply issued visas for those they were prepared to accept, and sent back those who arrived without a visa, the problem of illegal migration would disappear, to everyone's satisfaction. Unless they took some such measures to discourage illegal migration, the Cubans would stop the thankless task of trying to prevent people from leaving illegally.

Cuban migrants did indeed present the Americans with a dilemma. They did not want another flood. But it would be politically unacceptable to send Cubans back to Castro's Communist dungeon. Perhaps the problem would solve itself. The 6 August riot was seen by many people outside Cuba as a momentous event. It might look small compared with riots in Los Angeles or London, but once the monolithic Communist edifice was cracked, it could collapse very quickly, as events in Eastern Europe had shown. After thirty-five years, the myth of Castro's absolute control was broken. Or was it? Castro thought he knew better. The morning after the riot, having set his trap for the Americans, he set off for Cartagena in Colombia, to attend an Ibero-American summit conference. He looked relaxed and cheerful, even mischievous.

In the cafeteria of the Conference Centre in Cartagena, Castro stood up from his table in the section reserved for heads of government. He had spotted Gabriel García Márquez, and walked across to join his table. Then the Colombian Foreign Minister, Noemí Sanin, walked past. She was another of the women whom Castro fancied. 'Noemí,' said Castro, 'I've come to seek asylum over here.' 'Very well,' said Sanin, 'We welcome you.' 'Come on, Noemí,' said Castro, 'What kind of asylum do you think I meant? I sought asylum at this table, but I intend to return to Cuba. I want to find a small plot of land there where I can rest.'

19 Second Wind

It was unthinkable that a President of the United States should allow himself to be pushed around by Fidel Castro, of all people. There was no question of changing policy on immigration from Cuba, which in any case was established in law. So the answer to Castro's demand for a new approach was a brusque rejection. Accordingly, the decision foreshadowed by Castro in his 6 August interviews was implemented. Border guards were instructed not to prevent people from leaving Cuba, provided the vessels in which they travelled were their own property

So another exodus began. The angry young men stopped trying to steal or hijack government boats, and set about building their own. Tourists and diplomats could go to the beaches near Havana to watch the little boats and rafts being built and then paddled slowly out towards Florida, while tearful friends and relatives waved goodbye from the shore.

On 11 August 1994 the US State Department reiterated that policy would not change. Cuban boat people picked up in the Florida strait would continue to be accepted into the United States. But as they kept coming, and as the pressures to stop the flood grew, President Clinton was forced to announce a new policy. Cuban boat people picked up in the Florida strait would *not* be allowed into the United States. Instead, they would be taken to the US naval base at Guantánamo, in the east of Cuba, and kept there in temporary accommodation. They would be encouraged (but not forced), to return to Cuba and to apply for a visa at the US Interests Section in Havana.

To punish Castro for provoking this crisis, the President announced a package of further measures: Cubans in the United States would no longer be allowed to send money to relatives in Cuba; most flights between Cuba and Miami would be stopped; and broadcasts beamed at Cuba from Florida would be increased. These three measures had long been advocated by the CANF, and were agreed at a meeting which Clinton held with the CANF in the White House. In return the CANF accepted, albeit reluctantly, the abrogation of the long-established principle that the United States would automatically grant the right of residence to any person fleeing from Communist Cuba. Clinton had taken the money and the votes of the right-wing Cuban exiles. He had to take account of their views.

The new measures were announced on 19 August, Clinton's birthday. Castro offered some advice: 'I always try to avoid taking hasty and ill-considered measures on my birthday. He should have waited, and seen how events developed.' To raise some more laughs, Castro read out on Cuban television the full text of Clinton's statement (naturally directed to American opinion), together with a running commentary. '"The United States has done more than any other country to try to end Castro's government . . ." They call it Castro's government. It's Castro this and Castro that. They ignore the fact that there is a Revolution . . .'

The Guantánamo base provided only a temporary solution, and one which gave Castro some political benefits. It highlighted the continuing existence of an anachronistic American enclave on Cuban soil, with all the humiliation which that involved for Cuban national pride. Only a few emigrants chose to return to Cuban territory. Most preferred to sit it out. As frustration and boredom increased, and with it the risk of serious disturbances, the US authorities were obliged to move groups of migrants to longer-term transit camps in Panama.

Castro could sit back and wait. Many people had predicted that the 6 August riot would be quickly followed by more serious riots, and then by Castro's collapse. Instead the safety valve worked again. With thousands of the most disgruntled Cubans in Guantánamo and Panama, peace returned to Havana. The riot proved to be a one-off. Eventually the US government had to reverse course again, and accept all the migrants into the United States. A new bilateral migration agreement was quietly negotiated, under which the United States agreed to issue more visas, and Cuba agreed to restore controls on illegal departures. Clinton also phased out the measures which he had introduced on 19 August. The ban on flights and money transfers had proved unpopular and easy to evade. Perhaps, as Castro advised, Clinton should have been less hasty.

Castro often expressed outrage that the 'gangsters' of the CANF should be received as honoured guests in the White House, and should be giving advice to the President on policy towards Cuba. But he understood the pressures to which Clinton was subjected. Despite his public mockery of Clinton's erratic course, his overall view of the man was more balanced. One comment in this period was revealing both of Castro's prejudices and of his perceptiveness:

'I don't have a bad personal opinion of Clinton. It was the poorest people in the United States who elected him. I believe he is a man with good intentions. He wanted to help the unemployed, youth, older people, blacks and Hispanics. He wanted to improve health and education programmes. I would say his programme is good for the United States . . . But he has not been sufficiently firm in his positions. He has let the mafia-like groups influence him a great deal. This has enabled the far right to exert pressure on him. There was unrest fomented by the right and Clinton came out weakened . . .'

Towards the end of 1994 Castro was feeling confident that the worst was over, and that he had survived the crisis caused by the collapse of the Soviet Union. The economy, after two years of headlong decline, had bottomed out and was at last even showing some small signs of recovery. He described Cuba as a boxer who had been surprised by a flurry of heavy punches. It was still groggy, but its head was beginning to clear. In another variation on this metaphor, he said: 'It's like being hit on the head with a pole. One's vision is out of focus momentarily, until one regains control. We are already recovering from the trauma . . .'

To defeat the American 'blockade', Castro had to persuade the rest of the world, especially Europe and Latin America, that Cuba was indeed still in business; that his government was in firm control; and that Cuba was a reliable partner for trade and investment. Few foreign governments wanted to invite Castro to pay a bilateral visit. An impoverished and isolated Cuba had little to offer, and any government inviting Castro would incur disproportionate displeasure in Washington. But no country except the United States felt that Cuba should be excluded from multilateral gatherings. To make an impact overseas, Castro had to make the most of whatever opportunities arose to attend high-level international conferences or ceremonies. Hence his decision to attend the Ibero-American Conference in Cartagena, even though this meant leaving Cuba the day immediately following the 6 August riot.

Castro's charismatic presence usually enabled him to steal the show, even in the most exalted international company. In Cartagena he caused an even greater sensation than usual by appearing at the conference dressed in a *guayabera,* the typical Caribbean long-sleeved shirt, instead of his usual olive-green uniform. For thirty-seven years he had never ever worn civilian clothes. He wore pyjamas in bed, and shorts when swimming, but on all other occasions he had always stuck to an olive-green military uniform, either a plain cotton uniform buttoned up to the chin, or occasionally a more formal uniform with shirt and tie. He still carried the insignia of the rank of major (*Comandante*), with which he had set sail from Mexico on the *Granma* in 1956. On the *Granma* he was the only major, commanding two captains and several lieutenants. He liked to say that he was the only officer who had never been promoted. He was Commander in Chief, but still with the rank of major.

Why at this late stage in his life had he suddenly decided to appear as a civilian? Was he at last making a political concession? Was he recognising that the time had come to stop being a revolutionary guerrilla and become a civilian politician? Castro insisted that he wore a *guayabera* purely out of courtesy. The invitation to the conference in Cartagena specified that the dress to be worn was a suit or *guayabera*. He had neither, but a *guayabera* was easier to have made. Back in Cuba, he insisted, he would again wear his uniform. It was comfortable, practical and economical. He had no reason to change it.

All this was true, but not the whole truth. For all his protestations to the contrary, Castro was indeed sending a signal. The world had changed, and he was adapting to it. He would continue to wear his uniform in Cuba; but the invitation to Cartagena gave him a pretext to start wearing civilian clothes on trips abroad, when this helped to make the right impression. A few months later he appeared in Paris in a civilian dark suit. This time his explanation was different. 'It's because I'm a bit jealous of all you people. I didn't have a suit, and I was told that I absolutely had to be well dressed to come to Paris.' However, at a meeting of 'solidarity organisations' (i.e. supporters of Cuba) in Copenhagen, he made a point of wearing the olive-green uniform. The members of the solidarity organisations wanted to see their hero looking like a guerrilla leader, not like just another politician in a suit.

In a similar way, Castro became more willing than in the past to adjust his language to suit his audience. Sometimes, especially at home in Cuba, he continued to use the old radical Marxist rhetoric. On other occasions, especially with Western audiences, he defined the Cuban Revolution as meaning a mixed economy, social justice, and free education, health and social security for all, a programme to which even the most timid Social Democrat could subscribe. When he went to South Africa to attend the inauguration of President Mandela, he addressed a group of businessmen, one of whom asked if the future system in Cuba would be Communism. Castro said: 'We see it as Socialism. We want to maintain it, but we have left an economic opening . . . We need investment. There is a process of change under way in our country, to keep us in touch with the present realities of the world. But we have not given up our principles . . .'

Castro visited Colombia twice in 1994, the second time for the inauguration of President Samper. Colombia was the most violent country in Latin America, with large areas virtually outside government control. Some of the Colombian guerrilla organisations had in earlier years received support, weapons and training from Cuba. For many right-wing Colombians, including armed and ruthless paramilitaries, Castro was the devil incarnate, the man whom they blamed for the virtual state of civil war in the country. The Colombian officials responsible for Castro's security were therefore understandably nervous. Castro's own security officials also advised against taking part with other heads of government in a cavalcade through the narrow streets of the old colonial city of Cartagena.

Castro related the story to some Colombian friends. 'The security men were especially worried about the carriage ride. It was forty minutes among buildings, and with a horse that walked slowly. They thought I should not participate. They almost had me convinced. I was looking at the pictures in the Naval Museum, and I felt uneasy. I finally told the comrades that I was going on the carriage ride. I told them it was difficult for me to play the role of coward. I didn't want anyone to say that I came here to Barranquilla and didn't take the carriage ride . . .' 'Cartagena!' interjected an onlooker. Castro had made a Reagan-like mistake, confusing one Colombian port for another. But he recovered quickly. 'Cartagena! That's right, I came to Cartagena representing Barranquilla and all of Colombia . . .' (That got a round of applause.) 'Then I thought: whom will I invite? It occurred to me that I'd invite Gabo (García Márquez). I said to him: "Gabo, I invite you to come with me. I'm a bad friend. Climb aboard." I told Mercedes García Márquez: "Don't worry. If you're going to be widowed, it's best if it happens when you're still young . . ." Actually, our horse had a bad temper. We almost had an accident. It crashed into the carriage ahead of us . . .'

In a later private conversation, Castro said that the security men had also tried to persuade him not to go to the Lost City, a ruined Indian city high up in the mountains of the Sierra de Santa Marta. The only way to get there was by helicopter. The Colombians were worried that the helicopter might have to land in dangerous territory, or be fired on by guerrillas or paramilitaries. Castro thought that the risk was slight. He knew that he would travel in a modern American helicopter, with another helicopter as escort. 'I told them that their worries were excessive. I had confidence in the goodwill of the Colombian people, and in American technology.'

In Bogotá Castro revisited some of the places where he had been during the *Bogotazo* of 1948. He made no attempt to play down his role then in trying to foment an uprising. He described to Colombian journalists how he had taken a rifle and attached himself to a police unit which had joined the rebellion. He related his adventures in a jocular, self-deprecating manner. It had all happened nearly fifty years ago, and the world was now a very different place. But he did not present his role in 1948 as a youthful folly. On the contrary, he took pride in it. He had never felt more sure that his actions had been altruistic and honourable. He had been entirely alone, cut off from his friends and his country, his life in danger. He had been tempted to abandon the enterprise, as his friends had earlier advised. But in the end he had done his duty, and kept faith with his new Colombian comrades-in-arms whose leader, Gaitan, had been brutally murdered.

The past was easy to explain and justify. But what of the present? Many Colombians wanted Castro to use his influence to bring about an end to the country's crippling internal violence. The Colombian Marxist guerrillas held him in great esteem. Why did he not urge them publicly to lay down their weapons and negotiate a settlement? This presented Castro with a dilemma. It was many years since Cuba had been involved in active support for Colombian guerrillas. He could truthfully say that Cuba was not now co-operating with armed irregular groups anywhere in the world. 'In the past we believed that conditions existed for an armed struggle. In general, we do not believe that circumstances exist today for that type of struggle.' But Castro did not want to appear hypocritical and disloyal to his old friends and allies. 'When we are asked to intervene, we have to be careful. The armed groups do not appreciate paternalism, or people advising them, or meddling in their affairs.'

The same problem confronted Castro in 1995 over the Zapatista rebellion in Mexico. He came under pressure to urge the guerrillas to abandon violence. He said he had been as surprised as anyone by the uprising. Cuba had never had any involvement with any armed group in Mexico. 'I support political solutions to armed conflicts . . . We should not solve these problems through force, but through negotiations.' It was not quite an explicit repudiation of the Zapatistas' armed actions, but it went further than he had gone in Colombia.

During 1995 Castro made steady progress in creating a new image for himself as a moderate and reasonable leader, still irredeemably Communist, but willing to play a responsible role in international affairs. Cuba gained increasing sympathy as the victim of unreasonable, disproportionate and vindictive American hostility. In the United Nations 101 countries supported a resolution criticising the embargo, with only two opposed. At the 1995 Ibero-American summit in Bariloche, Argentina, Castro was on his most moderate behaviour, focussing on issues like United Nations reform, where his views enjoyed wide international support. He attended the UN General Assembly in New York, making a deliberate contrast with his last appearance three decades earlier, when he had harangued the Assembly for more than four hours. This time he spoke for only six minutes, on UN reform, disarmament and the environment.

Castro did not stop talking about Cuba's quarrel with the United States, but the tone was somewhat less combative, the emphasis on Cuba as the injured party. In a speech to a rally in Uruguay, he said that the blockade had been originally imposed not because Cuba took Communist or even Socialist measures, but in response to an agrarian reform which affected American land-holdings in Cuba. The United States was not blockading any other country, not China, not Vietnam. It had not blockaded the South Africa of apartheid. It had not blockaded South American countries when thousands of people there were being tortured and killed by brutally repressive military govern-ments. It only blockaded Cuba, the country with one of the lowest infant mortality rates in the world, where no child went without shelter or without a school or without medical care, where there were no death squads, no race discrimination, no criminal gangs, where no one was tortured or disappeared.

At a meeting with businessmen in Port of Spain, where Castro was attending a conference of the recently established Association of Caribbean States, he seemed to be making unprecedented concessions to the capitalist ethic, even if it was half in jest:

> There can be state enterprises that are not good businesses. The adversaries of our ideology will be pleased to hear this. The state makes good and bad businesses. In general businessmen, if they are genuine businessmen, run good businesses. At least their accounting is better. They take into account their costs, markets and investments. You are more guided by rationality. Our efforts are more often guided by, I would say, our feelings and our hearts. Very often we are dreamers. Very often we want impossible things. Generally, businessmen want to do possible things. When businessmen lose money, it is very painful for them. When politicians lose money, they don't care, and it doesn't hurt them. Of course this is a caricature . . .'

At home in Cuba Castro was not so polite about capitalist businessmen. But even with a domestic audience he argued that Cuba could learn something from them.

> The power of governments is declining, and that of multinationals is increasing. We are surrounded by capitalists on all sides . . . We cannot ignore capitalism, any more than we can ignore the sea around us. Besides – and this was pointed out by Marx – capitalism has made significant contributions to mankind's economic development, such as technological and scientific advances, such as new productive methods. There are things which were unknown in Marx's time, like management techniques and the use of computers in administration . . . It would be stupid not to make use of any useful experience which capitalism can contribute.

The Cubans, Castro was saying, were flexible and undogmatic. They wanted to keep their socialist system, but also understood the views and needs of

Western businessmen. What harm was this little island doing to the United States? Why did the American authorities go to such extreme lengths to prevent Western businessmen from investing in Cuba?

> If a dog goes into a park to relieve itself, US satellites are observing it, photographing it and reporting it. Satellites are all over the world spying on everything. Of course, that makes them the owners of communications. If we were to talk on the telephone with any country and say things that shouldn't be said on the telephone, we should be big fools. There is no government conversation in this country that they do not intercept. There are no conversations with political personalities or companies that they do not intercept. They intercept everything because the blockade is much more than the banning of buying or selling. The blockade is a tireless hounding of every commercial activity that the country might try to conduct . . .

Even in the United States, the trend of public opinion was running in favour of at least some relaxation of the embargo. The CANF had come to be seen as extreme and unreasonable. The Clinton administration did not have much enthusiasm for aggressive action against a country which no longer represented any threat to US security. It seemed that Cuba might even be preparing some small bilateral gestures of goodwill. The fugitive financier Robert Vesco, who had fled to Cuba to escape the threat of extradition from Costa Rica, was arrested in Havana and charged with breaking Cuban law. Was this a preamble to sending Vesco to face trial in the United States?

But on 24 February 1996, just when things seemed to be going Castro's way, he threw all the advantage away. Two light aircraft belonging to a Cuban exile organisation, *Hermanos al Rescate* (Brothers to the Rescue), were shot down by Cuban MiG fighters, and the pilots killed. The Cuban authorities said the aircraft had been violating Cuban airspace, and had ignored repeated warnings not to do so. The US authorities said the aircraft were shot down in international airspace. Whatever the exact position of the aircraft, scarcely anyone outside Cuba thought that it was remotely acceptable to shoot two civilian aircraft out of the sky. There was an outcry in the United States. In the new atmosphere, the Clinton administration felt it must change track and support the Helms–Burton Bill, extending the embargo by penalising companies in third countries which traded with Cuba.

How did it happen? No doubt, *Hermanos al Rescate* had indeed been engaging in increasingly provocative incursions, even dropping leaflets over Havana. Castro said the incident could easily have been avoided if Cuban warnings had been heeded. No country, he said, could tolerate the repeated violation of its sovereignty. *Hermanos al Rescate* worked closely with the

CANF, who had been responsible for organising assassination attempts and biological attacks. Light aircraft were perfectly capable of launching biological attacks. 'We are not to blame. We did not want anything like that to happen. We did not want to help the cause of the worst group of people.'

This last remark was an implicit recognition that the shooting down of the aircraft, whether or not a crime, was certainly a blunder. It helped Castro's bitterest enemies. Many months after the incident, Castro gave a fuller but still unsatisfactory explanation. He said the Cubans had to set up arrangements to stop further overflights of Havana. The decision to act could not be left until a violation actually took place, since it could happen in a few moments. According to Castro, when the US authorities conveyed an assurance that they would stop further overflights, the Cubans thought the problem had been resolved. But they forgot to stand down the aircraft which had been given orders to act.

The *Hermanos al Rescate* incident and its aftermath did not stop all new negotiations with foreign companies. Trade and tourism were only slightly affected. But it did put a significant brake on the gradual process of turning Cuba into a 'normal' market for European and other companies. Castro could justifiably joke that Helms and Burton wanted to preserve the purity of socialism in Cuba, by preventing capitalism from gaining a foothold. The affair also gave a new stimulus to the more extreme exile groups in Miami. There was a spate of bombings directed against the tourist industry in Cuba. And after a period of several relatively quiet years, Cuba's intelligence and security services began to pick up information about new plans by exile organisations to assassinate Castro during his visits abroad.

Throughout the 1990s there had been sporadic negotiations between the Cuban government and the Vatican over a possible visit to Cuba by the Pope. The Pope wanted to pay a visit. Cuba was one of the few countries with a significant Catholic population which he had never visited. The Cuban Church needed encouragement and inspiration. Castro was cautious, and in no hurry. He had seen the role played by the Catholic Church in undermining Communism in Eastern Europe. But he judged that if a visit took place on his terms, it would bring more benefits than problems. The negotiations were slow and complex, with long periods in which no progress was made. The Pope was unwilling to visit unless the Church had regained at least some of its pre-Revolutionary freedom of action. Nor would he come if his programme were to be tightly controlled by the Cuban government.

The Catholic Church was the only significant organisation in Cuba which had remained free of government control throughout the period of Castro's rule. In the first years of the Revolution it had openly opposed Castro's socialising measures. As a result, foreign priests had been expelled, Cuban priests harassed and sometimes imprisoned, seminaries closed down and Church publications prohibited. Later, the Church hierarchy accepted an unwritten compromise: they would be allowed to carry out their religious activities, provided they kept out of politics and refrained from criticising the government. Despite all this, and despite attempts by State Security to infiltrate agents into the Church's organisation, it never lost its nucleus of authenticity and independence. During the 1990s, while negotiations over a possible Papal Visit were proceeding, some of the constraints on the Church were gradually lifted. The intimidating presence of security men in churches was reduced. Some leading Churchmen became increasingly bold in demanding respect for fundamental rights and freedoms.

In 1994 some workmen from Rome carrying out repairs in the Papal Nunciature in Havana discovered a microphone in one of the chairs in the main reception room. This prompted further searches, during which numerous other microphones were found throughout the building. The Nuncio was outraged. His most confidential discussions with Cuban priests, not to mention other diplomats and ordinary Cuban visitors, had evidently been taped by the Cuban authorities.

It was an unusual misjudgement by the Cuban State Security. It was of course well known that the Cuban government, like other Communist governments, carried out extensive surveillance of their citizens and of foreign embassies. But the Cuban State Security was usually careful not to be caught. Fixed microphones were not usually planted in the embassies of countries with the technical capability to locate and remove them. Short-term plants or directional microphones were used instead. In this case the Interior Ministry had possibly made the mistake of assuming that the Holy See would be too engrossed in spiritual matters to organise a search for microphones. Castro was at this time trying hard to improve relations with the Vatican, and to pave the way for a Papal visit. His Foreign Minister, now Roberto Robaina, spent a weekend with the Nuncio, trying to undo the damage. He claimed that the microphones belonged to an earlier era, and were not active.

Castro had not completely changed his view of the Catholic Church. He still saw it as a reactionary relic of the bad old days. But it had emerged as a potential ally in a broader conflict. At least, under Pope John Paul, it had not sold out to the moral pollution of the consumer society. At the Social Development Conference in Copenhagen in 1995, Castro said: 'It must be stressed in today's world, a world which prefers to eat money, wear money and bathe in money, that there is something more valuable than money: people's souls, people's hearts, people's honour.' The Pope could have agreed with that.

In January 1998 the long-awaited Papal visit finally took place. It was an undoubted success, both for the Church and for Castro. The Church's position in Cuba was revived and strengthened. The Pope spoke his mind, sometimes speaking about the need for individual freedom and respect for human rights. But Castro could act as if the cap fitted someone else. He was the friendly and hospitable host, usually at the Pope's side. When the audience applauded, there was usually no way to tell if they were applauding the Pope or Castro. And the Pope said a lot of things which pleased Castro and reinforced his own message. He condemned embargoes which harmed innocent people. He and Castro talked in similar terms about social justice and the corrupting effects of Western consumerism. Many Cubans, being on the whole a hedonistic people, never liked the attacks on consumerism, but this time the message was coming more from the Pope than from Castro. The big losers from the visit were the right-wing exile organisations in Florida, who were left looking intransigent and marginalised.

The following year, Castro fought another arduous battle in the psychological war against his exiled opponents. It started when a raft carrying migrants to Florida capsized. A mother died, but her eight-year-old son, Elián González, was rescued. Elián's father in Cuba wanted the child to be returned to him. The mother's relatives in Florida insisted that the boy stay with them in Miami. Castro saw that the exiles, by denying a parent's most fundamental right, were putting themselves in the wrong even with sectors of American opinion which had no sympathy at all with Cuba's political system. Castro pulled out all the stops in a campaign for Elián's return. There were speeches, demonstrations, rallies. In April 2000 the US Federal authorities, under pressure from both public opinion and judicial rulings, seized Elián by force from the relatives who had refused to hand him over; and in June he was returned to a triumphal reception in Havana.

The Pope's extreme physical decrepitude made the seventy-two-year-old Castro look, by comparison, quite fit and sprightly. And during the Elián González campaign Castro showed that he was still capable of making long, emotive harangues, day after day. He could also still spend many hours talking to foreign diplomats or journalists, leaving younger men exhausted. 'One last question,' said a visiting journalist, thinking he must have outstayed his welcome. 'A last question?' said Castro. 'Why? Are you bored already?'

In his old age Castro's oratorical style had become sometimes mannered and repetitive. He had a few stylistic tricks which he repeated over and over again. He never said that Cuba had done a lot for children, but rather: 'I know of no country in the world which has done more for children . . .' (or done more to end discrimination, or suffered greater injustice, or whatever). Having in the past been accused of being a Soviet satellite, he now played repeatedly on the theme of being a satellite. Cuba was a satellite of ideas; a satellite of the sun of justice; not a satellite, but a star shining with its own light; and so on.

Intellectually, however, Castro was still more lively and creative than many of his opponents. He kept in touch with new political and scientific trends and theories, and tried to shackle them to his cause. He had been quick to see the growing importance of environmental issues. Since attending the Rio Summit of 1992 he talked and campaigned tirelessly on the need to stop the waste of natural resources, and to slow the process of global warming. Naturally, the environment served as a good stick with which to beat the great polluter and waster of resources, the United States.

Castro also took up with enthusiasm the cause of anti-globalisation. For him it was not a new cause, but the same one for which he had been fighting all his life. The big multinationals were acquiring ever-greater power, unrestrained by any democratic control. They could play off one national government against another. Developing countries tried to attract investment by offering conditions which favoured the multinationals, such as low wages, low taxation and the absence of effective trade unions. And the profits, as always, flowed back to the corporation headquarters and shareholders, mostly in the United States.

Above all, Castro felt indignant at the Americans' worldwide control of information. Everywhere, people's values and perceptions of the world were moulded by Hollywood films, by news distributed by US agencies, by books and magazines reflecting American popular culture. At the Conference against Racism in South Africa in August 2001, Castro described how racial stereotypes had been spread throughout the world through the Americans' domination of the film industry and of mass communications.

Most ordinary Americans, in Castro's view, did not deliberately set out to deceive. But they had become accustomed to applying double standards. Through the International Monetary Fund, they demanded that other countries must eliminate their budget deficits, while themselves running the world's biggest budget deficit. Belonging to the world's only superpower, they took it for granted that their way of life was superior to all others, and that they were helping humanity by spreading their own values and methods. With rare exceptions, they felt no need and no incentive to find out about other countries and other cultures. They shut themselves off from ideas or information which challenged their comfortable assumptions. 'They are afraid of ideas, of words, they are afraid of the truth.' The US Congress was constantly insisting that more information should be broadcast from the United States to Cuba, by television as well as radio. But it was the Americans who needed information. 'It is the most ill-informed population in the world. Statistics and surveys show that a huge number of Americans do not even know where Latin America is, nor what are the capitals of Mexico or Brazil, and they confuse Argentina with Brazil, Brazil with Colombia, and so forth. There is generalised ignorance. They know nothing at all about Cuba, but they want to inform us!'

20 End Game

On 23 June 2001 Castro (then aged seventy-five) was addressing yet another rally, this time in the Havana district of Cotorro. As usual, the speech was being transmitted direct on Cuban television. It was a stiflingly hot day. The midday sun beat down mercilessly on the 60,000 spectators. Fidel had been talking for more than two hours. He was venting his outrage over the long prison sentences imposed by a Miami court on five Cubans arrested in 1998 and charged with espionage. The only task of these brave men, said Castro, was to find out about terrorist actions against Cuba planned by extremist groups in Miami. These groups had become increasingly active and violent. They had organised the planting of bombs in hotels in Cuba, in order to wreck the Cuban tourist industry. They did not care how many innocent tourists they killed. They had made assassination attempts against himself and other Cuban leaders. When he visited Panama the previous year, the Panamanian police had arrested a six-man terrorist squad, organised and financed by the CANF, who had made arrangements to kill him with a 6-kg bomb, when he addressed supporters in the university. All these terrorist activities were prepared under the nose of the US authorities, and with their connivance. That was why the Cubans had to take measures themselves to pre-empt terrorist atrocities planned in the United States.

As Fidel grew angrier, his voice became hoarse and broken, his speech slower. Then he was silent. Slowly his body started to tip forward against the podium, his eyes and mouth still open. A bodyguard grabbed his arm. The young Foreign Minister, Felipe Pérez Roque, took hold of his other arm. Within seconds he was surrounded by aides, who hurried him from the platform to the ambulance which was always kept nearby. Carlos Lage and Felipe Roque exchanged a few brief words. Then Roque took the microphone. He called on everyone to remain calm and to have confidence. Fidel, he said, had been working all night, preparing a campaign to secure freedom for the Cubans sentenced in Miami. He had scarcely eaten. Everyone would be informed as soon as there were news. 'Long live Fidel! Long live Raúl!'

In the ambulance Castro was sweating profusely, but had regained consciousness. He was given oxygen. He said he must return to the platform. The doctors advised him to wait, but he insisted. Fifteen minutes after fainting, he reappeared on the platform. He apologised for the interruption. He was now fine, but thought it would be better if he finished his speech in the evening.

Six hours later he took the microphone again, this time in an air-conditioned television studio. He looked fit and cheerful. He apologised again for having interrupted his speech in the morning. He had worked late the previous night, and underestimated the heat. 'Anyone would think I was playing dead to see what sort of funeral I got.' During his speech in the morning, he added, 545 people in the audience had received first-aid treatment for heat exhaustion. This time it had also been his turn. After that brief introduction, he continued his speech from where he had left off at midday.

This was not the first time that Castro had fainted. Several years earlier, at a diplomatic lunch, he had lost consciousness and slumped forward against the table, only to recover after a few seconds and carry on as if nothing had happened. But such incidents could be covered up, or explained away as a momentary lapse of no significance. The fainting in Cotorro was in a different category. It was a public and dramatic reminder of Castro's age and mortality. The same thought was on the minds of both his friends and his enemies: he recovered this time, but how much longer could he last?

It was a warning also for Castro. He had often claimed to be attracted by the thought of rest and retirement. Should he not now take the idea seriously? How about spending more time with his family and friends? But what family and what friends? In some ways, Castro at seventy-five looked a lonely figure. He was always surrounded by people, but often seemed isolated by his own charisma and by the aura of his power. There had been several women in his life, but most of them, starting with his wife Mirta, had spent very little time with him, and did not seem to provide much real companionship and emotional support. Even brother Raúl, his designated successor, now lived an entirely separate life. His son Fidelito, to whom Fidel as a young man had shown such passionate attachment, swearing in prison to move heaven and earth to regain custody, was now never seen in his company. Fidelito had been appointed Chairman of the Nuclear Energy Commission in 1984, and for a few years it seemed that he was being groomed for an important role; but in 1992 he was abruptly dismissed, and disappeared from view. When a journalist asked Fidel about Fidelito's resignation, Fidel replied with brutal directness. 'There was no resignation. He was fired for incompetence. What's the problem? We don't have a monarchy here.'

But Fidel always vigorously denied being lonely. He claimed that at least in his case, the cliché about the loneliness of power was nonsense. And indeed, a few aides seemed to have become over the years more like family than mere political colleagues or supporters. Carlos Lage, in particular, had spent most of his adult life virtually living with Fidel. Fidel appreciated Lage's sharp intelligence, quick wit and total loyalty. The body language between them was that of father and son, with private jokes and little gestures of reassurance and support. In private, and even sometimes in public, Castro talked as if Lage was running the country, keeping Fidel informed but taking more and more decisions himself. 'Lage was telling me yesterday that we are going to . . .' And if Lage seemed like an eldest son, Felipe Roque was the favoured Benjamin, appointed Foreign Minister while still in his thirties. Before his appointment as Foreign Minister, Roque was Fidel's private secretary and personal fixer. Fidel seemed lost without him. Whenever he sat down at a meeting, he would check that Felipe was present, and ask for him if he was not.

In old age, Fidel had become easier to live with. His explosive temper was a thing of the past. As a young man, he was often rude and peremptory to his subordinates. As an old man, he was usually courteous and good-humoured. He spent less time in his office. He played the role of elder statesman, setting the general tone and direction of policy, but seldom involving himself in specific administrative decisions. He was still, however, the public face of the government. He still made long speeches, and organised campaigns, such as the campaign for the return of Elián González, and for the release of the five Cuban undercover agents. He still grasped most opportunities to appear on the international stage. The Ibero-American summit in Lima in November 2001 was the first in the series of eleven such meetings which he did not attend in person. He sent Lage, explaining that he wanted to stay in Cuba to direct rescue and repair work following the damage wrought by Hurricane Michelle.

From his earliest years in power, Castro was the subject of rumours about his health. Media reports claimed at different times that he suffered from numerous serious medical conditions, including diabetes, heart attacks and brain haemorrhages. Some of these reports may have been deliberate disinformation spread by Castro's enemies to create alarm and demoralisation, or by Castro himself to confuse the enemy. Most were probably the product of wishful thinking. At a conference in Barbados in 1994 Castro grumbled about the media interest in his health.

Recently they began to spread rumours again about my health. They have me dead every so often. I don't know who the people are who are wishing for my death so intensely. I am sure that the day I am dead, my enemies

are going to miss me. Do you understand? They are going to find themselves with nothing to do . . . Yesterday some journalists from Miami kept
asking about my health. To tell the truth, the day before yesterday I worked
fourteen hours. Yesterday I worked another fourteen hours. I listened to
every minute of every speech. If someone can listen to over a hundred
speeches, this is ample evidence of good health. If anything can kill a
person, it is a hundred speeches in a row . . .'

However, Castro knew that one day the rumours would be true. The
message he wanted to convey was that the Revolution would survive him.
When asked about his health on his seventieth birthday, he said that apart
from an occasional cold, he had excellent health. 'I'm also in good spirits,
which is important. The agencies are the ones who say that I'm ill.' 'What
agencies? The CIA or the news agencies?'

The CIA did everything it could to ruin my health, and in spite of everything, here we are. We have turned seventy. But I'm aware that I'm not
eternal. I'm flesh and blood like everyone else, and subject to the same
conditions that everyone faces. That doesn't bother me at all. I don't know
why people pay so much attention to my health. This revolution has been
made. No one can destroy it. Our health was more important during the
early days, when individuals played a more important role. But now we
have a fully fledged revolution with lots of people . . . Why are they so
impatient?

In fact, it had been many years since the CIA had tried to kill Castro.
When former US Defence Secretary McNamara went to Havana for an
academic conference on the missile crisis, he and Castro had a friendly argument about how many attempts the CIA had made. Castro claimed that it
was more than thirty. McNamara retorted that it was not more than half a
dozen. In any event it was enough to give Castro an almost obsessive interest
in the subject. He lost few opportunities to remind foreign journalists that an
official agency of the US government had repeatedly tried to kill him. When
Elle magazine asked when he would retire, he replied: 'It's not my fault that I
haven't died yet, or that the CIA hasn't been able to kill me. I am a revolutionary. Revolutionaries don't retire, just as writers don't retire. But no one is
irreplaceable, and I'm in need of a rest.' What would happen when he died?
'You should ask the CIA that question . . . Frankly I don't think anything will
happen. We have all the necessary political and legal instruments to deal with
the situation.'

Although the CIA had been prohibited from using assassination as a
weapon, there were still other would-be assassins who kept Castro's

indignation on the boil, such as the groups in Miami whom he had been denouncing when he collapsed in mid-speech in Cotorro. He treated them with a mixture of humour and bitterness. 'Animals are protected. You cannot kill lions or rhinoceros, especially rhinoceros . . . However, I am the only species for which there is no closed season throughout the year. Ever since the CIA first tried to eliminate me, I haven't had the good fortune to be left alone. But I am very difficult to catch. There are always people from Miami when I go to meetings abroad, not reporters but people posing as reporters.' On one occasion a hitman posing as a Venezuelan photographer got close to Castro with a pistol concealed in a false camera, but did not fire, evidently deterred by the bodyguards. 'Fortunately, they are not suicidal. They are not fanatics. They are crazy, but only crazy for money. They want to enjoy their money in this life . . .'

The renewal of assassination attempts was partly because Castro's opponents had lost hope that he would be forced out by political developments. In 1989, when Communism was collapsing in Europe, most observers expected Castro to be overthrown in months rather than years. By 2002 the general assumption was that only death or ill health would bring his rule to an end. How could a tired old man, who had put all his money on a losing horse, appear so secure? Why were so few people inside Cuba agitating for his removal?

Even in his old age, Castro was showing remarkable political skills. He had allowed no opposition for forty years, yet he made a surprisingly large number of Cubans feel that they were involved in the process of government. His National Assembly met only for a few days every year, and then acted as a rubber stamp; yet the process by which its members were chosen involved some real and even lively debate at the neighbourhood level. Certainly there was more public participation than there had been in the Communist countries of Eastern Europe. And unlike most other Communist leaders, Castro seldom tried to conceal bad news, or to sweep problems under the carpet. When thousands of workers lost their jobs due to the collapse of the project to build a nuclear power station, Castro twice addressed the workers in their workplace, making them feel that he shared their anger and frustration.

As an old man, Castro was constantly trying to demonstrate his concern for youth, and the problems of youth. He took the initiative in setting up a new type of school for social workers, focussed specifically on problems like truancy and youth alienation. He attended a concert in Havana given by the Manic Street Preachers. For an older generation, he unveiled a statue of John Lennon in a Havana park. After all, did not 'Imagine' reflect Fidel's own dream of a world with no heaven and no hell, no private property, only peace and brotherhood? And for the older still, Castro insisted that retired people still had a valuable contribution to make to society. As absolute ruler of Cuba, he had never had to face a genuinely contested election. Yet he never stopped worrying about how to maintain his popularity with all the different segments of the Cuban population.

Castro lost the great battle of his life, the battle against 'imperialism'. At the end of his life, the United States was even stronger than in 1958 when he swore to avenge the American bombs dropped on peasant houses in Oriente. But he had survived, and kept alive the flame of defiant independence. He felt no bitterness towards the American people. As a Marxist internationalist, he was confident that it would eventually be the American people themselves who put an end to the injustices of their political system. He took comfort from opinion polls in the United States which showed that 80 per cent had favoured the return of Elián González to his father in Cuba. He believed that Americans would themselves be shocked when the full truth was revealed about the dirty war waged by their government against Cuba, including acts of biological warfare. As for Cuba, Castro believed that merely by surviving during the most militant phase of American expansionism, the Revolution had ensured that Cuba would never again become the victim of exploitation which it had been in Castro's youth.

Whatever happened in the future, Castro thought, could never diminish the heroic role which Cuba had played:

> We are at the very doorstep of a powerful and expansionist nation that has never ceased expanding its borders, first at the expense of the Indians who lived in much of what is now the United States, who were practically exterminated, and secondly at the expense of the Latin American and Caribbean nations. Very few countries have had to face a challenge and a threat as huge as the one faced by Cuba – the ripe apple that was expected to fall of its own weight into the claws of the incipient empire. At that time there were already people who thought resistance was an impossible task, but there were also people who never resigned themselves to the idea of surrendering their independence, their culture and their national identity. We could not continue being a foreign colony, we could not remain obedient servants of the empire, or a country of landless peasants, of children without schools, of sick people without doctors, of exploited workers, of blacks without rights, of discriminated women, of young people without a future, of jobless people, of humiliated citizens, of mocked laws, of unstoppable corruption, of senseless flags and anthems. Evictions, police brutality, abominable crimes: this is the kind of makeshift republic which the imperialist intervention left for us in our homeland. Looters of the public treasury, corrupt politicians, people responsible for atrocious repressive crimes, had a sure refuge in the United States, especially if the crimes

were committed on behalf of US economic interests and the anti-Communist ideology of that country. The same has happened in recent years in many other countries of our hemisphere. Who has trained the repressive forces of Latin America in crime, torture, the massive elimination of citizens, death squads, clandestine cemeteries and other abominable practices? And here we are, not only resisting but beginning to gain ground . . .

When Castro received news of the terrorist attacks on the United States on 11 September 2001, he was not for a moment tempted to take satisfaction from the misfortune of his old adversary. Indeed, he realised at once that the destruction of the Twin Towers would be counter-productive in terms of the war against 'imperialism'. It would give the Americans a legitimate grievance, and make them more disposed than ever to use their overwhelming strength to hit back at real or assumed enemies. Since Cuba was still included in the State Department's list of countries which promoted terrorism, he feared that Cuba could become a target for reprisals. His immediate reaction, conveyed through Foreign Minister Roque, was to condemn and reject the attacks, to express sympathy and solidarity to the American people, and sincere condolences to the victims. He offered the use of Cuban airports for the diversion of aircraft in American airspace. Cuba also offered to give blood plasma and any other humanitarian assistance for the victims of the attacks.

Later, in a more measured statement, Castro said Cuba would never allow its territory to be used for terrorist attacks against the United States. Cuba was the country which had suffered most from terrorism. Cuba was against terrorism; but it was also against war. He feared that 'Infinite Justice', the military action which the US government promised, might become an infinite massacre of innocent civilians. He hoped that the United States would not strike at phantom enemies, and that its allies would urge restraint. As the American response developed, Castro expressed dismay at some of President Bush's statements. Bush said that everyone must make a choice: they were either with the United States, or with the terrorists. The implications of this, said Castro, were terrifying. By giving itself the right to strike out unilaterally, wherever it perceived a country which was not 'with the United States', the Americans were destroying the United Nations, destroying the independence of every other country in the world.

On 6 October 2001 Castro held a ceremony to mark the twenty-fifth anniversary of the destruction of a Cuban airliner near Barbados, with the death of seventy-three people. The two Venezuelans who planted the bomb were almost certainly agents of the CIA. The ceremony was Castro's way of reminding the world that Cuba had indeed been a victim of terrorism. But very few people outside Cuba heard about the ceremony, and fewer still remembered the original incident. The events of 11 September had further marginalised Cuba from the mainstream of international politics. The President of Russia showed his goodwill towards the United States by announcing the withdrawal from Cuba of the Lourdes intelligence facility. Like Khrushchev and Gorbachev before him, Putin had taken a decision affecting Cuba without consulting or even informing Castro, only to satisfy the United States.

Despite his annoyance with Putin, Castro was determined to keep plugging away at his more constructive objectives. These now included trying to play a role in conflict resolution, and helping to bring peace to countries like Colombia. In November 2001 he hosted talks in Havana bringing together the Colombian Government, the ELN guerrillas and the group of friendly countries which had agreed to help to promote peace.

He also continued to cultivate with loving care the groups of activists in many countries, including the United States, who campaigned in favour of Cuba and against the embargo. He addressed one such group with a biblical image which had impressed him as a young boy. 'With trumpets they destroyed the walls of Jericho. I say that men and women like you around the world will destroy the modern walls of this gigantic Jericho, which today attempts to defeat and crush Cuba, and to destroy the Cuban Revolution and Cuba's independence.'

Of course Castro knew that there were plenty of other people who regarded him as a repressive dictator, a dinosaur from the past, a ruler whose legacy would be wiped out immediately when he eventually departed. But he still found plenty of enthusiasm among the crowds which turned out for him when he travelled abroad. 'I have some evidence that despite all the propaganda against Cuba and against myself, there are many people in the world who appreciate Cuba. Could it be that we are right? Could it be that people admire our struggle? Could it be that people criticise the cruel blockade against our country that kills men, women and children, young and old?'

In old age Castro was often asked what he thought would be his place in history. At his trial after the assault on the Moncada barracks, he said: 'History will absolve me.' Did he still believe this? He claimed not to give the subject much thought. But was there in fact ever a man more conscious of his image? Precisely because of this, he was careful to show a proper modesty. He said he would be a sigh in history. He recalled that at school the Jesuits had often said: dust to dust, ashes to ashes. 'Very few people will remember me. Who remembers the dust, unless he was a saint like the apostle James?'

Comments like this became a standard reply to questions about his historical legacy. But occasionally his train of thought wandered on, and ended up revealing how he really wanted to be remembered.

When people die, they are usually forgotten. Only their closest relatives remember them. Time goes by. Some people live worrying about history and glory, but as Martí said, all the glory of the world fits into a kernel of maize. No glory lasts over two thousand years, except that of Christ, Julius Caesar and Charlemagne, or a few personalities from antiquity. No history has lasted more than five thousand years. No history will last a million years. No history will last a billion years. When the sun goes out, what history will be left? So why worry about history? I don't worry about history. I ask myself: What is my duty? What should I do? I am not bothered what people will say about me. What has been said already is enough, some good things and some bad things. In the end, people have to acknowledge that we have been steadfast, defended our beliefs, our independence, wanted to do justice, and were rebellious.

Select Bibliography

Sebastian Balfour, *Castro* (1990)

Frei Betto, *Fidel y la Religion* (1985)

Peter Bourne, *Castro* (1986)

Dino Brugioni, *Eyeball to Eyeball* (1990)

J. M. Bunck, *Fidel Castro and the Quest for a Revolutionary Culture in Cuba* (1994)

Fidel Castro, *Fidel: My Early Years* (reprinting various interviews and speeches from over the years) (1998)

Fidel Castro, *An Encounter with Fidel* (an interview by Gianni Mina) (1991)

Armando Hart Davalos, *Aldabonazo* (1997)

Jules Dubois, *Fidel Castro* (1959)

Jeffrey Elliot, *Fidel Castro: Nothing Can Stop the Course of History* (1986)

Alina Fernandez, *Alina, Memorias de la Hija Rebelde* (1997)

Clive Foss, *Fidel Castro* (Sutton Pocket Biographies) (2000)

Jane Franklin, *The Cuban Revolution and the United States* (1992)

Carlos Franqui, *Fidel* (1980)

Norberto Fuentes, *Dulces Guerreros Cubanos* (1999)

Claudia Furiati, *Fidel Castro, uma biografia consentida* (2001)

G. A. Geyer, *Guerilla Prince* (1991)

Tom Gibb, *Famous Lives: Fidel Castro* (2000)

Maurice Halperin, *Rise and Decline of Fidel Castro* (1973)

Warren Hinckle *et. al.*, *Deadly Secrets: The CIA-Mafia Wars against Castro* (1993)

John Krich, *A Totally Free Man: An Unauthorised Autobiography of Fidel Castro* (1981)

H. L. Matthews, *Castro: A Political Biography* (1969)

Mario Mencia, *The Fertile Prison: Fidel Castro in Batista's Jails* (1992)

Enrique Menesses, *Fidel Castro* (1966)

Gianni Mina, *An Encounter with Fidel* (1990)

Carlos Alberto Montaner, *Fidel Castro and the Cuban Revolution: Age, Position, Character, Destiny, Personality and Ambition* (1989)

Catherina Moses, *Real Life in Castro's Cuba* (2000)

Andrew Oppenheimer, *Castro's Final Hour* (1992)

Petra Press, *Fidel Castro* (2000)

Robert Quirk, *Fidel Castro* (1993)

Esther Selsdon, *The Life and Times of Fidel Castro* (1997)
Tad Szulc, *Fidel: A Critical Portrait* (1986)
Angelo Trento, *Castro and Cuba: From the Revolution to the Present* (2000)
Tim Wendal, *Castro's Curveball* (1999)

Index